ADVANCED GAME PROGRAMMING: A GAMEDEV.NET COLLECTION

JOHN HATTAN AND DREW SIKORA

SERIES EDITORS

Course Technology PTR

A part of Cengage Learning

COURSE TECHNOLOGY
CENGAGE Learning™

Australia • Brazil • Japan • Korea • Mexico • Singapore • Spain • United Kingdom • United States

COURSE TECHNOLOGY
CENGAGE Learning™

Advanced Game Programming:
A GameDev.net Collection
John Hattan and Drew Sikora

Publisher and General Manager, Course Technology PTR: Stacy L. Hiquet

Associate Director of Marketing: Sarah Panella

Manager of Editorial Services: Heather Talbot

Marketing Manager: Jordan Casey

Acquisitions Editor: Heather Hurley

Project Editor and Copy Editor: Kim Benbow

Editorial Services Coordinator: Jen Blaney

Interior Layout Tech: Macmillan Publishing Solutions

Cover Designer: Mike Tanamachi

Indexer: Broccoli Information Management

Proofreader: Laura Gabler

For product information and technology assistance, contact us at
Cengage Learning Customer & Sales Support, 1-800-354-9706

For permission to use material from this text or product, submit all requests online at **www.cengage.com/permissions**
Further permissions questions can be emailed to
permissionrequest@cengage.com

Microsoft, Windows, and Internet Explorer are either registered trademarks or trademarks of Microsoft Corporation in the United States and/or other countries.
All other trademarks are the property of their respective owners.

Library of Congress Control Number: 2008930424

ISBN-13: 978-1-59863-806-6

ISBN-10: 1-59863-806-8

Course Technology, a part of Cengage Learning
20 Channel Center Street
Boston, MA 02210
USA

Cengage Learning is a leading provider of customized learning solutions with office locations around the globe, including Singapore, the United Kingdom, Australia, Mexico, Brazil, and Japan. Locate your local office at: **international.cengage.com/region**

Cengage Learning products are represented in Canada by Nelson Education, Ltd.

For your lifelong learning solutions, visit **courseptr.com**

Visit our corporate website at **cengage.com**

Printed in Canada
1 2 3 4 5 6 7 11 10 09

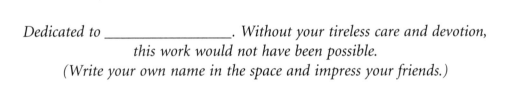

Dedicated to _____. Without your tireless care and devotion, this work would not have been possible.
(Write your own name in the space and impress your friends.)

Acknowledgments

There are plenty of people to acknowledge in the creation of this book. Ninety percent of 'em are mentioned in the table of contents, so I'm saving ink (going green is trendy) and will let you read the names there. Everyone who wrote an article for this book was helpful and was happy to contribute to this work. Many of those who submitted existing GameDev.net content went above and beyond the call of duty and provided updates and/or rewrites, sometimes without prompting. If you like what you see, scan the table of contents and thank those people. The bulk of the work is theirs.

Beyond the authors, I must thank my co-editor Drew Sikora for his advice in the process. This is the first book for both of us, and it's easier to scrabble around blindly in the dark if you have someone who can sanity-check your ideas.

Also big thanks to Heather Hurley and Kim Benbow at Cengage Learning. I know quite a few authors who told me horror stories about getting their works published. I don't know if it's those authors' fragile egos or Heather and Kim's skill at dealing with my own fragile ego, but the process was relatively painless.

John Hattan

ABOUT THE SERIES EDITORS

John Hattan has been working steadily in the casual game space since the TRS-80 days and professionally since 1990. After seeing his small-format games turned down for what ended up being Radio Shack's last store-brand PC, he took them independent, eventually releasing them as a set of discount game packs through a couple of shelf publishers. Following the demise of discount game shelf publishing, he sold his games on the Internet, both as pay-for-play and ad-supported. He continues to work in the casual game space as an independent developer, writing viral games for web portals and widget platforms. The games are always available on his web site, The Code Zone (www.thecodezone.com).

In addition to games, John writes weekly product reviews and blog entries for GameDev.net from his home office in Texas. When not working on games in one way or another, he manages his wife's civil engineering firm and helps raise their daughter.

Drew Sikora has been active in the games industry since 2001, when he co-founded the NJ North IGDA chapter with Darrell Porcher, which has since grown to become one of the leading IGDA chapters in the world. He's been involved with GameDev.net since 2000, becoming executive producer in 2006 and working hard with his team of awesome people to make GameDev.net a valuable resource for game developers of all trades. Drew has also worked with Game Institute since its conception in 2001, supporting the growing community, managing live seminars on game development topics by experienced industry members and judging the Institute's regular game programming challenges. His past writing credits include three chapters in *Game Design Perspectives* (Charles River Media, 2002) and well over 100 articles and interviews published on GameDev.net covering industry events and game development topics. Since 2008, he's been mentoring students attending the GDC as part of the IGDA's scholarship program. In whatever spare time he has, he likes to program small game projects whenever he gets the urge.

When Drew isn't doing anything industry-related, he can be found practicing martial arts, bouncing high on a trampoline or tumbling, doing stunt work, playing his PlayStation3, driving really fast in his car or on his motorcycle, hanging with friends or musing about something on his blog at www.blade-edge.com.

Contents

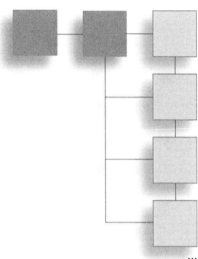

Chapter 22 20 Issues of Porting C++ Code on the 64-Bit Platform . . . 341
    Andrey Karpov and Evgeniy Ryzhkov

FOREWORD

Back when we launched GameDev.net, the world was a different place. There were only a handful of books covering game development, and many of those were rapidly becoming outdated. There were a lot of game development web sites, but the content they offered was sparse and intended primarily for hobbyists. Whether you were someone trying to break into the game industry, a developer trying to create a game in your spare time, or someone making games for a living, finding information or like-minded individuals was no easy task. Even your friend Google was still in diapers and not a lot of help yet!

Our goal in founding GameDev.net was simple: provide a place where game developers of all walks of life could come together, freely exchange information and ideas, and network. In the nearly 10 years since then, we've seen the site and community grow to reach hundreds of thousands of game developers all over the world. We've seen an increasing number of professional game developers join the community, and we've even seen people go from being complete newbies to joining the ranks of EA, Ubisoft, and many others.

Many people have given back to the community, sharing their time and knowledge through the over 4 million posts to our forums, and also by contributing articles.

Over the past decade, we've received literally thousands of articles covering a wide range of topics. The best of these have withstood the test of time, becoming staples in their respective topics. Working closely with our good friends at Cengage Learning, Drew and John have assembled these articles here, in printed form for the first time. They've also solicited new articles that will be exclusively available in these books, the GameDev.net Collection.

The GameDev.net community is a diverse and talented group, and this volume aims to capture those talents with advanced game programming topics that build on the foundations of the previous volume, *Beginning Game Programming*. While some of the topics explore the latest and greatest techniques in game programming, others revisit traditional concepts that provide the basis for much of the game technology you see today.

While *Beginning Game Programming* focused on introductory-level topics, *Advanced Game Programming* dives into the challenges game programmers face with optimization, physics and collision detection, scene management, multi-player gaming, advanced C++ topics, the latest graphics rendering techniques, and artificial intelligence. Continuing in our tradition of bringing a variety of topics together from a variety of sources, this volume captures the best of GameDev.net's community in advanced game programming topics. We hope you find the information invaluable in your pursuit of game development success.

Dave Astle
Kevin Hawkins
Founders, GameDev.net

PART 1

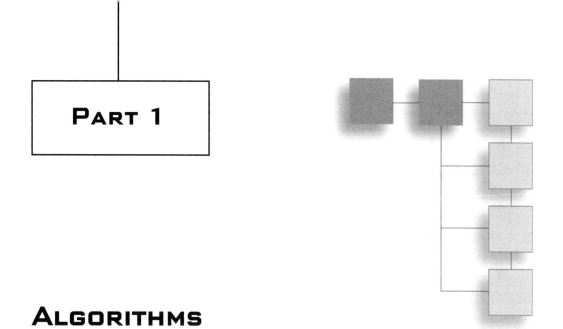

ALGORITHMS

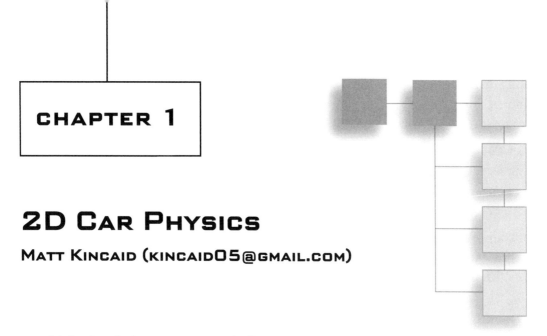

CHAPTER 1

2D CAR PHYSICS

MATT KINCAID (KINCAID05@GMAIL.COM)

A vehicle simulation may seem challenging at first glance, but the problem can actually be broken down into a few very fundamental parts of a game simulation. In this tutorial, you're going to learn how to make a basic 2D vehicle simulator using C#; and I'll attempt to make the simulation as accurate as possible without complicating the overall scope of the tutorial.

I've broken the process down into three steps. First, you will learn how to set up a basic game application in C#.NET and learn how to draw some basic graphics (emphasis on basic). Next, you will learn how to create a rigid body simulator using a simple Euler integrator with a variable time step. And last but not least, you will calculate vehicle forces simulating the tire patch contacting the road. And that's all there is to it! Let's get started.

Math Requirements

The math requirements for the 2D simulation are mostly in the form of a vector object. You'll need to be able to add, subtract, dot, and project two vectors. Also you'll need to be able to use a cross product. In 2D, this is kind of a fake situation, since you know the result will point in the screen's direction, so the result is returned as a scalar. If you're not familiar with any of these terms, please look them up now.

For matrix operations, you'll be using the .Net `Drawing2D.Matrix` object. A matrix will help to transform and inversely transform a vector between spaces. If you don't know what I'm talking about, let me give you an example.

Let's say you're facing forward in a vehicle. The forward direction is relative to the *local* space, and the world the vehicle exists in is called the *world* space. Let's say the vehicle is positioned in a way that, by you looking forward in local space, you are looking east in world space.

A transformation of the forward direction from local space to world space would result in east. A transformation of north direction from world space to local space (vehicle space) would result in left.

This is a critical concept, so please, if that example didn't make sense, do some searching on Google for transforming between spaces. The reason this is so important is because you will be doing all of your vehicle force calculations in local vehicle space. Yet the vehicle itself, and its integrator, persist in world space.

Phase One: Main Rendering Function

The first phase is to create the renderer, something graphical so you can actually see what the simulation is doing. This will make it a lot easier to debug.

Create a Windows form project in C# and place a picturebox control on it (name it "screen"). This control is where you will display the simulation. You could just start drawing to this screen, but you're going to be using double buffering to avoid flicker.

Creating the back buffer looks like this.

```
Graphics graphics; //gdi+
Bitmap backbuffer;
Size buffersize;
//initialize rendering
private void Init(Size size)
{
  //setup rendering device
  buffersize = size;
  backbuffer = new Bitmap(buffersize.Width, buffersize.Height);
  graphics = Graphics.FromImage(backbuffer);
}
```

The `Init` function must be called with the size of the screen control that you created on the form. This will create a bitmap `backbuffer` to which you can do your off-screen rendering. You then take this `backbuffer` and draw it to the screen, eliminating update flickering.

This is how you draw a basic shape to the `backbuffer` and present it to the screen.

```
//main rendering function
private void Render(Graphics g)
{
  //clear back buffer
  graphics.Clear(Color.Black);
  //draw to back buffer
  graphics.DrawLine(new Pen(Color.Yellow), 1, 0, 1, 5);
  //present back buffer
  g.DrawImage(backbuffer,
              new Rectangle(0, 0, buffersize.Width, buffersize.Height),
              0, 0, buffersize.Width, buffersize.Height,
              GraphicsUnit.Pixel);
}
```

This function is called from the `on_paint` method of the screen control placed on the form. The `on_paint` method has a parameter e that contains a graphics object you can use to draw to the control. You pass this graphics object to the render function and as you can see, you draw the `backbuffer` to it as the very last step.

Now by default, the graphics of a picturebox control has the origin in the top-left corner and extends downward for +y and to the right for +x. This is highly unnatural for most cases. In addition to that, it has extremely large units. Since you will be simulating in the metric system, I recommend introducing a scale factor to scale up the simulation and make it much more visible.

The transformation looks like this and takes place after `Graphics.Clear()` is called.

```
graphics.ResetTransform();
graphics.ScaleTransform(screenScale, -screenScale);
graphics.TranslateTransform(buffersize.Width / 2.0f / screenScale, -
buffersize.Height / 2.0f / screenScale);
```

That transformation flips the y axis so that +y points up. It simultaneously scales the space by the `screenScale` factor (something like 3.0f should work fine). Next, you translate the graphics space into the center of the screen control by half of the screen dimensions divided by your scale (since you are now in the scaled space.) The graphics are now drawn starting at the center of the screen.

Forms Wiring

Up until now, I haven't explained how to connect all the functions. The first thing you'll need to do is call the Render function from your on_paint event. Next, you'll need to create a function that gets called continuously, updating the simulation (referred to as DoFrame in this text). It is preferable to call this function on the Application_Idle event so that your simulation doesn't hog system resources.

Create an event handler for Application_Idle and have it call your DoFrame function. Inside this function you'll need to do the following:

1. Process input

2. Update the simulation

3. Invalidate the screen control

The last step is so that an on_paint gets triggered and the simulation gets redrawn. You'll also want to wire up key_down and key_up events to keep track of key states.

The Timer

Since you don't know how often your DoFrame function will be getting called, you need to code everything in a way to handle a variable time step. To utilize this, you must measure the time between DoFrame calls.

I introduce the timer, which simply queries the number of milliseconds that have passed since the computer was turned on. You store this number every frame, and on the next frame, you compute the difference. This gives you the time that has passed between frames. Here is a very simple timer object.

Note

You will need to call GetETime in your initialize function in order to clear the timer. Otherwise, the first call to it will return the amount of time that has passed since the computer was turned on.

```
class Timer
{
  //store last time sample
  private int lastTime = Environment.TickCount;
```

```
  private float etime;
  //calculate and return elapsed time since last call
  public float GetETime()
  {
    etime = (Environment.TickCount - lastTime) / 1000.0f;
    lastTime = Environment.TickCount;
    return etime;
  }
}
```

Conclusion of Phase One

So up to this point I've covered setting up a rendering surface using GDI, wiring a form to process a game loop and draw it to the screen, and computing the time that has passed between frames. The application so far looks like this:

```
using System;
using System.Collections.Generic;
using System.ComponentModel;
using System.Data;
using System.Drawing;
using System.Drawing.Drawing2D;
using System.Text;
using System.Windows.Forms;
namespace car_physics_2d
{
  //our main application form
  public partial class frmMain : Form
  {
    //graphics
    Graphics graphics; //gdi+
    Bitmap backbuffer;
    Size buffersize;
    const float screenScale = 3.0f;
    Timer timer = new Timer();
    //keyboard controls
    bool leftHeld = false, rightHeld = false;
    bool upHeld = false, downHeld = false;
    //vehicle controls
    float steering = 0; //-1 is left, 0 is center, 1 is right
    float throttle = 0; //0 is coasting, 1 is full throttle
    float brakes = 0; //0 is no brakes, 1 is full brakes
```

```csharp
public frmMain()
{
  InitializeComponent();
  Application.Idle += new EventHandler(ApplicationIdle);
  screen.Paint += new PaintEventHandler(screen_Paint);
  this.KeyDown += new KeyEventHandler(onKeyDown);
  this.KeyUp += new KeyEventHandler(onKeyUp);
  Init(screen.Size);
}
//initialize rendering
private void Init(Size size)
{
  //setup rendering device
  buffersize = size;
  backbuffer = new Bitmap(buffersize.Width, buffersize.Height);
  graphics = Graphics.FromImage(backbuffer);
  timer.GetETime(); //reset timer
}
//main rendering function
private void Render(Graphics g)
{
  //clear back buffer
  graphics.Clear(Color.Black);
  graphics.ResetTransform();
  graphics.ScaleTransform(screenScale, -screenScale);
  graphics.TranslateTransform(buffersize.Width / 2.0f /
      screenScale, -buffersize.Height / 2.0f / screenScale);
  //draw to back buffer
  DrawScreen();
  //present back buffer
  g.DrawImage(backbuffer, new Rectangle(0, 0, buffersize.Width,
   buffersize.Height), 0, 0, buffersize.Width,
   buffersize.Height, GraphicsUnit.Pixel);
}
//draw the screen
private void DrawScreen()
{
  //draw our simulation here
}
//process game logic
private void DoFrame()
{
  //get elapsed time since last frame
```

```
  float etime = timer.GetETime();
  //process input
  ProcessInput();
  ////////////////////////////////
  //integrate our simulation here
  ////////////////////////////////
  //redraw our screen
  screen.Invalidate();
}
//process keyboard input
private void ProcessInput()
{
  if (leftHeld)
    steering = -1;
  else if (rightHeld)
    steering = 1;
  else
    steering = 0;
  if (upHeld)
    throttle = 1;
  else
    throttle = 0;
  if (downHeld)
    brakes = 1;
  else
    brakes = 0;
}
private void onKeyDown(object sender, KeyEventArgs e)
{
  switch (e.KeyCode)
  {
    case Keys.Left:
      leftHeld = true;
      break;
    case Keys.Right:
      rightHeld = true;
      break;
    case Keys.Up:
      upHeld = true;
      break;
    case Keys.Down:
      downHeld = true;
      break;
```

```csharp
        default: //no match found
          return; //return so handled doesn't get set
      }
      //match found
      e.Handled = true;
    }
    private void onKeyUp(object sender, KeyEventArgs e)
    {
      switch (e.KeyCode)
      {
        case Keys.Left:
          leftHeld = false;
          break;
        case Keys.Right:
          rightHeld = false;
          break;
        case Keys.Up:
          upHeld = false;
          break;
        case Keys.Down:
          downHeld = false;
          break;
        default: //no match found
          return; //return so handled doesn't get set
      }
      //match found
      e.Handled = true;
    }
    //rendering - only when screen is invalidated
    private void screen_Paint(object sender, PaintEventArgs e)
    {
      Render(e.Graphics);
    }
    //when the os gives us time, run the game
    private void ApplicationIdle(object sender, EventArgs e)
    {
      // While the application is still idle, run frame routine.
      DoFrame();
    }
    private void MenuExit_Click(object sender, EventArgs e)
    {
      this.Close();
    }
  }
```

```
//keep track of time between frames
class Timer
{
  //store last time sample
  private int lastTime = Environment.TickCount;
  private float etime;
  //calculate and return elapsed time since last call
  public float GetETime()
  {
    etime = (Environment.TickCount - lastTime) / 1000.0f;
    lastTime = Environment.TickCount;
    return etime;
  }
 }
}
```

Phase Two: Rigid Body Simulation

Okay, now you're getting into some good stuff here. Let's put everything just covered on the back burner now and talk about some physics. You're going to be using a very simple Euler integration method.

Basically, each frame you accumulate a bunch of forces (in this case, from each wheel of the vehicle) and calculate the resultant acceleration, which is in the form of A = F/M (the same as F = MA, Newton's second law of motion). You use this to modify Newton's first law of motion, "an object in motion stays in motion. . . ." So you calculate A, and you integrate it into V. Without an A (the presence of forces), V would be constant, or stay in motion.

Newton's third law gets applied such that any potential force the vehicle is applying to the ground gets applied in the opposite direction to the vehicle. (I'll explain this later in the article in the section "Phase Three: The Vehicle.")

This topic is much easier to explain with symbols. P is the vehicle position, V is its linear velocity, F is the net force acting on it, M is its mass, A is the resultant acceleration, and T is the time step (the value the timer gave you from the last frame).

$$A = F / M$$

$$V = V + A * T$$

$$P = P + V * T$$

With a constant mass and some force, you will generate acceleration, which will in turn generate velocity, which will in turn generate a displacement (a change in P). This is a basic linear rigid body simulator. Each frame, you total up F, integrate it, and then zero out F to restart the accumulation in the next frame.

Now let's talk about rotation. The angular case is nearly identical to the linear case (especially in 2D). Instead of P you have an angle, instead of V you have an angular velocity, instead of F you have a torque, and instead of M you have inertia. So the angular model looks like this:

AngA = Torque / Inertia

AngV = AngV + AngA * T

Angle = Angle + AngV * T

Simple, right? Now, you may be wondering where this torque came from. A torque is generated every time you apply a force. Lay a book down on your desk and push on the corner of it. The book should slide across the desk, but it should also begin to rotate. The slide is caused by the force. This rotation is caused by the torque, and the magnitude of the torque is proportional to how far away from the center of the object the force was applied. If you applied the force directly to the center of the object, the torque would be zero.

You need to construct an AddForce function for your rigid body. This is what gets called every frame, once per wheel, to accumulate the chassis' rigid body forces and torques. The linear case is simple: Forces = Forces + newForce. The angular case is a little trickier. You take the cross product of the force direction and the torque arm (the offset between where the force was applied and the center of mass of the body). In 2D, this results in a scalar value that you can just add to torque. So, Torques = Torques + Cross(TorqueArm, Force). This is what that bit of code looks like:

```
public void AddForce(Vector worldForce, Vector worldOffset)
{
  //add linear force
  m_forces += worldForce;
  //and its associated torque
  m_torque += Vector.Cross(worldOffset, worldForce);
}
```

You'll notice the world prefix on the parameters. This is because all computation of the rigid body happens in world space. So as your book is rotating on the desk, the `worldOffset` value is changing, even though your finger is not moving on the book (this would be the `relativeOffset`). So if you know you're applying a force "across the book, at the top-right corner," you need to convert both "across" and "top-right corner" into world space vectors, then add them to the rigid body.

Code Dump

Here is the completed rigid body object. It includes all the properties previously mentioned, along with a `Draw` function, which will draw its rectangle to the provided graphics object, an `AddForce` function, a space conversion method, to and from world space (very handy), and a function that returns the velocity of a point on the body (in world space).

The point velocity is a combination of the linear velocity at the angular velocity. The angular velocity is converted to a linear one by scaling the angular velocity by the distance from the point to the center of rotation and in a direction perpendicular to the offset. So to kill two birds with one stone, find the orthogonal vector to the point offset and multiply it by the angular velocity (then add the linear velocity).

One thing you may be curious about is how to calculate the inertia value. That is a generalized formula that can easily be found in textbooks and on the web for different shapes. I used $1/12 * X^2 * Y^2$, which is the inertia of a rectangle rotating around a Z axis.

```
//physics simulation object
class RigidBody
{
  //linear properties
  private Vector m_position = new Vector();
  private Vector m_velocity = new Vector();
  private Vector m_forces = new Vector();
  private float m_mass;
  //angular properties
  private float m_angle;
  private float m_angularVelocity;
  private float m_torque;
  private float m_inertia;
  //cached output transforms
  private Matrix m_positionMatrix = new Matrix();
  private Matrix m_rotationMatrix = new Matrix();
  private Matrix m_invRotationMatrix = new Matrix();
```

```
//graphical properties
private Vector m_halfSize = new Vector();
private Rectangle rect = new Rectangle();
private Color m_color = new Color();
public RigidBody()
{
  //set these defaults so you don't get divide by zeros
  m_mass = 1.0f;
  m_inertia = 1.0f;
}
public void Setup(Vector halfSize, float mass, Color color)
{
  //store physical parameters
  m_halfSize = halfSize;
  m_mass = mass;
  m_color = color;
  m_inertia = (1.0f / 12.0f) * (halfSize.X * halfSize.X) *
               (halfSize.Y * halfSize.Y) * mass;
  //generate our viewable rectangle
  rect.X = (int)-m_halfSize.X;
  rect.Y = (int)-m_halfSize.Y;
  rect.Width = (int)(m_halfSize.X * 2.0f);
  rect.Height = (int)(m_halfSize.Y * 2.0f);
}
public void SetPosition(Vector position, float angle)
{
  m_position = position;
  m_angle = angle;
  CacheOutput();
}
public Vector GetPosition()
{
  return m_position;
}
public void Update(float timeStep)
{
  //integrate physics
  //linear
  Vector acceleration = m_forces / m_mass;
  m_velocity += acceleration * timeStep;
  m_position += m_velocity * timeStep;
  m_forces = new Vector(0,0); //clear forces
  //angular
```

```
    float angAcc = m_torque / m_inertia;
    m_angularVelocity += angAcc * timeStep;
    m_angle += m_angularVelocity * timeStep;
    m_torque = 0; //clear torque
    CacheOutput();
}
public void CacheOutput()
{
    //cache the output transforms
    m_positionMatrix.Reset();
    m_positionMatrix.Translate(m_position.X, m_position.Y);
    m_rotationMatrix.Reset();
    m_rotationMatrix.Rotate(m_angle / (float)Math.PI * 180.0f);
    m_invRotationMatrix = m_rotationMatrix.Clone();
    m_invRotationMatrix.Invert();
}
public void Draw(Graphics graphics, Size buffersize)
{
    //store transform, (like opengl's glPushMatrix())
    Matrix prevTransform = graphics.Transform;
    //transform into position
    graphics.MultiplyTransform(m_positionMatrix);
    graphics.MultiplyTransform(m_rotationMatrix);
    try
    {
        //draw body and line in the "forward direction"
        graphics.DrawRectangle(new Pen(m_color), rect);
        graphics.DrawLine(new Pen(Color.Yellow), 1, 0, 1, 5);
    }
    catch(OverflowException exc)
    {
        //physics overflow :(
    }
    //restore transform
    graphics.Transform = prevTransform;
}
//take a relative vector and make it a world vector
public Vector RelativeToWorld(Vector relative)
{
    PointF[] vectors = new PointF[1];
    vectors[0].X = relative.X;
    vectors[0].Y = relative.Y;
    m_rotationMatrix.TransformVectors(vectors);
```

```
      return new Vector(vectors[0].X, vectors[0].Y);
  }
  //take a world vector and make it a relative vector
  public Vector WorldToRelative(Vector world)
  {
    PointF[] vectors = new PointF[1];
    vectors[0].X = world.X;
    vectors[0].Y = world.Y;
    m_invRotationMatrix.TransformVectors(vectors);
    return new Vector(vectors[0].X, vectors[0].Y);
  }
  //velocity of a point on body
  public Vector PointVel(Vector worldOffset)
  {
    Vector tangent = new Vector(-worldOffset.Y, worldOffset.X);
    return tangent * m_angularVelocity + m_velocity;
  }
  public void AddForce(Vector worldForce, Vector worldOffset)
  {
    //add linear force
    m_forces += worldForce;
    //and its associated torque
    m_torque += Vector.Cross(worldOffset, worldForce);
  }
}
```

Testing

To make sure your rigid body works, instantiate one in your Init() function and apply a force with some offset in the DoFrame function. If you apply a constant worldOffset, the body will continue to accelerate its angular velocity. If you take your offset and run it through the RelativeToWorld function, the body will angularly accelerate in one direction and then come back the other way, like a pendulum, as the point the force is applied to changes. Play around with this for a while, as this has to work and make sense in order for the next section to work.

Phase Three: The Vehicle

Assuming everything has gone well so far, you should have a rigid body object in your scene that you can apply forces to and watch move around. Now all that's left is to calculate these forces in a way that will simulate a vehicle. For that, you are going to need a vehicle object. I recommend deriving directly from you rigid body object since the chassis is essentially a rigid body. In addition to the chassis, you will need to implement a "wheel" object. This wheel will handle the steering direction of each wheel, the velocity the wheel is spinning, and calculate the forces that that particular wheel applies to the chassis (all in vehicle space). Since the wheel is known to be constrained to the vehicle, you don't need to simulate it as another rigid body (though you could, but not in the 2D case). You will simply duplicate the angular properties of the rigid body in the wheel object.

The properties of the wheel are wheel velocity, wheel inertia, and wheel torque. You'll also need the relative offset of the wheel in the vehicle space and the angle the wheel is facing (this is constant for the back wheels, unless you want four-wheel steering). Just like the rigid body, the wheel's torque function acts as an accumulator, you add torques to it, and after it gets integrated the torque is zeroed. The AddTorque function allows you to apply a wheel torque from either the transmission (to make you go) or from the brakes (to make you stop). Internally, the wheel will generate a torque caused by the friction on the road.

The wheel object also needs a SetSteering function. This function calculates two vectors: an effective side direction, and an effective forward direction (both in vehicle space) that the tire patch will act on. The force applied on the tire by the ground acting in the side direction will directly translate into the chassis. Meanwhile, the force acting in the forward direction will not only act on the chassis, but it will cause a rotation of the tire.

Here is the SetSteering function. I used the Drawing2D.Matrix to transform the initial forward and side vectors by the steering angle. I had to convert the vectors to "points" in order to transform them by the matrix. And also, the Rotate function takes degrees, so I converted the steering angle as well.

```
public void SetSteeringAngle(float newAngle)
{
  Matrix mat = new Matrix();
  PointF[] vectors = new PointF[2];
  //forward vector
  vectors[0].X = 0;
  vectors[0].Y = 1;
  //side vector
  vectors[1].X = -1;
  vectors[1].Y = 0;
  mat.Rotate(newAngle / (float)Math.PI * 180.0f);
```

```
mat.TransformVectors(vectors);
m_forwardAxis = new Vector(vectors[0].X, vectors[0].Y);
m_sideAxis = new Vector(vectors[1].X, vectors[1].Y);
}
```

Force Calculation

If the vehicle were sitting there not moving with its front wheels turned, and you pushed it, a force would be generated in the opposite direction you push. This force gets projected onto these two directions. If the wheels were straight, there would be no side force, and the vehicle would simply roll forward. But since the wheels are turned, there is a bit of the force that acts in the "effective side direction," so you apply an opposite force to the chassis. This is what causes you to turn when you steer the wheels. To get the force that gets projected onto the two directions, you need to first determine the velocity difference between the tire patch and the road. If the wheel is spinning at the same speed as the ground is whizzing by, then there is effectively no force acting on the vehicle. But as soon as you slam on the brakes and stop the wheel, there is a huge velocity difference, and this is what causes the force that stops your car.

So here is the process broken down into six steps for each wheel:

1. Calculate the effective direction vectors (with the steering function).

2. Calculate velocity difference. The ground speed is determined via the PointVel function on the rigid body, given the wheel's world offset.

3. Project this velocity onto the two effective directions.

4. Generate an equal and opposite force for the two directions and call this the response force. This is what gets added to the chassis for each wheel.

5. Calculate the torque that the forward response force created on the wheel, and add this to the wheel torque.

6. Integrate the wheel torques into the wheel velocity.

That bit of code looks like this:

```
public Vector CalculateForce(Vector relativeGroundSpeed, float
timeStep)
{
    //calculate speed of tire patch at ground
```

```
  Vector patchSpeed = -m_forwardAxis * m_wheelSpeed * m_wheelRadius;
  //get velocity difference between ground and patch
  Vector velDifference = relativeGroundSpeed + patchSpeed;
  //project ground speed onto side axis
  Vector sideVel = velDifference.Project(m_sideAxis);
  //project ground speed onto forward axis
  float forwardMag = 0;
  Vector forwardVel = velDifference.Project(m_forwardAxis,
                      out forwardMag);
  //calculate super fake friction forces, this is the heart
  // of a vehicle simulation.
  // http://en.wikipedia.org/wiki/Friction
  //calculate response force from friction
  const float sideFrictionCoef = 2.0f;
  const float forwardFrictionCoef = 1.0f;
  Vector responseForce = -sideVel * sideFrictionCoef;
  responseForce -= forwardVel * forwardFrictionCoef;
  //calculate torque on wheel
  m_wheelTorque += forwardMag * m_wheelRadius;
  //integrate total torque into wheel
  m_wheelSpeed += m_wheelTorque / m_wheelInertia * timeStep;
  //clear our transmission torque accumulator
  m_wheelTorque = 0;
  //return force acting on body
  return responseForce;
}
```

Almost Done!

You're in the home stretch here now. Now you have a way to calculate the force each wheel generates on the chassis. Every frame, all you have to do is set your transmission and brake torques and also your steering angle, calculate each wheel force, add these to the chassis, and integrate the rigid body. And that's all there is to it!

Conclusion

Topics I've covered include simple forms wiring and double buffering, a simple Euler physics integration, and a very intuitive vehicle dynamics simulation. For your convenience, the entire source code to this project is available on the book's companion web site at www.courseptr.com/downloads. You can also download it from my web site at http://kincaid05.googlepages.com.

For bonus points, the vector object could easily be expanded to 3D and, with little effort, so could the rigid body object. The friction calculation could also be expanded in many ways. The implementation I've shown is a greatly simplified linear resistance. The Coulomb friction model is a lot more exciting with a distinction between static and kinetic friction.

For mega ultra bonus points, the vehicle integration can be unified in such a way that considers all the wheel forces and torques in a simultaneous calculation rather than an iterative one. This comes in handy when the vehicle is parked on a hill. The method I've described in this article will come to equilibrium at some velocity sliding down the hill. When you get that far, I'll leave it up to you to figure out how to prevent it.

Thanks for reading, and I hope this article was informative.

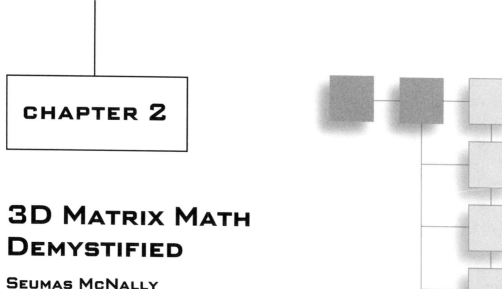

CHAPTER 2

3D MATRIX MATH DEMYSTIFIED

SEUMAS MCNALLY

Note

Note for Math Weenies

This is not meant to be a full tutorial on matrices, and it is also not intended to cover the math behind them in the usual manner. It is my personal way of thinking about rotation matrices in 3D graphics, and it will hopefully provide at least some people with a new (and possibly more intuitive) way of visualizing matrices that they may not have considered before.

For serious 3D graphics, you will need to use matrix math. The problem is that at first glance it seems bloody complicated. The truth is, there are simpler ways to think about matrix math than as abstract rectangular arrays of numbers. My personal favorite way of thinking about and visualizing 3D rotation matrices is this: simple 3-by-3 rotation matrices can be thought of simply as three 3D vectors. And those three vectors are usually unit-length (which means having a length of 1.0, where $sqrt(x*x + y*y + z*z) = 1.0$) and point along the x, y, and z axes, respectively, of the coordinate space the matrix represents.

Matrices can be thought of as representing the transformation (or change) in orientation and position required to get from one coordinate space, or frame of reference, to another one. Imagine two people, one standing up, and one lying down (or try it yourself). To the person who is standing, up is up, down is down, forward is forward, etc. But to the person lying down, forward is really up, and backward is really down, and down is forward, and up is backward. Earth's gravity dictates that our normal frame of reference has "down" pointing toward the center of the earth, but even then, everything has its own local frame of reference, where "up" and "down" are in relation to the person or thing and not in relation to the earth. All a matrix contains is a vector pointing in the direction that the local reference frame considers "up" when seen from the global, identity reference frame (you have to have some fixed frame that you measure everything else in relation to), plus another vector pointing "right," and another vector pointing either "forward" or "backward," depending on convention.

The identity matrix, which produces no rotation at all, simply has an x axis vector of (1, 0, 0), a y axis vector of (0, 1, 0), and a z axis vector of (0, 0, 1). Notice how each axis vector extends only along the same axis (x, y, or z) of the identity coordinate system. In matrix notation, this is usually represented (in column-major order) as follows:

```
           [1, 0, 0]   <- X Components of Axis Vectors
identity = [0, 1, 0]   <- Y Components of Axis Vectors
           [0, 0, 1]   <- Z Components of Axis Vectors
            ^  ^  ^- Z Axis Vector
            |  |---- Y Axis Vector
            |------- X Axis Vector
```

The cells are ordered (in RAM) like this:

```
[0, 3, 6]
[1, 4, 7]
[2, 5, 8]
```

This notation (which is OpenGL's notation style) fits perfectly into C's two-dimensional arrays, where the first index into the array is the axis vector you want (0 for x, 1 for y, and 2 for z), and the second index is the component (x, y, or z) of that axis vector. (It's also backward from C's normal syntax of [row][column], where in this case you specify [column][row] in the matrix.) For example, the number in "matrix[2][1]" is the y component of the z axis vector for the matrix. A very useful product of that arrangement in RAM is that if you take the address of the x component (second index is 0) of, say, the y axis vector (e.g., "&matrix[1][0]"), the result is a pointer to an ordinary 3D vector, which can be passed into vector math functions that expect a pointer to a 3-value vector. This leads into a different way of thinking about the actual calculation of rotations: rotating a 3D point through the use of a 3-by-3 rotation matrix can be thought of (and practiced) simply as the scaling and addition of vectors. You don't even need a "matrix" to be able to do it.

What you do is this: take the x axis vector of the rotation matrix, and scale it (multiply all three of its components by the same scaling factor) by the x component of the 3D point to be rotated, scale the y axis vector by the y component of the point, and scale the z axis vector by the z component of the point. Finally, take those three scaled vectors and add them together (add all of the x components to produce the new x, add all of the y components to produce the new y, etc.), and the result is your original 3D point, but rotated into the coordinate space defined by the axis vectors in your matrix. The end result is the same as doing a "normal" point times matrix operation, but with an entirely different way of thinking about it.

See "Visualizing Vector Addition" (www.gamedev.net/reference/articles/article1129.asp) for a visual representation of vector addition. *Vector scaling* is simply the act of changing the length of the vectors without changing their direction.

To help visualize a rotation matrix, hold out your right hand in a "hand gun" position with thumb up and index finger out, then extend your middle finger so it points out of your palm. Now rotate your whole hand so that your index finger points at you, and you have a standard right-handed identity matrix, with your index finger the z axis vector, your thumb the y axis vector, and your middle finger the x axis vector. As you rotate your hand, those vectors will rotate in 3D space, and any points multiplied by that matrix will follow. To see for yourself how points are rotated by the matrix using the preceding scaling and adding method, first start with a point lying along one of the axes, say the point (5, 0, 0) along the x axis. Now the y and z components are zero, so the y and z axis vectors of the matrix will be scaled to zero, and all you have to think about is the x axis vector, which is simply multiplied by 5 (made 5 times as long). So as the x axis vector of the matrix rotates, so does the point that lies on it.

In practice, the scaling and adding of vectors can be simplified to the following math, applicable for use in an actual program. Notice that the x coordinate of the point is only ever multiplied with a component of the x axis vector. This is just a simplification and condensation of the scaling and adding of vectors that is still going on under the covers.

```
NewX = X * Matrix[0][0] + Y * Matrix[1][0] + Z * Matrix[2][0];
NewY = X * Matrix[0][1] + Y * Matrix[1][1] + Z * Matrix[2][1];
NewZ = X * Matrix[0][2] + Y * Matrix[1][2] + Z * Matrix[2][2];
```

Extending to Affinity

The previous section only covered rotational or *linear* transformations. Usually, you also want to have a matrix be able to translate, or shift, a point through space as well as rotate it, and that sort of operation is called an *affine* transformation. You do that with either a 3 × 4 or a 4 × 4 matrix, but I'll deal with 3 × 4 matrices to keep things simpler. 4 × 4 matrices enter into the realm of homogeneous coordinates and perspective transforms, which are not things you usually have to deal with yourself. A 3 × 4 matrix (3 tall, 4 wide) basically just adds another vector to the matrix, but instead of being an axis vector, it is a translation vector. The representation is usually as follows:

```
                [1, 0, 0, 0]  <- X Components of Vectors
identity = [0, 1, 0, 0]  <- Y Components of Vectors
                [0, 0, 1, 0]  <- Z Components of Vectors
                 ^  ^  ^  ^- Translation Vector
                 |  |  |-----Z Axis Vector
                 |  |------- Y Axis Vector
                 |---------- X Axis Vector
```

The cells are ordered (in RAM) like this:

```
[0, 3, 6, 9 ]
[1, 4, 7, 10]
[2, 5, 8, 11]
```

The translation vector is merely the amount to shift the point in x, y, and z, as seen from the identity reference frame. It would work the same as if it were outside of the matrix, and you simply added it to the point after the matrix transform. If the matrix was representing a jet plane's orientation in the world, the translation vector would merely be the coordinates of the center of the jet plane in the world. When describing matrix multiplication as the scaling and adding of vectors before, the x, y, and z components of the point to be rotated scaled the x, y, or z axis vectors, respectively, but what scales the translation vector? If you're working with matrices that are larger in one or both dimensions than your vectors, you usually fill in the extra vector components with 1s. So a 3-component x, y, z vector gets an extra imaginary translation component added to the end, which is always a 1, and that translation component scales the translation vector of the matrix. Scaling by 1 is easy because it means no change at all. Here's the code to transform a point through a 3 × 4 matrix:

```
NewX = X * Matrix[0][0] + Y * Matrix[1][0] + Z * Matrix[2][0] + Matrix[3][0];
NewY = X * Matrix[0][1] + Y * Matrix[1][1] + Z * Matrix[2][1] + Matrix[3][1];
NewZ = X * Matrix[0][2] + Y * Matrix[1][2] + Z * Matrix[2][2] + Matrix[3][2];
```

Going in Reverse

Multiplying forward through a matrix is great, but what if you want to multiply "backward," to take a point that has been transformed through a matrix and bring it back into the identity reference frame where it started from? In the general case, this requires calculating the inverse of the matrix, which is a lot of work for general matrices. However, in the case of standard rotation matrices (said to represent an *orthonormal basis*) where the three axis vectors are at perfect right angles to each other, the transpose of the matrix happens also to be the inverse, and the transpose is created merely by flipping the matrix about its primary diagonal (which runs from the upper left to lower right). Here is a visual representation:

```
         [0,  0, -1]        T   [ 0, 1,  0]
matrix = [1,  0,  0]   matrix  = [ 0, 0, -1]
         [0, -1,  0]            [-1, 0,  0]
           ^   ^   ^
           |   |   |-- Z Axis Vector
           |   |------ Y Axis Vector
           | --------- X Axis Vector
```

Effective cell order change (in RAM):

```
           [0, 3, 6]                [0, 1, 2]
    normal [1, 4, 7]   transpose [3, 4, 5]
           [2, 5, 8]                [6, 7, 8]
```

You can either make a transposed version of your matrix and then multiply by that, or you can do the math to directly multiply through the transpose of the matrix without actually changing it. If you go for the latter, it just so happens that instead of scaling and adding, you do dot products. The dot product of the vectors (x, y, z) and (a, b, c) is X*A + Y*B + Z*C. The following code to multiply a point through the transpose of a matrix simply does three dot products, point dot x axis vector, point dot y axis vector, and point dot z axis vector.

```
NewX = X * Matrix[0][0] + Y * Matrix[0][1] + Z * Matrix[0][2];
NewY = X * Matrix[1][0] + Y * Matrix[1][1] + Z * Matrix[1][2];
NewZ = X * Matrix[2][0] + Y * Matrix[2][1] + Z * Matrix[2][2];
```

Going in reverse works similarly for 3×4 matrices with translation, except that you have to subtract the translation vector from the point *before* rotating it to properly reverse the order of operations, since when going forward, the translation vector was added to the point *after* rotation.

```
TX = X - Matrix[3][0];
TY = Y - Matrix[3][1];
TZ = Z - Matrix[3][2];
NewX = TX * Matrix[0][0] + TY * Matrix[0][1] + TZ * Matrix[0][2];
NewY = TX * Matrix[1][0] + TY * Matrix[1][1] + TZ * Matrix[1][2];
NewZ = TX * Matrix[2][0] + TY * Matrix[2][1] + TZ * Matrix[2][2];
```

Multiplying Matrices

Now things start to get really interesting. Multiplying matrices together, or *concatenating* them, allows you to combine the actions of multiple separate matrices into a single matrix such that when points are multiplied through it, will produce the same result as if you multiplied the points through each of the original matrices in turn. Imagine all the computation that can save you when you have a lot of points to transform!

I like to say that you multiply one matrix "through" another matrix, since that's what you're really doing mathematically. The process is astoundingly simple, and all you basically do is take the three axis vectors of the first matrix (for 3×3 matrices) and do a normal vector times matrix operation on each of them with the second matrix to produce the three axis vectors in the result matrix. The same is true for 3×4 matrices being multiplied through each other, in which case you multiply each of the x, y, and z axis vectors and the translation vector of the first matrix through the second matrix as normal, and you get your resultant 3×4 matrix out the other side. Keep in mind that you can also reverse multiply one matrix through another by using the transpose of the second matrix (or the appropriate code to do a transposed multiply directly). For a 3×3 matrix, the code for the normal forward case might look like this:

```
for(i = 0; i < 3; i++) //Cycle through each vector of first matrix.
{
    NewMatrix[i][0] = MatrixA[i][0] * MatrixB[0][0] +
        MatrixA[i][1] * MatrixB[1][0] + MatrixA[i][2] * MatrixB[2][0];
    NewMatrix[i][1] = MatrixA[i][0] * MatrixB[0][1] +
        MatrixA[i][1] * MatrixB[1][1] + MatrixA[i][2] * MatrixB[2][1];
```

```
  NewMatrix[i][2] = MatrixA[i][0] * MatrixB[0][2] +
     MatrixA[i][1] * MatrixB[1][2] + MatrixA[i][2] * MatrixB[2][2];
}
```

If you have two matrices, A and B, where A pitches forward a bit and B rotates to the right a bit, and you multiply A through B to produce matrix C, then multiplying a point through matrix C will produce the same result as if the point was first multiplied through matrix A, and the resulting point was multiplied through matrix B. *Note*: this is the way I prefer to think of my matrix operations right now, but it is actually the reverse of the normal way. When working with matrix operations in APIs, such as OpenGL, matrix concatenations actually work in reverse order. In the preceding example of concatenating A and B into C, multiplying a point by C would actually be the same as first multiplying the point by B, and then multiplying the result by A. You can think of it as each successively concatenated matrix acting in respect to the local coordinate reference frame built up by the previously concatenated matrices, whereas with my method each successive matrix acts in the identity reference frame, which keeps the same order as if you took the time to rotate the point by each original matrix in turn.

The End, For Now

This is by no means a complete treatment of matrix math, but hopefully it will help you to understand the basics better. Once you grasp this much, go dig up a few good books on matrices and learn some of their *real* power, while remembering that at their core, the simpler matrices don't have to be thought of as matrices at all.

[Editor's Note: Big thanks to Seumas' brother Jim McNally for giving us permission to reprint this excellent article.]

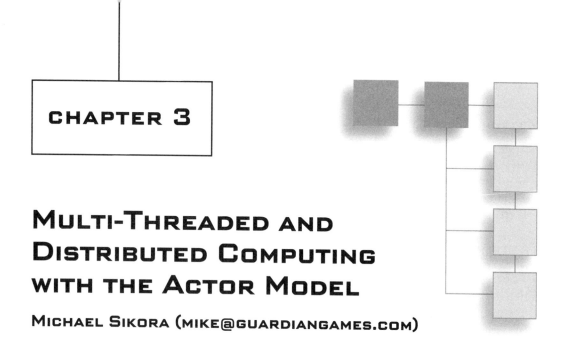

CHAPTER 3

MULTI-THREADED AND DISTRIBUTED COMPUTING WITH THE ACTOR MODEL

MICHAEL SIKORA (MIKE@GUARDIANGAMES.COM)

Are you are looking for a more effective technique with which to take advantage of multi-core CPU systems and/or with which to do distributed computing?[1] This article covers a single specific implementation of the Actor Model type of software architecture that will assist you in taking advantage of both computing resources. For the suitable type of problems in your game (particularly server components), liberal use of this architecture should give you near perfect scaling across multi-cores/machines. It will also provide a few unexpected side benefits that will decrease your development time and increase your confidence in the reliability of your code compared to other concurrency programming techniques. Pretty lofty promises, I know—but there will be trade-offs, and I will cover those, too.

In order to tie the whole article together, I will discuss one specific game programming problem: *computer-controlled players.*[2] I will take the premise that you are developing a massively multiplayer online game with thousands of computer-controlled players running in each game world instance. This is a relatively high-level problem that you will solve with parallel execution. The computer player units will not be doing anything particularly interesting, but they will be doing it in parallel, and they will not know or care what machine or thread they are on.

---

[1]The term *distributed computing* means doing computations in parallel on multiple computers.

[2]*Computer players* are also referred to as agents, nonplayer-controlled characters (NPCs), AI players, etc.

Many developers are accustomed to searching out much smaller, simpler problems to run in parallel. These include physics calculations, path finding problems, and so on. While it's great to run these tasks in parallel, it does not always lead to constant use of the available CPU resources over time. However, using the practical Actor-like model outlined here and breaking the problems into more naturally recurrent problems will lead to better CPU resource utilization. That's what I will show with the computer-controlled players example.

Multi-Threaded and Distributed Computing: Brothers or Second Cousins?

First, I'll look at the similarities and differences between multi-threaded and distributed computing. Are they closely related or just somewhat related? Most developers immediately recognize the obvious similarity between these two concepts—namely, that they do some form of processing in parallel. However, they are also similar in a few other respects:

Parallel execution: This is the definitive common feature. Both multi-threaded and distributed computing are based around this feature.

Shared memory: Most multi-core CPUs use shared memory that each core can access. Distributed computing rarely relies on using the same memory resource. Instead, it relies on distributing copies of the data used in calculations. There is, however, one extremely common system setup involving shared "memory" for distributed computing. Many distributed systems use a single database server, which provides the definitive state of a system to the rest of the non-database servers in real time.

Communication latency: It is easy to dismiss the latency considerations of sending a signal between multiple threads of execution, since they are directly comparable to the cost of copying the information in memory itself. In contrast, the latency between two computers on a network may be longer than the time it takes to compute the entire task itself!

Communication bandwidth: Again, sharing information across threads is similar to sharing information within a thread (copies of information or shared memory). Unfortunately, this is not the case with distributed computing. The amount of information that can be passed between computers is more limited, with the time required to transfer large amounts of information being unacceptable.

You might think that the communication bandwidth and latency issues with distributed computing are difficult to work around. In practice, however, server clusters on a private network often have reasonably low latency and high bandwidth. For this article, I'll assume that you are planning to run your system on a reasonably fast high-speed network—that means the Internet is generally out of the question, unless carefully planned for.

With that in mind, you can see that executing multiple tasks in parallel is, for the most part, similar with regard to both multi-threaded and distributed computing. Now I'll move on to how to abstract away the differences so you can work with one model (instead of two). This is where you get those side benefits with regard to development time and reliability. By working against one model, you can effectively test both ways of computing at the same time—making it easier to be confident in the code as a whole. Also, by having one common model, you can focus on the important thing—distributing tasks across all types of computing resources available to your game system.

The Actor Model

Distributed computing is not a new concept, so there are a lot of ideas out there already for how to best use a multi-computer system. The one I'll discuss here is the *Actor Model*. The Actor Model is a message passing system, where the message sender and receivers are known as Actors. Actors do all the real work in the system, and they all work in parallel by design. You may not have heard of the Actor Model before, so I will take you on a quick tour of its principal concepts before building a practical implementation.

The first thing to know about the Actor Model is that communication between parallel processes is driven by messaging. It is likely that you have come across various message passing systems before. Event-driven programming is generally message-based; so is most network programming. However, you may not have seen a general parallel computing model where all computation is based on the concept of message passing. There are a few important differences, as shown in Figure 3.1.

The key difference is that message passing in the Actor Model is asynchronous. Practical Actor Model implementations do not usually guarantee any form of message ordering. This one will because it is easier to work with. Asynchronous message passing is a requirement because Actors do not automatically block (i.e., stop executing) when they send or receive messages.

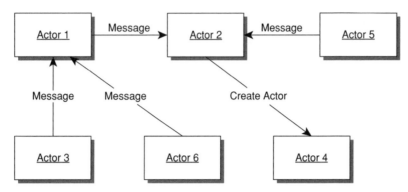

Figure 3.1
Actor Model in action. At any given instant, any and all Actors are performing some action, such as sending a message or creating a new Actor.

Now comes the most important part of the Actor Model: the Actors. Actors act (pardon the pun) like tasks or jobs do when run by a scheduler. Actors run independently of other Actors or systems, usually continuously. An Actor can receive messages, take actions (including creating more Actors), send messages, and continue to do computations. Often each Actor has an *address* that can be used to route messages to the Actor, used in conjunction with an *address space*. The actual implementation details of message routing can vary, so in Figure 3.1, the message routing mechanism is simply implied. Message routing aside, the key is that in a system of Actors, the primary way for Actors to communicate with each other is through asynchronous message passing.

Be aware that this is a very general definition of the Actor Model. It has been widely extended and written about since introduction in the 1970s. There are even Actor-oriented languages—interesting, but not very relevant to game development (at least, not yet).

Although I will not be implementing a full-out Actor Model in this article, it is the inspiration for the simplified model I will implement. If you are looking for more information on the Actor Model, there are some references included at the end of the article. There has been renewed interest in the field because of the wide availability of commodity multi-core CPUs and high-bandwidth interconnects, so what was once old has become new again.

When to Apply This Model

So for what type of problems should you consider the Actor Model for over other forms of concurrency programming? Generally speaking, there are a few questions you can ask yourself when considering a specific solution you want to run in parallel:

- Do you need to do parallel processing on different machines in real time?

- Do you need to do parallel processing on different threads in real time?

- Do you need to do seamless parallel processing on a local machine *and* other machines?

- Do you need dynamic load balancing for a series of machines?

- Do you have a high-speed network connecting the machines involved in the system?

If you answered yes to any of these, you should take a hard look at a message passing design. Generally, the one red flag warning for using the Actor Model is if your system is extremely memory-restrained. This could prevent you from breaking up your problem in such a way that each Actor has enough information to do continuous processing, but little enough that the sum total does not blow your memory budget.

For example, assume you adopt an Actor Model design for concurrently running your computer-controlled players. I'll also assume that your game is running on a console device (with notoriously harsh memory limitations) and that you have a few dozen computer players in use at a single time. If they all need to cache 10MB of game state data so that they can continue to make decisions concurrently, they will quickly eat up your entire memory budget. Is this a dead end? Not necessarily. If you plan carefully from the start and identify what information actually needs to be shared, you can distribute that information evenly among your Actors, and then let them transmit the information through messages on a needed basis. Interestingly, this was the way some researchers originally approached the model—under the assumption you could rapidly retransmit messages instead of storing information in each Actor.[3] This gave memory savings at the cost of CPU performance. It is ironic that in this article I advocate the opposite: spend your memory to make local copies of information for each Actor if you can afford it so that you can avoid resource contention issues and build multi-threaded and distributed computing solutions with one code path.

---

[3]See The Jellybean Machine (J-machine) home page for some historical insight <http://cva.stanford.edu/projects/j-machine/>.

To further expound on the virtues of the Actor Model, say that during the course of development, the design gets tweaked and now you want hundreds of computer players in multi-player matches. The question arises as to how you will run all those players on the host machine (assuming typical client/server architecture). Well, if you have been programming by the Actor Model from the start, it should take only a few hours to get your system distributing the computer players across the multiple console machines involved in the multi-player game.

In practice, it is easy to see how server-side development can benefit from sticking to the Actor Model as an architecture for parallel task execution: once you can get decent scaling, it's often cheaper to add more machines than it is to invest developer time into churning out marginally more efficient code. With server-side development, you can also ship with inefficient but correct code and just use more machines per game server instance. Post ship, if your new game is booming (particularly true for MMO subscription games) you can work on using fewer machines with more efficient code—and saving money, which is something managers love to hear. Tell them you will be able to ship on time with the option to reduce their ongoing costs, and you might just get a raise!

For client-side computing, it is somewhat more difficult to see the applications. This is particularly true where memory is limited (but can be shared). In this situation, most applications of the Actor Model can be found where multiple systems will be connected for multi-player matches. You can distribute computer players, physics calculations, and so on among the available machines. If you are worried about cheating by way of hacking, you might even have each Actor replicated on two different machines so the results can be compared.

In contrast to some consoles, most PCs are shipping with a lot of memory these days, so be sure to take advantage of it by applying the Actor Model where it makes sense.

Implementation Details

For this modified Actor Model framework, you are looking for a scalable parallel execution system that fits typical game programming problems. The one significant deviation I will make with regard to a typical Actor Model implementation is in the way that Actors pass messages around. With the goal of simplifying the example framework as much as possible, each Actor will route his message "directly" to the desired recipient Actor through a single intermediary

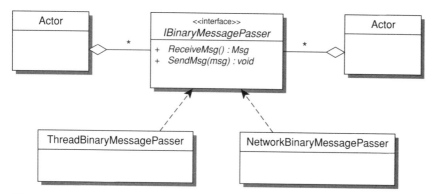

Figure 3.2
The basic message passing model for handling both local and networked parallel task execution with Actor objects.

that handles the synchronization, threading, and networking details. This intermediary will form a binary relationship between the two Actors that wish to communicate. To see how this specializes the general Actor Model, take a look at Figure 3.2. This is the simplified model, which you can use for treating multi-threaded and distributed computing as the same parallel execution system by way of an Actor-like model.

As you can see, the simplified model has different message passing implementations for messages passed between threads (i.e., `Server->ThreadBinary MessagePasser->Client`) and between computers (`Server->ThreadBinary MessagePasser->Client`). I still have not taken care of all the details regarding the creation of these message passers and hooking them up to their respective client and server components. These development details depend on what exactly the Actor objects will be doing. Let's first talk about the roles and responsibilities that each of these classes play in solving these problems.

> **Actor:** This is the computation workhorse object. It fulfills the normal Actor requirements by asynchronously passing and receiving messages, as well as executing in parallel with other Actors. You may have any number of these in your system, and they may be executing on separate threads or separate computers—it does not matter, since the message passer takes care of the communication details.
>
> **Message passer:** This is what makes the system easy to work with. Regardless of how you ultimately implement the message passing

mechanism, the message passer interface promises to fulfill these three requirements:

- To accept messages from one or more other objects. These messages will be held for the Server/Client Actor to retrieve at the client's convenience.
- To send messages to one or more other objects. If the message can't be sent, it is held and sent at the earliest possible opportunity.
- To completely encapsulate the details of message passing. This is what makes it possible to dynamically take advantage of both multiple threads and multiple systems for generic parallel execution.

Both[4] of the realized classes for message passing (ThreadBinaryMessagePasser and NetworkBinaryMessagePasser) fulfill each of these three requirements. The first two requirements (receiving and sending messages) are fulfilled by each by maintaining two queues. The first queue is for incoming (received) messages, and the second queue is for outgoing (sent) messages. Incoming messages are saved until the Actor retrieves them, at which point they are removed from the queue. Outgoing messages are stored until they can be passed to the other Actor or to some intermediate object, which will ensure the message reaches the intended recipient Actor.

The final requirement is fulfilled uniquely by each realized interface. Since I will be using TCP/IP for these network connections, I will actually have two IBinary MessagePasser realizations: a server and a client. The server will open a port on the host machine and wait for the client to connect, while the client will simply attempt to connect upon creation. That is the only notable difference. Once both are created, they behave in the same way through their shared interface.

Without further ado, here is the public interface for the various message passers:

```
class IBinaryMessagePasser
{
public:
    //Send a message as soon as possible
    virtual bool SendMessage(Message &msg) = 0;
    //Receive a message if any are available - returns true if msg
    //is filled with valid msg, false otherwise
    virtual bool ReceiveMessage(Message &msg) = 0;
    //Check if the connection relationship is still valid
    virtual bool IsValid() = 0;
};
```

---

[4]Technically, in this framework, the networking class is broken into two classes—a client and server component—since TCP is the underlying transport mechanism; but for something like UDP, you would likely have just one implementer.

```cpp
class ThreadBinaryMessagePasser : public IBinaryMessagePasser
{
public:
    ThreadBinaryMessagePasser();
    ~ThreadBinaryMessagePasser();
    //create a parent-partner
    void CreateParent();
    //create a child-partner - must be created with valid parent
    //already in existence
    void CreateChild( ThreadBinaryMessagePasser * ParentObject );
    //implement send message from IBinaryMessagePasser
    bool SendMessage(Message &Msg);
    //implement receive message from IBinaryMessagePasser
    bool ReceiveMessage(Message &MsgOut);
    //attempt to send messages held in the queue
    bool Update();
    //is binary relationship between communicating objects still
    //valid?
    bool IsValid();
    //check how many messages are queued
    int GetNumMsgsWaitingToBeSent();
    //destroy this side of the relationship (i.e. this object)
    void Destroy();
};
class ClientNetworkBinaryMessagePasser : public IBinaryMessagePasser
{
public:
    ClientNetworkBinaryMessagePasser();
    ~ClientNetworkBinaryMessagePasser();
    //Connect to server
    bool Connect(char * IP, int Port);
    //check the receive buffer for new *complete* messages
    bool ReceiveMessage(Message &MsgOut);
    //send a msg (immediately)
    bool SendMessage(Message &Msg);
    //Fill recv and send buffers (if possible)
    bool Update();
    //is binary relationship between communicating objects still
    //valid?
bool IsValid();
};
class ServerNetworkBinaryMessagePasser : public IBinaryMessagePasser
{
```

```
public:
    ServerNetworkBinaryMessagePasser();
    ~ServerNetworkBinaryMessagePasser();
    //create this object with an already connected client
    void Create(SOCKET ConnectedSocket, char * IPAddress);
    //check the receive buffer for new *complete* messages
    bool ReceiveMessage(Message &MsgOut);
    //send a msg (immediately)
    bool SendMessage(Message &Msg);
    //Fill recv and send buffers (if possible)
    bool Update();
    //Gracefully disconnect
    void Disconnect() { Socket.Disconnect(); };
    //is binary relationship between communicating objects still
    //valid?
    bool IsValid();
};
```

Finally, there is one last interface: the generic Actor. The Actor interface accepts generic IBinaryMessagePasser connections to other Actors. You do not define server and client Actor interfaces because not all problems will need to differentiate between Actors as being one or the other. This is where you save development time and increase the reliability of your code. Your Actors no longer care where their brethren are located (on the local system or on a completely different system). You can scale across multiple threads or multiple systems, and you do not have to make any changes to your code.

```
class Actor
{
public:
    //add an actor for communication to/from this actor
    virtual void addActor(IBinaryMessagePasser * actor);
};
```

Example Problem: Using Client Actors as Computer Players

Now that I've discussed the general framework, you can turn your attention to a specific example problem—how to run many computer players on a server back end. The computational cost of running all these computer-controlled players at once could easily chew through all your available CPU execution time on a single thread, or even on a single multi-core machine when you consider all the direct and indirect things these computer players might be computing, such as path finding, decision making, goal planning, and so on.

There is one significant difference between this framework and how the example problem is solved. Since I will be using this system to handle multiple computer players for a game where all players interact with the same "world" and many Actor objects may wish to change the world in parallel, I will lay a client-server architecture on top of the Actor Model framework. Non-Actor parts of the system need a common place to work on the game world with all the Actors. The Server Actor becomes the definitive game state object, and all changes must go through it. I also make this change on the assumption that you are unlikely to model your entire game system in terms of Actors. It may run on the same thread/computer as your non-Actor systems, allowing you to access the Server Actor directly, without having to use some thread/distributed computing safe method. You might think this means that the system will be bottlenecked by the server-to-client message passing, but I will at least discuss (if not implement) a way of alleviating that particular problem so that you get reasonably good performance scaling.

If you were developing such a game (maybe a massive online real-time strategy game), you might quickly find that no single server can possibly run a single instance of your game world on its own. Or you might have been able to pull it off in the original design, but during the first public beta, you realized that your fans are really clamoring for massive battles. Suddenly you end up with a design that requires you to run four times as many computer-controlled units, and your servers cannot keep up with the new demands. Now you have to turn to distributed computing. If you planned from the start to use an Actor Model implementation, like the one presented here, your game server system can safely scale across any reasonable number of servers. In fact, you can just throw as many servers as you need to at the problem.

The example problem will show just how that all works. In this case, you are moving a group of "player units" around in your game world. All of your players units are constantly moving away from one another (also known as *spreading out*). It is a very trivial use of the whole system, but it demonstrates very simply how a large group of computer players would continue to function in an asynchronous way while operating within the same game world (see Figure 3.3).

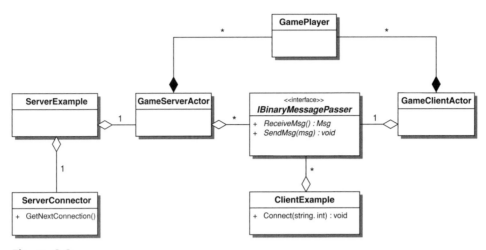

Figure 3.3
The general composition of the included example program.

The most interesting parts of the system are the GameServerActor and the GameClientActor, since they are the parts of the system running in parallel and still sharing information (through asynchronous messaging) with each other. The rest of the system is mostly networking and threading code designed to get you to the point where you can *just work* with Actor objects and forget about the details of how they run or on which machine they reside.

GamePlayerActor: The computer-controlled player attempts to continually move its assigned player units so that each is an equal distance between the closest objects around it. It does this by finding the closest object to it and moving perpendicularly away from it until another object is closer. There is not a one-to-one correspondence between "game player units" (points in the game world) and GamePlayerActor objects. A GamePlayerActor may be responsible for any number of player objects.

GameServerActor: The singleton game Server Actor keeps the definitive game state. For this little example, the "game" is a rectangular 2D space filled with computer-player units that can move. The "goal" of the game is for the computer players to evenly distribute themselves across the space, where each player is an equal distance from all the objects around it but still within the world bounds. This game example is exceedingly simple, but it parallels many flocking and formation problems that game artificial intelligence developers come across. The game server only moves player units based on the decisions that each PlayerActor makes with regard to which direction to be moving at any given time. The final result is that all players appear to "naturally" distribute themselves an equal distance from all the objects around them.

The entire example framework and example problem source code project are available on this book's companion web site at www.courseptr.com/downloads. The example framework here is designed for quick experimentation with new Actor ideas rather than production use, so be sure to use it for your problems and ideas but not your production projects. If you are going to run the system across multiple machines to do distributed computing, keep in mind that firewalls and networking routers can easily block connections, so check your settings if you have problems getting things to connect.

Extending the Framework with an Address Space

When you find a problem that might be a good fit for this system, the first limitation you might come across is the mechanism for message passing. The current system allows Actors to create new Actors and communicate with them, but you cannot route messages dynamically from any one Actor to another. It is arguably more efficient to keep your Actors directly communicating with each other, but it is not always practical. The solution is to move to a common address space where all your Actors register—then Actors can dynamically message each other.

You can easily add a common address space in the example code by changing each Actor to have a single asynchronous binary relationship with the address space object for sending and receiving messages. You can reuse the IBinary MessagePasser implementers practically as is, albeit with minor changes. Depending on your requirements, you might have each distributed Actor's messages sorted so that each machine maintains just one active network connection to any other given machine at a time. This can lead to better bandwidth utilization; and on most systems, network connections are not resource free, so you save those costs as well.

The last part is deciding how your Actors will identify themselves so that messages can be routed correctly. Using a simple integer-based ID is probably sufficient for most setups. You may wish to include the sender's ID by default as well, since two-way communication is normally assumed.

Beware of the drawbacks to using a common address space. First, there is no way to tell if an Actor exists when the message is sent. You can build tools into your address space so that it becomes possible to check the status of an Actor object, but because of the asynchronous communication links, the time it takes to receive a confirmation could be detrimental to performance.

On the topic of performance, one important thing to keep in mind when applying this system is that you can still use other forms of concurrency programming. Your individual Actors might choose to spawn multiple threads and use shared memory on their own. So, all the old concurrency techniques you know will still apply.

One warning though—if you are still looking for additional performance, particularly if your system is memory-limited, you might decide to do something a little more extreme. You might choose to group your Actors on local machines to use shared memory resources. This can be a particularly important optimization if the algorithms acting on these shared memory resources are of the lock-free variety. I would suggest you use this as a last resort, since, by doing so, you almost certainly give up the side benefits that come with using the Actor Model. Since you will have to differentiate between local and non-local actors, you lose the common interface for your actors. You also introduce the overhead of tracking which Actors are local and which are non-local. Now you have even more performance to make up by using shared memory resources between Actors. The bottom line is, if you find yourself working against the Actor Model that much, it might mean the Actor Model is not the right fit for your problem, and it is time to explore other solutions.

Dynamic Load Balancing

Dynamic load balancing is the process of distributing and scheduling the use of available computing resources to run tasks. In this case, tasks are equivalent to Actors. If your Actor system needs to do dynamic load balancing, it can be easy or hard, depending on the level of control you need.

The easy way is to create and initialize new Actors on other systems as one machine gets bogged down and as they are called for. If your Actors have relatively short life spans, this will likely be sufficient and requires little additional effort on your part. You simply keep track of the utilization of each server and place new Actors on the least utilized machine. The example here does not have any direct support for this, since the server passively waits for clients to join in, but it is not difficult to switch the system so that Actors can be created remotely on other machines.

The hard case for dynamically managing your Actors is when you need to transfer an Actor from one physical machine to another. It is not just a matter of copying the current state of the Actor and re-creating it (that is, unfortunately, the easy part). The hard part is making sure that your transferred Actor continues to receive messages from all the other Actors in the system. This means that your Actor either has to re-create its communication links directly with the Actors it is associated with, or a bridging object must be created to re-route messages. If you are using an address space, you have to make sure messages are correctly routed to the new physical location of the Actor. You also need to carefully manage the messages sent to the Actor during the transition so messages are not "lost" while the Actor is unavailable. Instead, they should be held until the intended Actor is ready to receive them.

If your Actors store significant amounts of data locally, the cost of transmitting them from one machine to another might be prohibitively expensive as a one-off event. You might be tempted to take the (rather difficult) engineering route of making your system capable of transferring the Actor over a reasonable period of time while continuing to operate the original—but there is an easier way. If you find your Actors contain so much information that it is hard to send them off in one go, that probably means your Actors are too large in general and should be broken down into more manageable pieces. This will help keep your system from becoming obscenely complex and also increase the scalability of your system in the process.

Conclusion

Actor Models use asynchronous message passing and multi-threaded and distributed computing to accomplish parallel execution with the use of Actor objects. Actor objects are like tasks in that each instance does a computing task in parallel to the others. You can use Actors as a replacement for other concurrency programming techniques or as a complement, depending on the situation.

This Actor Model example used direct message passing instead of an address space for improved efficiency and simplicity. It demonstrated how you might break up the typical tasks of computer players on a server back end so that you can utilize both multi-threaded concurrency and distributed computing.

The case for using an Actor Model instead of (or in addition to) other concurrency programming techniques is three-fold. First, you get the ability to scale your work across multiple threads of execution and multiple machines seamlessly. Second, you can trade memory for faster execution time or vice-versa (with regard to resource contention and message passing). Finally, you improve the speed of development by coding a single path for utilization of both multi-threaded and distributed computing. Now that you have a new tool for parallel execution, you just need to identify your own candidate problems that you can apply the Actor Model to, and then you can start reaping these benefits in your projects!

References

Agha, G. *ACTORS: A Model of Concurrent Computation in Distributed Systems.* MIT Press, 1986.

Heirich, A., and J. Arvo. "Parallel Rendering with an Actor Model." Proceedings of Eurographics '97, Workshop on Programming Paradigms for Graphics, Budapest, Hungary (September 1997).

Jamali, N., P. Thati, and G. Agha. "An Actor-Based Architecture for Customizing and Controlling Agent Ensembles." *IEEE Intelligent Systems.* 14(2), Mar/Apr 1999, pp. 38–44.

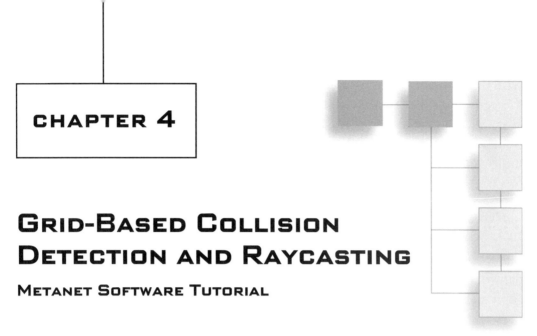

CHAPTER 4

GRID-BASED COLLISION DETECTION AND RAYCASTING

METANET SOFTWARE TUTORIAL

Note

Frequent mention is made to *N*. This is a freeware physics-based jumping game that's available on the authors' web site at www.thewayoftheninja.org.

You can find the previous Metanet Software tutorial, "Collision Detection and Response," in the companion book to this one in the GameDev.net Collection titled *Beginning Game Programming* (Cengage Learning).

SECTION 0: General Introduction

The previous tutorial examined how "narrow-phase" collision detection works in N; given two shapes (a dynamic AABB or circle and a static tile), we discussed how to project the dynamic object out of the tile.

This tutorial deals with "broad-phase" collision detection: given a dynamic object in a world full of tiles, how do you know which objects and tiles it should be tested with during the narrow phase? The solution used in N was to split the world into a uniform grid of square "cells"; instead of testing the dynamic object against all the tiles in the world, you only need to test against the tiles contained in the cells that are touching the dynamic object.

The one problem with our approach is that all dynamic objects must be smaller than a grid cell; while this limitation can be circumvented (for instance, by representing a single large object as multiple smaller objects), in ActionScript, it really helps keep things running fast. Thus it was a self-imposed design constraint.

Grids tend to work best when all game objects are of roughly the same size and the game world is relatively small; an N × N grid requires N^2 cells, so for larger worlds the memory requirements might be prohibitive. More complex structures, which are used to partition game worlds, such as quadtrees or multi-resolution grids, save memory and/or make it easier to support objects of vastly different size.

SECTION 1: Basic Tile Grid

The first use of the grid was to store the tilemap data, which defines the "solid" parts of the world; since tile-based games use a grid of tiles, a grid seemed like a good fit. The grid itself is simply a 2D array; each entry in the array is a cell object. In N, each cell is occupied by a single tile shape.

The first thing you need to be able to do is to determine, given a position, which cell contains this position. This is easily done:

```
grid_column = Math.floor(pos.x / cell_width);
grid_row = Math.floor(pos.y / cell_height);
```

Now you can easily determine which cell contains your dynamic object's center; you call this cell the *current cell* of the object. Since you've restricted the object's size to less than the size of a cell, you know that the object can only overlap, at most, four cells (see Figure 4.0).

Note

The grid cells touched by the box are highlighted. Note that if the object overlaps the current cell's right neighbor, it can't possibly overlap the left neighbor; likewise for the up/down neighbors.

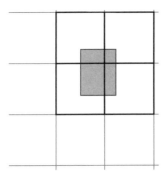

Figure 4.0
The cells touched by an object.

You can safely assume that the object will, at most, be overlapping the current cell, a horizontal neighbor of the current cell, a vertical neighbor of the current cell, and a diagonal neighbor of the current cell; the diagonal neighbor is also a neighbor of the horizontal/vertical neighbors. Determining which cells an object overlaps can be done in various ways:

- You can simply use four position lookups (one for each of the object's corners).

- You can use one position lookup (with the object's center) to determine the current cell's index in the 2D grid, and then use offsets from this index based on the object's position relative to the current cell's position—that is, if the object's center is left and below the current cell's center and the current cell's index is [i][j], you know you have to look at the left, down, and left/down neighbors, or [i−1][j], [i][j+1], [i−1][j+1].

You can run into problems if part of the object is outside of the boundary of the grid; this results in the preceding methods generating cell indices that don't exist. This can be avoided by using min/max to keep the indices within the limits of the grid, or by using modulo to "wrap" the indices to the other side of the grid. A much simpler solution is to pad the outside edges of the grid with "border" cells, which can't be occupied by an object; this prevents objects from leaving the boundary of the grid.

Collision vs. a Tilemap Using the Grid

Now that you know the four cells touched by your dynamic object, you need to collide the object against the tiles contained in those cells. Each cell in the grid stores tile information describing the tile contained in that cell. This includes a flag indicating the shape of the tile, as well as any tile-specific properties needed by the collision routines (i.e., x-width, center position, surface normal). To implement this, you can define a set of tile objects; each tile is responsible for generating collision results between itself and a dynamic object:

```
tile.Collide_Circle(myCircle)
```

Or you can use a simpler C-like approach where both the tile and the object are simply containers of data, and collision functions are stored in a 2D hash list of collision functions; the shape flags of the objects being collided are used as hash keys to select the appropriate function:

```
Collide[tile.shape][myObj.shape](tile, myObj)
```

SECTION 2: Advanced Tile Grid

Grid Improvements

Now that you have a simple grid in place for use with object-versus-tilemap collision, there are certain things you can do to make it more efficient. The first thing is to store, in each cell, direct references to that cell's four neighbors. This way, once you've determined an object's current cell, you can access the neighboring cells using a single property lookup; this results in a smaller number of calculations when accessing neighboring cells but causes each cell to occupy more memory. Since the cost of calculating cell indices is likely to be negligible in many programming environments, this trade-off might not always be worthwhile.

In N we implemented these neighbor "pointers" separately:

```
cell.nR //right, left, up, down neighbors
cell.nL
cell.nU
cell.nD
```

Edge Info

One major enhancement we made to our grid was to store information, not only about each cell, but about each of the cell's four edges. This idea was borrowed from an article by Tom Forsyth in *Game Programming Gems 3*, which mentioned that the game *X-Com* used a similar structure.

The edge data we stored was very minimal—a single flag that indicates the state of the edge:

- **Empty:** Neither of the cells that shares this edge contains a solid tile shape.

- **Solid:** Each tile shape has at least one edge that matches a grid edge perfectly; these edges were labelled "solid."

- **Interesting:** Edges that were adjacent to a cell containing a solid tile shape but that didn't match the shape perfectly were labelled "interesting," indicating that we needed to perform further collision tests. For instance, the two edges on the outside of a triangle's hypotenuse are "interesting."

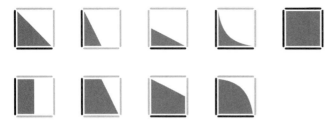

Figure 4.1
The nine tile shapes used in N and their corresponding edge states: solid edges are black and interesting edges are gray.

Once each tile has been assigned a set of edge states (see Figure 4.1), you then need to compare the edge states of neighboring tiles; any edge at which both tiles have solid edge states should be considered empty, as such a configuration only exists below the surface of the world. Such a change will have no impact on the correctness of the collision results, since objects should only collide with the world's surface.

Having this edge info let us skip a lot of tile-specific collision routines; if an object overlaps a solid edge (which is very common in tile-based games), you simply project it out of that edge instead of having to resort to a more complex object-versus-tile collision test. Since the only edges that were labeled solid were those that perfectly match the shape of a tile, the result was the same as if we had used an object-versus-tile test but much simpler to compute. The only time you have to resort to tile-specific collision routines is when an object touches an interesting edge.

This edge information can be considered a coarse approximation of the surface of the world described by the tilemap; this is sometimes useful, since a normal tilemap doesn't contain any explicit surface information. And knowing the surface of the world is often useful—for instance, to allow enemies to move along the world's surface. Having this extra edge info for each cell may or may not be useful in your game (see Figure 4.2).

In N, doors were easily implemented as objects, which changed the value of a cell's edge states. This was a pleasant side effect of using edges. Additionally, the enemy AI uses edge states for pathfinding; this lets enemies respond to doors and follow the (approximate) surface of the world. Our ray queries were also sped up by using this edge info.

Unfortunately, the state of each edge is determined by the state of the two cells adjacent to it; the logic we implemented to correctly set up the edges was complex and quite prone to bugs, since we had to consider each possible combination of

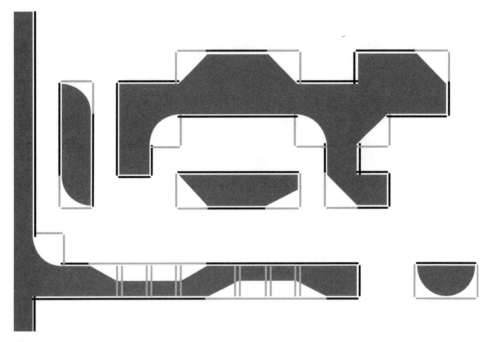

Figure 4.2
An example tilemap containing chunks of contiguous tiles and their edge states. Solid edges are black, and interesting edges are light grey. Note that the non-empty edges form a perimeter around each chunk, which approximates the chunk's surface.

cell states. A simpler method to set up/define edge states probably exists; please let us know if you come up with anything.

SECTION 3: Object Grid

The grid structure previously described can also double as a spatial database used to manage dynamic objects [Simpson]. Just as each cell contains information about the tile located in that cell, it can also contain information about each dynamic object currently located in the cell. Each cell contains a list of dynamic objects; as an object moves through the grid, you insert/remove it from each cell's list as appropriate.

There are two approaches that can be taken when using a grid with dynamic objects:

> **"Normal" grid:** Each object is associated with all of the cells it touches. In this case, it would be from one to four cells. Every time the object moves, it's removed from the cells that it used to touch and inserted into the cells it now

touches. When you collide an object, you only need to test it against the contents of any cell it touches.

- **Pros:** Each object needs to look in, at most, four cells to find other objects it might collide with.
- **Cons:** Each object needs to be inserted/removed from up to four cells every time it moves; also, additional logic needs to be added to the collision code to deal with a case where, for instance, two objects touch the same two cells. Since you only want to test that pair of objects once, you'd have to add a `tested` flag or similar code to deal with this.

"Loose" grid: Each object is placed in a single cell—that which contains its center. When an object moves, it's removed from that (single) cell and inserted into the cell that contains its new position. When testing for collision, you have to check not only the current cell, but also the eight cells neighboring the current cell. The idea of a loose grid can be a bit confusing until it clicks, at which point everything will make perfect sense. (You can find more details at www.tulrich.com/geekstuff/partitioning.html.)

- **Pros:** Each object needs to be inserted/removed from only one cell when it moves.
- **Cons:** Each object always needs to look in nine cells to find other objects it might collide with

We chose to use a loose grid in N because it simplified handling moving objects; however, most of the ideas mentioned in this tutorial apply to any kind of grid.

Each cell in our grid stores a double-linked-list of references to objects; the objects in a cell's list are those whose centers are contained in the cell. (If you're not familiar with linked lists, Googling "linked list" is probably a good way to learn about them.)

In our implementation, each cell has the following:

```
.next   //the head of the linked list
prev    //always equal to null since .next is the first list entry
and each object has:
    .cell   //reference to the cell in which it's contained
    .prev   //reference to the object before this object in .cell's linked list
    .next   //reference to the object after this object in .cell's linked list
```

Whenever an object moves, its position in the grid is updated, and changes to the linked lists are made as appropriate.

More Details

There are two ways to approach broad-phase collision. One is to let each object query the world to find other objects it might be colliding with. Another is for a manager to find all possible collisions and notify the objects involved.

In N, we used the first method because it allowed a very simple design: only the ninja queries for collision, and the other objects are notified if the ninja's query results in a collision event. While this is good from the point of view of execution speed, it also limits possible designs. For instance, enemies can't react to each other (as in *Super Mario Bros.*, where goombas that walk into each other change direction). So, each frame the ninja tests its current cell and the eight neighboring cells for objects; it tests for collision against any objects found.

A more general, elegant system, which is useful in simulation-type environments where all objects must collide with each other, is to iterate over all moving objects and test them against:

- Any objects after them in the current cell's list.

- Any objects in the lists of four cells that neighbor the current cell. You can use any contiguous set of four cells, for instance, [right, right-down, down, left-down], [up, up-left, left, left-down], and so on.

It might seem like this technique will miss some collisions; but if you work it out on paper, you'll see that every possible collision between objects is found. This lets you reduce the number of per-object cell-list tests to five (from nine), without resorting to flags or any other awkward solution.

Collision detection in any game is very specific to the game's design; usually, you can achieve significant increases in efficiency simply by choosing good rules for your game world. For instance, in a game such as *Soldat* (www.soldat.pl), where there are many moving objects, most of which are bullets, a very good idea is to decide that bullets should not collide against other bullets. This means that bullets don't have to be moved in the grid every time they change positions— instead of being *in* the grid, they simply read *from* the grid to determine which objects they might collide with. This saves the cost of numerous linked-list insertions/removals; the trade-off is that you can't stop your opponent's bullets with your own.

SECTION 4: Raycasting

Aside from projection/collision queries, games often also need other types of queries; objects can invoke these queries when they need to know something about the world. A good example of such a query is a *raycast*; a ray is simply a line with only one endpoint. Rays can be used to determine if two objects can "see" each other or can model a fast-moving projectile—for instance, in *Quake*, many weapons (such as the railgun) are modeled as rays.

You might want to know the first thing that the ray intersects (by *first* we mean the intersection point closest to the ray's origin); or, given two points you might want to know if the line that connects those two points intersects anything.

In N, we use raycasts to determine AI visibility, as well as for some of the weapons. Colliding the ray against the world requires the two (hopefully now familiar) steps:

- **Broad phase:** Determines which things (tiles and objects) the ray might collide with.

- **Narrow phase:** Tests the ray against each thing to determine collision information, such as the point of intersection.

Broad Phase

In our grid-based system, the broad phase amounts to determining which cells the ray touches; anything not contained in this set of cells can't possibly touch the ray. (Note: since we use a loose grid for our objects, this isn't strictly true; see the following sections for more details.)

A naive approach to determining which cells the ray touches might be to calculate the AABB containing the ray and consider all cells touching this AABB as touching the ray. While this works well for short rays, or rays that are almost vertical or horizontal, it requires testing up to n^2 cells, which will get very slow very fast.

A better solution would be to determine *exactly* which cells the ray touches; a great (and quite simple) algorithm to do this is described in [Amanatides] and [Bikker]; basically, it lets you step along the ray, visiting each cell the ray touches in the order that it is touched by the ray. For N, we simply implemented this algorithm; at each cell, we test the ray against the cell contents, using our narrow-phase routines.

Narrow Phase vs. Tiles

Not only does the preceding ray-traversal algorithm tell you which cells the ray touches, it also allows you to efficiently calculate the points at which the ray enters and exits each cell (i.e., the points at which the ray crosses the edges of the grid). This is very useful because, since the grid stores edge info, you can stop as soon as the ray crosses over a solid edge—you know that this is an intersection without having to perform any special ray-versus-tile intersection test.

If the ray crosses an interesting edge, you need to test the ray against the cell's tile shape using a tile shape–specific test. Most of the tests we used were implemented as ray-versus-line or ray-versus-line-segment tests, based on the following sources: Geometry Algorithms (www.geometryalgorithms.com) and [O'Rourke]. For the circular shapes, we adapted a swept-circle test [Gomez].

Narrow Phase vs. Objects

One major problem with using a loose grid is that objects that aren't contained in the cells touched by a ray might still touch the ray (see Figure 4.3).

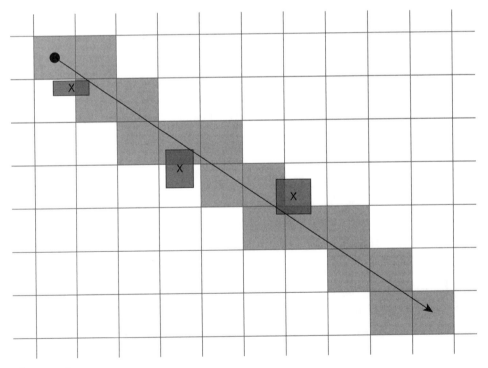

Figure 4.3
The cells touched by a ray.

In N, this was a problem we could ignore. Since the ninja was the only object that rays needed to be tested against, we simply performed a ray-versus-tiles test to find the point at which the ray hit the tiles, and then we performed a ray-versus-circle test against the ninja to see if the ray hit the ninja before hitting the tiles. If intersecting rays with dynamic objects is an important feature of your game, you might be better off using a regular/non-loose grid, which doesn't suffer from this problem.

SECTION 5: Conclusion

As we mentioned before, the one main limitation of our grid-based approach is that all objects must fit inside a grid cell (i.e., they can be no larger than a grid cell). This isn't really a limitation imposed by the use of a grid; it's a self-imposed limitation designed to increase the simplicity and speed of this approach.

To use a grid-based approach with any size of object, all that's necessary is to be able to (hopefully quickly) determine which cell(s) an object touches so that it can be inserted or deleted from those cells' linked lists. With objects smaller than a cell, this is very fast; as the size of an object grows, the number of cells it touches increases, and the cost of the linked-list insertions and deletions will become prohibitive. The *best* grid resolution to use is game-specific.

Another thing to note is that you don't need to have a tile-based world to use a grid. Using the previous tutorial's collision routines and a grid-based system, you could develop an engine that supports a world composed of arbitrarily placed and sized shapes; this way your world wouldn't have to be constrained to tile-sized blocks. All you need to be able to do is, given a shape, determine all of the tiles it overlaps. If you insert each static object into the grid this way, you can then use the grid as you would with tiles—to find all the static objects to test a dynamic object against.

Anyway, hopefully you've learned that a simple grid can often be an effective data structure to use as a spatial database in your game, as well as how to go about using it.

Source Code

A demo application containing the N source code relating to this tutorial is available on our web site at www.harveycartel.org/metanet/tutorials/tutorialB.html.

You are free to use this code however you'd like, provided you notify us if it's for commercial use; a link to our site would also be appreciated.

References

Amanatides, John and Andrew Woo. "A Fast Voxel Traversal Algorithm for Ray Tracing." (www.cse.yorku.ca/ ~ amana/research/grid.pdf).

Bikker, Jacco. "Raytracing Topics and Techniques - Part 4: Spatial Subdivision." 26 Oct 2004 (www.flipcode.com/archives/Raytracing_Topics_Techniques-Part_4_Spatial_Subdivisions.shtml).

Forsyth, Tom. "Cellular Automata for Physical Modeling." In *Game Programming Gems 3*, edited by Dante Treglia. Charles River Media, 2002.

Gomez, Miguel. "Simple Intersection Tests for Games." 18 Oct 1999 (www.gamasutra.com/features/19991018/Gomez_1.htm).

O'Rourke, Joseph. *Computational Geometry in C.* 2nd ed. Cambridge University Press, 2001.

Simpson, Zachary Booth. "Design Patterns for Computer Games." Computer Game Developer's Conference, Austin, TX, Nov 1998; San Jose, CA, May 1999 (www.mine-control.com/zack/patterns/gamepatterns.html).

Ulrich, Thatcher. "Spatial Partitioning with 'Loose' Octrees." (www.tulrich.com/geekstuff/partitioning.html).

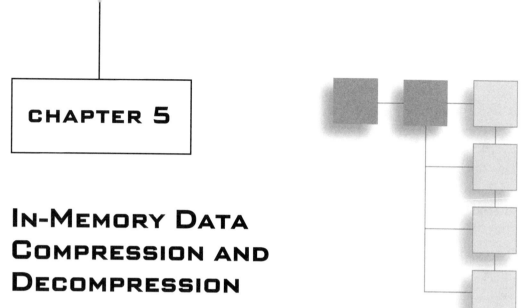

CHAPTER 5

IN-MEMORY DATA COMPRESSION AND DECOMPRESSION

LEE MILLWARD

Part One: Compression

This snippet will show you how easy it can be to perform compression/ decompression between data buffers in memory using the zlib library. I will go the easy route to get a simple example application going, which will read the contents of a file into memory, compress that data, and then write it back out to file. In Part Two, I will use the output from Part One to decompress the data, then write it back out to disk so you can check the results.

This code requires the zlib library, which is available for many platforms at www.zlib.net. Zlib provides two different functions for in-memory buffer-to-buffer compression, so let's have a look at them. Located in zlib.h at line 876, you will find the following declaration:

```
int ZEXPORT compress(Bytef* dest, uLongf *destLen, const Bytef *source,
                     uLong SourceLen);
```

dest: Pointer to the destination buffer where the compressed data will be written.

destLen: After the function has returned, this value will be the size in bytes of the destination buffer.

source: Pointer to the source buffer, which contains the data to be compressed.

sourceLen: Length of the source data in bytes.

This function is pretty simple to use—pass it pointers to two memory buffers, one containing the source data and one empty buffer for the compressed data. But what if you'd like a little more control about exactly *how* the data is compressed? For that you would need to use the following function instead, which is at line 891 in zlib.h:

```
int ZEXPORT compress2(Bytef *dest, uLongf *destLen,
                      const Bytef *source, uLong SourceLen, int level);
```

The parameters are identical to compress except for the addition of a new one: level. The value of this parameter will determine how the data is compressed, allowing you to achieve a trade-off between speed and compression ratio. The possible values are as follows:

Z_NO_COMPRESSION: Data is not compressed.

Z_BEST_SPEED: Sacrifices compression ratio for improved speed.

Z_BEST_COMPRESSION: Gain improved compression ratios, but at a cost of execution speed.

Z_DEFAULT_COMPRESSION: This is a compromise between compression ratios and speed of execution.

Both of these functions will return Z_OK on success; otherwise, an error code detailing a little more information about exactly why the call failed will be returned instead.

Now that you know what functions you can use, I'll go through a simple example:

```
// input and output files
FILE *FileIn = fopen("FileIn.bmp", "rb");
FILE *FileOut = fopen("FileOut.dat", "wb");
// get the file size of the input file
fseek(FileIn, 0, SEEK_END);
unsigned long FileInSize = ftell(FileIn);
// buffers for the raw and compressed data
void *RawDataBuff = malloc(FileInSize);
void *CompDataBuff = NULL;
```

```
// zlib states that the compressed buffer must be at least 0.1
// times larger than the source buffer plus 12 bytes
// to cope with the overhead of zlib data streams
uLongf CompBuffSize = (uLongf)(FileInSize + (FileInSize * 0.1) + 12);
CompDataBuff = malloc((size_t)(CompBuffSize));
// read in the contents of the file into the source buffer
fseek(FileIn, 0, SEEK_SET);
fread(RawDataBuff, FileInSize, 1, FileIn);
// now compress the data
uLongf DestBuffSize;
compress2((Bytef*)CompDataBuff, (uLongf*)&DestBuffSize,
          (const Bytef*)RawDataBuff, (uLongf)FileInSize,
           Z_BEST_COMPRESSION);
// write the compressed data to disk
fwrite(CompDataBuff, DestBuffSize, 1, FileOut);
```

I've not included any error checking in the preceding code for reasons of clarity; this is something you would obviously want to include in your own applications.

Part Two: Decompression

Having compressed data is of no use to anyone without a way of decompressing it back to the original form. Fortunately, zlib provides the following utility function to decompress a data buffer in memory:

```
int uncompress(Bytef *dest, uLongf *destLen,
               const Bytef *source, uLongf sourceLen);
```

dest: Pointer to the destination buffer where the decompressed data will be written to.

destLen: After the function has returned, this value will be the size in bytes of the decompressed data.

source: Pointer to the source buffer, which contains the data to be decompressed.

sourceLen: Length of the compressed data buffer in bytes.

Unlike its compression counterpart, there is only a single version of the decompression function, since there is not much customization you can apply to decompression—you generally want the function to operate as fast as possible. The `uncompress` function returns the same set of values as its compression counterparts regarding success and failures.

Now let's move on to an example of how to use this function to decompress the data from the file in Part One before writing the original contents back out to disk:

```
// the input file, this is the output file from part one
FILE *FileIn = fopen("FileOut.dat", "rb");
// output file
FILE *FileOut = fopen("OrigFile.bmp", "wb");
// get the file size of the input file
fseek(FileIn, 0, SEEK_END);
unsigned long FileInSize = ftell(FileIn);
// buffers for the raw and uncompressed data
void *RawDataBuff = malloc(FileInSize);
void *UnCompDataBuff = NULL;
// read in the contents of the file into the source buffer
fseek(FileIn, 0, SEEK_SET);
fread(RawDataBuff, FileInSize, 1, FileIn);
// allocate a buffer big enough to hold the uncompressed
// data, we can cheat here because we know the file size
// of the original
uLongf UnCompSize = 482000;
UnCompDataBuff = malloc(UnCompSize);
// all data we require is ready so compress it into the
// source buffer, the exact size will be stored
// in UnCompSize
uncompress((Bytef*)UnCompDataBuff, &UnCompSize,
           (const Bytef*)RawDataBuff, FileInSize);
// write the decompressed data to disk
fwrite(UnCompDataBuff, UnCompSize, 1, FileOut);
```

Again, error checking has been removed for this example; I also use a fixed file size for the uncompressed data, since I know how big the original file is. Ideally, you would want to store the size of the original uncompressed data along with the actual data itself for use when decompressing it.

That sums up compression between buffers in memory. The code for compression/decompression is ideally suited for utility functions to hide away all those details of buffer allocation, checking return values, and so forth.

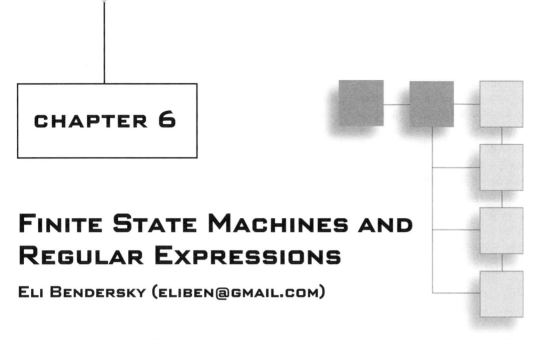

CHAPTER 6

Finite State Machines and Regular Expressions

Eli Bendersky (eliben@gmail.com)

I want to present an important and interesting topic in computer science, the finite state machine (FSM). I'll start with the basics: a discussion of FSMs and what they can be used for. This part is very elementary, so please be patient. In subsequent sections, things will become much more complicated and interesting.

Finite State Machines—What Are They?

A finite state machine is a conceptual model that can be used to describe how many things work. Think about a light bulb, for instance. The circuit consists of a switch that can be on or off, a few wires, and the bulb itself. At any moment in time, the bulb is in some state—it is either turned on (emits light) or turned off (no visible effect). For a more focused discussion, let's assume that you have two buttons: one for "turn on" and one for "turn off."

How would you describe the light bulb circuit? You could say that when it's dark and you press ON, the bulb starts emitting light. Then if you press ON again, nothing changes. If you press OFF, then the bulb is turned off. If you press OFF again, nothing changes. This description is very simple, but in fact it describes a state machine!

Think of it the following way: you have a machine (the bulb) with two states, ON and OFF. You have two inputs, an ON switch and an OFF switch. If you are in state ON, pressing ON changes nothing, but pressing OFF moves the machine to

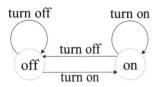

Figure 6.1

state OFF. If you are in state OFF, pressing OFF changes nothing, but pressing ON moves the machine to state ON.

The previous is a rephrasing of the first description, just a little more formal. It is, in fact, a formal description of a state machine. Another customary way to describe state machines is with a diagram (people like diagrams and drawings more than words for some insights), as shown in Figure 6.1.

Textual descriptions can become quite wordy, and a simple diagram like this can contain a lot of information. Note how states are represented by circles and transitions by arrows. This is almost all one needs to know, which makes diagrams very descriptive. This state machine can also be translated to (C++) code:

```
...
...
typedef enum {ON, OFF} bulb_state;
typedef enum {TURN_ON, TURN_OFF} switch_command;
...
...
bulb_state state;
switch_command command;
switch (state)
{
  case ON:
    if (command == TURN_ON)
    {
    }
    else if (command == TURN_OFF)
    {
      state = OFF;
    }
    break;
  case OFF:
    if (command == TURN_ON)
    {
      state = ON;
```

```
    }
    else if (command == TURN_OFF)
    {
    }
    break;
    default:
      assert(0);
}
```

If code such as this looks familiar, it's hardly surprising. Many of us write state machines in code without even noticing. Most of the state machines we write are "implicit" in the sense that there isn't a single switch statement that handles the whole machine, but rather it's distributed throughout the whole program. If, additionally, the state variables don't have the word state in their name, guessing that a certain code is a state machine in disguise is even harder.

Many programs you write are state machines. Think about a chess game for a moment. If you write a program to play chess against human beings, it's actually a state machine in some sense. It waits for the human to move—an idle state. Once the human moves, it goes into the active state of "thinking" about a move to make. A game can have an "end" state, such as a victory for one side or a draw. If you think of a GUI for a chess game, the state machine is even more obvious. There is a basic state, when it's a human's move. If a human clicks on some piece, you go into the "clicked" state. In this state, a click on an empty tile may produce a move by the piece. Note that if you click on an empty tile in the basic state (no pieces selected), nothing happens. Can you see an obvious state machine here?

Finite?

In the beginning of this section, I said I was going to discuss FSMs. By now I hope you already know what a state machine is, but what has "finite" got to do with it?

Well, computers are finite. There's only so much memory (even if it's quite large these days). Therefore, the applications are finite. Finite = limited. For state machines, it means that the amount of states is limited. One is limited, 2 is limited, but 10^7 is also limited, though quite large.

This point may seem banal to some of you, but it is important to emphasize. So now you know what an FSM is—a state machine with a finite number of states. It can be inferred that all state machines implemented in computer hardware and software must be FSMs.

Employing State Machines

State machines can be also used explicitly. You can benefit a lot from knowingly incorporating state machines in your code. First and foremost, it's a great way to reason out difficult problems. If you see that your code or a part of it can actually be in several states, with inputs affecting these states and outputs resulting from them, you can reason out this code using a state machine. Draw a diagram; visualizing always helps. With a diagram, errors can be spotted more easily. Think about all the inputs to your code—what should they change in every state? Does your code cover all possibilities (all inputs in all states)? Are some state transitions illegal?

Another use of state machines is for certain algorithms. In the next section, you'll see how essential state machines are for a very common and important application: regular expressions.

Regular Expressions

Think of an identifier in C++ (such as `this`, `temp_var2`, `assert`, and so on). How would you describe what qualifies for an identifier? Let's see if you remember— an identifier consists of letters, digits, and the underscore character (_), and it must start with a letter (though it's possible to start with an underscore, it's better not to, as these identifiers are reserved by the language).

A regular expression (regex) is a notation that allows you to define such things precisely:

```
letter (letter | digit | underscore) *
```

In regular expressions, the vertical bar | means "or," the parentheses are used to group subexpressions (just as in math), and the asterisk (*) means "zero or more instances of the previous." So the regular expression defines the set of all C++ identifiers (a letter followed by zero or more letters, digits or underscores). Here are some more examples:

- **abb*a:** All words starting with **a**, ending with **a**, and having at least one **b** in between. For example, **aba, abba,** and **abbbba** fit, but **aa** or **abab** do not.

- **0|1|2|3|4|5|6|7|8|9:** All digits. For example, **1** is a digit, but **fx** is not.

- **x(y|z)*(a|b|c):** All words starting with **x**, then zero or more, **y** or **z**, and end with **a**, **b**, or **c**. For example, **xa, xya, xzc,** and **xyzzzyzyyyzb**.

- **xyz:** Only **xyz**.

There is another symbol you'll use: *eps* (usually denoted with the Greek letter Epsilon) means "nothing." So, for example, the regular expression for "either xy or xyz" is **xy(z|*eps*)**.

People familiar with regexes know that there are more complicated forms than *and |. However, anything can be built from *, |, and *eps*. For instance, **x?** (zero or one instance of **x**) is shorthand for **(x|*eps*)**. **x+** (one or more instances of x) is shorthand for **xx***. Note also the interesting fact that * can be represented with +, namely, **x*** is equivalent to **(x+)|*eps***.

Note

Perl programmers and those familiar with Perl syntax (Python programmers, that would include you) will recognize *eps* as a more elegant alternative to the numerical notation {m, n} where both **m** and **n** are zero. In this notation, **x*** is equivalent to **x{0,}** (unbound upper limit). **x+** is **x{1,}** and all other cases can be built from these two base cases.

Recognizing Strings with Regexes

Usually a regex is implemented to solve some recognition problem. For example, suppose your application asks a question, and the user should answer yes or no. The legal input, expressed as a regex, is **(yes)|(no)**. Pretty simple and not too exciting—but things can get much more interesting.

Suppose you want to recognize the following regex: **(a|b)*abb**, namely all words consisting of almost any combination of **a** and **b** and ending with **abb**. For example, **ababb** or **aaabbbaaabbbabb**. Say you'd like to write the code that accepts such words and rejects others. The following function does the job:

```
bool recognize(string str)
{
  string::size_type len = str.length();
  // can't be shorter than 3 chars
  if (len < 3)
    return false;
  // last 3 chars must be "abb"
  if (str.substr(len - 3, 3) != "abb")
    return false;
  // must contain no chars other than "a" and "b"
  if (str.find_first_not_of("ab") != string::npos)
    return false;
  return true;
}
```

It's pretty clean and robust—it will recognize **(a|b)***abb** and reject anything else. However, it is clear that the techniques employed in the code are very "personal" to the regex at hand.

If you slightly change the regex to **(a|b)***abb(a|b)*** , for instance (all sequences of a's and b's that have abb somewhere in them), it would change the algorithm completely. (You'd then probably want to go over the string, a character at a time, and record the appearance of **abb**. If the string ends and **abb** wasn't found, it's a rejection, and so on.) It seems that for each regex, you should think of some algorithm to handle it, which can be completely different from algorithms for other regexes.

So what is the solution? Is there any standardized way to handle regexes? Can you even dream of a general algorithm that can produce a recognizer function given a regex? You sure can!

FSMs to the Rescue

It so happens that finite state machines are a very useful tool for regular expressions. More specifically, a regex (any regex!) can be represented as an FSM. To show how, you must present two additional definitions (which actually are very logical, assuming you use an FSM for a regex).

- A start state is the state in which an FSM starts.

- An accepting state is a final state in which the FSM returns with some answer.

This is best presented with an example, as shown in Figure 6.2.

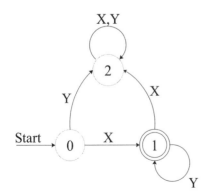

Figure 6.2

The start state 0 is denoted with a Start arrow. The number 1 is the accepting state (denoted with the double border). Now, try to figure out what regex this FSM represents.

It actually represents **xy***—x and then 0 or more of y. Do you see how? Note that x leads the FSM to state 1, which is the accepting state. Adding y keeps the FSM in the accepting state. If an x appears when in state 1, the FSM moves to state 2, which is non-accepting and "stuck," since any input keeps the FSM in state 2 (because **xy*** rejects strings where an x comes after y-s). But what happens with other letters? For simplicity, you can now assume that for this FSM the language consists of solely x and y. If the input set were larger (say the whole lowercase alphabet), you could define that each transition not shown (for instance, on input **z** in state 0) leads you into some "unaccepting" state.

I will now present the general algorithm for figuring out whether a given FSM recognizes a given word. It's called *FSM simulation*. But first I'll define an auxiliary function: `move(state, input)` returns the state resulting from getting `input` in state `state`. For the previous sample FSM, `move(0, X)` is 1, `move(0, Y)` is 0, and so on. So, the algorithm goes as follows:

```
state = start_state
input = get_next_input
while not end of input do
  state = move(state, input)
  input = get_next_input
end
if state is a final state
  return "ACCEPT"
else
  return "REJECT"
```

The algorithm is presented in very general terms and should be well understood. Let's "run" it on the simple **xy*** FSM, with the input **xyy**. You start from the start state 0. Get next input x. End of input? Not yet. `move(0, x)` moves you to state 1; input now becomes y. Not yet end of input. `move(1, y)` moves you to state 1; exactly the same with the second y. Now it's end of input. State 1 is a final state, so ''ACCEPT''. Piece of cake, isn't it ? Well, it really is! It's a straightforward algorithm and a very easy one for the computer to execute.

Let's go back to the regex you started with: **(a|b)*****abb**. Figure 6.3 shows the FSM that represents (recognizes) it.

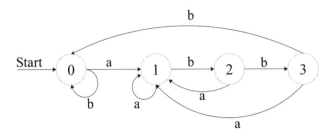

Figure 6.3

Although it is much more complicated than the previous FSM, it is still simple to comprehend. This is the nature of FSMs; looking at them you can easily characterize the states they can be in, what transitions occur, and when. Again, note that for simplicity, the alphabet consists of solely **a** and **b**.

Paper and pencil is all you need to "run" the FSM simulation algorithm on some simple string. I encourage you to do it, to better understand how this FSM relates to the (a|b)*abb regex.

Just for example, take a look at the final state 3. How can you reach it ? From 2 with the input b. How can you reach 2 ? From 1 with input b. How can you reach 1 ? Actually from any state with input **a**. So, **abb** leads you to accept a string, and it indeed fits the regex.

Coding It the FSM Way

As I said earlier, it is possible to generate code straight from any regex. That is, given a regular expression, a general tool can generate the code that will correctly recognize all strings that fit the regex and reject the others. Let's see what it takes. The task is indeed massive, but consider dividing it into two distinct stages:

1. Convert the regex to an FSM.

2. Write FSM code to recognize strings.

Hey, you already know how to do the second stage! It is actually the FSM simulation algorithm you saw earlier. Most of the algorithm is the same from FSM to FSM (just dealing with input). The only part that changes is the move function, which represents the transition diagram of some FSM. You learned how to code the transition function; the technique is the same for any FSM!

Let's now write down the full code that recognizes **(a|b)*****abb**.

```cpp
#include <iostream>
#include <cassert>
#include <string>
using namespace std;
typedef int     fsm_state;
typedef char    fsm_input;
bool is_final_state(fsm_state state)
{
  return (state == 3) ? true : false;
}
fsm_state get_start_state(void)
{
  return 0;
}
fsm_state move(fsm_state state, fsm_input input)
{
  // our alphabet includes only 'a' and 'b'
  if (input != 'a' && input != 'b')
    assert(0);
  switch (state)
  {
    case 0:
      if (input == 'a')
      {
        return 1;
      }
      else if (input == 'b')
      {
        return 0;
      }
      break;
    case 1:
      if (input == 'a')
      {
        return 1;
      }
      else if (input == 'b')
      {
        return 2;
      }
      break;
```

```
    case 2:
      if (input == 'a')
      {
        return 1;
      }
      else if (input == 'b')
      {
        return 3;
      }
      break;
    case 3:
      if (input == 'a')
      {
        return 1;
      }
      else if (input == 'b')
      {
        return 0;
      }
      break;
    default:
      assert(0);
  }
}
bool recognize(string str)
{
  if (str == "")
    return false;
  fsm_state state = get_start_state();
  string::const_iterator i = str.begin();
  fsm_input input = *i;
  while (i != str.end())
  {
    state = move(state, *i);
    ++i;
  }
  if (is_final_state(state))
    return true;
  else
    return false;
}
// simple driver for testing
int main(int argc, char** argv)
```

```
{
  recognize(argv[1]) ? cout << 1 : cout << 0;
  return 0;
}
```

Take a good look at the `recognize` function. You should immediately see how closely it follows the FSM simulation algorithm. The FSM is initialized to the start state, and the first input is read. Then, in a loop, the machine moves to its next state and fetches the next input, and so on, until the input string ends. Eventually, you check whether you reached a final state.

Note that this `recognize` function will be the same for *any* regex. The only functions that change are the trivial `is_final_state` and `get_start_state`, and the more complicated transition function `move`. But `move` is very structural—it closely follows the graphical description of the FSM. As you'll see later, such transition functions are easily generated from the description.

So, what have you got so far? You know how to write code that runs a state machine on a string. What don't you know? You still don't know how to generate the FSM from a regex.

DFA + NFA = FSM

FSM, as you already know, stands for finite state machine. A more scientific name for it is FA, or finite automaton (plural *automata*). Finite automata can be classified into several categories, but the one you need for the sake of regex recognition is the notion of *determinism*. Something is deterministic when it involves no *chance*—everything is known and can be prescribed and simulated beforehand. On the other hand, nondeterminism is about chance and probabilities. It is commonly defined as "a property of a computation which may have more than one result." Thus the world of FSMs can be divided into two: a deterministic FSM is called DFA (deterministic finite automaton) and a nondeterministic FSM is called NFA (nondeterministic finite automaton).

NFA

A *nondeterministic finite automaton* is a mathematical model that consists of the following:

1. A set of states S

2. A set of input symbols A (the input symbol alphabet)

3. A transition function move that maps state-symbol pairs to sets of states

4. A state s0 that is the start state

5. A set of states F that are the final states

I will now elaborate on a few fine points (trying to simplify and avoid mathematical implications). An NFA *accepts* an input string X if and only if there is some path in the transition graph from the start state to some accepting (final) state, such that the edge labels along this path spell out X.

The definition of an NFA doesn't pose a restriction on the number of states resulting in some input in some state. So, given you're in some state N, it is completely legal (in an NFA) to transition to several different states given the input a. Furthermore, epsilon (**eps**) transitions are allowed in an NFA. That is, there may be a transition from state to state given no input.

I know this must sound very confusing if it's the first time you've learned about NFAs, but an example I'll show a little later should make things more understandable.

DFA

By definition, a *deterministic finite automaton* is a special case of an NFA, in which

1. No state has an **eps**-transition.

2. For each state **S** and input **a**, there is at most one edge labeled a leaving **S**.

You can immediately see that a DFA is a more "normal" FSM. In fact, the FSMs discussed earlier are DFAs.

Recognizing Regexes with DFAs and NFAs

To make this more tolerable, consider an example comparing the DFA and the NFA for the regex **(a|b)*abb** you saw earlier (refer to Figure 6.3 for the DFA). The NFA is shown in Figure 6.4.

Can you see an NFA-unique feature in this diagram? Look at state 0. When the input is a, where can you move? To state 0 and state 1—a multiple transition, something that is illegal in a DFA. Take a minute to convince yourself that this NFA indeed accepts **(a|b)*abb**. For instance, consider the input string **abababb**.

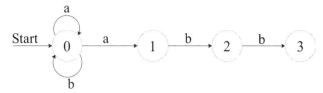

Figure 6.4

Recall how NFA's *acceptance* of a string is defined. So, is there a path in the NFA graph in Figure 6.4 that "spells out" **abababb**? There is indeed. The path will stay in state 0 for the first four characters, and then will move to states 1->2->3. Consider the input string **baabab**. Is there a path that spells out this string? No, there isn't; in order to reach the final state, you must go through **abb** in the end, which the input string lacks.

Both NFAs and DFAs are important in computer science theory and especially in regular expressions. Here are a few points of difference between these constructs:

- It is simpler to build an NFA directly from a regex than from a DFA.

- NFAs are more compact than DFAs. You must agree that the NFA diagram is much simpler for the **(a|b)*abb** regex. Due to its definition, an NFA doesn't explicitly need many of the transitions that a DFA needs. Note how elegantly state 0 in the NFA example handles the **(a|b)*** alternation of the regex. In the DFA, the character a can't both keep the automaton in state 0 and move it to state 1, so the many transitions on a to state 1 are required from any other state.

- The compactness also shows in storage requirements. For complex regexes, NFAs are often smaller than DFAs and, hence, consume less space. There are even cases when a DFA for some regex is exponential in size (while an NFA is always linear), though this is quite rare.

- NFAs can't be directly simulated in the sense DFAs can. This is due to them being nondeterministic "beings," while computers are deterministic. They must be simulated using a special technique that generates a DFA from their states on the fly. More on this later.

- The previous leads to NFAs being less time-efficient than DFAs. In fact, when large strings are searched for regex matches, DFAs will almost always be preferable.

There are several techniques involving DFAs and NFAs to build recognizers from regexes:

- Build an NFA from the regex. "Simulate" the NFA to recognize input.

- Build an NFA from the regex. Convert the NFA to a DFA. Simulate the DFA to recognize input.

- Build a DFA directly from the regex. Simulate the DFA to recognize input.

- A few hybrid methods that are too complicated for this discussion.

At first, I was determined to spare you from the whole DFA/NFA discussion and just use the third—direct DFA—technique for recognizer generation. Then, I changed my mind, for two reasons. First, the distinction between NFAs and DFAs in the regex world is important. Different tools use different techniques (for instance, Perl uses NFA while lex and egrep use DFA), and it is valuable to have at least a basic grasp of these topics. Second, and more important, I couldn't help falling to the charms of the NFA-from-regex construction algorithm. It is simple, robust, powerful, and complete—in one word, beautiful. So, I decided to go for the second technique.

Construction of an NFA from a Regular Expression

Recall the basic building blocks of regular expressions: **eps**, which represents "nothing" or "no input"; characters from the input alphabet (you used **a** and **b** most often here). Characters may be concatenated, like this: **abb**, alternation **a|b** meaning **a** or **b**, the star (*) meaning "zero or more of the previous," and grouping ().

What follows is *Thompson's construction*—an algorithm that builds an NFA from a regex. The algorithm is syntax directed, in the sense that it uses the syntactic structure of the regex to guide the construction process.

The beauty and simplicity of this algorithm is in its modularity. First, construction of trivial building blocks is presented. For **eps**, construct the NFA, as shown in Figure 6.5.

Figure 6.5

Here **i** is a new start state and **f** is a new accepting state. It's easy to see that this NFA recognizes the regex **eps**.

For some **a** from the input alphabet, construct the NFA, as shown in Figure 6.6.

Again, it's easy to see that this NFA recognizes the trivial regex **a**.

Now, the interesting part of the algorithm: an inductive construction of complex NFAs from simple NFAs. More specifically, given that **N(s)** and **N(t)** are NFAs for regular expressions **s** and **t**, you'll see how to combine the NFAs **N(s)** and **N(t)** according to the combination of their regexes. For the regular expression **s|t**, construct the composite NFA **N(s|t)**, as shown in Figure 6.7.

The **eps** transitions into and out of the simple NFAs assure that you can be in either of them when the match starts. Any path from the initial to the final state must pass through either **N(s)** or **N(t)** exclusively. Thus you can see that this composite NFA recognizes **s|t**.

For the regular expression **st** (**s** and then **t**), construct the composite NFA **NFA(st)**, as shown in Figure 6.8

Figure 6.6

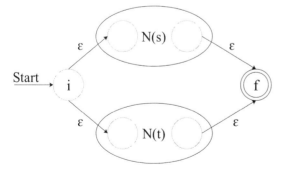

Figure 6.7

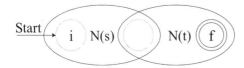

Figure 6.8

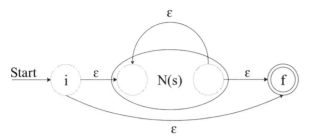

Figure 6.9

The composite NFA will have the start state of **N(s)** and the end state of **N(t)**. The accepting (final) state of **N(s)** is merged with the start state of **N(t)**. Therefore, all paths going through the composite NFA must go through **N(s)** and then through **N(t)**, so it indeed recognizes **N(st)**.

For the regular expression **s***, construct the composite NFA **N(s*)**, as shown in Figure 6.9.

Note how simply the notion of "zero or more" is represented by this NFA. From the initial state, either "nothing" is accepted with the **eps** transition to the final state or the "more than" is accepted by going into **N(s)**. The **eps** transition inside **N(s)** denotes that **N(s)** can appear again and again.

For the sake of completeness, a parenthesized regular expression **(s)** has the same NFA as **s**, namely **N(s)**. As you can see, the algorithm covers all the building blocks of regular expressions, denoting their translations into NFAs.

An Example

If you follow the algorithm closely, the NFA shown in Figure 6.10 will result for (our old friend) the regex **(a|b)*abb**.

Sure, it is much larger than the NFA you saw earlier for recognizing the same regex, but this NFA was automatically generated from a regex description using Thompson's construction, rather than crafted by hand.

Let's see how this NFA was constructed. First, it's easy to note that states 2 and 3 are the basic NFA for the regex **a**. Similarly, states 4 and 5 are the NFA for **b**. Can you see the **a|b** ? It clearly states 1,2,3,4,5,6 (without the **eps** transition from 6 to 1). Parenthesizing **(a|b)** doesn't change the NFA. The addition of states 0 and 7, plus the **eps** transition from 6 to 1, is the star on **NFA(a|b)**, namely that states 0–7 represent **(a|b)***. The rest is easy. States 8–10 are simply the concatenation of **(a|b)*** with **abb**.

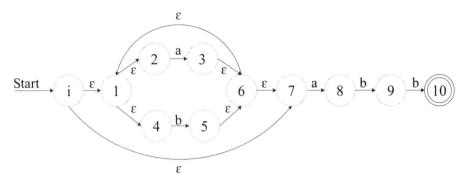

Figure 6.10

Try to run a few strings through this NFA until you convince yourself that it indeed recognizes **(a|b)*abb**. Recall that an NFA recognizes a string when the string's characters can be spelled out on some path from the initial to the final state.

Implementation of a Simple NFA

At last, you'll get your hands on some code. Now that you know the theory behind NFA-from-regex construction, it's clear that you will be doing some NFA manipulations. But how will you represent NFAs in code?

NFA is not a trivial concept, and there are full-blown implementations for general NFAs that are far too complex for the scope of this article. My plan is to code as simple an implementation as possible. After all, the regex recognizing engine is not supposed to expose its NFAs to the outer world—for our purposes, an NFA is only an intermediate representation of a regular expression, which you want to simulate in order to "accept" or "reject" input strings.

My philosophy in such cases is the KISS principle: keep it simple, stupid. The goal is first to code the simplest implementation that fits my needs. Later, I have no problem refactoring parts of the code and inserting new features, on an as-needed basis.

A very simple NFA implementation is presented here. You will build upon it later, but for now it is enough just to demonstrate the concept:

```
#ifndef NFA_H
#define NFA_H
#include <vector>
using namespace std;
// Convenience types and constants
```

```
typedef unsigned state;
typedef char input;
enum {EPS = -1, NONE = 0};
class NFA
{
  public:
    // Constructed with the NFA size (amount of
    // states), the initial state and the final state
    NFA(unsigned size_, state initial_, state final_);
    // Adds a transition between two states
    void add_trans(state from, state to, input in);
    // Prints out the NFA
    void show(void);
  private:
    bool is_legal_state(state s);
    state initial;
    state final;
    unsigned size;
    vector<vector<input> > trans_table;
};
#endif // NFA_H
```

As promised, the public interface is kept trivial, for now. All you can do is create an NFA object (specifying the amount of states, the start state, and the final state), add transitions to it, and print it out. This NFA will then consist of states 0 .. size-1, with the given transitions (which are single characters). Note that you use only one final state for now, for the sake of simplicity. Should you need more than one, it won't be difficult to add.

A word about the implementation: I don't want to go deep into graph theory here (if you're not familiar with the basics, a web search can be very helpful), but basically an NFA is a directed graph. It is most common to implement a graph using either a matrix or an array of linked lists. The first implementation is more speed efficient, but the second is better space-wise. For this NFA, I picked the matrix (vector of vectors), mostly because (in my opinion) it is simpler.

The classic matrix implementation of a graph has 1 in cell (i, j) when there is an edge between vertex i and vertex j, and 0 otherwise.

A NFA is a special graph, in the sense that you are interested not only in whether there is an edge, but also in the condition for the edge (the input that leads from one state to another in FSM terminology). Thus the matrix holds inputs (a nickname for chars, as you can see). So, for instance, **c** in `trans_table[i][j]` means that the input **c** leads from state **i** to state **j** in the NFA.

Here is the implementation of the NFA class:

```
#include <iostream>
#include <string>
#include <cassert>
#include <cstdlib>
#include "nfa.h"
using namespace std;
NFA::NFA(unsigned size_, state initial_, state final_)
{
  size = size_;
  initial = initial_;
  final = final_;
  assert(is_legal_state(initial));
  assert(is_legal_state(final));
  // Initialize trans_table with an "empty graph",
  // no transitions between its states
  for (unsigned i = 0; i < size; ++i)
  {
    vector<input> v;
    for (unsigned j = 0; j < size; ++j)
    {
      v.push_back(NONE);
    }
    trans_table.push_back(v);
  }
}
bool NFA::is_legal_state(state s)
{
  // You have 'size' states, numbered 0 to size -1
  if (s < 0 || s >= size)
    return false;
  return true;
}
void NFA::add_trans(state from, state to, input in)
{
  assert(is_legal_state(from));
  assert(is_legal_state(to));
  trans_table[from][to] = in;
}
```

```
void NFA::show(void)
{
  cout << "This NFA has " << size << " states: 0 - " << size - 1 << endl;
  cout << "The initial state is " << initial << endl;
  cout << "The final state is " << final << endl << endl;
  for (unsigned from = 0; from < size; ++from)
  {
    for (unsigned to = 0; to < size; ++to)
    {
      input in = trans_table[from][to];
      if (in != NONE)
      {
        cout << "Transition from " << from << " to " << to << "
        on input ";
        if (in == EPS)
        {
          cout << "EPS" << endl;
        }
        else
        {
          cout << in << endl;
        }
      }
    }
  }
}
```

The code is very simple, so you should have no problem understanding what every part of it does. To demonstrate, let's see how you would use this class to create the NFA for **(a|b)*abb**—the one you built using Thompson's construction earlier (only the driver code is included):

```
#include "nfa.h"
int main()
{
  NFA n(11, 0, 10);
  n.add_trans(0, 1, EPS);
  n.add_trans(0, 7, EPS);
  n.add_trans(1, 2, EPS);
  n.add_trans(1, 4, EPS);
  n.add_trans(2, 3, 'a');
  n.add_trans(4, 5, 'b');
  n.add_trans(3, 6, EPS);
```

```
    n.add_trans(5, 6, EPS);
    n.add_trans(6, 1, EPS);
    n.add_trans(6, 7, EPS);
    n.add_trans(7, 8, 'a');
    n.add_trans(8, 9, 'b');
    n.add_trans(9, 10, 'b');
    n.show();
    return 0;
}
```

This would (quite expectedly) result in the following output:

```
This NFA has 11 states: 0 - 10
The initial state is 0
The final state is 10
Transition from 0 to 1 on input EPS
Transition from 0 to 7 on input EPS
Transition from 1 to 2 on input EPS
Transition from 1 to 4 on input EPS
Transition from 2 to 3 on input a
Transition from 3 to 6 on input EPS
Transition from 4 to 5 on input b
Transition from 5 to 6 on input EPS
Transition from 6 to 1 on input EPS
Transition from 6 to 7 on input EPS
Transition from 7 to 8 on input a
Transition from 8 to 9 on input b
Transition from 9 to 10 on input b
```

As I mentioned earlier, as trivial as this implementation may seem at the moment, it is the basis I will build upon later. Presenting it in small pieces will, hopefully, make the learning curve of this difficult subject less steep for you.

Implementing Thompson's Construction

Thompson's construction tells you how to build NFAs from trivial regular expressions, and then compose them into more complex NFAs. Let's start with the basics.

The Simplest Regular Expression

The most basic regular expression is just some single character, for example **a**. The NFA for such a regex is shown in Figure 6.11.

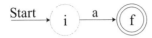

Figure 6.11

Here is the implementation:

```
// Builds a basic, single input NFA
NFA build_nfa_basic(input in)
{
  NFA basic(2, 0, 1);
  basic.add_trans(0, 1, in);
  return basic;
}
```

Just to remind you about the NFA implementation, the first line of the function creates a new (with no transitions yet) NFA of size 2 (that is, with 2 states), and sets state 0 to be the initial state and state 1 to be the final state. The second line adds a transition to the NFA that says "in moves from state 0 to state 1." That's it—a simple regex, a simple construction procedure.

Note

Note that this procedure is suited for the construction of an **eps** transition as well.

Some Changes to the NFA Class

The previous implementation of a simple NFA class was just a starting point, and you have quite a few changes to make. First of all, you need direct access to all of the class's data. Instead of providing get and set accessors (which I personally dislike), all of the class members (size, initial, final, and trans_table) have been made public.

Recall what I told you about the internal representation inside the NFA class: it's a matrix representing the transition table of a graph. For each **i** and **j**, trans_table[i][j] is the input that takes the NFA from state **i** to state **j**. It's NONE if there's no such transition (hence, a lot of space is wasted—the matrix representation, while fast, is inefficient in memory).

Several new operations were added to the NFA class to use in the NFA building functions. Their implementation can be found in nfa.cpp (included in the source code on this book's companion web site at www.courseptr/downloads). For now, try to understand how they work (it's really simple stuff); later you'll see why you need them for the implementation of various Thompson construction stages. It may be useful to have the code of nfa.cpp in front of your eyes and to follow the code for the operations while reading these explanations. Here they are:

append_empty_state: I want to append a new, empty state to the NFA. This state will have no transitions to it and no transitions from it. This is the transition table before the appending (a sample table with size 5—states 0 to 4).

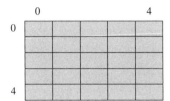

Following is the table after the appending. The shaded cells are the transitions of the original table (be they empty or not), and the white cells are the new table cells, containing NONE.

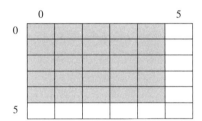

shift_states: I want to rename all NFA's states, shifting them "higher" by some given number. For instance, if I have five states numbered 0 to 4, and I want to have the same states, just named 2 to 6, I will call `shift_states(2)`, and will get the following table:

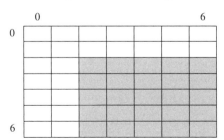

fill_states: I want to copy the states of some other NFA into the first table cells of my NFA. For instance, if I take the previous shifted table and fill its first two states with a new small NFA, I will get this (the new NFA's states are darkest):

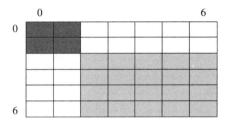

Note that using fill_states after shift_states is not incidental. These two operations were created to be used together to concatenate two NFAs. You'll see how they are employed shortly.

Now I will explain how the more complex operations of Thompson's construction are implemented. You should understand how the operations work that were previously demonstrated and also have looked at their source code (a good example of the NFA's internal table manipulation). You may still lack the "feel" of why these operations are needed, but this will soon be discussed. Just understand how they work, for now.

Implementing Alternation: alb

Figure 6.12 shows the diagram of the NFA alternation from earlier.

Given two NFAs, you must build another one that includes all the states of both NFAs, plus additional, unified initial and final states. The function that implements this in nfa.cpp is build_nfa_alter. Take a look at its source code now—it

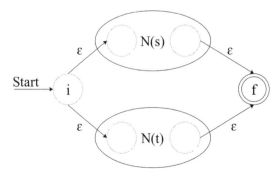

Figure 6.12

is well commented, and you should be able to follow all the steps with little difficulty. Note the usage of the new NFA operations to complete the task. First, the NFA's states are shifted to make room for the full NFA. `fill_states` is used to copy the contents of nfa1 to the unified NFA. Finally, `append_empty_state` is used to add another state at the end—the new final state.

Implementing Concatenation: ab

Figure 6.13 shows the diagram of NFA concatenation from earlier.

Given two NFAs, you must build another one that includes all the states of both NFAs (note that nfa1's final and nfa2's initial states are overlapping). The function that implements this in nfa.cpp is `build_nfa_concat`. Just as in `build_nfa_alter`, the new NFA operations are used to construct, step by step, a bigger NFA that contains all the needed states of the concatenation.

Implementing Star: a*

Figure 6.14 shows the diagram of the NFA for **a*** from earlier.

Although the diagram looks complex, the implementation of this construction is relatively simple, as you'll see in `build_nfa_star`. There's no need to shift states because no two NFAs are joined together. There's only a creation of new initial and final states, and new **eps** transitions added to implement the star operation.

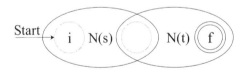

Figure 6.13

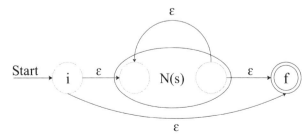

Figure 6.14

Specialty of NFAs Constructed by Thompson's Construction

You might have observed that all the NFAs constructed by Thompson's construction have some very specific behavior. For instance, all the basic building blocks for single letters are similar, and the rest of the constructions just create new links between these states to allow for the alternation, concatenation, and star operations. These NFAs are also special implementation-wise. For instance, note that in this NFA implementation, the first state is always the initial, and the last state is always final. You may have noted that this is useful in several operations.

A Complete NFA Construction Implementation

With these operations implemented, you now have a full NFA construction implementation in nfa.cpp! For instance, the regex **(a|b)*****abb** can be built as follows:

```
NFA a = build_nfa_basic('a');
NFA b = build_nfa_basic('b');
NFA alt = build_nfa_alter(a, b);
NFA str = build_nfa_star(alt);
NFA sa = build_nfa_concat(str, a);
NFA sab = build_nfa_concat(sa, b);
NFA sabb = build_nfa_concat(sab, b);
```

With these steps completed, **sabb** is the NFA representing **(a|b)*****abb**. Note how simple it is to build NFAs this way! There's no need to specify individual transitions like you did before. In fact, it's not necessary to understand NFAs at all—just build the desired regex from its basic blocks, and that's it.

Even Closer to Complete Automation

Though it has now become much simpler to construct NFAs from regular expressions, it still may not be as automatic as you'd like. You still have to explicitly specify the regex structure. A useful representation of structure is an expression tree. For example, the construction in Figure 6.15 closely reflects this tree structure.

In this tree, . is concatenation, | is alternation, and * is star. So, the regex **(a|b)*****abb** is represented here in a tree form, just like an arithmetic expression.

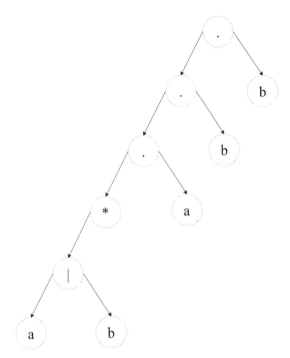

Figure 6.15

Such trees in the world of parsing and compilation are called *expression* trees, or *parse* trees. For example, to implement an infix calculator (one that can calculate, for example, 3*4 + 5), the expressions are first turned into parse trees, and then these parse trees are walked to make the calculations.

Note, this is, as always, an issue of representation. You have the regex in a textual representation—**(a|b)*abb**—and you want it in NFA representation. Now you're wondering how to turn it from one representation to the other. My solution is to use an intermediate representation—a parse tree. Going from a regex to a parse tree is similar to parsing arithmetic expressions; and going from a parse tree to an NFA will now be demonstrated, using the Thompson's construction building blocks described in this chapter.

From a Parse Tree to an NFA

A parse tree in this case is just a binary tree, since no operation has more than two arguments. Concatenation and alternations have two arguments; therefore, their nodes in the tree have two children. Star has one argument—hence, only the left child. Chars are the tree leaves. Take a good look at the tree from Figure 6.15; you'll see this very clearly.

Take a look at the file regex_parse.cpp from the source code archive on the book's companion web site. It has a lot in it, but you only need to focus on some specific things for now. First, let's look at the definition of parse_node:

```
typedef enum {CHR, STAR, ALTER, CONCAT} node_type;
// Parse node
struct parse_node
{
  parse_node(node_type type_, char data_, parse_node* left_,
  parse_node* right_) :
    type(type_),
    data(data_),
    left(left_),
    right(right_)
  {
  }
  node_type type;
  char data;
  parse_node* left;
  parse_node* right;
};
```

This is a completely normal definition of a binary tree node that contains data and some type by which it is identified. For the moment you can ignore the question of how such trees are built from regexes (if you're very curious, it's all in regex_parse.cpp), and instead think about how to build NFAs from such trees. It's very straightforward, since the parse tree representation is natural for regexes. Here is the code of the tree_to_nfa function from regex_parse.cpp:

```
NFA tree_to_nfa(parse_node* tree)
{
  assert(tree);
  switch (tree-<type)
  {
    case CHR:
      return build_nfa_basic(tree-<data);
    case ALTER:
      return build_nfa_alter(tree_to_nfa(tree-<left),
      tree_to_nfa(tree-<right));
```

```
  case CONCAT:
    return build_nfa_concat(tree_to_nfa(tree->left),
    tree_to_nfa(tree->right));
  case STAR:
    return build_nfa_star(tree_to_nfa(tree->left));
  default:
    assert(0);
  }
}
```

Not much of a rocket science, is it? The power of recursion and trees allows you to build NFAs from parse trees in just 18 lines of code.

From a Regex to a Parse Tree

If you've already looked at regex_parse.cpp, you surely noted that it contains quite a lot of code, much more than I've shown so far. This code is the construction of parse trees from actual regexes [strings like (a|b)*abb].

I really hate to do this, but I won't explain how this regex-to-tree code works. You'll just have to believe that it works (or study the code—it's there!). As a note, the parsing technique I employ to turn regexes into parse trees is called *recursive descent* parsing. It's an exciting topic, and there is plenty of information available on it if you are interested.

Converting NFAs to DFAs

The N in NFA stands for *nondeterministic*. Computers, however, are utterly deterministic beasts, which makes "true" simulation of an NFA impossible. But you know how to simulate DFAs, so what's left is to see how NFAs can be converted to DFAs.

The algorithm for constructing from an NFA a DFA that recognizes the same language is called *subset construction*. The main idea of this algorithm is in the following observations:

- In the transition table of an NFA, given a state and an input, there's a set of states you can move to. In a DFA, however, there's only one state you can move to.

- Because of **eps** transitions, even without an input, there's a set of states an NFA can be in at any given moment. Not so with the DFA, for which you always know exactly in what state it is.

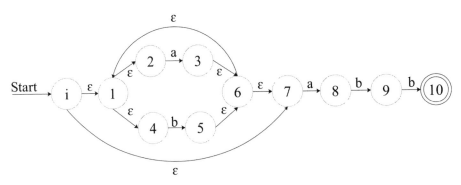

Figure 6.16

- Although you can't know from the sets previously described in which state the NFA is, the set *is* known. Therefore, I will represent each set of NFA states by a DFA state. The DFA uses its state to keep track of all possible states the NFA can be in after reading each input symbol.

Take, for example, the familiar NFA of the **(a|b)***abb** regex, as shown in Figure 6.16 (generated automatically by Thompson's construction, with the code from the last column).

The initial state of this NFA is 0—or is it? Take a look at Figure 6.16, and count in how many states this NFA can be *before* any input is read. If you remember the previous columns where I explained how **eps** transitions work, you should have no trouble noticing that initially, the NFA can be in any of the states {0, 1, 2, 4, 7}, because these are the states reachable by **eps** transitions from the initial state.

Note

The set T is reachable by **eps** from itself *by definition*. (The NFA doesn't have to take an **eps** transition—it can also stay in its current state.)

Now imagine you received the input **a**. What happens next? In which states can the NFA be now? This should be easy to answer. Just go over all the states the NFA can be in *before* the input, and see where the input **a** leads from them. This way, a new set emerges: {1, 2, 3, 4, 6, 7, 8}. I hope you understand why. Initially, the NFA can be in states {0, 1, 2, 4, 7}. But from states 0, 1, and 4, there are no transitions on **a**. The only transitions on **a** from that set are from state 2 (to state 3) and from state 7 (to state 8). However, the states {3, 8} is an incomplete answer. There are **eps** transitions from these states to states {1, 2, 4, 6, 7}, so the NFA can actually be in any of the states {1, 2, 3, 4, 6, 7, 8}.

If you understand this, you understand mostly how the subset construction algorithm works. All that's left is the implementation details. But before you get to the implementation of the conversion algorithm itself, there are a couple of prerequisites.

eps-closure

Given N (an NFA) and T (a set of NFA states), which states in N are reachable from states T by **eps** transitions. eps-closure is the procedure that answers this question. Here is the algorithm:

```
algorithm eps-closure
inputs: N - NFA, T - set of NFA states
output: eps-closure(T) - states reachable from T by eps transitions
  eps-closure(T) = T
  foreach state t in T
    push(t, stack)
  while stack is not empty do
    t = pop(stack)
    foreach state u with an eps edge from t to u
      if u is not in eps-closure(T)
        add u to eps-closure(T)
        push(u, stack)
  end
  return eps-closure(T)
```

This algorithm iteratively finds all the states reachable by **eps** transitions from the states T. First, the states T themselves are added to the output. Then, one by one, the states are checked for **eps** transitions. The states these transitions lead to are also added to the output and are pushed onto the stack (in order to be checked for **eps** transitions). The process proceeds iteratively, until no more states can be reached with **eps** transitions only. For instance, for the **(a|b)*abb** NFA, eps-closure({0}) = {0, 1, 2, 4, 7}, eps-closure({8, 9}) = {8, 9}, and so on.

In the source code, the implementation of eps-closure is in the file subset_construct.cpp, function build_eps_closure. It follows the algorithm previously outlined very closely, so you should have no trouble understanding it.

move: A New NFA Member Function

Given T (a set of NFA states) and A (an input), which states in the NFA are reachable from T with the input A? This operation was implemented in the move function in nfa.cpp (member of the NFA class). The function is very simple. It traverses the set T and looks for transitions on the given input, returning the states that can be reached. It doesn't take into account the **eps** transitions from those states—there's eps-closure for that.

Keeping Track of the Input Language of an NFA

For reasons that will soon become obvious, you must keep track of the input language used in the NFA. For example, for the regex **(a|b)*abb**, the language is {a, b}. A new member was added to the NFA class for this purpose—inputs. Take a look at the implementation in nfa.cpp to see how it's managed.

DFA Implementation

Since I intend to build DFAs in this column, I need a DFA implementation. A very basic implementation was coded in dfa.h—take a look at it now. The DFA's transition table is implemented with a map that maps (state, input) pairs to states. For example, **(t1, i)** will be mapped to **t2** if input **i** in state **t1** leads to state **t2**. Note that it's not the same representation as the one I used for the NFA. There are two reasons for this difference:

- I want you to see two different implementations of a graph (which is what a transition table is, as I told you before). Both are legitimate for certain purposes.

- A little bit of cheating—I know which operations I'll need from the DFA, so I'm tailoring the representation to these operations. This is a very common programming trick: you should always think about the ways a data structure will be used before you design its exact implementation.

So take a look at dfa.h—the DFA implementation is very simple—only a transition table, a start state, and a set of final states. There are also methods for showing the DFA and for simulating it.

To remind you, this is the algorithm for the DFA simulation:

```
algorithm dfa-simulate
inputs: D - DFA, I - Input
output: ACCEPT or REJECT
  s = start state of D
  i = get next input character from I
```

```
while not end of I do
  s = state reached with input i from state s
  i = get next input character from I
end
if s is a final state
  return ACCEPT
else
  return REJECT
```

Let's now finally learn how the DFA is built.

Subset Construction

At the beginning of this article, I provided some observations about following NFA states and gave an example. You saw that while it's impossible to know in what state an NFA is at any given moment, it's possible to know the set of states it can be in. Then you can say with certainty that the NFA is in one of the states in this set and not in any state that's not in the set.

So the idea of subset construction is to build a DFA that keeps track of where the NFA can be. Each state in this DFA stands for a set of states the NFA can be in after some transition. You may ask yourself, "How is this going to help me?" Good question.

Recall how you simulate a DFA. When can you say that a DFA recognizes an input string? When the input string ends, you look at the state you're left in. If this is a final state, ACCEPT; if it's not a final state, REJECT.

So, say that you have a DFA, each state of which represents a set of NFA states. Since an NFA will always "pick the correct path," you can assume that if the set contains a final state, the NFA will be in it, and the string is accepted. More formally—a DFA state D represents S, a set of NFA states. If (and only if) one or more of the states in S is a final state, then D is a final state. Therefore, if a simulation ends in D, the input string is accepted.

So, you see, it's useful to keep track of sets of NFA states. This will allow you to correctly "simulate" an NFA by simulating a DFA that represents it.

Here's the subset construction algorithm:

```
algorithm subset-construction
inputs: N - NFA
output: D - DFA
```

```
add eps-closure(N.start) to dfa_states, unmarked
D.start = eps-closure(N.start)
while there is an unmarked state T in dfa_states do
  mark(T)
  if T contains a final state of N
    add T to D.final
  foreach input symbol i in N.inputs
    U = eps-closure(N.move(T, i))
    if U is not in dfa_states
      add U to dfa_states, unmarked
    D.trans_table(T, i) = U
end
```

The result of this procedure is D—a DFA with a transition table, a start state, and a set of final states (incidentally, not what you need for the DFA class).

Here are some points to help you understand how subset-construction works:

▪ It starts by creating the initial state for the DFA. Since an initial state is really the NFA's initial state, plus all the states reachable by **eps** transitions from it, the DFA initial state is the eps-closure of the NFA's initial state.

▪ A state is "marked" if all the transitions from it were explored.

▪ A state is added to the final states of the DFA if the set it represents contains the NFA's final state.

▪ The rest of the algorithm is a simple iterative graph search. Transitions are added to the DFA transition table for each symbol in the alphabet of the regex. So the DFA transition actually represents a transition to the eps-closure in each case. Recall once again that a DFA state represents a set of states the NFA can be in after a transition.

This algorithm is implemented in the function subset_construct in subset_construct.cpp; take a look at it now. Here are some points about the implementation:

▪ dfa_states from the algorithm is represented by two sets—marked_states and unmarked_states, with the obvious meanings.

▪ Since DFA states are really sets of NFA states (see the state_rep typedef), something must be done about numbering them properly. (You want a state to be represented by a simple number in the DFA.) So, the dfa_state_num

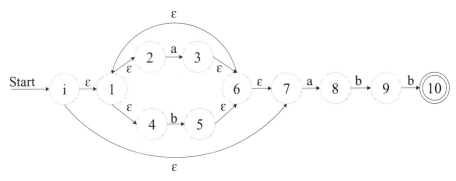

Figure 6.17

map takes care of it, with the numbers generated on demand by gen_new_state.

- The loop runs while the unmarked_states set is not empty. Then, some state is marked by taking it out of the unmarked set (the first member of the set is picked arbitrarily) and putting it into the marked set.

I hope an example will clear it all up. Let's take our favorite regex—**(a|b)*abb**—and show how the algorithm runs on the NFA created from it (see Figure 6.17).

Following the algorithm, the start state of the equivalent DFA is the eps-closure of NFA state 0, which is A = {0, 1, 2, 4, 7}. So, you enter into the loop and mark A. A doesn't contain a final state, so you don't add it to the DFA's final set. The input symbol alphabet of the regex **(a|b)*abb** is {a, b}, so first you compute eps-closure(move(A, a)). Let's expand this:

eps-closure(move({0, 1, 2, 4, 7}, a)) = eps-closure({3, 8}) = {1, 2, 3, 4, 6, 7, 8}

Let's call this set B. B is not a member of dfa_states yet, so you add it there, unmarked. You also create the DFA transition D.trans_table(A, a) = B. Now you're back to the inner loop, with the input **b**. Of all the states in set A, the only transition on **b** is from 4 to 5, so you create a new set:

C = eps-closure((move(A, b)) = eps-closure({5}) = {1, 2, 4, 5, 6, 7}

So C is added, unmarked, to dfa_states. Since all the alphabet symbols are done for A, you go back to the outer loop. Are there any unmarked states? Yes, there are B and C. So you pick B and go over the process again and again, until all the sets that are states of the DFA are marked. Then, the algorithm terminates, and D.trans_table contains all the relevant transitions for the DFA. The five different sets you get for DFA states are as follows:

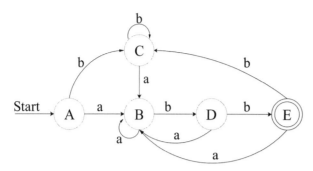

Figure 6.18

```
A = {0, 1, 2, 4, 7}
B = {1, 2, 3, 4, 6, 7, 8}
C = {1, 2, 4, 5, 6, 7}
D = {1, 2, 4, 5, 6, 7, 9}
E = {1, 2, 4, 5, 6, 7, 10}
```

A is the initial state of the DFA, since it contains the NFA initial state 0. E is obviously the only final state of the NFA, since it's the only one containing the NFA final state 10. If you follow the whole algorithm through and take note of the DFA transitions created, you get the resulting diagram in Figure 6.18.

You can easily

1. See that this is a DFA—no **eps** transitions, and no more than a single transition on each input from a state.

2. Verify that it indeed recognizes the regular expression **(a|b)*abb**.

Conclusion

You've come a long way, and finally your mission is accomplished. You've created a real regular expression engine. It's not a complete engine like the one Lex or Perl have, but it's a start. The basis has been laid, and the rest is just extensions. Let's see what you have learned:

1. A regular expression is read into a parse tree (implemented in regex_parse.cpp). I didn't actually explain how this part is done, but you can trust me (and I hope you verified!) that it works.

2. An NFA is built from the regular expression, using Thompson's construction (implemented in nfa.h/cpp).

3. The NFA is converted to a DFA, using the subset construction algorithm (implemented in subset_construct.h/cpp and dfa.h).

4. The resulting DFA is simulated using the DFA simulation algorithm (implemented in dfa.h).

A small `main` function is implemented in regex_parse.cpp. It reads a regex and a string as arguments and says whether the string fits the regex. It does this by going through the steps previously mentioned, so I advise you to take a look at it and make sure that you understand the order in which things are called.

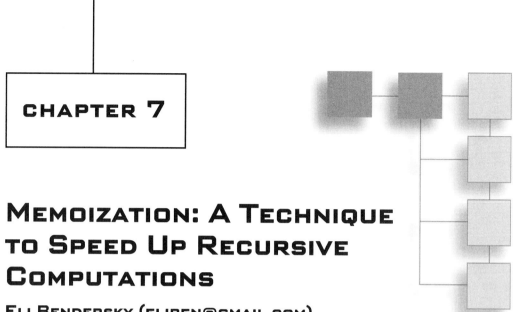

CHAPTER 7

MEMOIZATION: A TECHNIQUE TO SPEED UP RECURSIVE COMPUTATIONS

ELI BENDERSKY (ELIBEN@GMAIL.COM)

In mathematics and computer science, *recursion* is a way of specifying something (usually a mathematical object or part of a computer program) by a reference to itself. More precisely (and to dispel the appearance of circularity in the definition), "complicated" instances are defined in terms of "simpler" instances, and the "simplest" instances are given explicitly.

One interesting application of recursion is the definition of the set of natural numbers. You can define a natural number recursively, as follows:

- 0 is natural.

- If n is natural, then $n + 1$ is also natural.

So 0 is natural by definition. 1 is natural because 0 is natural, and $1 = 0 + 1$. 2 is natural because $2 = 1 + 1$, and 1 is natural, and so on.

Fibonacci Numbers

A canonical example of recursion is the computation of Fibonacci numbers:

0, 1, 1, 2, 3, 5, 8, 13, 21, 34, 55, 89, 144, 233, 377, 610, 987, 1597, 2584, 4181, 6765, 10946 . . .

This sequence can be defined recursively as follows [F(n) is the nth Fibonacci number]:

- If n = 0, F(n)= 0

- If n = 1, F(n) = 1

- Otherwise, F(n) = F(n − 1) + F(n − 2)

You can easily follow this definition and generate some Fibonacci numbers for yourself—you will get the preceding sequence.

How would you generate this sequence in code? It's quite simple—recursive definitions are easily reflected in recursive function calls. Here is the C++ code that returns any Fibonacci number (constrained by execution time and limitations of the C++ long type):

```
long fib_rec( long index )
{
  if (index < 2)
    return index;
  else
    return fib_rec(index - 1) + fib_rec(index - 2);
}
```

Note how gracefully the mathematical definition is translated to the code of fib_rec. This is the beauty and elegance of recursion. Unfortunately, everything has its price. While often being the most natural way to express algorithms, recursion can suffer from performance problems.

For example, finding the 40th Fibonacci number (which is, by the way, 102,334,155) using this routine takes about 4 seconds on my machine. The 42nd number (267,914,296) takes 11 seconds to compute, and the time grows very quickly (the 45th, which is 1,134,903,170, takes 47 seconds, and so on).

One reason for this is the cost of function calls (of which there are many in the recursive solution). When a function is called, there is always a certain amount of overhead. For small functions, this overhead can be comparable to the time required to execute the function itself. This results in a performance hit.

However, this is not the main reason for recursion being slow for the computation of Fibonacci numbers. The principal cause, in this case, is the vast amount of repetition involved. To demonstrate this, let's try to trace a sample execution of the recursive computation fib_rec, taking a call with index set to 5 as an example:

```
fib_rec(5)
|
|---fib_rec(4)
|   |
|   |---fib_rec(3)
|   |   |
|   |   |---fib_rec(2)
|   |   |   |
|   |   |   |---fib_rec(1)
|   |   |   |---fib_rec(0)
|   |   |
|   |   |---fib_rec(1)
|   |
|   |---fib_rec(2)
|       |
|       |---fib_rec(1)
|       |---fib_rec(0)
|
|---fib_rec(3)
    |
    |   fib_rec(2)
    |   |
    |   |---fib_rec(1)
    |   |---fib_rec(0)
    |
    |---fib_rec(1)
```

When fib_rec(5) is called, it calls fib_rec with 4 and fib_rec with 3. Each of those makes the appropriate calls, and so on. What you see is the complete call tree that results from the fib_rec(5). You can generate it yourself by inserting a tracing printout at the beginning of the function.

Now, do you notice anything funny about this call tree? It shouldn't be hard to spot the scandalous number of times the same calls are made. For instance, the call fib_rec(1) is made five times. The result of fib_rec(i) surely doesn't change between calls (the first Fibonacci number is, by definition, 1); so why is there a need for so much repetition? This, in fact, is the reason for the unfortunate inefficiency of recursive algorithms for many computations. So can you really write nice recursive algorithms and not be daunted by their performance problems? The answer to this question is fortunately positive!

Memoized Fibonacci

Memoization literally means "putting into memory." An alternative name for it is *caching*. Caching is familiar from the hardware world, where a cache is that small amount of fast but expensive memory where the CPU keeps recent data from the RAM (which is considerably slower than cache), thus avoiding some costly RAM accesses and saving execution time.

In programming, memoization plays a role similar to a hardware cache. It is a technique used to speed up computer programs by saving intermediary answers for later use rather than recomputing them. If you look at the call tree for fib_rec(5), you can see that many (most!) of the calls may be avoided by saving their results in earlier calls. In fact, there's no real need to compute the Fibonacci number at any index more than once, so five fib_rec calls would do for fib_rec(5), and not 15 as it currently is.

So what should you do in order to memoize the Fibonacci computation? First, you would set up some data structure to serve as a cache of computations. Then, when being asked to compute a Fibonacci number, you would first consult the cache. If the result is in the cache, it can be returned without any further computations. If it isn't in the cache, it means you haven't computed it yet; so you compute it and add it to the cache. Let's see how this is translated to code:

```
long fib_memoized_aux(vector<long>& cache, long
index)
{
  if (cache[index] >= 0)
    return cache[index];
  cache[index] = fib_memoized_aux(cache, index - 1) +
                 fib_memoized_aux(cache, index - 2);
  return cache[index];
}
long fib_memoized(long index)
{
  vector<long> cache(index + 1, -1);
  cache[0] = 0;
```

```
  cache[1] = 1;
  return fib_memoized_aux(cache, index);
}
```

Here, fib_memoized acts exactly as the simple fib_rec—it takes an index as an argument and returns the Fibonacci number at this index. Internally, it first sets up a cache (for such a simple task a vector is enough—the ith vector cell holds the computed i^{th} Fibonacci number, with −1 meaning a yet-uncomputed result), and uses fib_memoized_aux as a helper function for the computations. In fib_memoized_aux, you can see memoization in action, just as previously described.

What about performance, then? While up to about 30, fib_rec and fib_rec_memoized are comparable in execution time, but afterward the difference is staggering. For example, computing the 47th Fibonacci number takes around 47 seconds with fib_rec. With fib_rec_memoized, it takes 0 (below resolution of system clock). There's no doubt that the difference gets bigger and bigger after that.

There's another major speed improvement here, which may not be immediately obvious. Imagine that during the runtime of your program, you need to calculate Fibonacci numbers not just once, but many times. While using the plain method, you'd go through the computations again and again; but using memoization, you can just reuse the cache from call to call. Chances are that most of the computations will be answered in constant time—because the result will already be in the cache!

The assiduous reader may implement a simple class for Fibonacci number calculation. This class will have the cache as a member, which will be initialized only once. The Fibonacci calculation method will use this cache and update it at times (when yet-uncalculated results are requested).

Alternative Fibonacci Implementations

Personally, I don't feel good about the Fibonacci calculation example. Though it's educationally sound, I find it somewhat contrived. This is because there are fast implementations for Fibonacci calculations that don't require memoization. For example, it's very easy to come up with a simple iterative solution. Since a Fibonacci number is simply a sum of the previous two, you can use a loop and keep track of just two numbers to generate any Fibonacci:

```
long fib_iter(long index)
{
  if (index < 2)
```

```
    return index;
  long cur = 1;
  long one_back = 0;
  for (long i = 2; i <= index; ++i)
  {
    long temp = cur;
    cur = cur + one_back;
    one_back = temp;
  }
  return cur;
}
```

This will calculate Fibonacci numbers as fast as the memoized implementation—in linear time. An even faster solution can utilize Binet's Fibonacci number formula:

```
long fib_binet(long index)
{
  double sqrt_5 =
2.2360679774997896964091736687313;
  return (long) floor(((pow(1 + sqrt_5, index)
          - pow(1 - sqrt_5, index)) / (pow(2,
index) * sqrt_5));
}
```

Don't just sit there and gasp in horror. :-) The calculation of Fibonacci numbers is a fascinating topic, and you can learn a lot by browsing the web a little. Start by Googling the phrase "Fibonacci numbers."

I must note, just to be fair, that these fast non-recursive implementations lack the caching-between-calls property of memoization—that is, if you use memoization to save results between function calls. You can get most results at a cost of a trivial array lookup—faster than the non-recursive implementations.

But to be even more fair, huge Fibonacci numbers are rarely needed in practice. And even when they are, the iterative or the formula implementations can provide you with as many big numbers as you'll need in negligible time. So let's examine another problem, where there is no simple alternative to the recursive solution.

Counting Change

As you saw, it isn't hard to come up with a simple iterative Fibonacci algorithm. (The same goes for the factorial function, another common example of recursion in programming books and tutorials.)

In contrast, consider the following problem. How many different ways can you make change for $1.00, given half dollars, quarters ($0.25), dimes ($0.10), nickels ($0.05), and pennies ($0.01)? More generally, can you design an algorithm to compute the number of ways to change any given amount of money? While at first sight, it's an innocuous problem that might interest supermarket cashiers, this is a close relative of an important algorithm—the subset sum problem. (Once again, Google can be your guide to enlightenment.)

Let's start with an example to make sure that the problem is understood. In how many ways can you make change from 10 cents? One is 10 cents. Two is one nickel and five cents. Three is two nickels. Four is a dime. So, there are four ways.

In fact, this problem has a simple recursive solution. Suppose you think of the types of coins available as arranged in some order. Then the following relation holds: the number of ways to change amount a using n kinds of coins equals

- The number of ways to change amount a using all but the first kind of coin, plus

- The number of ways to change amount $a - d$ using all n kinds of coins, where d is the denomination of the first coin.

Rationale: note that given a task to make change, you can divide it into two complementary groups—ways that don't use the first kind of coin, and ways that do. The total number of ways is the sum of those two groups—that is, the number of ways to make change without using the first kind of coin, plus the number of ways to make change assuming that you do use the first kind of coin. But if you've used the first kind, what remains is the amount minus the denomination of the first kind.

Thus you've found a way to solve the problem by reducing it to two smaller problems. (In the first, the amount of coins is smaller, and in the second, the sum is smaller.) This is just what recursion is about—reducing problems to simpler problems. What we're lacking is an explicit solution for the "simplest" problems:

- If the amount a is 0, there's only one way to make change (no coins).

- If the amount a is negative, there is no way to make change.

- If n is 0, there's only one way to make change. (You don't have any choice.)

To convince you that the reduction and boundary cases work, let's look again at the 10-cent problem (note that you're not interested in 25- and 50-cent coins in this case). So to change 10 using the coins 10, 5, and 1 (ordered thus), you sum (1) the number of ways to change 10 using all but the first kind of coin (that is, using 5 and 1 only) and (2) the number of ways to change amount $10 - 10 = 0$ using all kinds of coins. Number (2) is simple; there's one way to change amount 0 (by the first boundary case). (1) can be further reduced to (3) the number of ways to change amount 10 using 1 cent only, plus (4) the number of ways to change $10 - 5 = 5$ using all kinds of coins. Number (3) is only one way, 10 one-cent coins (4) can be reduced, and so on. You get two ways from (4): one five-cent coin and five one-cent coins. When the algorithm finishes, you'll end up with four ways.

To take care of the coins ordering, I'll define a helper function:

```
long first_denomination(long n_kinds_of_coins)
{
  switch (n_kinds_of_coins)
  {
    case 5: return 50;
    case 4: return 25;
    case 3: return 10;
    case 2: return 5;
    case 1: return 1;
    default: assert(0);
  }
}
```

Given how many coins you can use, this function returns the denomination of the first coin. It sets up the following ordering of the coins: 50, then 25, then 10, then 5, then 1.

Now you're ready to implement the change counting procedure itself. As a true recursive algorithm, it translates into code very naturally:

```
long count_change_aux(long amount, long
n_kinds_of_coins)
{
  if (amount == 0)
    return 1;
  else if (amount < 0 || n_kinds_of_coins == 0)
    return 0;
  else
  {
    return
```

```
      count_change_aux(amount, n_kinds_of_coins -
1) +
      count_change_aux(amount -
         first_denomination(n_kinds_of_coins),
n_kinds_of_coins);
   }
}
long count_change(long amount)
{
   return count_change_aux(amount, 5);
}
```

count_change is the procedure to be called to get an answer, and it uses count_change_aux as a helper function. If you understood the algorithm and the boundary cases, there's really not much left to explain, since the code is just the algorithm "paraphrased" (to be exact, written in another language; C++ instead of English). On to some benchmarking.

count_change answers the original question (how many ways are there to make change of a dollar?) in no time—below resolution of system clock. (The answer is 292, by the way.) However, when you start raising the stakes, the runtime grows quickly. It takes 5 seconds for 1000 cents, 2.5 minutes for 2000, and the time soars rapidly, on and on. Care to throw a guess at the cause of this slowness? Right. It's the same problem you had with fib_rec—multiple repetitions of the same calculations.

To get some intuition of the problem, suppose that you run count_change on 2000 cents. Consider an intermediate sum of 1000 cents. How many ways are there to reach 1000 cents from 2000 cents? Quite a lot. But each time you reach 1000 cents, you go on and compute the ways to change 1000 cents; you saw that it takes 5 seconds each time, so it's not surprising that the runtime grows so quickly.

Contrary to the Fibonacci problem, here you don't have any simple way to formulate a swift iterative algorithm that will complete the same task. (If you find one, let me know!) But I'd still like to compute change for large sums in a reasonable time. The solution is memoization.

Memoized Change Counting

I will proceed in a manner similar to the memoization of fib_rec: I'd like to keep the results of count_change_aux computations in some cache and return immediately with a cached result when requested to do some computation for the second time. The only slightly problematic point is that you can't just use a simple array for the cache as you did in fib_memoized, since count_change_aux takes two arguments. However, as this code demonstrates, there's really no problem expanding the memoization technique to use multiple arguments.

```
long count_change_memoized_aux(map<pair<long,
long>,
  long>& cache, long amount, long
n_kinds_of_coins)
{
  pair<long, long> entry = make_pair(amount,
n_kinds_of_coins);
  if (cache.find(entry) != cache.end())
    return cache[entry];
  if (amount == 0)
    cache[entry] = 1;
  else if (amount < 0 || n_kinds_of_coins == 0)
    cache[entry] = 0;
  else
  {
    cache[entry] =
      count_change_memoized_aux(cache, amount,
        n_kinds_of_coins - 1) +
        count_change_memoized_aux(cache, amount -
          first_denomination(n_kinds_of_coins),
          n_kinds_of_coins);
  }
  return cache[entry];
}
long count_change_memoized(long amount)
{
  map<pair<long, long>, long> cache;
  return count_change_memoized_aux(cache, amount,
5);
}
```

Note that first_denomination remains the same as in the simple recursive version, so I didn't reproduce it here. Here I use a map as the cache. It maps argument pairs to results: for a pair of (amount n_kinds_of_coins), the cache holds the number of ways to change this amount with this number of kinds of coins. Except for the different data structure used as a cache, the changes are very similar to the ones in fib_memoized—first of all, the cache is consulted, and if the desired result is already there, it's simply returned. Then the real calculation is performed and added to the cache. The next time the function runs with the same arguments—the computation will be immediate, simply a fetch from the cache.

And, indeed, benchmarking shows considerable improvement in speed. Change from 2000 cents now takes only 0.02 seconds to compute (versus 2.5 minutes for the non-memoized version). Change from 5000 takes 0.06 seconds. (I gave up waiting for the non-memoized version to finish this calculation.) The runtime increase for the memoized version increases linearly with the size of the problem, as expected.

Wrapping Up

In this article, you've been introduced to memoization—an important programming technique used to speed up computations. In particular, memoization often allows one to considerably improve the runtime of a crawling recursive algorithm that may be just the right solution for a problem but is too slow to use. You learned about the inherent slowness in some recursive computations due to repetitions and saw how to use memoization to eliminate this problem.

You probably noticed the similarity between memoizing the Fibonacci implementation and memoizing the change counting algorithm. Indeed, memoization is quite simple to apply automatically, if the programming language allows it. For example, in Lisp where functions are data just like any other data, memoizing an arbitrary function is trivial. In Perl it is a little bit trickier, but there exists an excellent module called Memoize that will automatically memoize any function for you. As far as I know, there is no simple way to achieve this in C++.

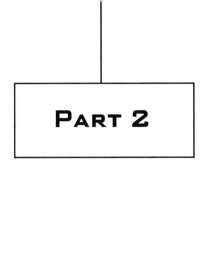

PART 2

AI

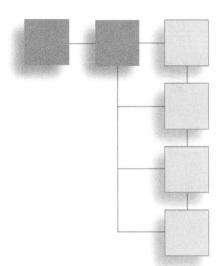

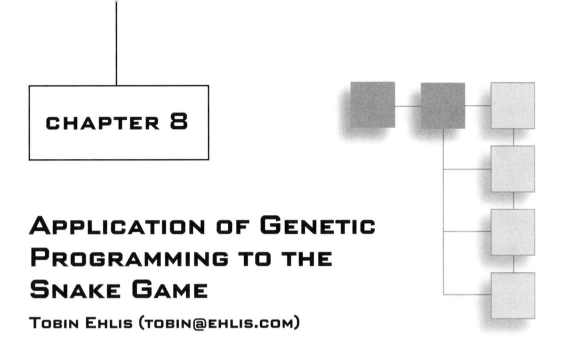

CHAPTER 8

APPLICATION OF GENETIC PROGRAMMING TO THE SNAKE GAME

TOBIN EHLIS (TOBIN@EHLIS.COM)

This article describes the evolution of a genetic program to optimize a problem featuring task prioritization in a dynamic, randomly updated environment. The specific problem approached is the Snake game in which a snake confined to a rectangular board attempts to avoid the walls and its own body while eating pieces of food. The problem is particularly interesting because as the snake eats the food its body grows, causing the space through which the snake can navigate to become more confined. Furthermore, with each piece of food eaten, a new piece of food is generated in a random location in the playing field, adding an element of uncertainty to the program. This article will focus on the development and analysis of a successful function set that will allow the evolution of a genetic program that causes the snake to eat the maximum possible pieces of food.

Introduction and Overview

Artificial intelligence techniques have been proven highly successful for the problems of navigation, task prioritization, and problem avoidance. Traditionally, humans have encoded rule-based AIs to create the behaviors necessary to allow an automaton to achieve a specific task or set of tasks. Genetic programming (GP), however, has been proven to allow a computer to create human-competitive results. Specifically, examples such as the wall-following robot (Koza 1992) and *Pac-Man* (Koza 1992) demonstrate the effectiveness of GP at evolving programs capable of navigation and task prioritization behaviors that are competitive with human-produced results.

xIn an original approach to demonstrating the effectiveness of GP at producing human-competitive results, this article describes the evolution of a genetic program that can successfully achieve a maximum score in the Snake game. The problem posed by the Snake game is of particular interest for two main reasons. First, the size and shape of the area through which the main game character, the snake, can move is constantly changing as the game progresses. Second, as the snake eats the single available piece of food in the game world, a new piece is generated in a random location. Because of these two factors, the Snake game presents a unique challenge in developing a function and terminal set to allow GP to evolve an optimal solution that is generalized for successive runs of the Snake game.

The "Background" section of this article outlines the rules and discusses the specific details of the Snake game. Next, the "Statement of the Problem" section explains the problem being addressed by this article. The "Methods" section provides the GP specifics of how the problem was approached. The "Results" section gives numerous examples of results produced by the GP runs along with a discussion and analysis of those results. The "Conclusion" section summarizes the ultimate results achieved by this work. The "Future Work" section discusses potential for further study in line with the work discussed in this article.

Background

The Snake game has existed for over two decades and seen incarnations on nearly every popular computing platform. The game begins with a snake having a fixed number of body segments confined to a rectangular board. With each time step that passes, the snake can either change direction to the right or left, or move forward—hence, the snake is always moving. Within the game board there is always one piece of food available. If the snake is able to maneuver its head onto the food, its tail will then grow by a single body segment, and another piece of food will randomly appear in an open portion of the game board during the next time step. The game ends when the snake's head advances into a game square that is filled with either a snake body segment, or a section of the wall surrounding the game board. From a task prioritization standpoint, then, the snake's primary goal is to avoid running into an occupied square. To the extent that this first priority is being achieved, its second priority is to pursue the food.

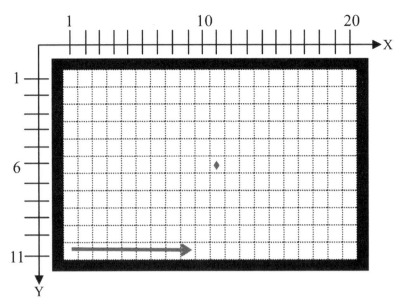

Figure 8.1
Initial position of the Snake game.

The version of the game used for this article, shown in Figure 8.1, is a replica of the first Snake game that was featured on Nokia cell phones. In this version, the game board is made up of 220 total squares, 20 horizontal and 11 vertical, and the food begins in position (11,6) on the game board, represented by a diamond in the figure. The snake is initially made up of nine body segments, occupying positions (1,11) through (9,11) on the board, with the head in position (9,11) and the snake moving to the right, represented by the arrow in the figure. The maximum number of pieces of food that can be eaten is the size of the game board minus the initial size of the snake. With the given parameters, then, this equates to $220 - 9 = 211$ pieces of food. This is because with each piece of food eaten, the snake grows by a body segment, reducing the amount of free space in which it can move. Hence, when it has eaten 211 pieces of food, its body will fill the entire game board, rendering any further movement impossible. One critical piece of information is whether or not it is even possible for the snake to eat the maximum amount of food. Indeed, it is conceivable that after eating a certain amount of food, the snake will have grown so large that it restricts itself from access to a portion of the board. Upon close inspection, however, the reader will note that by tracing certain patterns repeatedly over the board, it is possible for the snake to cover every square exactly once and return to its initial position. One such pattern is shown in Figure 8.2, which features a snake of 210 body segments

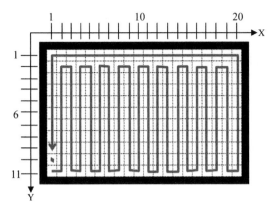

Figure 8.2
Movement pattern to achieve maximum score.

about to eat the final piece of food. Thus by continually tracing the pattern shown, the snake can eat the maximum possible pieces of food.

In evolving a genetic program to successfully eat the maximum amount of food, a human-competitive solution, in terms of score, will have been obtained. With that in mind, there are some important differences in the game when being played by a human as opposed to a computer-generated program.

For a human player, the fact that the snake is always moving adds an element of pressure, forcing the player to make decisions in a timely manner. When using a computer to play the game, this is not a concern, as the computer will have the time between each move to parse through a program tree and determine the next move. The nearest equivalent to "pressure" for a computer is any limitation imposed on the size and depth of the genetic program's function tree. These limitations restrict the possible number of decision trees that can be generated, thereby ensuring that the computer will have a finite amount of time in which to determine the next move for the snake. The particular function tree limitations imposed for this problem will be discussed in the following "Methods" section.

Statement of the Problem

The fundamental problem of the Snake game is to eat the maximum number of food pieces before "dying" by running into either a wall or a segment of the snake's body. The problem being addressed in this article is to provide a function and terminal set that will allow for the evolution of a GP that will maximize the number of food pieces eaten by the snake. The maximum goal for the particular configuration of the Snake game used in this article is 211 pieces of food.

Methods

Table 8.1 shows the initial runs of the Snake game. Following over 20 initial runs of the program, the maximum score that had been achieved was 123 hits. As it was apparent that a maximum solution would not be obtained using the initial function set, the function set was expanded to enhance the snake's movement and environment-sensing capabilities. For the remainder of the article, any GP runs performed with the function and terminal sets given in Table 8.1 will be referred to as a run made with the "initial" function set. Any run made with the enhanced function set, which includes the complete initial function set as a subset, will be referred to as having been made with the "final" function set. A discussion of both the initial and final function sets follows.

Terminals

The terminal set chosen for the problem was right, left, and forward. Each terminal was a macro that would cause the snake to take the corresponding action during a time step as follows:

- **Right**: The snake would change its current direction, making a move to the right.

- **Left**: The snake would change its current direction, making a move to the left.

Table 8.1 Tableau for Snake Game Problem

Objective	Find a computer program that eats the maximum possible pieces of food.
Terminal set	(forward), (left), (right)
Function set	ifFoodAhead, ifDangerAhead, ifDangerRight, ifDangerLeft, progn2
Fitness cases	One fitness case.
Raw fitness	Pieces of food eaten.
Standardized fitness	Maximum possible pieces of food eaten (211) minus the raw fitness.
Hits	Total pieces of food eaten during a run of the program (same as raw fitness).
Wrapper	None.
Parameters	M = 10000. G = 500.
Success predicate	A program scores 211 hits.

■ **Forward**: The snake would maintain its current direction and move forward. This is the same as a no-op, as the snake must make a move during each time step.

These three terminals represent the minimal terminal set with which the snake can effectively navigate its surroundings. While some navigation problems in a two-dimensional grid can be successfully solved by way of only one direction changing terminal, that is impractical for the Snake game because the facts that the game board is enclosed and that the snake has an extended body that is impassible necessitate the ability for the snake to move in either direction in order to avoid death. More advanced terminals, such as moving the snake along the shortest path to the food, were not implemented. Rather, the function set was constructed in such a manner that the GP could evolve the necessary capabilities to achieve the maximum score.

Functions

Initially, the snake was given very limited functionality. One function gave it information about the location of the food, three other functions gave it information about any immediately accessible danger, and progn2 was provided as connective "glue" to allow a function tree to make multiple moves in a single pass. All functions were implemented as macros of parity two, and therefore would only execute one of their arguments depending on the current state of the game, except for progn2, which would execute both of its arguments. Even though no expressions evolved from this initial function and terminal set were able to achieve the optimum score of 211 pieces of food, this set served as a baseline by which to evaluate progress and determine enhancements that would lead to the optimal solution. Following is a description of the initial function set:

■ ifFoodAhead: If there is food in line with the snake's current direction, this function will execute its first argument; otherwise, it will execute the second argument. This was the only initial function that gave the snake information beyond its immediate surroundings.

■ ifDangerAhead: If the game square immediately in front of the snake is occupied with either a snake body segment or the wall, this function will execute its first argument; otherwise, it will execute its second argument.

- **ifDangerRight:** If the game square immediately to the right of the snake is occupied with either a snake body segment or the wall, this function will execute its first argument; otherwise, it will execute its second argument.

- **ifDangerLeft:** If the game square immediately to the left of the snake is occupied with either a snake body segment or the wall, this function will execute its first argument; otherwise, it will execute its second argument.

- **progn2:** This is a connectivity function that will first execute its right argument, then its left. It is the only function that allows execution of more than one terminal in a single parse of the function tree. Although this function will always execute both of its arguments, it was necessary to implement it as a macro because of the way that the software used to make GP runs, Dave's Genetic Programming in C (DGPC), evaluated functions versus macros. To avoid unnecessary modification of DGPC, implementing progn2 as a macro proved the simplest option.

As mentioned previously, no GP runs performed with the initial function set were able to score greater than 123 hits. In order to increase the probability of evolving a function tree capable of achieving the maximum number of hits, the initial function set was enhanced. Following is a discussion of the additional functions that, along with the initial function set, make up the final function set (all of parity two):

- **ifDangerTwoAhead:** If the game square two spaces immediately in front of the snake is occupied by either the wall or a segment of the snake's body, this function will execute the first parameter; otherwise, it will execute the second.

- **ifFoodUp:** If the current piece of food on the board is closer to the top of the game board than the snake's head, then the first parameter of this function will be executed; otherwise, the second parameter will be executed.

- **ifFoodRight:** If the current piece of food on the board is farther to the right of the game board than the snake's head, then the first parameter of this function will be executed; otherwise, the second parameter will be executed.

- **ifMovingRight:** If the snake is moving right, then the first parameter of this function will be executed; otherwise, the second parameter will be executed.

- **ifMovingLeft:** If the snake is moving left, then the first parameter of this function will be executed; otherwise, the second parameter will be executed.

- **ifMovingUp:** If the snake is moving upward, then the first parameter of this function will be executed; otherwise, the second parameter will be executed.

- **ifMovingDown:** If the snake is moving downward, then the first parameter of this function will be executed; otherwise, the second parameter will be executed.

There are two characteristics of the final function set that should be given special attention. First, note that the ifFoodUp and ifFoodDown functions are direction-independent, meaning that the direction in which the snake is moving has no impact on the function's behavior. This is in contrast to the initial set of functions, such as ifDangerAhead, in which the direction that the snake was traveling would have an impact on the return value of the function.

The reason for the difference is to maintain simplicity in the function set. The snake can potentially be surrounded by danger, but there will only be one piece of food on the board at any one time. If the ifDanger* functions were direction-independent, then two significant complexities would be added to the problem. Also an additional function would be required, as there would need to be one for all cardinal directions in order to account for all possible surrounding dangers. An added downfall of this complexity is that one of the ifDanger* functions will be virtually meaningless, depending on the direction of the snake's travel, since the snake's neck segment adjacent to the snake's head is always an adjacent danger, although not one of any consequence to the snake, since it is unable to move back on itself. Any time an ifDanger* function was used, it would need the aid of a helper function, such as the new ifMoving* functions in order to make intelligent moves based on an assessment of the danger.

Taking the second complexity into account, the reader may now note that the same disadvantage is true of the two new functions, ifFoodUp and ifFoodRight. Indeed this is true, but an important difference between the role of food and the role of danger in the game makes for a worthwhile trade-off. The difference is that there will only be one piece of food on the board at any time. This allows the new ifFood* functions to serve as two functions each. To clarify, consider the ifFoodUp function. When not true, it is indicating that the food is either down or on the same horizontal plane as the snake's head. Now consider a hypothetical ifDangerUp function. If this function were not true, it would tell nothing about whether or not danger is down because it can be anywhere simultaneously.

Likewise, it would not even tell whether an existing "up" danger posed an immediate threat to the snake, as the further information of the snake's current moving direction would need to be known, as discussed earlier. For the second special characteristic of the new functions, consider the new ifMoving* functions. Clearly, they can be used as helper functions with the two new ifFood* functions to create beneficial schemata.

As an example of a beneficial schemata, consider ifFoodUp(ifMovingRight(left, ifMovingUp(fwd, right)))), which orients the snake to pursue food that is upward. As will be seen in the "Results" section, not only does the GP learn how to use these functions in conjunction with the two new ifFood* functions, but they also prove useful in helping the snake discover patterns that greatly extend its life.

Fitness Cases

For initial runs of the problem, only a single fitness case was used to determine the fitness for each individual. Because the food placement is random both during a single run and from one run to another, occasionally individuals would score a number of hits because of fortuitous placement of the food, not on the merit of their function tree.

To better ensure that the most successful individuals achieved high fitness measures primarily on the basis of their function tree, new GP runs were often made featuring a "primed" population in which the fitness was measured as the average of four runs of an individual. The procedure for this is as follows: once a run had completed without obtaining a solution, or if a run had stalled on a single individual for a large number (100 or more) of generations, a new run was begun with this final individual as one of the initial individuals. For this new run, however, the fitness was taken as the average fitness of an individual over four runs instead of merely a single run. The averaging of the fitness over four runs helped eliminate the possibility of an individual having a high fitness due simply to lucky placement of the food. Using this averaging method to determine fitness was only used in primed populations because it increased the time of a GP run fourfold. Furthermore, it was common for the generations that timed out to feature an individual who had scored a high fitness as a result of a lucky run. By beginning a new run with this individual in the initial population, it not only assured a more realistic fitness measure, but it also introduced an entirely new mix of randomly generated schemata that could potentially benefit the stalled individual. Details of results produced by primed runs are given in the "Results" section.

Fitness Measure

The fitness measure used is the maximum possible pieces of food eaten (211) minus the actual number of pieces of food eaten. Furthermore, if the snake was unsuccessful at eating any food, the fitness would be penalized by the number of board squares that it was from the food. This additional criterion was added to favor individuals who moved toward the food in early generations of snakes who were unable eat any food.

Parameters

Population was set to 10,000. The maximum number of generations was set to 500. The size of a function tree was limited to 150 points. These parameters were mainly chosen based on available computer resources, covered in computer equipment and runtime explanation below.

Designating a Result and Criterion for Terminating a Run

The best generation individual will be the one that is able to eat the most pieces of food. A run will end when one of three termination criteria is met:

- The snake runs into a section of the game board occupied by a wall.

- The snake runs into a section of the game board occupied by a segment of the snake's body.

- The number of moves made by the snake exceeds a set limit. This limit was set to 300, slightly larger than the size of the game board. This will prevent a snake from wandering aimlessly around a small portion of the board.

The reader may note that there is no termination criterion for the completely successful snake. That is because upon eating the final piece of food, the snake's tail will grow onto its head, causing it to satisfy the second termination criteria. Hence, even the optimal solution will end in death for the snake.

Crossover and Mutation Rates

Crossover of nodes was the primary genetic operator employed during the GP runs. The crossover fraction for leaves was set to .10, the crossover fraction for a node was set to .80, and the mutation fraction was set to 0. Additionally, primed

GP runs were used to improve genetic diversity, as previously described in the discussion of fitness cases.

Computer Equipment and Runtime

The software used was Dave's Genetic Programming in C (DGPC), and Microsoft Visual Studio. In addition, a standalone simulation of the Snake game was created that was able to read in the function trees produced by DGPC and display a graphical (using ASCII graphics) run of a particular function tree. This utility proved invaluable, as it provided a fast, visual method to determine the overall optimization strategy represented by the function tree. The alternative of hand-evaluating each function tree would have proven not only more time-consuming, but much less conclusive. A complete run of two simultaneous sets of 500 generations (1000 total generations) took approximately 1.5 hours to complete on an Intel Core 2 Duo 6600 Processor at 2.4GHz with 2GB of RAM.

Schemata

Given the initial function set, there were a few highly desirable sub-tree schemata that could be produced. First, considering a minimal sub-tree of three points, any sub-tree that would evade impending danger by changing directions is certainly the key to an individual's survival. One such sub-tree is ifDangerAhead(right, forward). Secondly, a basic sub-tree that will avoid changing directions into impending danger is solely beneficial to an individual. One example is ifDanger Right(forward, right). The reader will note that any time a change in direction is about to be undertaken, it would be wise to have such a check before making the move. Thirdly, a three-pointed sub-tree that aims at pursuing the food, and modifying directions if no food is ahead, is required to give the individual more than a random opportunity to eat the food pieces. One such individual is ifFoodAhead(forward, right).

As explained previously, the ifFoodAhead function will return true for a piece of food any number of squares in front of the snake. Therefore, in addition to seeking the food, it would also be desirable for the individual to continually scan for impending danger while the food is being sought. Thus a final example of a desirable schemata is any combination of the preceding three examples that effectively combines the goals of each. For example, consider the following function tree of seven points that will pursue food ahead as long as no immediate threat is observed. If, however, there is a threat or no food ahead, the sub-tree will cause the individual to change direction, avoiding any observed danger, or pursue a new vector to find food. (Specific examples of the emergence of such schemata will be given in the "Results" section.)

```
ifFoodAhead(ifDangerAhead(right, forward), ifDangerRight(left, right))
```

In addition to the potential beneficial schemata, touched on previously, there are also *detrimental* schemata. The detrimental schemata would be any function branch whose primary goal is either to seek danger or avoid food. Examples of detrimental schemata are essentially the converse of the previously outlined beneficial schemata, and their further consideration is left to the reader.

Certainly all schemata are not strictly beneficial or detrimental, and any such schemata will be called *neutral* schemata. Consider, for example, the simple sub-tree `ifDangerRight(left, forward)`. This function will turn left if danger is present to the right and continue forward otherwise. This schemata makes either a left or forward move without having any apparent knowledge of what lies in those directions. This could certainly prove to be detrimental, but the move to the left when danger is right is at least avoiding the danger to the right. Schemata such as this can actually prove beneficial when placed in the context of a complete function tree. An examination of actual schemata produced during the GP runs in question follows in the "Results" section.

Results

As mentioned in the "Methods" section, there were three types of GP runs made in an attempt to evolve a solution to the Snake game: runs using the initial function set, the final function set, and primed runs, also using the final function set. The highest number of hits generated by a run using the initial function set was 123. Three separate solutions were generated using the final function set, although none of them was found to consistently generate a solution. The number of hits achieved by each solution depended on the placement of the food. It was not until the method of "priming" a run, described in the "Methods" section, was used that a consistent solution was generated. Of 10 primed runs, using various initial seeds, exactly five of them evolved a solution, all of which were consistent solutions over multiple runs. Comparatively, over 20 runs using the full function set were made, and only three of them produced solutions (none consistent).

A summary of the overall results achieved in each type of run is given in Figure 8.3. Each line on the graph is the average of 10 runs. Note that the initial and final

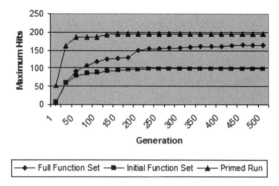

Figure 8.3
Average results of different runs.

function sets produce a roughly equivalent maximum number of hits until about generation 50. At this point, the final function set continues to improve while the initial function set levels off. By generation 200, the initial function set has virtually no improvement, while the final function set continues improving past generation 400. Because the final function set is both more complete and larger, new and more successful individuals continue to evolve while individuals produced by the initial function set max out around 100 hits. Another feature to note in Figure 8.3 is the impressive results achieved by the primed runs. All primed runs were begun with an individual from a final function set run who had achieved at least 150 hits. When taken as the average over four runs, however, these individuals were only able to achieve about 50 hits, as shown in the first generation of the primed runs. These individuals jumpstart the population to great success, and by generation 25 the maximum number of hits has more than tripled to around 160. By generation 150, the primed runs level off to about 200 hits. Following is an evaluation of some of the most prominent strategies evolved during the various GP runs. Specific examples of individuals from each type of run are presented and analyzed, and all function trees are reduced for simplicity's sake.

Zig-Zagger

One strategy that was prevalent in individuals across multiple runs is the "zig-zagger." These individuals would trace the board diagonally in a stair-stepper pattern until they either reached a wall or had lined up the direction of their movement with the food. Upon reaching a wall, they would change their direction as if bouncing off of the wall and continue diagonally, tracing the board in a new direction. If they were successful in aligning their movement with the piece of food, they would typically head directly toward the food, perhaps avoiding danger, depending on the particular individual. Variations in zig-zaggers occurred between which directions they would head when hitting the wall, how often they would seek the food, and how they would react in enclosed situations, such as in corners or heading toward food that was blocked by their body. Obviously, the more successful individuals evolved traits that allowed them to avoid danger in close quarters and dodge their body when it blocked progress toward the food. Following is an example of a zig-zagger that was able to score a maximum of 33 hits in one particular run:

```
(ifFoodAhead
  (ifDangerLeft
    (right)
    (ifDangerRight
      (¹forward)
      (ifDangerAhead
        (left)
        (¹forward)
      )
    )
  )
  (ifDangerAhead
    (ifDangerLeft
      (right)
      (left)
    )
    (ifDangerLeft
      (ifDangerRight
        (forward)
        (²right)
      )
      (progn2
        (left)
        (right)
      )
    )
  )
)
```

Consider initially the rightmost sub-tree of the function tree, which is given on the last line as progn2 (left)(right). This is the branch executed initially and for the majority of this zig-zagger's run. When executed repeatedly, this sub-tree will cause the snake to move left then right, progressing diagonally across the board. For this example, the sub-tree is executed whenever there is no food ahead of the snake's line of movement, and there is no danger in front of or to the left of the snake's head. This continuous zig-zagging motion allows the snake to examine successive rows or columns of the board in search of the food. Because both branches of `progn2` are executed before returning to the beginning of the function tree, however, the snake will only detect the food if the second argument of the `progn2`, `right`, leaves the snake's head in line with the food.

Once the food is directly in line with the movement of the snake's head, the left-hand sub-tree, given on the first line of the preceding code, is executed. As noted with a superscript 1, the snake will continue forward if there is no danger to the left, and either there is danger to the right or there is no danger to the right or ahead. Unfortunately for the snake, if there is no danger to the left, but danger to the right and ahead, this function tree will lead it directly into the danger ahead, noted with the first 1 in the code. This is exactly what happened to the snake in Figure 8.4, shown one time step before its demise after having eaten 24 pieces of food. This snake, whose head is in (14,5), began moving toward the food in (4,5) after having released from the wall.

Finally, note that when the `right` portion of the `progn2` sub-tree causes the snake to be either facing or next to a wall, the sub-trees on the second and third lines of the code will be executed respectively. Further investigation reveals that each of these sub-trees will cause the snake to move away from the wall in a direction that avoids danger, even in corners. In this fashion, the snake appears to bounce from

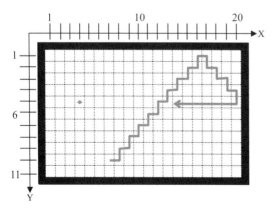

Figure 8.4
Zig-zagger near death.

the walls and proceed to zig-zag in an alternate direction. Two examples of this are seen at positions (17,1) and (20,5) of Figure 8.4. In both of these cases, the snake made the right turn (noted with a 2) in order to avoid the wall.

Wall-Slitherer

The strategy that scored the highest out of all individuals using the initial function and terminal set is the "wall-slitherer." These individuals would follow along the wall, not simply moving forward, but rather slithering back and forth between the two squares closest to the wall. Once able to align its head with the food, the individual would move away from the wall in a straight line to obtain the food. Then, when the food was eaten, successful wall-slitherers would either double-back along their own body and head for the wall or head in a random direction toward a wall. Variations on wall-slitherers occurred in the direction they would take around the wall and when they would leave the wall to pursue the food. One highly successful wall-slitherer is shown in the following code. This individual scored a maximum of 107 hits in one particular run, and an evaluation of its important characteristics follows:

```
(ifFoodAhead
  (ifDangerAhead
    (left)
    (forward )
  )
  (¹ifDangerAhead
    (ifDangerRight
      (left)
      (progn2
        (right)
        (ifFoodAhead
          (ifDangerRight
            (forward)
            (right)
          )
        )
        (ifDangerRight
          (forward)
          (right)
        )
      )
    )
  )
)
```

```
(²ifDangerRight
  (ifDangerLeft
    (forward)
    (left)
  )
  (³ifDangerLeft
    (right)
    (⁴progn2
      (left)
      (ifFoodAhead
        (ifDangerLeft
          (right)
          (left)
        )
        (ifDangerRight
          (left)
          (⁵progn2
            (ifDangerAhead
              (right)
              (ifDangerLeft
                (right)
                (left)
              )
            )
            (ifDangerRight
              (forward)
              (right)
            )
          )
        )
      )
    )
  )
)
```

In evaluating this individual, first consider the root, which consists of the ifFoodAhead function. For any case in which there is food ahead, the very simple left sub-tree is executed. This sub-tree simply checks for danger ahead and attempts to avoid it to the left if present; otherwise, the snake will continue along its current path toward the food. While this sub-tree proves both simple and effective, the fact is clear that the individual spends the majority of its run without the food immediately ahead, which is handled by the much larger right-hand sub-tree.

While it appears much more complicated than the left-hand sub-tree, the fundamental strategy of the right-hand sub-tree is to avoid danger. This strategy is executed impressively by the three different ifDanger* functions (noted with the superscripts 1, 2, and 3). These functions provide the roots for the three sub-trees along the right-hand side of the main function tree. The reader can verify that each of these three sub-trees contains schemata that are highly effective at avoiding any impending danger to the snake. Having already taken precautions to pursue food and avoid danger, the final sub-tree provides the snake with its wall-slithering motion, in which it spends the majority of its time.

The final sub-tree, noted with a 4, is rooted with a progn2. This indicates that multiple actions will be carried out every time this sub-tree is reached, which proves to be very frequently. Initially, the branch will make a move to the left, which is already known to be safe. Following this move, if there is no food ahead and no food to the right, then the second progn2, noted with a 5, is reached, making for a total of three moves to be executed on this single pass of the function tree. This three-move sequence is both common and highly beneficial to the success of this wall-slitherer.

In Figure 8.5, note the snake's body segment at (19,8). At this point in the past, the snake was facing downward and a new parse of the function tree was beginning. As no danger was immediately present, sub-tree 4 was reached, and the snake turned left toward the wall. Needing to complete the second argument

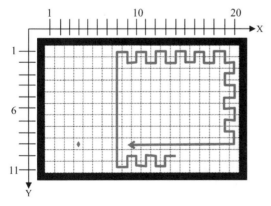

Figure 8.5
Wall-slitherer near death.

of the progn2, and with no food ahead or danger to the right, the progn2 at 5 was reached, which caused the snake to turn right twice, leading to the next parse of the function tree. Looking back in history through the illustration, note that the same pattern was carried out at points (19,6), (19,4), (19,2), as well as numerous other times in the brief potion of the snake's run demonstrated here. This repeated slithering pattern served to maximize the amount of ground covered by the snake while minimizing the danger that its body would pose to itself. A time step prior to a fatal flaw in the snake's movement, however, is illustrated.

As the food is in front of the snake's head, the simple sub-tree on the left is entered. Since there is danger ahead of the snake, it will simply turn left. As shown in the illustration, this turn will lead to the snake's death as it hits its own body after having eaten 61 pieces of food. While it may seem surprising that this flaw in the left-hand function tree was not encountered sooner, the snake survives by keeping its body along the walls as much as possible. In the illustration, it is clear that the snake left the wall 57 time steps earlier in order to pursue a piece of food across the board. Once the food was eaten, the snake resumed its slither pattern clockwise around the edge of the board. Unfortunately, its body had grown so long that by the time its head was in line with the food at position (19,9), its body was still blocking its path to the food. The snake's evasion tactic of going to the left when danger is encountered with the food ahead had saved it in previous similar situations: once a single successful left was made, the snake was no longer in line with the food, and it would continue any necessary evasive maneuvers via the much more robust sub-trees 1, 2, and 3. In this final, fatal case, however, the combination of the snake's long body, its previous cross-board pursuit of the food, and the placement of the next piece of food three board squares off of the wall caused the evasive left to lead the snake directly into its own body.

Circler

After the function set was enhanced to include the further food-sensing capabilities of ifFoodUp and ifFoodRight, as well as the four ifMoving* functions, a new strategy of behavior evolved called the "circler." These individuals would follow along the outside of the wall in a circular pattern and only leave the wall to get the food. Once they reached the food, they would continue forward until they reached the wall; then they'd start to circle again. Typically, they would only attempt to eat the food while moving in one particular direction. While similar to the wall-slitherer, they differ in two key ways. The first is that the circler will always remain directly next to the wall and not move back and forth like the wall-slitherer. The second is that the circler will typically only leave the wall while headed in one direction. Both of these differences are a direct result of the new functions. Before further discussion, consider the following circler, who scored a maximum of 80 hits over a single run:

```
(ifDangerAhead
  (ifDangerTwoAhead
    (ifDangerLeft
      (right)
      (left)
    )
    (ifFoodUp
      (ifDangerLeft
        (right)
        (²left)
      )
      (forward)
    )
  )
  (ifMovingUp
    (ifDangerRight
      (ifFoodUp
        (forward)
        (³left)
      )
      (right)
    )
    (¹forward)
  )
)
```

First note the leftmost branch of the function tree, in which the snake will primarily avoid danger to both the front and the left. Certainly, the left-hand sub-tree, though simple, proves highly effective at achieving the snake's primary goal of avoiding danger. Secondly, take note of the right-hand sub-tree, which is parsed whenever danger is not immediately ahead of the snake. If the snake is not moving upward, it simply continues forward, which is already known to be a safe move. This proves to be the move that the snake most commonly makes. If, however, the snake is moving upward and there is danger to the right, then it will turn left as soon as the food is no longer above it. The primary moves of this snake, then, are to continue forward around the outside of the board until either there is danger ahead and it turns left, or the snake is moving upward and there is food to left, when it turns left. Note that these moves are marked 1, 2, 3, respectively, in the preceding function tree. Hence, when seen in action, the snake will make a counterclockwise circular motion around the outside of the board with the top of the circle determined by the current piece of food.

Pattern-Following Solution

As a final example of an evolved strategy, an individual that was able to score the maximum number of hits, 211, will be considered. All individuals who were able to score the maximum number of hits demonstrated some pattern similar to that shown in Figure 8.2. All of these individuals took little to no consideration of where the food was on the board, but rather followed a set pattern that would cover the entire board, eventually causing them to eat the food. Furthermore, the pattern they followed would be continuous, meaning that their head would eventually reach its original starting position, allowing the pattern to continue indefinitely. The following is one such pattern follower, produced in generation 27 of a primed run:

```
(ifDangerRight
  (ifDangerAhead
    (ifDangerTwoAhead
      (⁸left)
      (forward)
    )
    (ifMovingRight
      (⁶left)
      (⁴·⁷forward)
    )
  )
  (ifDangerAhead
    (ifDangerLeft
      (ifFoodUp
        (right)
        (right)
      )
      (ifDangerTwoAhead
        (left)
        (forward)
      )
    )
    (ifMovingUp
```

```
(ifDangerTwoAhead
  (ifFoodAhead
    (ifMovingRight
      (³right)
      (⁹forward)
    )
    (ifMovingDown
      (left)
      (²right)
    )
  )
  (¹progn2
    (forward)
    (forward)
  )
)
(ifMovingRight
  (right)
  (forward)
  )
  )
  )
)
```

This individual followed a pattern exactly the same as that shown in Figure 8.2. There were only a few minor deviations from the pattern that would occur during very infrequent states of the game board. Before considering any such deviations, an examination of the major pattern-following steps will be made.

The overall pattern followed by the preceding individual is as follows, with the movement steps noted by superscripts. To simplify the analysis, consider that the snake has already eaten enough food to be as long as the board is high, 11 segments, and that the snake is currently moving upward with its head at position (2,10) on the board:

1. While moving upward, if there is not danger two ahead, move forward twice.

2. Once there is danger two ahead, turn right; snake now moving right one row from the top of the board.

3. Turn right again, to begin heading downward.

4. Continue moving downward until there is danger directly ahead.

5. Once there is danger ahead, turn left; snake now moving right at the bottom of the board.

6. Turn left again and return to step 1 until there is danger to the right of the snake.

7. Danger right indicated the final right-hand column, so the snake now moves up until danger is one ahead.

8. Once there is danger ahead, turn left to follow the top row of the board (4,7) while moving left; repeat this same step to move down the left-hand side of the board, and when the bottom of the board is reached, return to step 5.

While it is clear that by repeatedly following this pattern, the snake will continually trace the whole board, causing it to eat at least one piece of food on each pass of the board, there is one notable exception from the pattern that is made whenever the food is in the top row of the board and the snake is moving upward toward it. In this rare case, when step 2 of the pattern is reached, rather than turning right, the snake will continue forward to eat the food, as noted with a 9 in the function tree. When this case occurs the snake will resume the pattern to the right following its consumption of the food. If, however, this case occurs too far to the right and the snake's body is long enough, the snake can trap itself on the right side of the board, causing it to die. This is the only way that the individual shown will not successfully eat 211 pieces of food.

Conclusion

This article has presented the development and evaluation of a function set capable of evolving an optimal solution to the Snake game. An initial function set was presented and evaluated, but it proved unsuccessful at evolving an optimal solution. The initial function set was then expanded upon to create the successful final function set, and consistently optimal solutions were generated using primed GP runs. A comparison was made of the results achieved by each function set, as well as by the primed GP runs. Examples of commonly evolved strategies were presented and evaluated, and a final analysis of a consistently successful optimal solution was given.

Future Work

The work presented in this article provides innumerable opportunities for further investigation into the evolution of a task prioritization scheme within a dynamically changing, randomly updated environment. Specific to the snake problem, modifications can be made to create completely new and interesting problems, such as a non-rectangular game board, obstacles within the game board, or multiple pieces of food. Multiple snakes could be co-evolved to competitively pursue the food. The function set could be modified to feature enhanced detection capabilities and more advanced navigational options. The techniques used for navigating the snake could be generalized to apply to various other problems of interest. Possibilities include automated navigation of multiple robots through a crowded workspace, an automaton for tracking fleeing police suspects through harsh environments, or a control scheme for an exploratory vehicle seeking a particular goal on a harsh alien planet. The possibilities are limited only by the imagination.

References

Koza, John R. *Genetic Programming: On the Programming of Computers by Means of Natural Selection.* Cambridge, MA: MIT Press, 1992.

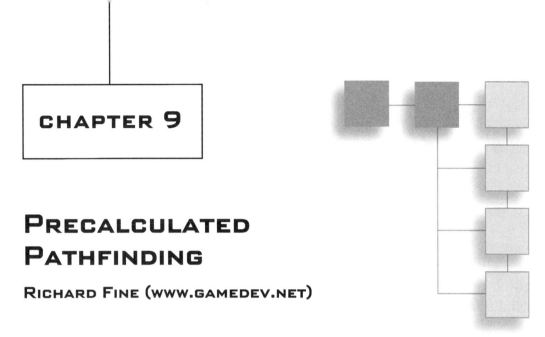

CHAPTER 9

PRECALCULATED PATHFINDING

RICHARD FINE (WWW.GAMEDEV.NET)

The player is presented with a new environment, having just battled his way past a hoard of enemies. The new environment is a network of corridors and rooms, and throughout the environment are enemies, bonuses, and other interactive items. The player explores the environment, taking out the enemies, collecting the bonuses, and discovering the interactive items.

The NPC is presented with a new environment, having just been generated by the engine. The NPC heads straight for the nearest room because it can see from the node graph that a bonus is there, and then takes a route through the environment that avoids and evades all enemies. The frame rate drops a little as the route is recalculated each step to account for enemy movements. The player watches in disbelief.

Giving NPCs perfect knowledge of the game world can often lead to frustratingly unrealistic behavior. Yet, ironically, it's easier to give them perfect knowledge than imperfect knowledge—after all, the computer *needs* perfect knowledge of the environment in order to render or update it, and in order for that computer to model an AI agent that doesn't have perfect knowledge, it will have to deliberately "feign ignorance."

A* searches also aren't free. They're cheaper than some other search techniques if your heuristic is good, but they do still take some time; in environments with complex costs and heuristics, you may have to count every search you perform against your frame rate.

In this article, I'll present a dynamic programming technique that you can use to precalculate all the paths through the environment, allowing you to replace all your runtime A* searches with table lookups—in essence, trading memory for speed. You'll examine how this technique can be used to model an agent's imperfect knowledge of the environment, how behaviors such as exploration can be built on top, how the technique can be extended to account for a changing environment, and I'll discuss some ways of mitigating the memory cost. If you're familiar with things like the Internet routing protocols, then you'll probably find this reminds you of something. . . .

Initial Concept

The technique stems from the fact that pathfinding has "optimal sub-structure": you can take any segment between two points on a shortest path, and that segment is guaranteed to be the shortest path between the two points. Say you have a route ABCDE, and you're claiming that it's the shortest route between A and E. Because pathfinding has optimal substructure, you can take any segment of that path (say, BCD), and it's guaranteed to be the shortest path between B and D. The cost (distance) of the route ABCDE is cost of AB + cost of BCD + cost of DE. If BCD were anything other than the shortest route, ABCDE would not be a shortest route either. So, you can say something like this:

```
route(A->E) = AB + route(B->E)
```

You know because of the optimal substructure property that it's the shortest route.

Here's the next key observation: when your agent is currently at A, you don't actually *need* to calculate route(B->D). You don't need to know any of it until you're actually at B, and even then, you only need to know the first step of the route. People often navigate this way in the real world—they establish the beginning of their route enough that they can start moving, but they leave the rest to be determined as they proceed. All they need to know, at any given time, is where to go next.

Foundations

That "where to go next" is a pretty powerful concept. Imagine that once you're at B, your target changes and you want to get to E? You won't have wasted any time calculating the rest of the route to D; you can instantly change your target and say, "Okay, so where do I go next to get to E?' These where-to-go-next values can be stored neatly in a lookup table. Let's take the sample network, as shown in Figure 9.1.

From this network, using any pathfinding algorithm you feel like, you can build a table of where-next nodes:

		To				
		A	B	C	D	E
From	A	-	B	C	C	E
	B	A	-	C	C	A
	C	A	B	-	D	A
	D	C	C	C	-	E
	E	A	A	A	D	-

To recap: I built this table by finding the route *from* each given node *to* each given node, storing the first node in the route (excluding the start node). Naturally, an actual implementation of this would store numeric node identifiers instead of string-based names.

To use the table, all you need to know is your current location and your destination. Using the current location as the `from` value and the destination as the `to` value, you get the next node you should move to. I'll assume that your network has been constructed in such a way that each connection is easy to actually move along (i.e., that a connection between two nodes represents a direct line of sight between them), so actually moving to the next node should be a cinch. Effectively, you've amortized the cost of calculating the path over the entire time taken to travel it.

This technique also has the advantage that it can cope instantly with changes, both in position and destination, without having wasted any processing time at

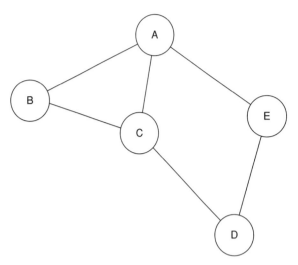

Figure 9.1

runtime. Using conventional pathfinding techniques, you have to calculate the entire route to the target. If you don't, then you might inadvertently select a path that becomes a dead-end at the last minute. And even if you store that path until you've finished travelling along it, you still run the risk that, a couple of nodes into your path, the target will move and you'll have wasted time calculating parts of the path that never got used. With this technique, however, you process all the nodes before the game starts (perhaps even at development time, where the table can be stored in a file), and once you're in-game, you never have to waste time looking at nodes that don't get used. Potentially, you're wasting a lot of time calculating routes that won't get used, but now you're doing it offline instead of at runtime.

To drive the point home, let's play a little game with the network. You'll place a hare at A, set to follow the path AEDCA repeatedly. You then place a dog at D and watch it track (and, finally, catch) the hare.

Hare Position	Dog Position	Dog moves to...
A	D	C
E	C	A
D	A	C
C	C	...eat the hare!

Notice how in the third row the dog actually doubles back on itself. That's because you've only been tracking the hare's current position, and you haven't made any attempts to predict where it will be. To do so, you may find it useful to augment the where-next table with an indication of the remaining distance to the stated target, allowing you to begin predicting what state the world will be in by the time you get there. Distance information will also become extremely useful when you move on to making the table adapt to changes in the network in the next section.

In fact, there's quite a bit more information you could store within the table—you'd effectively be storing information per route. For instance, you could store some value representing whether the route is mostly in confined spaces or mostly in open areas, allowing the AI to make a decision about which weapon would be the best to equip. You could store information about the shortest detour required to collect health packs or ammo so that the AI could decide whether it needs to stock up before leaving. Naturally, each extra piece of information consumes more memory, so each inclusion needs to be carefully considered.

Dynamic Worlds

What you've established so far will work very well for environments in which the network is unchanging. Unfortunately, that's too limiting for many games to use. The ability to account for the fact that a door has now been unlocked, or that a corridor has collapsed, would be a very useful addition to this system. Of course, you could always recalculate the entire table, but that would be horribly inefficient and slow; a more intelligent algorithm is required.

Let's consider the situation where one edge has been removed from the network. You can't recalculate *nothing* if your network is to be properly dynamic, and you don't want to recalculate everything. So let's say that you wish to minimize the number of nodes you process (see Figure 9.2).

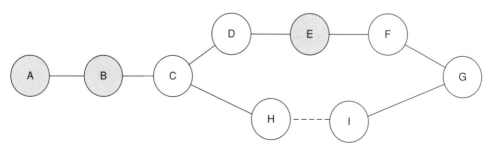

Figure 9.2

In this diagram, the nodes shaded gray will be unaffected by the removal of the edge from H to I. Node E is a fairly obvious one; if you consider the shortest path from E to every other node, then none of them would use the edge HI even if it *were* present, so none of its directions needs amending. A and B are not so simple, though. It's clear that if the edge HI were in the network, then the route B->I would be BCHI, and now that it's gone, the route must be BCDEFGI. The important thing to note is that both paths begin with BC, and you are only recording beginnings in your table. Thus your table does not need to change for B->I. Can you determine when this will be the case without computing full paths?

The concept is simple: the bare minimum number of nodes that you must at least *check* for changes are the two nodes that the absent edge used to connect. Starting with these two nodes, you determine if any changes need to be made, and if so, move outward to any of their neighboring nodes that direct some route through them. If a node has not changed, its neighbors do not need to be recomputed. In the network shown in Figure 9.2, you would find that B does not change (as it directs all affected routes through C, both before and after edge removal), and so you do not need both checking node A. You keep going until you've run out of nodes to check. The change "propagates" through the network like a ripple on a puddle, affecting fewer and fewer nodes as it goes. The process is very similar when an edge is being added.

There's one very important exception. What happens if an edge is removed that causes the network to split into two disconnected islands? Every single node in the network has to be updated because there will now be at least one other node for which it has no path at all, and thus no beginning to store. There's really no way around this for a table that you wish to keep "perfect." Fortunately, though, it's not often that you would actually do this without deleting the nodes in one of the two islands (e.g., when permanently blocking off an entire area). If the nodes are being deleted, then the rows and columns relevant to them should be deleted from the table first, and then the remaining affected node can propagate as normal; changes should then be minimized. Similarly, if you intend to close one route and open an alternative one at roughly the same time, you should add the new edge before deleting the old one; that way you will avoid splitting the network between steps (see Figure 9.3).

Let's take the network from earlier and remove the path BC. The original path table looked like this:

		To				
		A	B	C	D	E
	A	-	B	C	C	E
	B	A	-	C	C	A
From	C	A	B	-	D	A
	D	C	C	C	-	E
	E	A	A	A	D	-

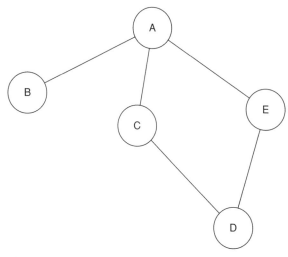

Figure 9.3

You'll keep two lists: an open list and a closed list. The open list represents nodes that you need to check for updates, and the closed list represents nodes you have already checked. To begin with, the open list contains nodes B and C, and the closed list is empty. When implementing this, it would be more efficient to store both lists as a single closed list followed by an open list, and then simply keep a counter as to how many of the nodes are in the closed list—but for clarity here, I'll use two lists.

You process the first node on the open list, B. Using the pathfinding method of your choice, you rebuild B's row in the table. In fact, in this case, you can see that B only has one edge left, so all its values will have to use that edge. So, the original row was:

From	B	A	-	C	C	A

And the newly calculated row is:

From	B	A	-	A	A	A

You can see that the row has changed. So you take all of B's neighbors and add any that are not yet open or closed to the open list. As noted, it only has one edge, one neighbor, node A. You also remove B from the open list and add it to the closed list. So, now, the open nodes are {C, A}, and the closed nodes are {B}.

Now you start processing node C. The original row for C was:

From	C	A	B	-	D	A

The newly calculated row is:

From	C	A	A	-	D	A

It's only a small change, but it's a change. So, you take C's neighbors, A and D. A is already on the open list, so you skip it; but D is on neither list, so you add it to the open list. Now you close C, moving it from the open to closed lists, giving you open nodes {A, D} and closed nodes {B, C}.

Now you try node A. The original row for A was:

From	A	-	B	C	C	E

The newly calculated row is:

From	A	-	B	C	C	E

The row hasn't changed, so you can skip checking its neighbors and close it straight away. This leaves you with only one open node, {D}, and three closed nodes, {B, C, A}.

Original row for D:

From	D	C	C	C	-	E

New row for D:

From	D	C	C	C	-	E

Again, there's no change, so you close D immediately. The open list is now empty, which means you've finished. The new path table in its entirety is as follows:

		To				
		A	B	C	D	E
From	A	-	B	C	C	E
	B	A	-	A	A	A
	C	A	A	-	D	A
	D	C	C	C	-	E
	E	A	A	A	D	-

Notice that you didn't even check node E. None of its neighbors actually changed as a result of the missing path, and thus it's guaranteed not to need updating.

It's worth observing that if you are making multiple changes to the network in one go, you don't need to perform the algorithm for each individual change. Provided you collect all the affected nodes across every change into a single open list, you can make a collection of changes and then run the algorithm a single time to update the network, which will be more efficient than running it separately for each change.

Education

There's another interesting thing about this technique. Let's say that rather than having one globally shared table, you give each AI agent in the world its own table—and this table starts with one row/column for the node the agent is currently at.

Now, you add all the nodes that the agent can "see," updating the table using the propagation method described earlier. So your agent has a limited knowledge of the world: it can traverse the part of the graph that it "knows" about. It won't use routes that it hasn't yet seen, even if they're much shorter (see Figure 9.4).

You're about to need another table. You can call this a *degree* table—it's a table of the number of connections each node in the network has to other nodes. For the network you've been using, it looks like this:

Node	Degree
A	3
B	2
C	3
D	2
E	2

Again, you let the agent keep its own copy constructed only from information that he can "see." So, how does this help you? Well, your agent can take his degree table and compare it to the global degree table. If, for a given node, his value is smaller than the global value, then it means he hasn't fully explored that node yet (there are routes beyond that node that he doesn't know about yet).

So, let's give the agent a new type of idle behavior: *explore*. He can do it when he has no achievable goal. When exploring, he picks a nearby node with a degree less than the global one and goes to it. When he reaches it, he should be able to see other routes, thus increasing his perceived degree for that node until it reaches its maximum. The degree alone is enough information to do this; you don't need to store a flag against every single route.

This behavior could be linked to other ideas—for example, he could be instructed to stay within a certain radius of a point or within the line of sight of a

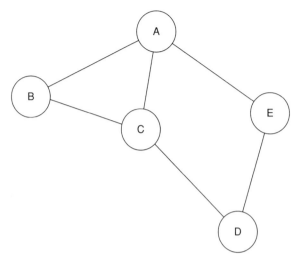

Figure 9.4

given node. It could be linked to a more complex idea—for example, the agent finds a trail of blood on the floor, increasing the probability of nearby nodes being explored relative to other nodes (*investigation*). Maybe he sees a sign saying "danger," which decreases the probability of nearby nodes being explored (*caution*). Simply adding a heuristic to the choice of node to start exploring from can give surprisingly good results.

It would also not be too difficult to implement *forgetfulness*. Every now and then, decrement the agent's perceived degree of a given node a little or update the where-next table as if a given edge has been removed from the graph. You could also try adding a nonexistent route, though you'd then have to account for the degree of a node being greater than the global value. Ideally, you should also make these changes to a part of the network far away from the agent's current position, just because he's less likely to forget things that are nearest him.

What are the problems with this technique? The first, and most obvious one, is that of memory usage. With a large network, keeping a path table for each agent in the world may be totally unfeasible, especially if they will cover a large part of the world. Keeping the agent constrained to a section of the network will help to mitigate this; most games have very few unconstrained agents anyway (i.e., "sidekick" characters). If you have multiple agents in the same area, then you could also try grouping them together into squads and have each squad share a single path table.

Progressive Nets and Subnets

Another problem is dealing with networks over large worlds—not necessarily large networks, just networks that need to cover large distances, particularly over open terrain. If you consider the way people navigate over large distances, you realize that they tend to split their networks into levels. At the top level are the major node routes, like states and interstates. At the next level down, the nodes are towns and the main roads between them; this continues right down to individual buildings and suburban driveways. Paths are considered primarily on the top level, and then segments of the path are broken down into lower levels as you travel along that part of the path.

You can do the same thing for agents. You break your world up into rough regions—in some way that makes sense for the particular structure of your world. Each region has some defined area: it might be carefully bound by the world geometry, or it might be just a vague ellipsoid. Regions can overlap if necessary. You define the network between regions at this level.

Then you step to the next level. Within each region, you build another node network. The edges of the region require some special handling; you want to build connections from the region's node network to the next region's node network (if there is a connection from this region to that region). You could do this by simply referencing the nodes in the next region directly or by establishing particular nodes as being "boundary" nodes shared by both regions. You can then repeat this process, if you wish, for another level, giving all the nodes at this level some volume, and then establishing a more detailed network again within each node.

By storing a link from each subnetwork back up to the region containing it, you can follow a node back up to the "interstate," find the next region to go to, and drop back down to navigate straight to that region.

This approach can be extremely useful in terms of memory consumption, as a region's subnet does not need to be loaded into memory until you are doing detailed navigation within that region. Imagine a world containing many buildings that can be explored. The nodes in each building can be grouped into a subnet and only loaded when the building is actually being traversed.

Echoes of the Past

When tracking prey by scent, a predator will follow by picking up the scent and then continually checking in which direction the scent is strongest. If tracking is left too late, then the scent may have faded, and so the prey cannot be tracked.

Here's an idea inspired by that. Have moving entities leave "scents" in the network that can be followed by others. This would deal with the problem of tracking more than one moving target (the most recent scent would indicate the nearest entity) and the problem of an entity moving out of sight (perhaps even out of the network, if the agent has only partial information). A scent is stored within a node as an entity ID (to identify what the scent is of) and a strength value, stored as the timestamp that the entity visited the node. A node might store only a single scent—such that any new entity visiting the node drowns out the old scent—or it may store a fixed or variable length list.

When tracking by scent, the predator agent needs the entity ID of its prey (or some way of checking any entity ID to pick out interesting scents—for example, a test to see whether a given entity ID is a particular creature type) and a node that the prey has visited. Then, it searches all connected nodes and finds the node with the most recent timestamp for the given entity ID. It moves to that node. Scent fading can be implemented by ignoring any scents with a timestamp that is sufficiently old; timestamps approaching that threshold could also be used to cue agent behavior (i.e., the agent has to visibly try harder to detect a fainter scent). If multiple scents are present at a node, then perhaps a predator with a less sensitive nose is unable to identify scents other than the strongest ones.

Why use timestamps rather than a simple decrementing counter? A decrementing counter still needs to be decremented. Every game loop you'd have to process the entire network, decrementing all the counters—and that's not a nice performance hit, especially for a large network. When you take into account that many nodes may not have scents attached to them anyway, it is obviously inefficient. Timestamps only need to be calculated once and are unchanging until they are updated or removed; they're also much more versatile in that different entities can use them in different ways. A decrementing counter only tells you the number of iterations left until the scent disappears; a timestamp, on the other hand, tells you how long the scent has been there.

Another interesting variation would be to link the scent threshold times into the nodes themselves. Perhaps nodes in a small river would fade much more quickly, while nodes in an enclosed corridor fade more slowly.

Conclusion

Much of the information needed for pathfinding is static and can be pre-calculated—found by a compiler tool, stored to a file, and then loaded and decompressed for instant use in-game. The network can be used not just for finding a route, but also for deciding whether to use it.

Remember to be lazy. When nodes and routes are changing over time, consider whether you can process them on demand rather than forcing the whole network to be touched frequently.

Keep good connectivity in your game worlds to make the networks efficient and close up paths behind points of articulation; using the subnet approach can make unloading a region very straightforward.

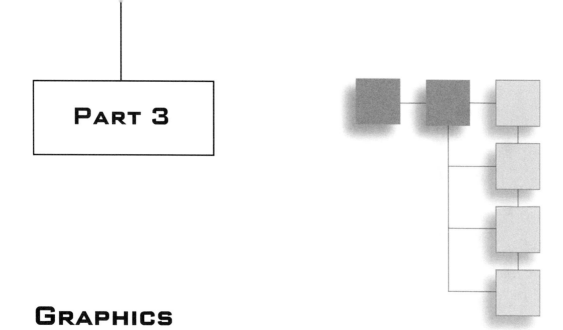

PART 3

GRAPHICS

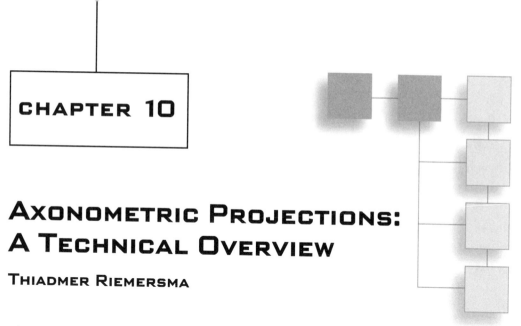

CHAPTER 10

Axonometric Projections: A Technical Overview

Thiadmer Riemersma

This chapter discusses how axonometric projections may be used in computer graphics, multimedia applications, and computer games. It compares the axonometric projection, or *parallel perspective*, to the linear perspective, lists the major properties, and tackles some implementation details.

The focus of this article is on isometric and dimetric projections, the most widely used varieties of the axonometric projection. This article also presents two dimetric projections that are suitable for (tiled) computer graphics.

Introduction—First Attempt

In the Western world, we are accustomed to the linear perspective, which tries to achieve visual realism in paintings of three-dimensional environments. The linear perspective, which was perfected throughout the 17th century in Europe, is based on Euclidean optics: the eye as a point object catches straight light rays and senses only the color, the intensity, and the angle of the rays, not their length.

Another perspective had developed in Asian art: the "Chinese perspective" was an intrinsic part of classical scroll painting. (Actually, "Chinese perspective" is a bit of a misnomer because the same perspective was also used in Japanese art and that of other Asian countries.) A typical Chinese scroll painting measured approximately 40 centimeters high by several meters wide. One views the painting by unrolling it (from right to left) on a table in segments of about

60 centimeters wide. Chinese scroll paintings show a development in time—a form of "narrative art"—in contrast to the paintings that were made in Europe at the time, which show a "situation" rather than a development.

For these scroll paintings, the Chinese painters needed a perspective that had no explicit vanishing points; every scene of the scroll painting would be seen individually and a vanishing point that lies outside the viewport creates a disoriented view of the scene. (For the same reason, the Chinese scroll paintings usually do not have an explicit light source or cast shadows.) The Chinese painters solved the problem by drawing the lines along the z axis as parallel lines in the scroll painting (see Figure 10.1). This has the effect of placing the horizon at an imaginary line, infinitely high above the painting. The axonometric projection is a technical term for a class of perspectives to which the Chinese parallel perspective also belongs. These perspectives not only lack a vanishing point, but they also have a few other, mostly useful, characteristics. These are discussed in the next section.

Figure 10.1
A scroll painting (broken into thirds for printing).

Introduction—Second Attempt

Technical drawings need to be precise, accurate, and unambiguous. Technical drawings are for engineers and fitters. National institutes formally standardize technical drawings so that a carpenter will build the particular chair that the furniture designer imagined. Technical drawings are a means of communication, for those who can understand it.

If the world were populated by engineers, nothing else would matter—but it isn't, and engineers (as well as fitters and carpenters) need to communicate with managers and customers. The problem is, of course, that technical drawings are difficult to decipher for the uninitiated. Although they show an object from up to six angles, all of those angles are unrealistic: directly from the front, directly from above, and so on. What is needed to convey the general shape of the object is a perspective drawing that shows three sides of a cube at once.

At this point, the next issue is "how"? Engineers being as they are, they want a simple technique that does not lose much of the accuracy of the original drawings and does not require artistic skills. Also note that in most cases the object you must draw does not yet exist, so usually you cannot take a look at the object to get a sense for its proportions. That makes it nearly undoable to adequately position the vanishing points and to estimate the foreshortening.

The compromise, which came to be known as *axonometry*, is a drawing technique where the orthogonal x, y, and z axes of the (three-dimensional) world space are projected to (non-orthogonal) axes on paper. In the projection, the y axis usually remains the vertical axis, the z axis is skewed, and the x axis may be horizontal, as in Figure 10.2, or may be skewed as well. A more important property of

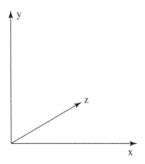

Figure 10.2
The axonometric drawing technique.

axonometry is its fixed relation between sizes of objects in world space and those on projected space, independent of the positions of the objects in projected space. In linear perspective, objects become smaller when they move farther away; not so in axonometric perspective. This means that you can measure the size of an object of an axonometric drawing and know how big the real object is (you need to know the scale of the drawing and the properties of the projection, but nothing else), something that cannot be done with linear perspective. This leads to the name of the projection: the word "axonometry" means "measurable from the axes." Although there are countless possible axonometric projections, only two are standardized for technical drawings, which are described in the next section.

Introduction—Third Attempt

Computer games have traditionally been brimming with graphics and animation. In fact, games are categorized according to the kind of graphics they used. Two popular types of games are *platform games,* where you look from the side, and *board games,* where you look mostly from above. These games also commonly use tiles to build the game world from. Given these similarities, and given the dullness of the unrealistic viewpoints of both platform games and board games, the attempt to make a compromise between these extreme viewpoints is a logical next step.

So what one does is take a board of a board game, scale its height (the z axis), and skew it so that the z axis on the computer display is a diagonal line. For a better appearance, you can also skew the x axis. The y axis remains vertical. This is all you need, provided you get the proportions (for scaling and skewing) right.

Due to the coarseness of digital coordinates and the requirement that the edges of (checkerboard) tiles should match precisely, without any pixel overlaps or gaps, the skewing angles and scaling factors that game designers use are an approximation of the visually optimal proportions. One of the simplifications that game designers have made is to use an axonometric projection where a unit along an axis is equally long for all three of the axes. Every axis has the same metric; hence, the projection is named *isometric.* Axonometric projections and tile-based images are not necessarily related. But most computer games that use an isometric perspective also use tile-based images.

And Now, Onward. . .

The three questions that occupied me when planning this article were the following:

- What are common (or well-proportioned) axonometric projections, and how persuasive does each look?

- At what angles does one look at a board in an axonometric projection? It is tempting to use rendered 3D objects on an axonometric map as sprites. To specify the position and orientation of the "camera" in relation to the object, you will need to know the intrinsic angles of the axonometric map that you are using.

- What does one write in an introduction anyway?

The goal of this article is to present two common axonometric projections, the isometric projection (already briefly introduced) and the diametrical projection, and to provide answers to the questions here.

I am intentionally neglecting the proper definitions of terms and categories; axonometric projections and "oblique parallel" projections are so similar that I lumped them under the term "axonometry." In any case, an oblique parallel projection should be seen as just a special case of a dimetric (or sometimes isometric) projection. Oblique parallel projections, cavalier projections, cabinet projections, military projections, axonometric projections—different names, same concept.

To repeat, the main properties of axonometric projections are as follows:

- No vanishing points. This allows you to scroll a large image below a viewport and to have the same perspective at any point. In the case of tile-based images, an image is constructed on the fly and need not have physical bounds or edges.

- Lines that are parallel in the three-dimensional space remain parallel in the two-dimensional picture. This is in contrast to the *linear perspective*, where parallel lines along the z axis in the three-dimensional space collapse to a single vanishing point at the horizon in the two-dimensional picture.

- Objects that are distant have the same size as objects that are close; objects do not get smaller as they move away from the viewer. If you know the scale of the axes, you can measure the size (width, height, length, depth) of an object directly from the picture, regardless of its position on the z axis; hence, the name *axonometry.*

- The axonometric projections are standardized for technical drawings. These standards are optimized for ease of use versus visual realism. Even if you choose to deviate from the standards, use them as an inspiration. The two projections standardized by the Dutch standardization institute are presented in this article.

One word of caution regarding any of the figures shown in this article and the projection angles that these figures present: the angles are only approximate. I calculated the angles based on the shapes of the rhombuses of one or two sides of the projected cube. These calculations would be valid if the perspective projections had not distorted the original cube. Now, especially the projections standardized for technical drawings were chosen to minimize the distortion, but they are nevertheless not *exact.* The angles that I give are likewise a good approximation, but no more than that.

The Isometric Projection

In an isometric projection, the x, y, and z axes have the same metric: a unit (say, a centimeter) along the x axis is equally long along the y and z axes. In other words, if you render a wire frame cube, all edges in the two-dimensional picture are equally long. Another property of the isometric projection is that the projected wire frame cube is also symmetric. All sides of the projected cube are rhombuses.

NEN 2536 (see the section "References and Further Information") describes an isometric projection that is symmetric with regard to the vertical axis; the angle between the x and y axes, and between the z and y axes, is 60 degrees. The projection shows three sides of a cube, and the surfaces of each side are equal. The 30° angle between the x and z axes and the "horizon" is convenient for technical drawings because the sine of 30° is 1/2. This projection is attributed to William Farish, who published a treatise about it in 1822 (Krikke 2000).

Figure 10.3 shows a cube in the isometric projection as defined by NEN 2536. The first object from the left in the figure is the cube unadorned; the second object is the same cube with angles and measures annotated around it. The third and fourth graphics are the top and side views of the perspective scene, and they give the camera position that fits the perspective view. The camera position is what

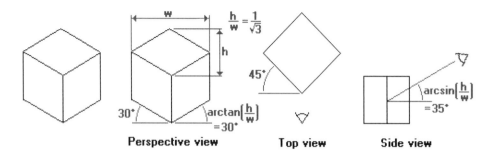

Figure 10.3
The 30° isometric projection.

you would feed into a 3D renderer (or ray tracer) to create the sprites or tiles for the isometric projection.

Computer games with isometric maps are often tile-based. To make tiles match, the game designer must take into account how diagonal lines are plotted in discrete steps (Bresenham and all that). As it turns out, a line at 30 degrees (sine is 0.5) produces steps that are too irregular. A line at an angle where the tangent is 0.5 *does* have a nice regular pattern: two steps to the right, one step up. Thus the isometric projection used by most games tilts the x and z axes with approximately 27 degrees [the exact angle is arctangent(0.5)]. By the way, because the tangent of the angle of the rhombus is 0.5, the rhombus is twice as wide as it is high. This is why many sources mention a 1:2 scale for isometric perspectives. (To make the edges of the rhombuses match, the width of the rhombus should be a multiple of four pixels, and the height should be one pixel less than 1/2 width. In other words, the height:width ratio of a rhombus is usually not *exactly* 1:2, but rather near 1:2.1. This makes no difference for the principles of the isometric perspective.)

Again, Figure 10.4 shows what this isometric projection looks like. The two isometric projections previously mentioned "skew" all faces of the example cube. In applications where the most important faces are the horizontal ones—for example, in applications where maps or floor plans are paramount—another isometric projection is common. It is called the "military" projection, probably because of its origin or use.

In the military projection (see Figure 10.5), the angles of the x and z axes are at 45°, meaning that the angle *between* the x axis and the z axis is 90°. That is, the x-z plane is *not* skewed. It *is* rotated over 45°, though.

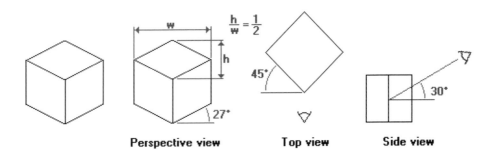

Figure 10.4
The 1:2 isometric projection.

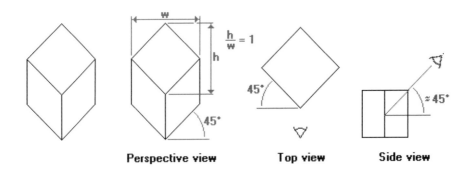

Figure 10.5
The "military" projection.

In the side view of the military projection, I have indicated that the viewing angle downward onto the object (the cube) is *approximately* 45°. The military projection gives quite an inaccurate perspective (numerically speaking), and the scheme that I used to calculate the angles does not work on this projection. This angle is therefore just an estimate, based on a concept of symmetry rather than visual accuracy.

The Dimetric Projection

In the dimetric projection, one of the three axes has a different scale than the other two. In practice, the scaled axis is the z axis and, hence, a cube drawn in a dimetric projection is not a symmetrical graphic (as in the isometric projection).

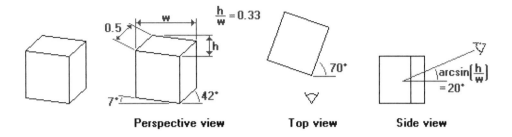

Figure 10.6
The 42°/7° projection.

Dimetric projections are more flexible than the isometric projections, as you vary the scale factor (and adjust other parameters in accordance). The asymmetry in the dimetric projection also provides you with an additional angle to play with. From an artistic viewpoint, I also like dimetric projections better than isometric projections because of the asymmetry. Or, rather, the symmetry of an isometric projection makes the scene look artificial or surrealistic. Another advantage, in a computer game, is that if you mirror the graphics of a dimetric projection, you are looking at a scene in a new, fresh perspective, while the basic computations for the coordinate system stay the same.

NEN 2536 also presents a dimetric projection for technical drawings, summarized in Figure 10.6. Any distance along the z axis (drawn at 42°) is scaled at a factor 1/2.

I mentioned Chinese scroll paintings at the beginning of the article, and I took some time taking the metrics of the reproductions of two scroll paintings. The projection is different in these two paintings, and I assume that more variations exist. Noticeable in all scroll paintings that I have seen so far is that the x axis stays horizontal.

The first scroll painting projects the z axis to quite a low angle (approximately 30 degrees). As a result, the perspective view is, computationally, far from accurate. The reasons that we still see a three-dimensional cube, rather than some kind of flat polygon, is that the angle in the side view of the perspective view is also low and because our visual system is quite forgiving for errors in perspective correction.

The scale of the z axis could not be accurately determined from the scroll painting. My estimate is that the z axis on the painting (with a 30° projected

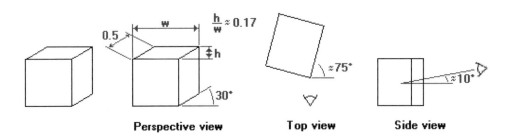

Figure 10.7
The "Chinese perspective."

Figure 10.8
A reproduction from an 18th-century remake of an 11-meter hand scroll by artists of the Qing court, published in "A City of Cathay."

z axis) is scaled by half (50%). (See Figure 10.7.) Also note (again) that the perspective is distorted and that the angles of the top view and the side view should be taken as a rule of thumb; I calculated these angles in the same way as the angles in the dimetric projection presented in NEN 2536, but these calculations are, actually, no longer applicable.

The other painting, reproduced in Figure 10.8, has the projected z axis at a bit less than 40 degrees, but slanted in the other direction. On the one hand, I could say that the z axis is slanted to approximately 130° (90° + 40°); but on the other hand, the direction of the slant is insignificant for the discussion of axonometric projection. I can give only a *rough* estimate of the scaling of the z axis in this scroll painting ("A City of Cathay"): between 0.6 and 0.7 (but probably closer to 0.6).

Dimetric Projections for Computer Graphics and Games

As was the case with the isometric projection, in computer graphics some angles are preferable to others. The first dimetric projection that I propose for (tiled) computer graphics is very similar to the projection of Chinese scroll paintings. The difference is the scale of the z axis and the angle that it makes with the x axis. To start with the angle, the z axis is slanted with approximately 27 degrees [the exact angle is arctangent(0.5)]. This is the same angle as the isometric projection for computer graphics uses. The scale is such that the width of the side view of a cube, when measured along the x axis, is half of the width of the front face. The key phrase in the previous sentence is "when measured along the x axis." In the two former projections, the scale factor applied to distances measured along the z axis.

The projection shown in Figure 10.9 gives a perspective that is viewed mostly from the side. It might be useful to add some depth to a side-scrolling (or platform) game. For board-like games, a perspective that is viewed from a greater height is more appropriate. The second proposed dimetric projection for games serves this end (see Figure 10.10).

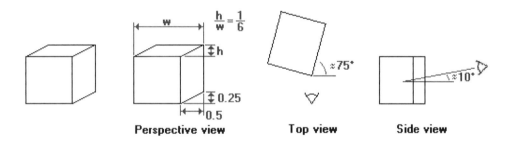

Figure 10.9
Dimetric 1:2 projection side view.

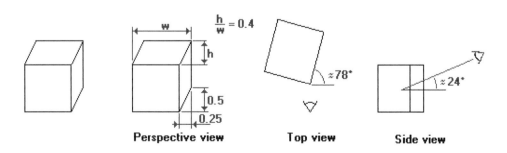

Figure 10.10
Dimetric 1:2 projection top view.

Again, note that the perspective of the two projections is distorted. The angles in the top and side views are *really* approximate. For example, in the second projection, the angle at which one looks from above at the scene is given as 24 degrees. However, using an angle of 30 degrees may actually look better. In addition, a 30-degree angle lets you use the same objects for both the dimetric and the isometric projections for games.

Other dimetric projections are summarized in the following table. These projections were taken from the CARTESIO program. For each projection, I give the name that the program gives to the projection, the slant for the x and z axes, and the scale for the z axis. In all the projections presented here, the y axis remains vertical and the x and y axes have the same scale.

projection name	x-axis angle	z-axis angle	z-axis scale
130, 130, 100	10	40	0.59
1, 1, 2/3	12.8	38.6	0.667
1, 1, 3/4	16.3	36.8	0.75

The CARTESIO program lists more projections than the few listed here, including those of the NEN 2536 standard and a few that are so distorted that I see no practical use for them.

Moving Across an Axonometric Projection

Converting from space coordinates (x,y,z) to a pixel coordinate (x′,y′) in the projection requires only trivial geometry. The following table presents the formulae for completeness.

Isometric	NEN 2536	$x' = (x - z) \cdot \cos(30°)$ $y' = y + (x + z) \cdot \sin(30°)$
	Computer games	$' = x - z$ $y' = y + \frac{1}{2}(x + z)$
Dimetric	NEN 2536	$x' = x \cdot \cos(7°) + \frac{1}{2} z \cdot \cos(42°)$ $' = y + \frac{1}{2} z \cdot \sin(42°) - x \cdot \sin(7°)$

(Continued)

Chinese scroll paintings	$x' = x + n \cdot z \cdot \cos(T)$ $y' = y + n \cdot z \cdot \sin(T)$ here n is 0.5 to 0.7 and T is 30° to 40°
Computer games: side view	$x' = x + \frac{1}{2} z$ $y' = y + \frac{1}{4} z$
Computer games: top view	$x' = x + \frac{1}{4} z$ $y' = y + \frac{1}{2} z$

Converting coordinates in the projection to space coordinates is a different matter. In its general form, it simply cannot be done: you cannot calculate three independent output parameters from two input parameters. If you can "fix" one of the output parameters, the other two can be calculated from the input parameters. An example: if the axonometric projection represents a map, and you can assume that the area on the map has little or no relief, then you can fix the position on the y axis to zero (ground level), and you only have to calculate x and z from x' and y'.

A refinement of this is to support some amount of relief. The calculation of the output coordinates starts as before, only now the y-coordinate is an estimate, rather than a "known" value. After calculating the x- and z-coordinates, you can look up the corresponding "height" value at the position (x, z). Typically, they will not match with the y-coordinate that you guessed when calculating the x- and z-coordinates. Now you can adjust your estimate of the y-coordinate and calculate the matching x- and z-coordinates again. This iteration continues until the estimated y-coordinate (before calculating x and z) comes close enough to the looked-up value (after calculating x and z).

The principal question in following this iterative procedure is, "Does it converge?" Following intuition, the procedure is considered to converge if no spot on the project surface obscures another location in 3D space—that is, if the slopes of the surface relief stay below the viewing angle (in the "view direction"), every location on the map in 3D space has a unique "sibling" location in the axonometric projection, which is visible from the view point. In Figure 10.11, the

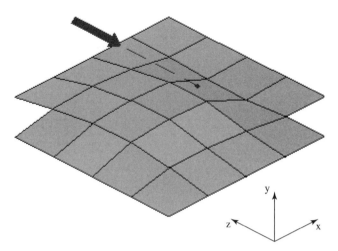

Figure 10.11
The viewing angle from the horizontal plane is 30 degrees.

viewing angle from the horizontal plane is 30 degrees, and the steepest slope in the view direction is approximately half of that.

If you have extreme relief, or overlapping ground levels, such as bridges or buildings, I suggest that you separate the projected map into parts that, themselves, adhere to the limitation of no steeper angles than the viewing angle. These parts can be separate layers or sprites, and you build the full map by combining them. To calculate (x,y,z) from (x′,y′), you first decide on what layer/sprite the location (x′,y′) is, and then use the iterative procedure to find the values of x, y, and z.

References and Further Information

Cultural Cafe, The. "A City of Cathay: View Chinese Life through a Famous Painting." CD-ROM, Vol. 2, *no date.* [This CD-ROM contains a detailed presentation of the famous scroll painting.]

Foley, James D., Andries van Dam, Steven K. Feiner, and John F. Hughes. *Computer Graphics: Principles and Practice.* 2nd ed. Addison-Wesley, 1990. [This encyclopedic book covers perspective projections in Chapter 5.]

Krikke, J. "Axonometry: A Matter of Perspective," *IEEE Computer Graphics and Applications.* Vol. 20 (4), July/August 2000, pp. – . [A (historic) overview of axonometric projections from the viewpoints of Asian art, technical drawings, and computer games—in the same spirit as the three introductions to this article, but in a more detailed and coherent example. The article argues that the word "axonometry" should refer only to the particular projection used by Asian artists (the so-called "Chinese perspective"), whereas the generic term is "orthographic projections." Citing NEN 2536 and Foley et al. as references, I treat axonometric projections and parallel projections as synonyms, while an orthographic projection is one where the viewing direction is perpendicular to a plane, showing no perspective at all.]

NEN 2536. "Engineering Drawing. Axonometric Projection." Nederlands Normalisatie Instituut, August 1966. [A Dutch standard for axonometric projections for technical drawings.]

Trevisan, Camillo. the CARTESIO program, version 3.03e. [An educational and interactive application that features many geometric projections. It is free for personal use.]

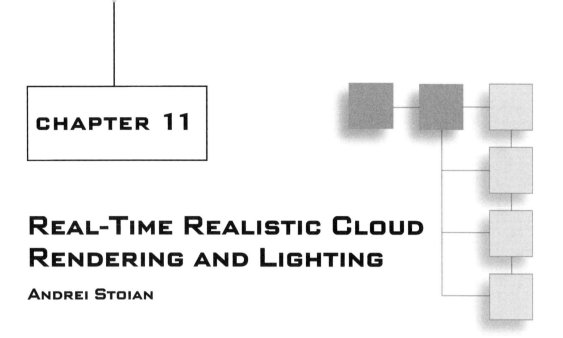

CHAPTER 11

REAL-TIME REALISTIC CLOUD RENDERING AND LIGHTING

ANDREI STOIAN

As a ray of light travels through a medium, the radiance, commonly called the intensity, may change depending on the contents of the medium. A medium that affects the radiance of light is called a *participating medium* and such a medium can influence light in several ways. Scattering of light happens in a vast variety of environments and is used in creating visual effects such as atmospheric haze, skylight computation, light passing through clouds or smoke, light passing through water, and sub-surface scattering. These effects are very complex and usually require large amounts of computation due to the mathematical functions that need to be evaluated.

For the purpose of real-time computer graphics, scattering algorithms are often simplified and adapted to run on graphics hardware. Another option is to allow artists to set up functions and parameters that mimic real light scattering, thus saving computation time.

Harris' Model for Cloud Rendering and Lighting

The solution proposed by Harris is to approximate the scattering integral over the volume of the cloud using graphics hardware to speed up the process. The basic ideas are as follows:

1. The radiance absorbed in each cloud volume unit, modeled as a metaball, is stored in a texture that is used for splatting.

2. The product that approximates the integral is calculated by reading from the draw buffer the previous splat result and using it for the current splat, which is blended back into the buffer.

3. Two scattering directions are used: from the sun to the cloud center and from the eye point to the cloud center. This accounts for most of the light scattered in the cloud.

To improve the system, the clouds can be rendered in impostor textures at a resolution based on distance from the camera. The impostors are updated when the change in angle between the camera and the cloud center increases above a certain threshold.

Cloud Lighting

First of all, the clouds are stored as an array of particles that represents the metaballs. The shapes can be modeled in various ways—by an artist, using a fluid motion equation solver, using procedural noise techniques—but that is beyond the scope of this article. The particles have position, color, size, *albedo* (the ratio of reflected light to the incoming light), and extinction (reduction of the intensity of light), and an alpha component can be added for simulating cloud formation and extinction.

When lighting the clouds, you are approximating light scattered in the light's direction (from the cloud center to the sun). To do this, you sort your particles away from the light position; thus the closest particle will be rendered first. This is fairly obvious, since the particle that is not occluded in any way should receive the most amount of light. You can use the square of the distance to the point for sorting, and this is stored in the `DistanceToCam` member. Following is a function that can sort an array of particles both away and toward a point:

```
switch (mode)
{
  case SORT_AWAY:
    sort(Cloud->Puffs.begin(), Cloud->Puffs.end(), SortAway);
    break;
  case SORT_TOWARD:
    sort(Cloud->Puffs.begin(), Cloud->Puffs.end(), SortToward);
    break;
}
class SortAwayComparison
{
public:
    bool operator () (CloudPuff puff1, CloudPuff puff2)
    {
      return puff1.DistanceToCam < puff2.DistanceToCam;
    }
} SortAway;
class SortTowardComparison
{
public:
    bool operator () (CloudPuff puff1, CloudPuff puff2)
    {
      return puff1.DistanceToCam > puff2.DistanceToCam;
    }
} SortToward;
```

First of all, after sorting your particles, you need to set up the camera to be placed in the sun's position, viewing the cloud center, and the projection should map the cloud onto the whole viewport. The size of the viewport can be chosen arbitrarily, but a value of 32, proposed by Harris, is fine. I will use an orthographic projection because it will not deform faraway particles.

```
glMatrixMode(GL_PROJECTION);
glPushMatrix();
glLoadIdentity();
```

```
glOrtho(-Cloud->Radius-pr, Cloud->Radius+pr,
    -Cloud->Radius-pr, Cloud->Radius+pr, d - r, d + r);

glMatrixMode(GL_MODELVIEW);
glPushMatrix();
glLoadIdentity();
gluLookAt(Sun.x, Sun.y, Sun.z,
    Cloud->Center.x, Cloud->Center.y, Cloud->Center.z,
    0, 1, 0);

glPushAttrib(GL_VIEWPORT_BIT);
glViewport(0, 0, SplatBufferSize, SplatBufferSize);
```

The lighting equation given by Harris is as follows:

$$I_k = \begin{cases} k > 0 : g_{k-1} + T_{k-1} \times I_{k-1} \\ k = 0 : I_0 \end{cases}$$

This equation relates the intensity of the current particle I_k with the intensity of the previous particle I_{k-1} and the transparency of the previous particle T_{k-1}. The other term is g_{k-1}, where $g_k = a_k \, x \, \tau_k \, x \, p(l, -l) \, x \, I_k \, x \, \gamma/4\pi$. As you can see, g_{k-1} is related to the intensity of the $k-1$ fragment, so you will have to read this value from the frame buffer. All the other values in the equation (albedo, extinction, solid angle) are constants, and the $p(l, -l)$ element is a phase function that will be discussed later. The original intensity I_0 is fully bright; thus the buffer is first cleared to white.

This equation can be encoded for graphics hardware through blending. Blending calculates the sum of the incoming fragment multiplied with the "source factor" and the existing fragment in the buffer multiplied with a "destination factor." In this case, the source factor is 1 (as g_{k-1} has no coefficient) and the destination factor is T_{k-1}, the transmittance of the fragment in the splat texture. The result of the blend operation is a color that is then read back for the next particle. Since opacity is stored in the splat texture, transmittance T_{k-1} will equal one minus opacity. This gives the blend function with parameters GL_ONE, GL_ONE_MINUS_SRC_ALPHA.

A rough description of the lighting process can be formulated: you start from a fully bright buffer and use the splat textures to decrease the luminance, thus "darkening" the color of the particles as they get farther from the light. You start by looping over the particles and calculating the screen position of its center using projection:

```
double CenterX, CenterY, CenterZ;
gluProject(Cloud->Puffs[i].Position.x,
     Cloud->Puffs[i].Position.y,
     Cloud->Puffs[i].Position.z,
     mm, mp, vp, &CenterX, &CenterY, &CenterZ);
```

Note

Here the puffs were in world space.

Then, using the solid angle over which you will read back the pixels from the buffer, the size of the splat buffer, and the cloud radius, you compute the area, which will be read as follows:

```
Area = Cloud->Puffs[i].DistanceToCam * SolidAngle; //squared distance
Pixels = (int)(sqrt(Area) * SplatBufferSize / (2 * Cloud->Radius));
if (Pixels < 1) Pixels = 1;

ReadX = (int)(CenterX-Pixels/2);
if (ReadX < 0) ReadX = 0;
ReadY = (int)(CenterY-Pixels/2);
if (ReadY < 0) ReadY = 0;

buf = new float[Pixels * Pixels];

//we only need the red component since this is grayscale
glReadBuffer(GL_BACK);
glReadPixels(ReadX, ReadY, Pixels, Pixels, GL_RED, GL_FLOAT, buf);
```

Finally, you compute the average intensity in the area and calculate the color of the current particle that will be splatted, following the previous equation:

```
avg = 0.0f;
for (j = 0; j < Pixels * Pixels; j++) avg += buf[j];
avg /= (Pixels * Pixels);

delete [] buf;

//Light color *
// average color from solid angle (sum * solidangle / (pixels^2 * 4pi))
// * albedo * extinction
```

```
// * rayleigh scattering in the direction of the sun (1.5f)
// (only for rendering, don't store)

factor = SolidAngle / (4 * PI);

ParticleColor.R = LightColor.R * Albedo * Extinction * avg * factor;
ParticleColor.G = LightColor.G * Albedo * Extinction * avg * factor;
ParticleColor.B = LightColor.B * Albedo * Extinction * avg * factor;
ParticleColor.A = 1.0f - exp(-Extinction);
```

This color, stored in `ParticleColor`, will be stored as the color that will be used for rendering later on; but when you are splatting the particles for lighting, you need to include the phase function. This is always equal to 1.5 in the direction of the light, so you scale up your color by this value before rendering this particle as a billboard.

The Phase Function: Scattering in the Eye Direction

To simulate multiple scattering in the eye direction, a phase function is used. The phase function allows the calculation of the distribution of light scattering for a given direction of incident light.

The phase function takes as parameters two directions—in this case, the light direction and the direction of light arriving at the observer. Thus when doing lighting, the direction of incident light is the negative of the direction of the light. When rendering normally, the direction the light arrives at the observer is the vector between the particle position and the camera eye point. The function Harris uses is a simple Rayleigh scattering function:

$$p(\omega, \omega') = 0.75 \times (1 + (\cos \theta)^2)$$

Where θ is the angle between ω and ω' and thus equal to their dot product if they are normalized. When ω is in the direction of ω' the function is equal to 1.5, giving the value used in lighting.

Creating Cloud Impostors

To speed up rendering, the 3D clouds, composed of particles, can be rendered to a 2D surface, which is then mapped onto a billboard. This saves fill-rate, as the impostor is only updated when the change in angle between the camera and the cloud center exceeds a certain threshold.

The hardest part in rendering the impostor is setting up the camera. In this case, the camera will lie at the eye position and will point at the cloud center. The particles are sorted from back to front to eliminate transparent blending problems. Setting up the camera is easily done with OpenGL's functions, and again I will use an orthographic projection.

```
glMatrixMode(GL_PROJECTION);
glPushMatrix();
glLoadIdentity();
glOrtho(-Cloud->Radius-pr, Cloud->Radius+pr,
    -Cloud->Radius-pr, Cloud->Radius+pr, d - r, d + r);

glMatrixMode(GL_MODELVIEW);
glPushMatrix();
glLoadIdentity();
gluLookAt(Camera.x, Camera.y, Camera.z,
    Cloud->Center.x, Cloud->Center.y, Cloud->Center.z,
        0, 1, 0);

glPushAttrib(GL_VIEWPORT_BIT);
glViewport(0, 0, ViewportSize, ViewportSize);
```

The viewport size can be set to trade between speed and quality. A more advanced implementation will set the viewport size, depending on the distance of the cloud center to the camera.

After the viewport is set up, you can simply render the particles with their respective colors as billboards. Again, enable blending and set the blend function to GL_ONE, GL_ONE_MINUS_SRC_ALPHA. The up and right vectors for the billboards can be obtained straight from the modelview matrix as follows:

```
float mat[16];
glGetFloatv(GL_MODELVIEW_MATRIX, mat);

Vector3 vx(mat[0], mat[4], mat[8] );
Vector3 vy(mat[1], mat[5], mat[9] );
```

When rendering each cloud particle, you have to calculate the phase function and modulate the particle color with it:

```
costheta = Dot(Omega, Light);
phase = 0.75f * (1.0f + costheta * costheta);
```

Now you can upload the frame buffer into a texture that will be used for creating the cloud billboard:

```
glBindTexture(GL_TEXTURE_2D, Cloud->ImpostorTex);
glCopyTexImage2D(GL_TEXTURE_2D, 0, GL_RGBA8, 0, 0, ViewportSize,
ViewportSize, 0);
```

Now the cloud can be simply rendered as a billboard with the texture that was uploaded. To detect when an impostor update is needed, you store the vector from the cloud to the camera of the last update, and then compute the angle between it and the current vector.

```
float dot = Dot(ToCam, Clouds[i].LastCamera);
bool in_frustum = Frustum.SphereInFrustum(Clouds[i]
Center, Clouds[i].Radius);
int mip_size = GetImpostorSize(SqDist(Camera, Clouds[i].Center));

if ((dot < 0.99f || Clouds[i].ImpostorSize < mip_size) && in_frustum)
{
    RenderCloudImpostor(&Clouds[i], Sun, Camera);
    Clouds[i].LastCamera = ToCam;
}
```

Creating the Splat Texture

The splat texture used encodes the intensity of light lost as the light passes through the cloud particle's volume. Thus as less light passes through the center than through the edges, the texture needs to exhibit a falloff from the center to the edges. To your aid comes a nice interpolating polynomial, which, using an interpolant between 0 and 1, varies from 1 to 0 in a smooth way. Since you are interpolating between a value in the center of the texture and 0 on the outside, the polynomial can be further simplified to give a function of the center value and the interpolant:

$$v = v_1 \times (2f^3 - 3f^2 + 1)$$

v_1 can be chosen arbitrarily to give a good result, and f is the distance between the pixel you are coloring and the center divided by the radius of the texture. Instead of computing the distance in pixels, you can have variables that vary from -1 to 1 from left to right, top to bottom on the texture, and thus also eliminate the need for division by the texture radius:

```
Y = -1.0f;
for (int y = 0; y < N; y++)
{
    X = -1.0f;
    for (int x=0; x<N; x++, i++, j+=4)
    {
        Dist = (float)sqrt(X*X+Y*Y);
        if (Dist > 1) Dist=1;

        value = 2*Dist*Dist*Dist - 3*Dist*Dist + 1;
        value *= 0.4f;

        B[j+3] = B[j+2] = B[j+1] = B[j] = (unsigned char)(value * 255);

        X+=Incr;
    }

    Y+=Incr;
}
```

From Impostors to Full 3D Models

You can obtain visual improvement by changing between rendering impostors and rendering the full 3D cloud. This helps when objects pass through clouds, as they won't simply show up as clipping the cloud impostor billboard—they will appear to really travel through the cloud.

First of all, you need to determine below which distance the cloud should look fully 3D and above which distance the cloud should appear only as an impostor, taking into account the size of the cloud. Through experimentation, good values for these distances are two times the radius of the cloud and four times the radius, respectively. In between these distances, you fade the impostor out from fully opaque to fully transparent. The 3D will also be faded, but it will go from transparent to opaque as the camera draws nearer. To calculate the alpha value when the impostor and the 3D model are fading, use the following:

```
alpha = (Clouds[i].DistanceFromCamera - dist_3D) / (dist_impostor - dist_3D);
```

The main problem is that the texture already contains an alpha channel, and you need to blend it with the GL_ONE, GL_ONE_MINUS_SRC_ALPHA factors. Thus you cannot simply use the alpha value of the color to fade. Setting all the components of the color to the color will achieve this. Thus in the impostor rendering function, use the following:

```
glColor4f(alpha, alpha, alpha, alpha);
```

The 3D rendering function looks very similar to the impostor creation function, excluding the viewport and camera changes. To fade the particles, you must multiply their colors by the alpha value, and then send it to OpenGL:

```
ParticleColor.R = (0.3f + Puff->Color.R * phase) * alpha;
ParticleColor.G = (0.3f + Puff->Color.G * phase) * alpha;
ParticleColor.B = (0.3f + Puff->Color.B * phase) * alpha;
ParticleColor.A = Puff->Color.A * Puff->Life * alpha;
```

The conditions for determining which way to draw the cloud are these:

```
//beyond this render only the impostor
dist_impostor = Clouds[i].Radius * 4;

//square this since the camera distance is also squared
dist_impostor *= dist_impostor;

//closer than this render only the 3D model
dist_3D = Clouds[i].Radius * 2;

//square
dist_3D *= dist_3D;

if (Clouds[i].DistanceFromCamera > dist_impostor)
    RenderCloudImpostor(&Clouds[i], 1.0f);
else
    if (Clouds[i].DistanceFromCamera < dist_3D)
        RenderCloud3D(&Clouds[i], Camera, Sun, 1.0f);
    else
    {
        alpha = (Clouds[i].DistanceFromCamera - dist_3D) /
        (dist_impostor - dist_3D);
        RenderCloudImpostor(&Clouds[i], alpha);
        RenderCloud3D(&Clouds[i], Camera, Sun, 1.0f - alpha);
    }
```

Conclusion

Harris' method for cloud rendering is suitable for real-time applications requiring a realistic model for clouds that one can fly through. With the added advantage of impostors, the performance is good even for a large number of clouds. However, the method does present some disadvantages.

If the light direction changes, the whole lighting algorithm has to be executed again, which is expensive if it is to be done in real time. This can be alleviated by distributing the calculations over several frames and storing intermediate results in a separate texture. Loading the texture from the frame buffer is a rather inexpensive operation and can be performed each frame to store the calculations. Another advantage of using such a texture is that it can be used as a lightmap, projecting it on geometry underneath to achieve correct shading.

The time required by the lighting algorithm is significant, and for many clouds the processing time can slow down the loading of the game. This is, however, a fair trade-off for having realistic clouds.

Using the splat texture, the clouds always look very fluffy, but there is a lack of detail. Niniane Wang proposes a different, artistically based method, used in Microsoft Flight Simulator 2004, which gives better detail in the clouds and uses fewer particles. This comes as a trade-off to physically correct lighting.

A problem arises when objects are in the clouds, as sharp edges will be visible. This can be solved, as Harris shows, by splitting the impostor with a plane on which the object resides. For further details, refer to the original paper.

References

Harris, Mark J. and Anselmo Lastra. "Real-Time Cloud Rendering." Computer Graphics Forum (Eurographics 2001 Proceedings), 20(3):76–84, September 2001.

Pharr, Matt and Greg Humphreys. *Physically Based Rendering: From Theory to Implementation.* San Francisco, CA: Morgan Kaufmann, 2004.

Wang, Niniane. "Realistic and Fast Cloud Rendering," *Journal of Graphics Tools*, 9(3):21–40, 2004.

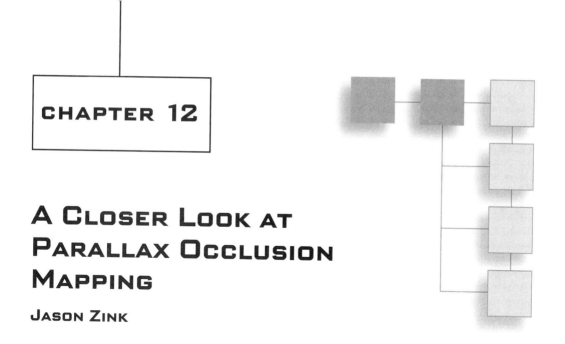

CHAPTER 12

A Closer Look at Parallax Occlusion Mapping

Jason Zink

Parallax occlusion mapping is a technique that reduces a geometric model's complexity by encoding surface detail information in a texture. The surface information typically used is a height-map representation of the replaced geometry. When the model is rendered, the surface details are reconstructed in the pixel shader from the height-map texture information.

I recently read through the GDC 2006 presentation on parallax occlusion mapping titled "Practical Parallax Occlusion Mapping for Highly Detailed Surface Rendering" by Natalya Tatarchuk of ATI Research, Inc. (http://ati.amd.com/developer/gdc/2006/GDC06-Tatarchuk-Parallax_Occlusion_Mapping.pdf). In the presentation, an improved version of parallax occlusion mapping is discussed along with possible optimizations that can be used to accelerate the technique on current and next-generation hardware. Of course, after reading the presentation, I had to implement the technique for myself to evaluate its performance and better understand its inner workings. This article attempts to present an easy-to-understand guide to the theory behind the algorithm as well as to provide a reference implementation of basic parallax occlusion mapping algorithm.

This investigation is focused on the surface reconstruction calculations and what parameters come into play when using this technique. I have decided to implement a simple Phong lighting model. However, as you will see shortly, this algorithm is very flexible and can easily be adapted to just about any lighting model that you would like to work with. In addition, a brief discussion of how to light a parallax occlusion mapped surface is also provided.

The reference implementation is written in Direct3D 10 HLSL. A demonstration program is also available on this book's companion web site (www.courseptr.com/downloads) that shows the algorithm in action. The demo program and the associated effect files that have been developed for this article are provided with it and may be used in whatever manner you desire.

Algorithm Overview

So what exactly is parallax occlusion mapping? First, let's look at an image of a standard polygonal surface that you would apply this technique to. Let's assume that this polygonal surface is a cube, consisting of six faces with two triangles each for a total of 12 triangles. I will set the texture coordinates of each vertex such that each face of the cube will include an entire copy of the given texture. Figure 12.1 shows this simple polygonal surface, with normal mapping used to provide simple diffuse lighting.

The basic idea behind parallax occlusion mapping is relatively simple. For each pixel of a rendered polygonal surface, we would like to simulate a complex volumetric shape. This shape is represented by a height-map encoded into a texture that is applied to the polygonal surface. The height-map basically adds a

Figure 12.1
Flat polygonal surface.

Figure 12.2
Flat polygonal surface approximating a volumetric shape.

Figure 12.3
Gridlines projected onto the simulated surface.

depth component to the otherwise flat surface. Figure 12.2 shows the results of simulating this height-mapped surface on the sample cube.

The modification of the surface position can also be visualized more clearly with a grid projected onto the simulated volume. This shows the various contours that are created by modifying the surface's texture coordinates. Figure 12.3 demonstrates such a contour pattern.

You can assume that the height-map will range in value from [0.0,1.0], with a value of 1.0 representing the polygonal surface and 0.0 representing the deepest

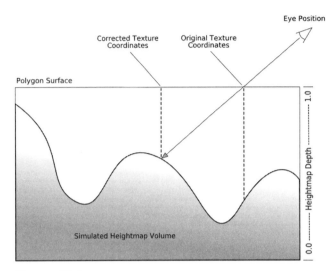

Figure 12.4
View vector intersecting the virtual volume.

possible position of the simulated volumetric shape. To be able to correctly reconstruct the volumetric shape represented by the height-map, the viewing direction must be used in conjunction with the height-map data to calculate which parts of the surface would be visible at each screen pixel of the polygonal surface for the given viewing direction.

This is accomplished by using a simplified ray tracer in the pixel shader. The ray that you will be tracing is formed from the vector from the eye (or camera) location to the current rasterized pixel. Imagine this vector piercing the polygonal surface and travelling until it hits the bottom of the virtual volume. Figure 12.4 shows a profile of this intersection taking place.

The line segment from the polygonal surface to the bottom of the virtual volume represents the line of sight for the surface. The task at hand is to figure out the first point on this segment that intersects with the height-map. That point is what would be visible to the viewer if you were to render a full geometric model of the height-map surface.

Since the point of intersection between the line segment and the height-map surface represents the visible surface point at that pixel, it also implicitly describes the corrected offset texture coordinates that should be used to look up a diffuse color map, a normal map, or whatever other textures you use to illuminate the surface. If this correction is carried out on all of the pixels that the polygonal surface is rendered to, then the overall effect is to reconstruct the volumetric surface—which is what I originally set out to do.

Implementing Parallax Occlusion Mapping

Now that you have a better understanding of the parallax occlusion mapping algorithm, it is time to put your newly acquired knowledge to use. First, I will discuss the required input texture data and how it is formatted. Then I will step through a sample implementation line by line with a thorough explanation of what is being accomplished with each section of code. The sample effect file is written in Direct3D 10 HLSL, but the implementation should apply to other shading languages as well.

Before writing the parallax occlusion map effect file, let's examine the texture data that you will be using. The standard diffuse color map is provided in the RGB channels of a texture. The only additional data required is a height-map of the volumetric surface that you are trying to simulate. In this example, the height data will be stored in the alpha channel of a normal map where a value of 0 (shown in black) corresponds to the deepest point, and a value of 1 (shown in white) corresponds to the original polygonal surface. Figure 12.5 shows the color texture, the alpha channel height-map, and the normal map that it will be coupled with.

It is worth noting that the normal map is not required to implement this technique. It is used here for simplified shading purposes, but is not required to perform the parallax occlusion mapping technique.

With a clear picture of the texture data that will be used, you will now look into the vertex shader to see how to set up the parallax occlusion mapping pixel shader. The first step in the vertex shader is to calculate the vector from the eye

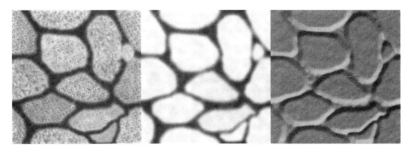

Figure 12.5
A sample color map, normal map, and height-map.

(or camera) position to the vertex. This is done by transforming the vertex position to world space, and then subtracting its position from the eye position. The world space vertex position is also used to find the eye vector and the light direction vector.

```
float3 P = mul( float4( IN.position, 1 ), mW ).xyz;
float3 N = IN.normal;
float3 E = P - EyePosition.xyz;
float3 L = LightPosition.xyz - P;
```

Next, you must transform the eye vector, light direction vector, and the vertex normal to tangent space. The transformation matrix that I will use is based on the vertex normal, binormal, and tangent vectors.

```
float3x3 tangentToWorldSpace;

tangentToWorldSpace[0] = mul( normalize( IN.tangent ), mW );
tangentToWorldSpace[1] = mul( normalize( IN.binormal ), mW );
tangentToWorldSpace[2] = mul( normalize( IN.normal ), mW );
```

Each of these vectors is transformed to world space and then used to form the basis of the rotation matrix for converting a vector from *tangent* to *world* space. Since this is a rotation-only matrix, if you transpose the matrix it becomes its own inverse. This produces the *world* to *tangent* space rotation matrix needed:

```
float3x3 worldToTangentSpace = transpose(tangentToWorldSpace);
```

Now the output vertex position and the output texture coordinates are trivially calculated:

```
OUT.position = mul( float4(IN.position, 1), mWVP );
OUT.texcoord = IN.texcoord;
```

And finally, you use the world to tangent space rotation matrix to transform the eye vector, light direction vector, and the vertex normal to tangent space:

```
OUT.eye = mul( E, worldToTangentSpace );
OUT.normal = mul( N, worldToTangentSpace );
OUT.light = mul( L, worldToTangentSpace );
```

That is all there is for the vertex shader. Now I'll move on to the pixel shader, which contains the actual parallax occlusion mapping code. The first calculation in the pixel shader is to determine the maximum parallax offset length that can be allowed. This is calculated in the same way that standard parallax mapping does it.

The maximum parallax offset is a function of the depth of the surface (specified here as `fHeightMapScale`), as well as the orientation of the eye vector to the surface. For a further explanation, see "Parallax Mapping with Offset Limiting: A Per-Pixel Approximation of Uneven Surfaces" by Terry Welsh (www.cs.ualberta.ca/~keith/610/papers/parallax_mapping.pdf).

```
float fParallaxLimit = -length( IN.eye.xy ) / IN.eye.z;
fParallaxLimit *= fHeightMapScale;
```

Next you calculate the direction of the offset vector. This is essentially a two-dimensional vector that exists in the x/y plane of the tangent space. This must be the case, since the texture coordinates are on the polygon surface with z = 0 (in tangent space) for the entire surface. The calculation is performed by finding the normalized vector in the direction of offset, which is essentially the vector formed from the x and y components of the eye vector. This direction is then scaled by the maximum parallax offset calculated in the previous step:

```
float2 vOffsetDir = normalize( IN.eye.xy );
float2 vMaxOffset = vOffsetDir * fParallaxLimit;
```

Now you must determine how many height-map samples you are going to take while determining where the eye vector intersects it. This is done by using a dot product of the surface normal and the eye vector as a measure of how "straight on" the surface is to the viewing direction. First you find the normalized normal and eye vectors:

```
float3 E = normalize( IN.eye );
float3 N = normalize( IN.normal );
```

Then the number of samples is determined by lerping between a user-specified minimum and maximum number of samples:

```
int nNumSamples = (int)lerp( nMaxSamples, nMinSamples, dot( E, N ) );
```

Since the total height of the simulated volume is 1.0, then starting from the top of the volume where the eye vector intersects the polygon surface provides an initial height of 1.0. As you take each additional sample, the height of the vector at the point that you are sampling is reduced by the reciprocal of the number of samples. This effectively splits up the 0.0–1.0 height into n chunks where n is the number of samples. This means that the larger the number of samples, the finer the height variation you can detect in the height-map:

```
float fStepSize = 1.0 / (float)nNumSamples;
```

Since I would like to use dynamic branching in the sampling algorithm, I cannot use any instructions that require gradient calculations within the dynamic loop section. This means that for the texture sampling, I must use a `SampleGrad` instruction instead of a plain `Sample` instruction. In order to use `SampleGrad`, I must manually calculate the texture coordinate gradients in screen space outside of the dynamic loop. This is done with the intrinsic `ddx` and `ddy` instructions:

```
float2 dx = ddx( IN.texcoord );
float2 dy = ddy( IN.texcoord );
```

Now you initialize the required variables for the dynamic loop. The purpose of the loop is to find the intersection of the eye vector with the height-map as efficiently as possible. So when you find the intersection, you want to terminate the loop early and save any unnecessary texture sampling efforts. You start with a comparison height of 1.0 (corresponding to the top of the virtual volume), initial parallax offset vectors of (0,0), and at the 0th sample:

```
float fCurrRayHeight = 1.0;
float2 vCurrOffset = float2( 0, 0 );
float2 vLastOffset = float2( 0, 0 );

float fLastSampledHeight = 1;
float fCurrSampledHeight = 1;

int nCurrSample = 0;
```

Next is the dynamic loop itself. For each iteration of the loop, you sample the texture coordinates along the parallax offset vector. For each of these samples, you compare the alpha component value to the current height of the eye vector. If the eye vector has a larger height value than the height-map, then you have not found the intersection yet. If the eye vector has a smaller height value than the height-map, then you have found the intersection, and it exists somewhere between the current sample and the previous sample:

```
while ( nCurrSample < nNumSamples )
{
    fCurrSampledHeight = NormalHeightMap.SampleGrad( LinearSampler,
    IN.texcoord + vCurrOffset, dx, dy ).a;
    if ( fCurrSampledHeight > fCurrRayHeight )
    {
        float delta1 = fCurrSampledHeight - fCurrRayHeight;
        float delta2 = ( fCurrRayHeight + fStepSize ) - fLastSampledHeight;
```

```
    float ratio = delta1/(delta1+delta2);

    vCurrOffset = (ratio) * vLastOffset + (1.0-ratio) * vCurrOffset;

    nCurrSample = nNumSamples + 1;
  }
  else
  {
    nCurrSample++;

    fCurrRayHeight -= fStepSize;

    vLastOffset = vCurrOffset;
    vCurrOffset += fStepSize * vMaxOffset;

    fLastSampledHeight = fCurrSampledHeight;
  }
}
```

Once the pre- and post-intersection samples have been found, you solve for the linearly approximated intersection point between the last two samples. This is done by finding the intersection of the two line segments formed between the last two samples and the last two eye vector heights. Then a final sample is taken at this interpolated final offset, which is considered the final intersection point:

```
float2 vFinalCoords = IN.texcoord + vCurrOffset;

float4 vFinalNormal = NormalHeightMap.Sample
( LinearSampler, vFinalCoords ); //.a;

float4 vFinalColor = ColorMap.Sample( LinearSampler, vFinalCoords );

// Expand the final normal vector from [0,1] to [-1,1] range.
vFinalNormal = vFinalNormal * 2.0f - 1.0f;
```

Now all that is left is to illuminate the pixel based on these new offset texture coordinates. In the example here, you utilize the normal map normal vector to calculate a diffuse and ambient lighting term. Since the height-map is stored in the alpha channel of the normal map, you already have the normal map sample available to you. These diffuse and ambient terms are then used to modulate the color map sample from the final intersection point. In place of this simple lighting model, you could use the offset texture coordinates to sample a normal map, a gloss map, or whatever other textures are needed to implement your favorite lighting model:

```
float3 vAmbient = vFinalColor.rgb * 0.1f;
float3 vDiffuse = vFinalColor.rgb * max
( 0.0f, dot( L, vFinalNormal.xyz ) ) * 0.5f;

vFinalColor.rgb = vAmbient + vDiffuse;

OUT.color = vFinalColor;
```

Now that you have seen parallax occlusion mapping at work, let's consider some of the parameters important to the visual quality and speed of the algorithm.

Algorithm Metrics

The algorithm as presented in the demonstration program's effect file runs faster than the 60Hz refresh rate of my laptop with a Geforce 8600M GT at a screen resolution of 640x480, with the minimum and maximum number of samples set to 4 and 20, respectively. Of course, this will vary by machine, but it will serve as a good metric to base performance characteristics on since you know that the algorithm is pixel-shader bound.

The algorithm is implemented using shader model 3.0 and later constructs—specifically, it uses dynamic branching in the pixel shader to reduce the number of unnecessary loops after the surface intersection has already been found. Thus relatively modern hardware is needed to run this effect in hardware. Even with newer hardware, the algorithm is pixel-shader intensive. Each iteration of the dynamic loop that does not find the intersection requires a texture lookup along with all of the ALU and logical instructions used to test if the intersection has occurred.

Considering that the sample images were generated with a minimum sample count of 4 and a maximum sample count of 20, you can see that the number of times the loop is performed to find the intersection is going to be the most performance-critical parameter. With this in mind, you should develop some methodology for determining how many samples are required for an acceptable image quality. Figure 12.6 compares images generated with 20 and then 6 maximum samples, respectively.

Figure 12.6
A 20-sample maximum image (top) and a 6-sample maximum image (bottom).

As you can see, there are aliasing artifacts along the left-hand side of the 6-sample image where the height-map makes any sharp transitions. Even so, the parts of the image that do not have such a sharp transition still have acceptable image quality. Thus if you will be using low-frequency height-map textures, you may be able to significantly reduce your sampling rate without any visual impact. It should also be noted that the aliasing is more severe when the original polygon surface normal is closer to perpendicular to the viewing direction. This allows you to adjust the number of samples based on the average viewing angle that will be used for the object being rendered. For example, if a wall is being rendered that will always be some distance from the viewer, then a much lower sampling rate can be used than if the viewer can stand next to the wall and look straight down its entire length.

Another very important parameter that must be taken into consideration is the height-map scale, named `fHeightMapScale` in the sample effect file. If you imagine a 1-meter by 1-meter square (in world space coordinates), then the height-map scale is how deep of a simulated volume you are trying to represent. For example, if the height-map scale is 0.04, then the 1x1 square would have a potential depth of 0.04 meters. Figure 12.7 shows two images generated with a scale height of 0.1 and 0.4 with the same sampling rates (20 samples maximum).

It is easy to see the dramatic amount of occlusion caused by the increased scale height, making the contours appear much deeper than in the original image. Also notice in the bottom image that the aliasing artifacts are back—even though the sampling rates are the same. With this in mind, you can see that the height scale also determines how "sharp" the features are with respect to the eye vector. The taller the features are, the harder they will be to detect intersections with the eye vector. This means that you would need more samples per pixel to obtain similar image quality if the height scale is larger. So a smaller height scale is "a good thing."

In addition, let's look deeper into how the algorithm will react when viewing polygonal surfaces nearly edge on. The current algorithm uses a maximum of 20 samples to determine where the intersections are. This is already a significant number of instructions to run, but the image quality is going to be low when viewed from an oblique angle. Here's why. If your height-map is 256x256, and you view the 1x1 square from the edge on, then in the worst case, you can potentially have a single screen pixel be required to test 256 texels for intersections before it finds the surface of the height-map. You would need approximately 12 times more samples than this maximum sampling rate to get an accurate intersection point! Figure 12.8 shows an edge on an image generated with 50 samples and 0.1 height-map scale.

Mip-mapping would help this situation by using a smaller dimension version of the texture when at extreme angles like this; but by each level of mip-map reducing the resolution of the height-map, it could potentially introduce additional artifacts. Care must be taken to restrict the number of situations where an object would be viewed edge on, or to switch to a constant time algorithm like bump mapping at sharp angles.

Figure 12.7
A 0.1 height-map scale image (top) and a 0.4 height-map scale image (bottom).

Figure 12.8
A 50-sample 0.04 height-map scale image from an oblique angle.

The ideal sampling situation would be to have one sample for each texel that the eye vector could possibly pass through during the intersection test. So a straight on view would only require a single sample, and an edge on view would require as many samples as there are texels in line with the pixel (up to a maximum of the number of texels per edge).

This information is already available in the pixel shader. The maximum parallax offset vector length, named `fParallaxLimit` in the pixel shader, is a measure of the possible intersection test travel in texture units (the x/y plane in tangent space). It is shorter for straight on views and longer for edge on views, which is what you want to base the number of samples on anyway. For example, if the parallax limit is 0.5, then a 256x256 height-map should sample, at most, 128 texels. This sampling method will provide the best quality results but will run slower due to the larger number of iterations.

Whatever sampling algorithm is used, it should be chosen to afford the minimum number of samples that provides acceptable image quality. Another consideration should be given to how large an object is going to appear on screen. If you are using parallax occlusion mapping on an object that takes up 80% of the frame buffer's pixels, then it will be much more prohibitive than an object that will take up 20% of the screen. So even if your target hardware can't handle full-screen parallax occlusion mapping, you could still use it for smaller objects.

Conclusion

I decided to write this article to provide some insight into the parallax occlusion mapping algorithm. Hopefully it is easy to understand and will provide some help in implementing the basic algorithm in addition to giving some hints about the performance versus quality trade-off that must be made. I think that the next advance in this algorithm will probably make it more efficient, most likely with either a better sampling rate metric or with a data structure built into the texture data to accelerate the searching process.

If you have questions or comments on this document, please feel free to contact me as "Jason Z" on the GameDev.net forums, or you can also PM me on GameDev.net.

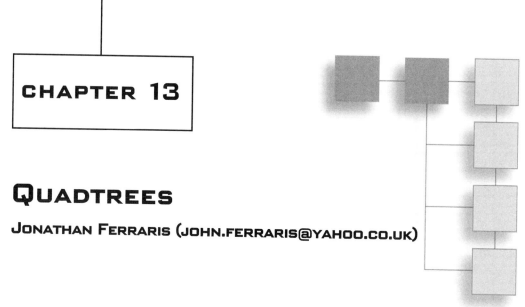

CHAPTER 13

Quadtrees

Jonathan Ferraris (john.ferraris@yahoo.co.uk)

With the revolution of consumer 3D graphics cards, there was a boom in 3D games. Most of these were first-person shooters, and for a very good reason—indoor environments, when compared to outdoor environments, are far simpler. With the great outdoors, there are no convenient staircases to the next level or doors and walls blocking your view. Believable outdoor environments go on for *miles*. The sheer geometry involved is phenomenal, and any steps to cut this down are welcomed. Enter quadtrees.

Note

The following diagrams are a top-down view of a 3D terrain. The grid shows the terrain on the x/z axis, as the actual "height" (i.e., hills) isn't visible, as you are looking down the y axis.

Imagine your terrain as a large grid, extending in the x/z plane. Take a look at Figure 13.1. Here, the camera is located in the bottom right of the terrain, with the viewing *frustum* (the triangle) extending a few cells in the same direction. So, before any optimizations, the routine for drawing the terrain would look like this:

```
for (int ctr=0; ctr<num_of_cells; ctr++)
{
  DrawCell();
}
```

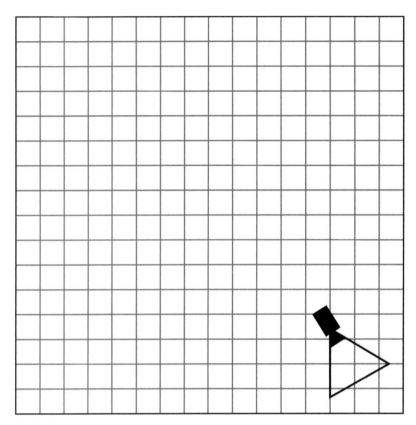

Figure 13.1

Note

A *cell* is just a square containing a number of triangles that are part of the terrain.

This is all very nice, but as the terrain is 16×16 cells, 256 cells are being drawn. This is a lot of waste, as only five cells are in your viewing frustum! Now for the first optimization: you'll test each cell to see if it lies in your viewing frustum, and if it does, draw it. Now the code looks a little like this:

```
for (int ctr=0; ctr<num_of_cells; ctr++)
{
  if(cell is in frustum) DrawCell();
}
```

If the cell is in the frustum, you'll draw it. Right, now you're only drawing five cells, as opposed to 256. With that bit of modified code, you've saved yourself drawing 251 cells! But, once again, it is very inefficient. Take a look at Figure 13.2.

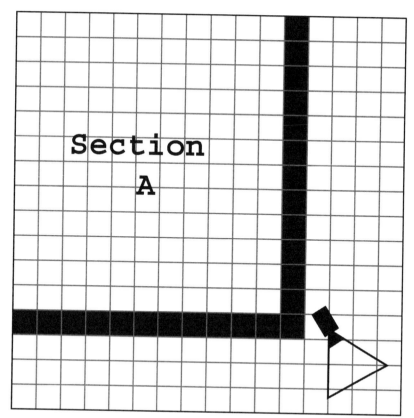

Figure 13.2

I've shaded certain cells so they create a bounding box. If the shaded cells aren't in the frustum, then you can safely say that the cells inside Section A won't be either. If you know that the shaded cells aren't in the frustum, why bother testing the other 144 cells in Section A? That's where quadtrees come into play.

Quadtrees take the terrain and divide it up into four smaller parts, then those smaller parts into four smaller parts, and so on, until it reaches a set size. That may seem a little confusing, but let me explain with pictures. First, you start off with your grid and divide it into four smaller sections, as shown in Figure 13.3.

As you can see, you now have four subsections of terrain. You now need to keep dividing into four sections until you reach, say, a section of only one cell. So, in Figure 13.4, the first section is divided into four smaller parts.

Again, divide one section into four smaller parts (see Figure 13.5).

And again, divide a section into four more parts (see Figure 13.6).

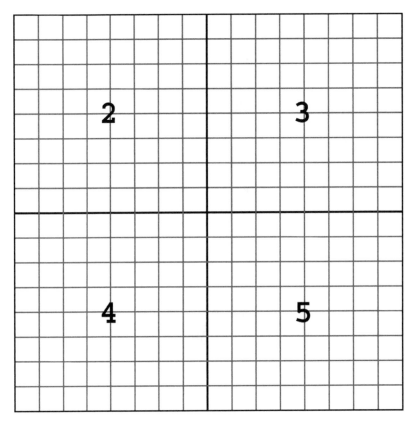

Figure 13.3

Okay. You've divided your section again, and its subsections are only one cell wide and tall. You tell your tree to stop dividing this section and carry on to the next. Eventually, the whole tree will be divided up. So, to recap, to create a quadtree, you divide it into four sections, then divide those sections into four sections, then divide those smaller sections into four sections, and so on. When do you stop? When you reach a certain size. This size is arbitrary, so make it up yourself. In this example, each cell contains 16 triangles (4 × 4), so you'll stop when the subdivisions are one cell by one cell. One thing I haven't discussed is the parent/child relationship. Each subdivision (called a *node*) has one parent (the node that it was split from) and four children. The exceptions are leaves, which only have a parent. A *leaf* is the smallest subdivision allowed, in this case, one cell by one cell. Another thing—before you subdivide, you have a root. The root has no parent, but, like the rules, has four children. Still don't get it? Let's take an example. You know those chain letters? It's like that. One person (the root) sends a letter to four people (the root's children). Now, these four people (nodes) share

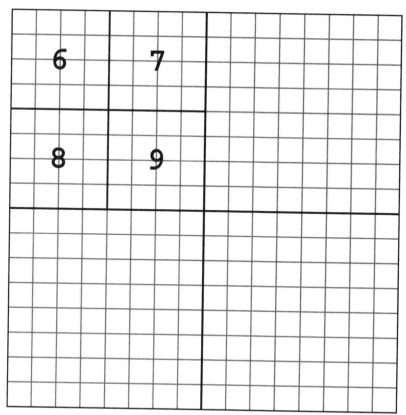

Figure 13.4

the same parent: the evil conspirator (the root). The letter says, "Send this letter to four more people, else you'll have seven years of bad luck/unlimited fame/ whatever." So each one of those four people send the letter to four more people, and so on.

Look at Figure 13.1 again. The border is the root. In Figure 13.3, the four squares are the root's children. I'll call them nodes 2, 3, 4, and 5, respectively. In Figure 13.4, the first child of the root (node 2) is divided up into four more squares. These squares are node 2's children. All of those children share the same parent: the first child of the root, or node 2. These are nodes 6, 7, 8, and 9. Once again, node 2's children are divided into four more squares (nodes), which are 10, 11, 12, and 13 (refer to Figure 13.5). Nodes 10–13's parent is node 6. In Figure 13.6, node 10 is divided, giving you leaves 14, 15, 16, and 17. As they are leaves, you don't divide them; you can go back and carry on dividing the next node, node 11. When node 11 is done, you divide 12, then 13, then 7, 8, and 9, then 3, 4, and 5. Then you're done.

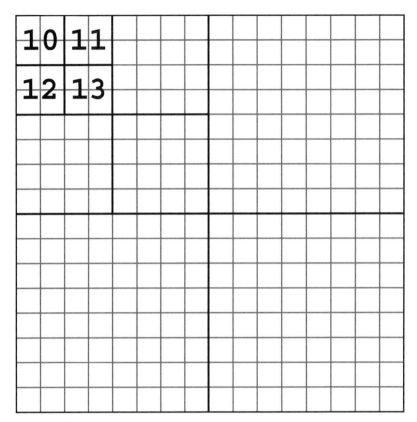

Figure 13.5

I know that's a really jagged piece of toast to swallow, but read it carefully. Then read it again. If you're still unsure, have a gander round the web. It'll probably click eventually, as they are easy to understand if explained correctly. In a final desperate attempt, I'll walk you through the process of using a quadtree. But first, here's a nice summary:

> A quadtree divides terrain into four pieces, and then divides those pieces into four pieces, and so on, until it reaches a certain size and stops dividing.

Quadtrees work by using the bounding coordinates of a node. Let's say your map goes from 0–16 in the x axis and 0–16 in the z axis. In that case, the bounding coordinates of your whole map are as follows: top left = (0,0,0), top right = (16,0,0), bottom left = (16,0,0), and bottom right = (16,0,16). When you split the root node, you split its bounding coordinates as well, so node 2 has these bounding coordinates: top left = (0,0,0), top right = (8,0,0), bottom left = (0,0,8), and bottom right = (8,0,8), as shown in Figure 13.7.

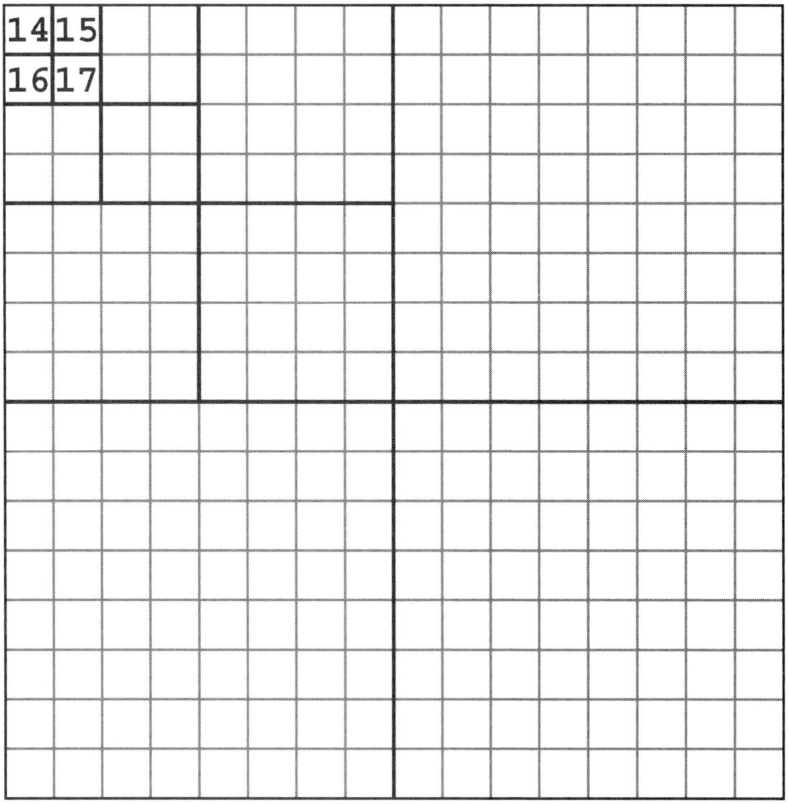

Figure 13.6

Test 1

The way it works is you start at the root and ask, "Is the camera within the root's bounding coordinates?" Unless something is wrong, the answer is yes. You know the camera is within the root's children, so now you test them. "Is the camera within node 2's bounding coordinates?" The answer here is no, so you can dismiss node 2 and all its children (see Figure 13.8). So far, you have dismissed testing 64 cells (the number of leaves in node 2). Not bad, not bad.

Test 2

As you can see in Figure 13.8, I've removed node 2 and all its children for the sake of clarity. Once again, you test the tree: "Is the camera within node 3's bounding coordinates?" Again, the answer is no, so you can safely dismiss node 3 and all its children (see Figure 13.9).

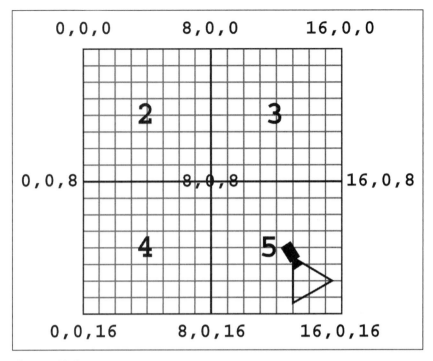

Figure 13.7

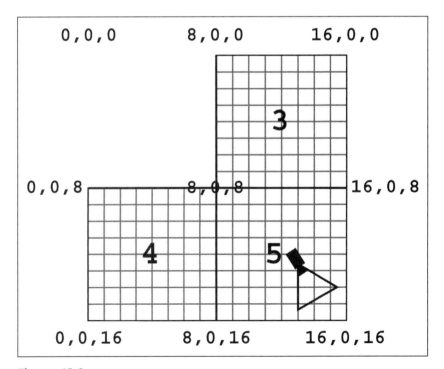

Figure 13.8

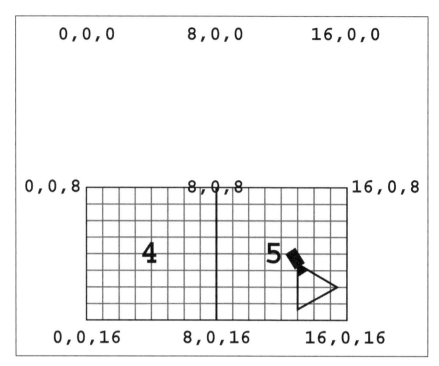

Figure 13.9

Test 3

So, here you go. "Is the camera within node 4's bounding coordinates?" No surprise, the answer is no (see Figure 13.10). It is time to test node 5.

Test 4

This time, the camera is within node 5's bounding coordinates, so you test its children. I've named node 5's four children A, B, C, and D for clarity. Time to test node 5's first child. "Is the camera within node A's bounding coordinates?" Looking at the figure, you can see that it isn't, so you dismiss node A and its children (see Figure 13.11).

Test 5

Now let's test node 5's second child: "Is the camera within node B's bounding coordinates?" Looking at Figure 13.11, you can see that it isn't, so you dismiss node B and its children (see Figure 13.12).

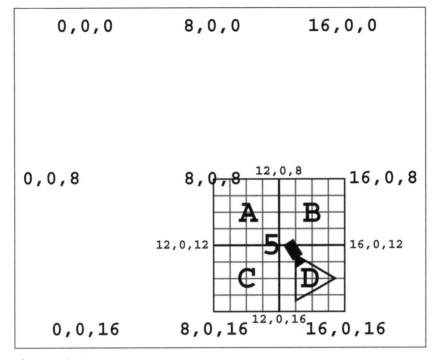

Figure 13.10

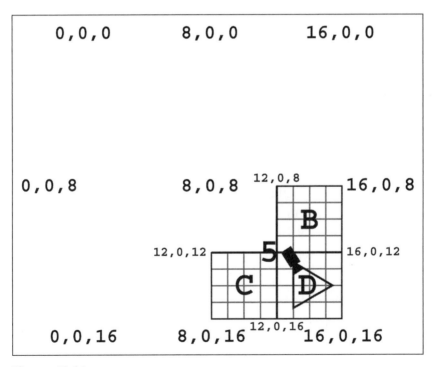

Figure 13.11

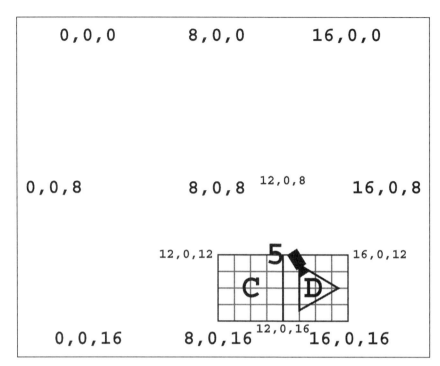

Figure 13.12

Test 6

Right, let's test node C, node 5's third child: "Is the camera within node C's bounding coordinates?" 'Course it's not, so let's just get rid of node C altogether (see Figure 13.13).

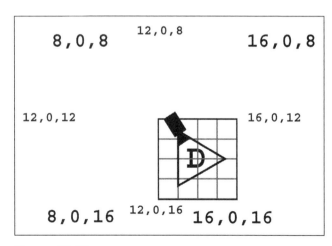

Figure 13.13

Test 7

Okay, it *has* to be in node D. "Is the camera within node D's bounding coordinates?" Yes, yes it is. Finally. Now all you have to do is test all of node D's children (groan). Well, I'm going to stop here. Think of working out the rest as an exercise. For your information, there are 16 more tests, resulting in five cells being visible. Let's total up the number of tests: $7 + 16 = 23$. You've gone from 256 tests to 23. (Actually, it's 22 tests, as it wasn't worth testing the root. The camera must lie within the root, or else nothing would be visible.) With a quadtree, you've done approximately 11.6% of the work of the previous method of testing every cell/leaf. By now you should have a firm understanding of the theory of quadtrees, so put on your coding socks, because you're going to make one. Not so fast, Sonny Jim. I'll just summarize what's been discussed:

> A quadtree is used to dismiss large chunks of terrain at a time. If an apple is on a tree's leaf, chopping off the branches the apple is nowhere near saves you looking on every leaf.

Putting It Together: Coding a Quadtree

Note

The following code assumes an indexed list. There are several implementations of these available.

So, now you've got the theory under your belt. How do you put it together? You will need the following:

- A structure to hold the quadtree data

- A function to create the tree

- A structure to hold triangle data

```
typedef struct node
{
  int bType;
  VERTEX vBoundingCoordinates[4];
  unsigned int uiBranches[4];
  unsigned int uiVertexStrip1[8];
  unsigned int uiVertexStrip2[8];
  unsigned int uiVertexStrip3[8];
  unsigned int uiVertexStrip4[8];
  unsigned int uiID;
  unsigned int uiParentID;
}NODE;
```

The variable bType tells you what type this node is. It can either be NODE_TYPE or LEAF_TYPE. If you are drawing your tree (terrain), it is used as a flag to tell the program to either stop and draw some triangles (LEAF_TYPE) or carry on reading through the tree (NODE_TYPE).

Next is an array of four vertices. These hold the node's bounding coordinates. The layout for the structure VERTEX is as follows:

```
typedef struct vertex
{
   float x,y,z;
}VERTEX;
```

Now you have an array called uiBranches. This is an array of four indexes to the quadtree array. These indexes are the children of the node. If the bType is LEAF_TYPE, this isn't used.

As mentioned, each leaf would hold 16 triangles, so you have four arrays named uiVertexStrip1 to uiVertexStrip 4. Each of these arrays holds four indexed triangles in the form of a triangle strip. In this tutorial, I won't be using these, so I won't go into detail about them (which also saves me an explanation). The variable uiID holds the node's ID in the quadtree. As I said before, the quadtree is just an array of nodes. The ID is just an index in that array.

Then you have the last variable, the uiParentID. This is the ID (index) of the parent. This, coupled with the uiBranches array, lets you navigate your way around the tree by jumping from node to node. At any given node, you can go to its parent or its children, which, if you follow the tree, will take you to the root or to all of the leaves:

```
NODE *pNodeList;
```

The preceding code line creates a pointer structure called pNodeList. It can be called anything. Basically, it is your quadtree. (Note: you'll use array element pNodeList[0] as your root.)

$$\frac{(\text{Grid Width})^2}{\text{Leaf Width}}$$

Formula 13.1

The preceding formula gives you the number of leaves. Leaf Width is the number of triangles across in each leaf. As I said, each leaf will be one cell by one cell; I also said each cell contains 16 triangles. In this case, as cells are 16x16 triangles, the

Leaf Width will be 4. Grid Width is the width of the grid in triangles. As each cell is four triangles across, 16 cells multiplied by 4 is 64. To find out the total number of nodes in the tree, you call the function CalcNodeNum:

```
unsigned int CalcNodeNum(unsigned int max,unsigned int min)
{
  int ctr=0;
  int var = 0;
  while(var==0)
  {
    ctr+=max;
    max=max/min;
    if(max==1)
    {
      var=1;
    }
  }
  ctr++;
  return ctr;
}
```

Here, CalcNodeNum takes two parameters: the total number of leaves (max) and the leaf width (min). In this case, the leaf width is four triangles. The total number of leaves was obtained in the previous formula. What CalcNodeNum does is keep on dividing the grid by min to get the total number of leaves. You can step through the function to understand it better. So, let's get the next bit of code done:

```
unsigned int Temp =(GridWidth/4)*(GridWidth/4);
unsigned int Temp2 = CalcNodeNum(Temp,4);
pNodeList = (NODE*)malloc(sizeof(NODE)*Temp2);
```

Okay. The first line uses Formula 13.1 to calculate the total number of leaves. The second line stores the total number of nodes in an unsigned integer called Temp2. The third line allocates memory for pNodeList. You typecast the function malloc with the structure NODE. Then, you allocate memory for Temp2 nodes by multiplying the number of nodes by the size of the NODE structure. For more information, check out the malloc and sizeof functions in your compiler's help file. Now that you've calculated the number of nodes and allocated memory for your quadtree, let's call the quadtree creation function. But first, let's lay the foundation knowledge for recursive code. I'll use a number counter as an example. If you want to display the numbers 1 to 10, you could do this:

```
void Count(int num)
{
   cout<<num<<"\n";
}
void main()
{
   Count(0);
   Count(1);
   Count(2);
   Count(3);
   Count(4);
   Count(5);
   Count(6);
   Count(7);
   Count(8);
   Count(9);
   return;
}
```

But as you know, that would be tedious to do every time you wanted to count with numbers. So the natural progression would be something like this:

```
for (int ctr=0;ctr<10;ctr++)
{
   Count(ctr);
}
```

Although there is nothing wrong with the preceding code, using it for your quadtree would be a real nightmare. This would involve having lots of temporary values and would take a lot of time to get right. You'll understand why once you've coded your quadtree. In the preceding code, you have actually implicitly called Count 10 times. If you wanted to call it 20 times, you would have to explicitly call the for statement 20 times. Recursive code needs only to be called once. There is no need for for or while statements. The reason is that you call the recursive function, and it calls itself however many times you tell it to. So, to the code:

```
void Count(int num)
{
   static int ctr = 0;
   if(ctr>num)
   {
      return;
   }
```

```
  else
  {
    cout<<ctr<<"\n";
    ctr++;
    Count(num);
  }
}
void main()
{
  Count(ctr);
  return;
}
```

The static integer `ctr` means that `ctr` is declared once (the first time the function is called), but its value is used by subsequent calls to the function. It is like a global variable that only `Count` can see. As is shown here, you only call `Count` once. It keeps on calling itself until a certain condition is met (in this case, when `ctr` reaches the value of `num`). So when you, the programmer, call `Count` for the first time, you have to set it up. You give it a condition to meet, in this case the number 10. If you wanted it to count to 20, you would pass 20 to `Count` when you call it. Right, let's summarize that:

> The programmer only calls a recursive function once. The first call (made by the programmer) tends to initialize the function, telling it what to do and what conditions are needed to stop calling itself.

Well, I'm glad that's out of the way. On with the code. Now, let's look at the function `CreateNode`. As the name suggests, this creates nodes. If only it were that simple. As this function is recursive, not only does it create a node, but by calling itself, it creates the whole quadtree! You only need to call the function `CreateNode` once, and it does all the hard work. The format for `CreateNode` is as follows:

```
void CreateNode(unsigned int Bounding[4],unsigned int ParentID,
                unsigned int NodeID)
```

This function returns nothing. Nil. Void. If you want, you could make it return something like a `BOOL` for error checking; but for this tutorial, I know the code works, so I'll leave it as `void`. `CreateNode` takes three parameters. The first is the bounding coordinate for the node. These bounding coordinates are index values for the grid/terrain. They are in the following order: top left, top right, bottom left, and bottom right. The next value is the ID (index) for the node's parent. Last, but by no means least, is the ID (index) for the node. As I said, when you, the programmer, call `CreateNode`, you need to initialize it. As the first node is the root, you need to set the parameters for the root. The bounding coordinates for the root are that of the whole terrain. In this case, they would be as follows: (0,0,0) (16,0,0) (0,0,16) (16,0,16). The only problem is that you just blurted some vertex data. `Bounding[4]` uses vertex *indexes*, so you need to find the indexes for the terrain. Put that calculator away, as I have done the work for you.

In a 2D array extending in the x/z plane with height values of 0 (i.e., the grid), to find the top left, you use the following equation:

```
0
```

Wow, that'll get you scratching your head. Don't get too cocky, as that was the easy bit. To find the top right, you use the following equation:

```
GridWidth
```

Easy, easy. Now let's try the bottom left:

```
GridHeight * (GridWidth + 1)
```

And now the bottom right:

```
((GridHeight) * (GridWidth + 1)) + GridWidth
```

The mathematics isn't hard, but if you're having trouble understanding it, then just plot a grid on some paper (or better yet, squared paper), and step through it. Now you're ready to call `CreateNode`:

```
unsigned int uiBoundingCoordinates[] =
  {0,GridWidth,(GridHeight*(GridWidth+1)),
  ((GridHeight)*(GridWidth+1))+GridWidth};
CreateNode(uiBoundingCoordinates,0,0);
```

What you have done is set up the root node. The root node has the bounding box previously described and no parent (so a parent ID of 0), and its ID is 0 (i.e., the first element in your quadtree array). You are now prepared to walk through the `CreateNode` code:

```
void CreateNode(unsigned int Bounding[4],unsigned int ParentID,
                unsigned int NodeID)
{
  static unsigned int TotalTreeID = 0;
  unsigned int uiNodeType;
  unsigned int uiWidth,uiHeight;
```

Okay, the static unsigned int TotalTreeID holds the current number of nodes. You'll use this later on to assign the nodes children their IDs. The unsigned int uiNodeType holds the node's type, either a leaf (LEAF_TYPE) or a node (NODE_TYPE). The unsigned ints uiWidth and uiHeight will hold the width and height of the node. As you are passed just bounding coordinates, you don't actually know the dimensions of the node. You use the uiWidth and uiHeight to tell whether the node is a leaf or node. Now you need to get the width and height from the bounding coordinates:

```
uiWidth = fVerts[(Bounding[1]*3)] - fVerts[(Bounding[0]*3)];
uiHeight = fVerts[(Bounding[2]*3)+2] - fVerts[(Bounding[0]*3)+2];
```

This assumes fVerts is an array containing a list of vertices, which build up your grid. As a vertex contains three parts, x, y, and z, each vertex in the array will occupy three elements. Normally, if you have an index of value 3, it would point to the third element. But, as each vertex occupies three elements, an index of 3 would point to the third element (i.e., vertex 0's Z component):

```
fVerts[0] = Vertex 0's X component
fVerts[1] = Vertex 0's Y component
fVerts[2] = Vertex 0's Z component
fVerts[3] = Vertex 1's X component
fVerts[4] = Vertex 1's Y component
fVerts[5] = Vertex 1's Z component
fVerts[6] = Vertex 2's X component
fVerts[7] = Vertex 2's Y component
fVerts[8] = Vertex 2's Z component
fVerts[9] = Vertex 3's X component
fVerts[10] = Vertex 3's Y component
fVerts[11] = Vertex 3's Z component
```

As you can see, an index of 0 points to element [0]. Element [0] is vertex 0's X component. Element [3] is vertex 1's X component. This is all very nice, but the indices are wrong, right? Surely if Bounding[0] was 3, it wouldn't point to the third vertex, but the second vertex's X component? Well, you multiply the index by 3 for the vertex's X component, add 1 for the Y component, and add one more for the Z component. So, if you have an index of 3, it's supposed to point to vertex 3. Okay, 3*3 is 9, and the ninth element is vertex 3's X component. So, if you wanted index 3's Z component, you would do (3*3)+2, which gives you element 11, vertex 3's Z component! To find the width of the node, you subtract the top-left vertex's X component (remember, x values in the grid go across, so they represent width) from the top-right vertex's X component. And to find the height, you subtract the top-left vertex's Z component (by *height*, I mean the *depth*, but I call it height to make it easier to picture as a 2D grid) from the bottom-left vertex's Z component.

Now, I said that the leaves are 4x4 triangles. This implies that leaves are four triangles wide. As you know the width of the node (stored in `uiWidth`), if you divide the width by 2 and get a result of 2, then the width is 4—hence, your node is a leaf:

```
if (0.5*uiWidth == 2)
{
   uiNodeType = LEAF_TYPE;
}
else
{
   uiNodeType = NODE_TYPE;
}
```

Notice that multiplying by 0.5 is the same as dividing by 2. Next, you want a pointer to your node. The reason for this is to save you getting RSI from typing the same thing about 50 times. So, `pNodeList` contains all your nodes, and you just need to select your node:

```
NODE *pNode = &pNodeList[NodeID];
```

All this means is that instead of doing stuff with your node like so:

```
pNodeList[NodeID].uID = Whatever;
```

you can simply do this:

```
pNode->uiID = Whatever;
```

The next bit just fills your node with values already discussed:

```
pNode->uiID = NodeID;
pNode->uiParentID = ParentID;
pNode->vBoundingCoordinates[0].x = fVerts[(Bounding[0]*3)];
pNode->vBoundingCoordinates[0].y = fVerts[(Bounding[0]*3)+1];
pNode->vBoundingCoordinates[0].z = fVerts[(Bounding[0]*3)+2];
pNode->vBoundingCoordinates[1].x = fVerts[(Bounding[1]*3)];
pNode->vBoundingCoordinates[1].y = fVerts[(Bounding[1]*3)+1];
pNode->vBoundingCoordinates[1].z = fVerts[(Bounding[1]*3)+2];
pNode->vBoundingCoordinates[2].x = fVerts[(Bounding[2]*3)];
```

```
pNode->vBoundingCoordinates[2].y = fVerts[(Bounding[2]*3)+1];
pNode->vBoundingCoordinates[2].z = fVerts[(Bounding[2]*3)+2];
pNode->vBoundingCoordinates[3].x = fVerts[(Bounding[3]*3)];
pNode->vBoundingCoordinates[3].y = fVerts[(Bounding[3]*3)+1];
pNode->vBoundingCoordinates[3].z = fVerts[(Bounding[3]*3)+2];
pNode->bType = uiNodeType;
```

Now, in this tutorial I won't deal with leaf nodes. Once I've assigned a leaf node its type (LEAF_TYPE), I'm going to just return to the calling function (i.e., do nothing). In the real world, you may wish to have a leaf point to an array or triangles. If you have a look at the NODE structure, you'll notice I left four vertex strips (uiVertexStrip1...4), which, if you want, you can fill with triangles. This is so that when you are drawing the terrain and you hit a leaf, you can tell it to draw those triangle strips (which represent that portion of the terrain).

```
if(uiNodeType == LEAF_TYPE)
{
  return;
}
else
{
```

Next, you need to do the following for each of the node's children: add one to uiTotalTreeID; create a new bounding volume for that child; and call CreateNode, passing the new bounding volume, NodeID, for the parent ID and uiTotalTreeID for the new node's (child's) ID.

```
unsigned int BoundingBox[4];
TotalTreeID++;
pNode->uiBranches[0] = TotalTreeID;
//Top-Left i.e. b[0]
BoundingBox[0] = Bounding[0];
//Between b[0] and b[1]
BoundingBox[1] = Bounding[0]+((Bounding[1]-Bounding[0])/2);
//[between b[0] and b[2]
BoundingBox[2] = Bounding[0]+((Bounding[2]-Bounding[0])/2);
//middle of node
BoundingBox[3] = Bounding[0]+((Bounding[2]-Bounding[0])/2)+
                ((Bounding[1]-Bounding[0])/2);
CreateNode(BoundingBox,NodeID,TotalTreeID);
```

What you have done is split the bounding volume to 1/4 of its size. You do this differently for each child, as the previous code shows, splitting for the top-left child. Notice for the top left of the child, it is the same as the top left of the node. The top right of the child will be halfway between the nodes `Bounding[0]` and `Bounding[1]`. I'll show you the rest, just so you get the idea:

```
//*****************************************************************
TotalTreeID++;
pNode->uiBranches[1] = TotalTreeID;
// Between b[0] and b[1]
BoundingBox[0] = Bounding[0]+((Bounding[1]-Bounding[0])/2);
//Top-Right i.e. b[1]
BoundingBox[1] = Bounding[1];
//middle of node
BoundingBox[2] = Bounding[0]+((Bounding[2]-Bounding[0])/2)+
                ((Bounding[1]-Bounding[0])/2);
//between b[1] & b[3]
BoundingBox[3] = Bounding[0]+((Bounding[2]-Bounding[0])/2)+
                ((Bounding[1]-Bounding[0]));
CreateNode(BoundingBox,NodeID,TotalTreeID);
//*****************************************************************
TotalTreeID++;
pNode->uiBranches[2] = TotalTreeID;
//between b[0] and b[2]
BoundingBox[0] = Bounding[0]+((Bounding[2]-Bounding[0])/2);
//middle of node
BoundingBox[1] = Bounding[0]+((Bounding[2]-Bounding[0])/2)+
                ((Bounding[1]-Bounding[0])/2);
//Bottom-Left i.e. b[2]
BoundingBox[2] = Bounding[2];
//between b[2] and b[3]
BoundingBox[3] = Bounding[2]+((Bounding[3]-Bounding[2])/2);
CreateNode(BoundingBox,NodeID,TotalTreeID);
//*****************************************************************
TotalTreeID++;
pNode->uiBranches[3] = TotalTreeID;
//middle of node
BoundingBox[0] = Bounding[0]+((Bounding[2]-Bounding[0])/2)+
                ((Bounding[1]-Bounding[0])/2);
//between b[1] and b[3]
BoundingBox[1] = Bounding[0]+((Bounding[2]-Bounding[0])/2) + uiWidth;
//between b[2] and b[3]
BoundingBox[2] = Bounding[2]+((Bounding[3]-Bounding[2])/2);
//Bottom-Right i.e. b[3]
```

```
    BoundingBox[3] = Bounding[3];
    CreateNode(BoundingBox,NodeID,TotalTreeID);
}
```

All you need to do is return nothing and end `CreateNode`'s curly braces:

```
    return;
}
```

And that's about it. You can download the fully annotated source and executable at the book's companion web site: www.courseptr.com/downloads.

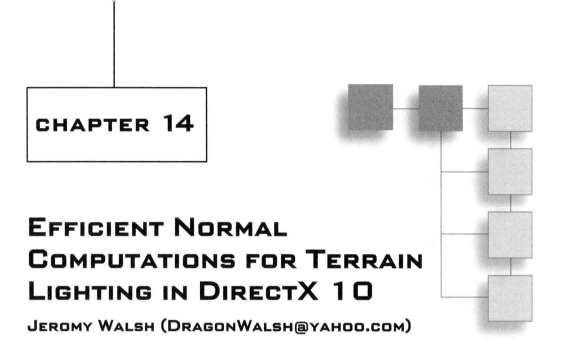

CHAPTER 14

EFFICIENT NORMAL COMPUTATIONS FOR TERRAIN LIGHTING IN DIRECTX 10

JEROMY WALSH (DRAGONWALSH@YAHOO.COM)

In 2005, I spent a good amount of time answering questions in the For Beginners forums of GameDev.net. One question I frequently saw was how to compute the vertex normals required for various diffuse lighting models used in games. After answering the question three or four times, I aimed to write an introductory article that would explain the most commonly used algorithms for computing surface and vertex normals to date and to compare and contrast their performance and rendering quality. However, times and technology have changed.

At the time of my first article, real-time shaders were just becoming the *de facto* standard method for implementing graphics among video game developers, and the lack of texture fetches for vertex shaders and the limited instruction count prevented people from performing many of the operations they would have liked on a per-frame basis directly on the GPU. However, with the introduction of DirectX 10, geometry shaders, streamed output, and Shader Model 4.0, it's now possible to move the workload of transforming and lighting your scenes entirely to the GPU.

In this article, I will be utilizing the new uniform interface for texture fetching and shader resources of DirectX 10, along with the new Geometry Shader Stage to allow you to efficiently compute per-frame, per-vertex normals for dynamic terrain, such as rolling ocean waves or evolving meshes—entirely on the GPU. To make sure I cover all the bases, I will be computing the normals for terrain lighting using two distinct algorithms, each of which addresses a specific type of terrain. It is my hope that by the end of this article, you will have discovered some efficient and exciting ways to take advantage of current-generation hardware to compute the surface and vertex normals necessary for the complex lighting algorithms that will be popping up with the new generation of rendering hardware.

Height-Map-Based Terrain

Depending upon the genre of game you're making, players may spend a significant amount of time looking at the terrain or ocean waves passing them by. With this in mind, it is desirable to have a terrain that is both realistic and attractive. Among the simplest methods of creating attractive terrain are those based on height-maps.

A *height-map* is a one- or two-dimensional array of data that represents the height of a piece of terrain at a specific (x,z) point in space. In other words, if you were to look at the [x][z] offset within a 2D array or compute the associated index into a one-dimensional array, the value at that location in memory would be the height at point X,Z in 3D space.

The value in memory can be stored as either a floating-point value or an integer, and in the case of an integer, the values are often stored as either a 1-byte (8 bits) or 4-byte (32 bits) block of memory. When the height values are stored as 8-bit integers, the height-map can easily be saved and loaded to disk in the form of a grayscale image. This makes it possible to use a standard image editing application to modify the terrain offline. Figure 14.1 shows an example grayscale height-map.

Fortunately, technology has advanced a great deal in recent years, and floating-point buffers and textures are now frequently used. For the purposes of this article, I will use 32-bit, single precision floating-point values to represent height.

When working with static terrain, or when it's necessary to perform collision detection, the values from the height-map can be read from memory and then assigned to a grid-shaped mesh that contains the same number of rows and columns of vertices as the dimension of the height-map. Once this is done, the newly generated mesh can be triangulated and passed to the renderer for drawing, or it can be used for picking and collision detection. This "field of vertices," which is used for rendering and collision, is called the *heightfield*.

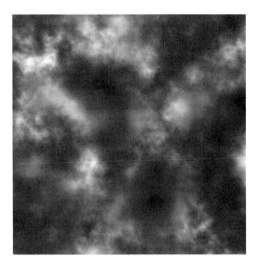

Figure 14.1
An example height-map taken from Wikipedia.

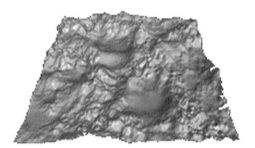

Figure 14.2
An example 3D heightfield taken from Wikipedia.

Figure 14.2 shows a 3D heightfield representation of the height-map used in Figure 14.1.

Because the distance between pixels in a height-map are uniformly treated as one, it is common to generate a heightfield with similarly distributed vertices. However, forcing your vertices to exist in increments of 1 can cause the terrain to seem unnatural. For this reason, a horizontal scale factor, sometimes called *scale* or *units per vertex*, is added to allow your vertices to be spaced in distances greater or smaller than 1.0.

When it is not necessary for actors to collide against the terrain, or when it's possible for the collisions to be computed on the GPU, it is more common to pass the height-map directly to the GPU along with a flat mesh. In this case, the scaling and displacement of the vertices are performed by the GPU, and the method is referred to as *displacement mapping*. This is the method I'll use in this article.

Slope Method of Computing Heightfield Normals

Because heightfields are generated from height-maps, the vertices are always evenly spaced and are never overlapping (resulting in the Y component of the normal always facing "up"). This makes it possible to break the three-dimensional heightfield into two, two-dimensional coordinate systems, one in the x/y plane and one in the z/y plane. You can then use the simple and well-known phrase *rise above run* from elementary geometry to compute the X and Z component normals from each of the coordinate systems, while leaving the Y component one. Consider the line shown in Figure 14.3.

In Figure 14.3, you can see that the slope for the line segment is 2. If you assume for a moment that the line segment represents a 3D triangle lying on its side, and that the front face of the triangle points up, then the surface normal for such a triangle (in the x direction) can be determined by finding the negative reciprocal of the slope. In this case, the negative reciprocal is $-(1/2)$. At the beginning of this explanation, I made a point of indicating that you can express the 3D heightfield as a pair of 2D coordinate systems because the Y component of the normal always points up. That implies that you want to keep the Y component positive. So the slope for the normal is better expressed as $1/-2$. Note that this means the *dy* is 1 and *dx* is -2 and that if you use those values as the X and Y components of a 2D normal vector, you get the vector $(-2,1)$. Once normalized, that would indeed represent a vector that is normal to the triangle lying on its side in the x/y plane.

In the discussion of heightfields, I also noted that the distance between pixels is always 1, and consequently, the distance between vertices in the heightfield

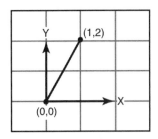

Figure 14.3
A simple 2D line.

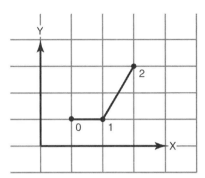

Figure 14.4
A series of 2D line segments.

(before scaling) is also 1. This further simplifies the computation of normals because it means that the denominator of the expression rise/run is always 1, and that the X component can be computed simply by subtracting the Y components (the rise) of the two points that make up the line segment. Assume y is 1, and then subtract the first height (1) from the first height (3), and you get –2.

So now you have a fast and efficient method of computing the normal for a line segment, the 2D equivalent of a surface normal; but you still need to take one more step to compute the normal for each vertex. Consider the graph in Figure 14.4.

Here you can see three vertices, each separated by a line segment. Visually, the normal at point 0 would just be the up vector, the normal at point 2 would be the same as the line segment that you computed previously, and point 1 would be halfway in between. From this observation, you can generalize an algorithm for computing the component normal for a point in a 2D coordinate system:

> The vertex normal in a 2D coordinate system is the average of the normals of the attached line segments.

Or, when expressed using standard equation speak:

$$\text{Component Normal} = \Sigma(\text{line Normals})/N$$

where N is the number of normals.

Up until this point, I've attempted to consistently use the term *component normal* to remind you that what you've been computing so far is simply the X component of the normal in the 3D heightfield at any given vertex. Fortunately, computing the Z component is exactly the same. That is, you can compute the *dy*

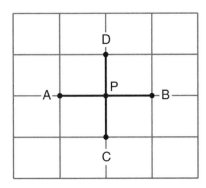

Figure 14.5
An overhead view of a heightfield.

in the z direction to get the Z component of the normal, just as you computed *dy* in the x direction to get the X component. When you combine the two equations, you get the following:

$$\text{Normal.x} = \Sigma\,(x - \text{segments})/\text{Nx};$$
$$\text{Normal.y} = 1.0$$
$$\text{Normal.z} = \Sigma(z - \text{segments})/\text{Nz};$$

The preceding algorithm can be shown more effectively using a visual aid (see Figure 14.5).

If you take the example shown in Figure 14.5, you'll see the algorithm can be filled in to get the following equations:

$$\text{Normal.x} = [(A - P) + (P - B)]/2.0$$
$$\text{Normal.y} = 1.0$$
$$\text{Normal.z} = [(C - P) + (P - D)]/2.0$$

During implementation, the algorithm becomes a little more complicated because you must do the following:

- Find the indices of your points in the height data.

- Handle edge cases in which there are fewer points to sample.

Rather than describe the special cases here, let's look at them in the context of an implementation in DirectX 10 using vertex shaders.

Implementing the Algorithm with DirectX 10

In the explanation that follows, I will try and address the most relevant components of implementing the preceding algorithm within a DirectX 10 application. However, I will be using the source code from the associated demo program, which you may examine for a more complete listing and an idea of how it may fit into your own games. You can find it at this book's companion web site at www.courseptr .com/downloads.

Before you do anything else you need to define the custom vertex format. For the 3D heightfield, you're only going to need two floating-point values, x and z. This is because the normal values, along with the Y component of your position, will be pulled from the height-map and procedurally computed within the vertex shader. When initializing the X and Z components within your program, you are going to set them to simple integer increments: 0, 1, 2, and so on. You do this so you can compute an index into your height-map in order to determine the height at any given vertex:

```
struct FilterVertex      // 8 Bytes per vertex
{
  float x, z;
};
```

The index into a one-dimensional height-map can be computed with the following equation, where numVertsWide is how many pixels are in your height-map in the x dimension:

```
index =  z * numVertsWide + x
```

DirectX 10 is unique from DirectX 9 and is particularly suited for this type of problem because, unlike DirectX 9, DirectX 10 provides uniform interfaces for each stage in the graphics pipeline. This allows you to create buffers, textures, and constants, which can be accessed the same across all stages. For this particular purpose, you're going to need a buffer to store your heights in. In DirectX 9 with Shader Model 3, you could have done this by stuffing your heights into a texture, and then accessing it using the SM 3.0 vertex texture fetching operations. However, with DirectX 10, it's even easier. You can define a buffer that will store your heights, and then bind it to the graphics pipeline as a shader resource. Once you do this, you access the buffer as though it were any other global variable within your shaders. To make this possible you need to define three different fields:

```
ID3D10Buffer* m_pHeightBuffer;
ID3D10ShaderResourceView* m_pHeightBufferRV;
ID3D10EffectShaderResourceVariable* m_pHeightsRV;
```

First, you'll need the buffer itself. This is what ultimately contains your float values and what you'll be updating each frame to contain your new heights. Next, all resources that derive from `ID3D10Resource` (which includes textures and buffers) require an associated resource view, which tells the shader how to fetch data from the resource. While you fill your buffer with data, it is the resource view that will be passed to your HLSL Effect. Finally, you're going to need an Effect Variable. In DirectX 10, all effect fields can be bound to one of several variable types. Shader resources such as generic buffers and textures use the shader resource variable type.

While I won't demonstrate it here, you will need to define your vertex and index buffers and fill them with the corresponding values. Once you've done that, you'll want to create the shader resources previously discussed. To do this you create an instance of the `D3D10_BUFFER_DESC` and `D3D10_SHADER_RESOURCE_VIEW_DESC` structures and fill them in using the following code:

```
void Heightfield::CreateShaderResources(int numSurfaces)
{
  // Create the non-streamed shader resources
  D3D10_BUFFER_DESC desc;
  D3D10_SHADER_RESOURCE_VIEW_DESC SRVDesc;
  // Create the height buffer for the Filter method
  ZeroMemory(&desc, sizeof(D3D10_BUFFER_DESC));
  ZeroMemory(&SRVDesc, sizeof(SRVDesc));
  desc.ByteWidth = m_NumVertsDeep * m_NumVertsWide * sizeof(float);
  desc.Usage               = D3D10_USAGE_DYNAMIC;
  desc.BindFlags           = D3D10_BIND_SHADER_RESOURCE;
  desc.CPUAccessFlags      = D3D10_CPU_ACCESS_WRITE;
  SRVDesc.Format           = DXGI_FORMAT_R32_FLOAT;
  SRVDesc.ViewDimension    = D3D10_SRV_DIMENSION_BUFFER;
  SRVDesc.Buffer.ElementWidth = m_NumVertsDeep * m_NumVertsWide;
  m_pDevice->CreateBuffer(&desc, NULL, &m_pHeightBuffer);
  m_pDevice->CreateShaderResourceView(m_pHeightBuffer, &SRVDesc,
    &m_pHeightBufferRV);
}
```

For the filter normal algorithm, you're going to be writing to the height-map buffer once every frame, so you'll want to specify it as a writeable, dynamic resource. You also want to make sure it's bound as a shader resource and has a format that supports the 32-bit floating-point values. Finally, as seen in the previous code listing, you need to specify the number of elements in your buffer.

Unfortunately, the field you use to do this is horribly misnamed, and in the documentation it is described as containing a value that it should not. The field you're looking for is ElementWidth. The documentation says it should contain the size of an element in bytes; however, this is incorrect. This field should contain the total number of elements. Don't be fooled.

After you've created your index, vertex, and height buffers and filled them in with the correct values, you'll need to draw your heightfield. But, before you pass your buffers off to the GPU, you need to make sure to set the relevant properties for the different stages and set your buffers. So let's examine the Draw call a little bit at a time. First, you'll define a few local variables to make the rest of the method cleaner:

```
void Heightfield::Draw()
{
  // Init some locals
  int numRows = m_NumVertsDeep - 1;
  int numIndices = 2 * m_NumVertsWide;
  UINT offset = 0;
  UINT stride = sizeof(FilterVertex);
```

Next, you need to tell the vertex shader the dimensions of your heightfield so that it can determine whether a vertex lies on an edge, a corner, or in the middle of the heightfield. This is important, as the number of line segments included in the algorithm is dependent upon where the current vertex lies in the heightfield:

```
m_pNumVertsDeep->SetInt(m_NumVertsDeep);
m_pNumVertsWide->SetInt(m_NumVertsWide);
m_pMetersPerVertex->SetFloat(m_MetersPerVertex);
```

Next, you're going to follow the usual procedure of specifying the topology, index buffer, input layout, and vertex buffer for your terrain:

```
m_pDevice->IASetPrimitiveTopology
(D3D10_PRIMITIVE_TOPOLOGY_TRIANGLESTRIP);
m_pDevice->IASetIndexBuffer(m_pIndexBuffer,DXGI_FORMAT_R32_UINT,0);
m_pDevice->IASetInputLayout(m_pHeightfieldIL);
m_pDevice->IASetVertexBuffers(0, 1, &m_pHeightfieldVB, &stride, &offset);
```

Next, and this is perhaps the most important step, you're going to bind the resource view of the buffer to the established effect variable. Once you've done this, any references to the buffer inside of the HLSL will be accessing the data you've provided within your height-map buffer.

```
m_pHeightsRV->SetResource(m_pHeightBufferRV);
```

Finally, you're going to apply the first pass of the technique in order to set the required stages, vertex and pixel shaders, and then you're going to draw your terrain.

```
m_pFilterSimpleTech->GetPassByIndex(0)->Apply(0);
for (int j = 0; j < numRows; j++)
    m_pDevice->DrawIndexed( numIndices, j * numIndices, 0 );
}
```

In my demo, I treated the terrain as a series of rows, where each row contained a triangle strip. Previous to DirectX 10, it might have been better to render the entire heightfield as a triangle list in order to reduce the number of Draw calls. However, in DirectX 10, the performance penalty for calling Draw has been amortized and is significantly less. As a result, I chose to use triangle strips to reduce the number of vertices being sent to the GPU. Feel free to implement the underlying topology of your heightfield however you like.

Now that I've taken care of the C++ code, let's move on to the HLSL. The first thing you're going to do is define a helper function that you will use to obtain the height values from your buffer. The Load function on the templated Buffer class can be used to access the values in any buffer. It takes int2 as the parameter, where the first integer is the index into the buffer and the second is the sample level. This should just be 0, as it's unlikely your buffer has samples. As I mentioned previously, DirectX 10 provides a uniform interface for many types of related resources. The second parameter of the Load method is more predominately used for Texture objects, which may actually have samples:

```
float Height(int index)
{
    return g_Heights.Load(int2(index, 0));
}
```

Now that you've got your helper function in place, let's implement the Filter method. In this method, you declare a normal with the Y component facing up, and then you set the x and z values to be the average of the computed segment normals, depending on whether the current vertex is on the bottom, middle, or top rows, and whether it's on the left, center, or right side of the terrain. Finally, you normalize the vector and return it to the calling method:

```
float3 FilterNormal( float2 pos, int index )
{
    float3 normal = float3(0, 1, 0);
```

```
  if(pos.y == 0)
    normal.z = Height(index) - Height(index + g_NumVertsWide);
  else if(pos.y == g_NumVertsDeep - 1)
    normal.z = Height(index - g_NumVertsWide) - Height(index);
  else
    normal.z = ((Height(index) - Height(index + g_NumVertsWide)) +
          (Height(index - g_NumVertsWide) - Height(index))) * 0.5;
  if(pos.x == 0)
    normal.x = Height(index) - Height(index + 1);
  else if(pos.x == g_NumVertsWide - 1)
    normal.x = Height(index - 1) - Height(index);
  else
    normal.x = ((Height(index) - Height(index + 1)) +
          (Height(index - 1) - Height(index))) * 0.5;
      return normalize(normal);
}
```

For each vertex, you're going to execute the following vertex shader:

```
VS_OUTPUT FilterHeightfieldVS( float2 vPos : POSITION )
{
  VS_OUTPUT Output = (VS_OUTPUT)0;
  float4 position    = 1.0f;
  position.xz       = vPos * g_MetersPerVertex;
```

First, you take the 2D position that was passed in and compute the index into your buffer. Once you've got the index, you use the Load method on the Texture object in order to obtain the height at the current position, and use that to set the Y component of your vertex's position:

```
  // Pull the height from the buffer
  int index        = (vPos.y * g_NumVertsWide) + vPos.x;
  position.y       = g_Heights.Load(int2(index, 0)) * g_MetersPerVertex;
  Output.Position = mul(position, g_ViewProjectionMatrix);
```

Next, you pass the 2D position and the index into the previously shown Filter method. You pass the index into the function in order to prevent having to compute it again, and you pass in the position as the x and z values are used to determine whether the vertex lies on the edge of the terrain:

```
  // Compute the normal using a filter kernel
  float3 vNormalWorldSpace = FilterNormal(vPos, index);
  // Compute simple directional lighting equation
  float3 vTotalLightDiffuse = g_LightDiffuse *
```

```
      max(0,dot(vNormalWorldSpace, g_LightDir));
    Output.Diffuse.rgb = g_MaterialDiffuseColor * vTotalLightDiffuse;
    Output.Diffuse.a   = 1.0f;
    return Output;
}
```

As an additional note about this implementation, with DirectX 10 and the introduction of the geometry shader, it's now possible to generate geometry directly on the GPU. If someone were interested, they could completely avoid the need to pass a mesh to the GPU and instead generate it along with the normals inside of the geometry shader. However, as most games are not bus-bound, there would be no noticeable performance benefit, as simply creating a static vertex buffer and passing it to the GPU each frame requires little overhead by the CPU.

Mesh-Based Terrain

While the previous algorithm works effectively for height-map-based terrain, it's unacceptable for mesh-based terrain. In this case, caves, chasms, overhangs, and waves prevent you from performing any type of optimizations because you can make no guarantees about the direction of the Y component. For this reason, it becomes necessary to compute the full normal. The following algorithm is a fast and efficient method for computing cross-products for mesh-based terrain entirely on the GPU, so long as certain assumptions and constraints are made.

Grid-Mesh Smooth Shading Algorithm

I refer to this algorithm as the *grid-mesh smooth shading* algorithm because it is a combination of two principles. The first principle, smooth shading, was set forth by Henri Gouraud. Gouraud suggested that if you were to compute the normals of each of the facets (surfaces) of a polyhedron, then you could get relatively smooth shading by taking all of the facets that are "attached" to a single vertex and averaging the surface normals.

Gouraud shading is thus a two-stage algorithm for computing the normal at a vertex. The first stage is to compute the surface normals of each of the triangles in the heightfield using cross-product calculations. The second stage is to sum the surface normals attached to any given vertex, and then normalize the result.

The following two equations are the mathematical definitions for the surface and vertex normals:

$$\text{Surface Normal} : \mathbf{N}_s = \mathbf{A} \times \mathbf{B}$$
$$\text{Vertex Normal} : \mathbf{N} = \text{Norm}\left(\Sigma(\mathbf{N}_{si})\right)$$

While I won't demonstrate all the methods here (though they are included in the associated demo), there are actually three different ways for computing the vertex normals that distribute the workload differently. In order of efficiency, they are as follows:

1. Compute both the surface and vertex normals on the CPU.

2. Compute the surface normals on the CPU and the vertex normals on the GPU.

3. Compute both the surface and vertex normals on the GPU.

Until DirectX 10, only the first two options were available and were still expensive, as computing the cross-products for a large number of triangles on the CPU means each frame can become unreasonable. With DirectX 10 and geometry shaders, it is now possible to compute both the surface and vertex normals entirely on the GPU. This method is significantly faster than computing the surface normals on the CPU, and it allows you to get much closer in performance of complex, mesh-based terrain to the methods used for height-map-based terrain.

The geometry shader stage is unique in its functionality in that, unlike the vertex shader stage, which receives a single vertex at a time, or the pixel shader stage, which receives a single pixel at a time, the geometry shader stage can receive a single primitive at a time. With a single triangle, you can compute the cross-product using each of the three points of the triangle and can then stream the surface normal back out of the graphics pipeline to be used in a second pass.

With all of this said, having both the current vertex position and the surface normals only solves half the problem. Without a method for determining which surfaces are attached to the current vertex, there's no way to determine which of the surfaces in the buffer should be summed and normalized. This leads to the grid-mesh portion of the algorithm.

While this algorithm is intended to work with irregular meshes that may contain overhangs, vertical triangles, caves, and so on, one thing must remain consistent—in

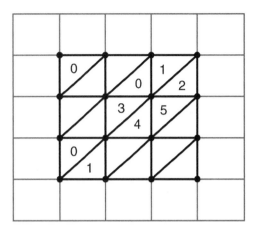

Figure 14.6
A simple grid-based mesh with triangles.

order for you to quickly and predictably determine the surfaces attached to any given vertex, the mesh must have a fixed and well-understood topology. One method of ensuring this is to derive your terrain mesh from a grid. Every grid, even one containing extruded, scaled, or otherwise manipulated triangles, has a unique and predictable topology. Specifically, each vertex in a grid-based mesh has between one and six attached surfaces, depending on the orientation of the triangles and the position of the vertex within the mesh. Consider the diagram of a grid-based mesh in Figure 14.6, which shows a few different cases and the related surface normals.

Having a fixed topology that is based on a grid allows you to compute an index into a buffer, as you did in the Filter method. As before, depending upon which corner or edge the vertex is on will change the number and indices of the surfaces that will be used in computing the normal. Let's take a look at an implementation that uses DirectX 10 to compute both surface and vertex normals on the GPU.

Implementing the Algorithm with DirectX 10 (Again)

As with the Filter method, the first thing you must do is define your vertex format:

```
struct MeshVertex
{
    D3DXVECTOR3 pos;
    unsigned i;
};
```

Rather than having a 2D position vector containing an X and Z component, you've now got a full 3D position. The second parameter, an unsigned integer, which I call i, will be used as the vertex's index. This index was unnecessary with the Filter method because the x and z values combined could be used to compute where in the heightfield the vertex lay. However, the arbitrary nature of vertices within a mesh makes it impossible to determine its relationship to other vertices based solely on its position. Thus the index helps you to identify which normals are attached to any given vertex within the surface normal buffer.

Next, you'll need to create a buffer and associated view resources. Unlike before, this buffer will be used to store your surface normals rather than simple height values, and it will need to be both read from and written to by the geometry shader.

```
ID3D10Buffer* m_pNormalBufferSO;
ID3D10ShaderResourceView* m_pNormalBufferRVSO;
ID3D10EffectShaderResourceVariable* m_pSurfaceNormalsRV;
```

When creating the buffer, you need to make sure that, in addition to being bound as a shader resource, it is also bound as a stream output buffer so that it can be set as a stream output target:

```
void Heightfield::CreateShaderResources( int numSurfaces )
{
  // Create the non-streamed shader resources
  D3D10_BUFFER_DESC desc;
  D3D10_SHADER_RESOURCE_VIEW_DESC SRVDesc;
  // Create output normal buffer for the stream output
  ZeroMemory(&desc, sizeof(D3D10_BUFFER_DESC));
  ZeroMemory(&SRVDesc, sizeof(SRVDesc));
  desc.ByteWidth = numSurfaces * sizeof(D3DXVECTOR4);
  desc.Usage     = D3D10_USAGE_DEFAULT;
  desc.BindFlags = D3D10_BIND_SHADER_RESOURCE | D3D10_BIND_STREAM_OUTPUT;
```

Next, you need to make sure that the buffer format is compatible with the stream output stage and that it can be used as a stream output target. The only format I was able to successfully bind was DXGI_FORMAT_R32G32B32A32_FLOAT. I attempted to get it working with R32G32B32_FLOAT, a full four bytes smaller per buffer element, but the compiler claimed it was an incompatible type. This may suggest the stream output stage must treat each element as a full float4.

```
SRVDesc.Format              = DXGI_FORMAT_R32G32B32A32_FLOAT;
SRVDesc.ViewDimension       = D3D10_SRV_DIMENSION_BUFFER;
SRVDesc.Buffer.ElementWidth = numSurfaces;
```

```
  m_pDevice->CreateBuffer(&desc, NULL, &m_pNormalBufferSO);
  m_pDevice->CreateShaderResourceView(m_pNormalBufferSO, &SRVDesc,
    &m_pNormalBufferRVSO);
}
```

After initializing all of your buffers and updating your mesh positions, the next step is to draw your mesh. As before, you're going to create some local variables, set some necessary constants within the HLSL, and set the input layout, index buffer, and vertex buffers so that the input assembler knows how to construct and process your vertices for use by the vertex shader:

```
void Heightfield::Draw()
{
  int numRows   = m_NumVertsDeep - 1;
  int numIndices = 2 * m_NumVertsWide;
  m_pNumVertsDeep->SetInt(m_NumVertsDeep);
  m_pNumVertsWide->SetInt(m_NumVertsWide);
  m_pMetersPerVertex->SetFloat(m_MetersPerVertex);
  m_pDevice->IASetPrimitiveTopology
    (D3D10_PRIMITIVE_TOPOLOGY_TRIANGLESTRIP);
  m_pDevice->IASetIndexBuffer(m_pIndexBuffer, DXGI_FORMAT_R32_UINT,0);
  UINT offset = 0;
  UINT stride = sizeof(MeshVertex);
  m_pDevice->IASetInputLayout(m_pMeshIL);
  m_pDevice->IASetVertexBuffers(0, 1, &m_pMeshVB, &stride, &offset);
```

Next, you get a chance to take a look at some new stuff. Here you're creating an array of ID3D10ShaderResourceViews containing a single element, NULL, and setting it as the shader resource array of the vertex shader. This is because you're using the same buffer for the stream output stage as input for your vertex shader. In order to do this, you need to ensure that it's not still bound to the vertex shader from a previous pass when you attempt to write to it:

```
  ID3D10ShaderResourceView* pViews[] = {NULL};
  m_pDevice->VSSetShaderResources(0, 1, pViews);
```

Once you've cleared the shader resources attached to slot 0, you're going to set the surface normal buffer as the output for the stream output stage. This makes it so that any vertices you add to the stream get stored within your buffer. Because you don't actually read from that buffer until the second pass, it's also fine to bind it to the vertex shader at this point.

```
  m_pDevice->SOSetTargets(1, &m_pNormalBufferSO, &offset);
  m_pSurfaceNormalsRV->SetResource(m_pNormalBufferRVSO);
```

Unlike the `Filter` method, you take a few additional steps when calling `Draw` here. First, because you're working with a technique that you know has more than one pass, you're going to be polite and actually ask the technique how many passes it has, and then iterate over both:

```
D3D10_TECHNIQUE_DESC desc;
m_pMeshWithNormalMapSOTech->GetDesc(&desc);
for(unsigned i = 0; i < desc.Passes; i++)
{
  m_pMeshWithNormalMapSOTech->GetPassByIndex(i)->Apply(0);
  for (int j = 0; j < numRows; j++)
    m_pDevice->DrawIndexed(numIndices, j * numIndices, 0 );
```

At the end of your first pass, after iterating over each of the rows in your mesh and drawing them, you need to make sure to clear the stream output targets so that in pass 1, you can use the surface normal buffer as an input to the vertex shader.

```
    m_pDevice->SOSetTargets(0, NULL, &offset);
  }
}
```

Next, you move on to the HLSL. While the technique declaration comes last within the HLSL file, I'm going to show it to you here first so you have a clear picture of how the technique is structured and how the two passes are broken down. In the first pass, pass `P0`, you're setting the vertex shader to contain a simple pass-through shader. All this shader does is take the input from the input assembler and pass it along to the geometry shader.

```
GeometryShader gsNormalBuffer = ConstructGSWithSO( CompileShader( gs_4_0,
  SurfaceNormalGS() ), "POSITION.xyzw" );
technique10 MeshWithNormalMapSOTech
{
  pass P0
  {
    SetVertexShader( CompileShader( vs_4_0, PassThroughVS() ) );
    SetGeometryShader( gsNormalBuffer );
    SetPixelShader( NULL );
  }
```

The next part of the declaration is assignment of the geometry shader. For clarity, the geometry shader is built before the pass declaration using the `ConstructGSwithSO` HLSL method. Of importance, the last parameter of the

ConstructGSWithSO method is the output format of the primitives that are added to the streamed output. In this case, you're simply passing out a four-component position value, which, incidentally doesn't represent position, but represents your surface normal vectors. The final part of P0 is setting the pixel shader. Because P0 is strictly for computing your surface normals, you're going to set the pixel shader to NULL.

Once pass 0 is complete, you render your mesh a second time using pass 1. In pass 1, you set a vertex shader that looks almost identical to the vertex shader you used for the Filter method. The primary difference is that this vertex shader calls ComputeNormal instead of FilterNormal, resulting in a different approach to obtaining the vertex normal. Because pass 1 is ultimately responsible for rendering your mesh to the screen, you're going to leave the geometry shader at NULL for this pass and instead provide a pixel shader. The pixel shader is just a standard shader for drawing a pixel at a given point using the color and position interpolated from the previous stage. Note that you also enable depth buffering so that the mesh waves don't draw over themselves:

```
pass P1
{
  SetVertexShader( CompileShader( vs_4_0, RenderNormalMapScene() ) );
  SetGeometryShader( NULL );
  SetPixelShader( CompileShader( ps_4_0, RenderScenePS() ) );
  SetDepthStencilState( EnableDepth, 0 );
}
}
```

Now let's take a look at the most important of those shaders one at a time. The first item on the list is the geometry shader.

```
[maxvertexcount(1)]
void SurfaceNormalGS( triangle GS_INPUT input[3], inout
PointStream<GS_INPUT> PStream )
{
  GS_INPUT Output = (GS_INPUT)0;
  float3 edge1 = input[1].Position - input[0].Position;
  float3 edge2 = input[2].Position - input[0].Position;
  Output.Position.xyz = normalize( cross( edge2, edge1 ) );
  PStream.Append(Output);
}
```

Here you declare a simple geometry shader that takes as input a triangle and a point stream. Inside of the geometry shader, you implement the first part of Gouraud's smooth shading algorithm by computing the cross-product of the provided triangle. Once you've done so, you normalize it, and then add it as a 4-component point to your point stream. This stream, which will be filled with float4 values, will serve as the surface normal buffer in the second pass.

This leads to the second part of Gouraud's smooth shading algorithm. Rather than list the entire vertex shader here, let's focus on the code that actually does most of the work: ComputeNormal.

```
float3 ComputeNormal(uint index)
{
  float3 normal      = 0.0;
  int topVertex      = g_NumVertsDeep - 1;
  int rightVertex    = g_NumVertsWide - 1;
  int normalsPerRow = rightVertex * 2;
  int numRows        = topVertex;
  float top          = normalsPerRow * (numRows - 1);
  int x = index % g_NumVertsWide;
  int z = index / g_NumVertsWide;
  // Bottom
  if(z == 0)
  {
    if(x == 0)
    {
      float3 normal0 = g_SurfaceNormals.Load(int2( 0, 0 ));
      float3 normal1 = g_SurfaceNormals.Load(int2( 1, 0 ));
      normal = normal0 + normal1;
    }
    else if(x == rightVertex)
    {
      index = (normalsPerRow - 1);
      normal = g_SurfaceNormals.Load(int2( index, 0 ));
    }
    else
    {
      index = (2 * x);
      normal = g_SurfaceNormals.Load(int2( index-1, 0 )) +
        g_SurfaceNormals.Load(int2( index,   0 )) +
        g_SurfaceNormals.Load(int2( index+1, 0 ));
    }
  }
}
```

```
// Top
else if(z == topVertex)
{
  if(x == 0)
  {
    normal = g_SurfaceNormals.Load(int2( top, 0 ));
  }
  else if(x == rightVertex)
  {
    index = (normalsPerRow * numRows) - 1;
    normal = g_SurfaceNormals.Load(int2( index,   0 )) +
          g_SurfaceNormals.Load(int2( index-1, 0 ));
  }
  else
  {
    index = top + (2 * x);
    normal = g_SurfaceNormals.Load(int2( index-2, 0)) +
          g_SurfaceNormals.Load(int2( index,   0)) +
          g_SurfaceNormals.Load(int2( index-1, 0));
  }
}
// Middle
else
{
  if(x == 0)
  {
    int index1 = z * normalsPerRow;
    int index2 = index1 - normalsPerRow;
    normal = g_SurfaceNormals.Load(int2( index1,   0 )) +
          g_SurfaceNormals.Load(int2( index1+1, 0 )) +
          g_SurfaceNormals.Load(int2( index2,   0 ));
  }
  else if(x == rightVertex)
  {
    int index1 = (z + 1) * normalsPerRow - 1;
    int index2 = index1 - normalsPerRow;
    normal = g_SurfaceNormals.Load(int2( index1,   0 )) +
          g_SurfaceNormals.Load(int2( index2,   0 )) +
          g_SurfaceNormals.Load(int2( index2-1, 0 ));
  }
  else
  {
    int index1 = (z * normalsPerRow) + (2 * x);
```

```
    int index2 = index1 - normalsPerRow;
    normal = g_SurfaceNormals.Load(int2( index1-1, 0 )) +
        g_SurfaceNormals.Load(int2( index1,   0 )) +
        g_SurfaceNormals.Load(int2( index1+1, 0 )) +
        g_SurfaceNormals.Load(int2( index2-2, 0 )) +
        g_SurfaceNormals.Load(int2( index2-1, 0 )) +
        g_SurfaceNormals.Load(int2( index2,   0 ));
    }
  }
  return normal;
}
```

As with the filter algorithm for height-map-based terrain, the `ComputeNormal` method performs a series of checks to determine whether the vertex is on the left, middle, or right edge, and whether it's on the bottom, center, or top edge of the grid. Depending on the answer, between one and six surface normals are sampled from the buffer, and then summed together. The result is then returned to the main entry function for the vertex shader, where it is normalized and used in computing the final color of the vertex.

Conclusion

The code snippets contained within this article are based on the accompanying demo, which is written in C++ using DirectX 10 and HLSL; it contains not only the algorithms detailed here but also the two remaining methods for computing vertex normals for a grid-based mesh—that is, it computes the surface and vertex normals on the CPU and also computes the surface normals on the CPU while using the GPU for the vertex normals. Please make sure to download those files (see www.courseptr.com/downloads), run the demo for yourself, and evaluate the remaining source code. You can then perform a personal comparison of the performance afforded to you by each method. For an idea of what the demo looks like, refer to Figure 14.7.

As the demo uses DirectX 10 and SM 4.0, you will need a computer running Windows Vista and a compatible video card with the most up-to-date DirectX SDK and drivers in order to successfully run the application.

The limited documentation for the demo can be displayed within the application by pressing the F1 key. Additionally, at the lower-right corner of the screen, there are four controls that can be used to configure the demonstration. The resolution

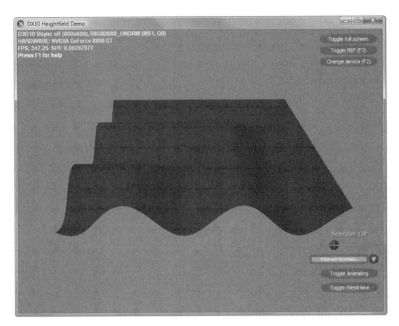

Figure 14.7
A screenshot of the demo program for this article.

slider identifies the number of vertices across and how deep the terrain sample will be. The slider ranges from 17 to 512.

Below the Resolution slider is a combo box that allows the user to select from one of the four different methods of implementation within the demo: Filtered Normals, CPU Normals, GPU Normals, and Streamed Normals.

Below the Normal mode combo boxes are two buttons: Toggle Animation and Toggle Wireframe. No surprise, these either toggle on/off the animation or toggle on/off Wireframe mode, respectively.

References

Walsh, Jeromy. "Normal Computations for Heightfield Lighting." (2005) www.gamedev.net/reference/programming/features/normalheightfield/.

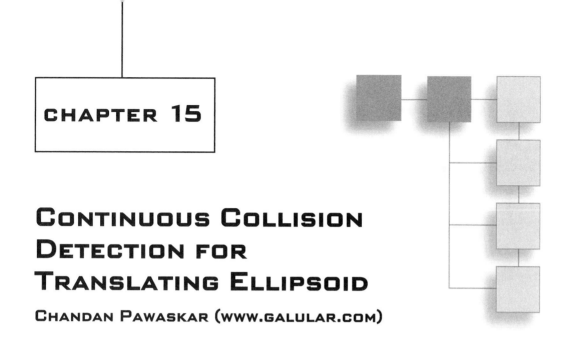

CHAPTER 15

Continuous Collision Detection for Translating Ellipsoid

Chandan Pawaskar (www.galular.com)

Discrete collision detection (overlap test) can be fast and simple to implement, but it suffers from the tunneling effect wherein very thin or fast-moving objects can move through each other without being detected. Things become worse at low frame rates, as objects displace more space between frames.

Continuous collision detection (CCD) doesn't suffer from the tunneling effect, and no collisions are missed even when the frame rate is low. Furthermore, accurate collision detection data, such as *point of contact*, *time of contact*, and *normal of contact*, are readily available.

Paul Nettle in his excellent article titled "General Collision Detection for Games Using Ellipsoids" (www.gamedev.net/reference/articles/article1026.asp) provides details on implementation of CCD for sphere against triangle. At the end of his article, he provides information on how the sphere test could be extended to support ellipsoids. However, the implied statement that the normal to the surface of the ellipsoid passes through its center is incorrect—hence, the approach outlined therein for ellipsoidal collision is misleading and will provide inaccurate results.

In this article, I will look at extending the sphere CCD algorithm described in Paul's article to the ellipsoidal case. I will use a more accurate formulation for the ellipsoid surface normal. (It is assumed that the reader has basic understanding of vectors.)

CCD for Ellipsoids

Consider an ellipsoid (**E**) to be a sphere of radius (rad) that is scaled by Sx, Sy, and Sz along its local x, y, and z axes, respectively (see Figure 15.1). You also constrain the scales such that $Max(Sx,Sy,Sz) = 1$.

For example, $rad = 100$, $(Sx, Sy, Sz) = (1, 0.5, 0.25)$

Position and orientation of **E** are determined by:

Ctr: Center in world space

TMRot: Orientation matrix

Let the triangle be represented by a plane that it lies on {**N**, **d**} (**N** being the plane's normal, and **d** its distance from the origin) and three vertices **V1**, **V2**, and **V3**. You need to see if the ellipsoid collides with the triangle for a displacement $\overline{disp}$. Let dispN be the magnitude of displacement along the plane normal (see Figure 15.2).

Then $dispN = \overline{disp} \cdot \hat{N}$. So if dispN is $>= 0$, there is no collision, as the ellipsoid would be moving away from the plane.

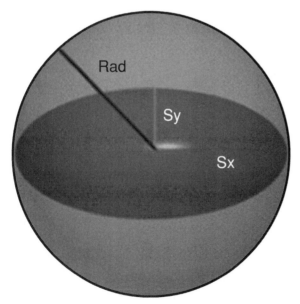

Figure 15.1

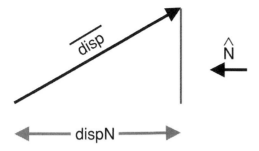

Figure 15.2

The distance of the ellipsoid center from the plane is $ElCtrDisp = Ctr \cdot \hat{N}+d$. It is clear from Figure 15.3 that collision will not occur if $ElCtrDisp - Rad > dispN$. This is an inexpensive check that will allow you to exit the collision detection routing early.

Next you need to find point on ellipsoid that is closest to the plane, namely, **ClsPt**. It's easier to solve this problem if the ellipsoid is axis-aligned. Hence, you transform the plane to the ellipsoid's object space.

The transformed plane is simply $\{\hat{N}_e, ElCtrDisp\}$ where $\hat{N}_e = TMRot^{-1} * \hat{N}$.

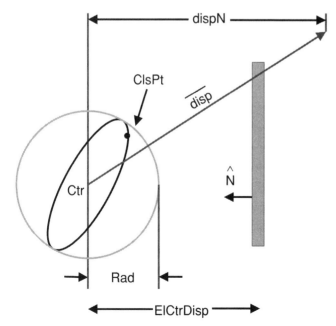

Figure 15.3

See Appendix A at the end of this article for a formulation of point on ellipsoid that is closest to a given plane. Remember to transform the point back to world space.

Now that you have the closest point, you will find its distance from the plane. This will be the ellipsoid-plane separation:

$$\text{elSep} = \text{ClsPt} \cdot \hat{N} + d$$

Let **t** be time defined over the ellipsoid displacement such that at $t = 0$, the ellipsoid is displaced by **0**, and at $t = 1$, the ellipsoid is displaced by $\overline{\text{disp}}$. Then time at which ellipsoid will touch the plane is given by t = elSep / dispN.

If $t > 1$, clearly there is no collision!

The point at which ellipsoid touches the plane is **ClsPtPl** (closest point on plane) and is given by $\text{ClsPtPl} = \text{ClsPt} - \hat{N} * \text{elSep}$.

If you were colliding with an infinite plane, your detection would stop here. However, since you are more interested in colliding with triangles, you need to do a few more checks. First you check to see if **ClsPtPl** is inside the triangle. (See Appendix B at the end of this article for a point-in-triangle test algorithm.) If it is, you are done, as you already have all the collision data:

Time of contact: t

Point of contact: ClsPtPl

E's center of contact: $\text{Ctr} + \overline{\text{disp}} * t$

Contact normal: $\hat{N}$

If **ClsPtPl** is outside triangle, the ellipsoid is probably going to collide with one of the three edges.

It is clear from Figure 15.4 that the ellipsoid will collide with the edge (and point on edge) that is closest to **ClsPtPl**. Let us call this the contact point **CtPt**.

Please see Appendix C for a formulation of distance between point and line segment (along with closest point on line segment). Now you know that the ellipsoid would collide at **CtPt**. To get the time of contact, you shoot a ray from **CtPt** in direction $-\overline{\text{disp}}$ to collide with the ellipsoid. (For a ray-ellipsoid collision algorithm, please see Appendix D.)

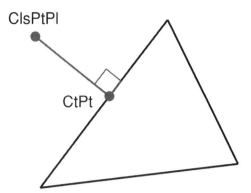

Figure 15.4

The normal of contact is determined using this intersected point. The normal would simply be along the ellipsoid gradient at this point. The equation of the ellipsoid in its object space is

$$x^2/Sx^2 + y^2/Sy^2 + z^2/Sz^2 = Rad^2$$

The gradient is given by $\{2x/Sx^2, 2y/Sy^2, 2z/Sz^2\}$. The 2s can be removed, as you would be normalizing the vector.

Note

The intersection point needs to be transformed to ellipsoid's object space; the gradient is then computed and normalized. This normal is then transformed back to world space.

The collision data is then given by

Time of contact: t

Point of contact: CtPt

E's center of contact: $Ctr + \overline{disp}^*t$

Contact normal: Gradient

Appendix A: Point on Ellipsoid Closest to Given Plane

Let the ellipsoid be defined by $\dfrac{x^2}{Sx^2} + \dfrac{y^2}{Sy^2} + \dfrac{z^2}{Sz^2} = rad^2$.

Let the plane be defined by $ax + by + cz + d = 0$.

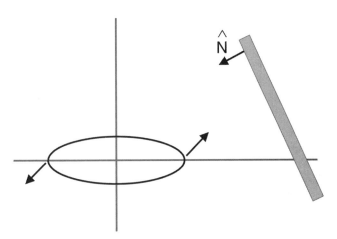

Figure 15.5

As can be seen from Figure 15.5, the closest and farthest point on ellipsoid from plane will be such that the ellipsoid's surface normal at this point will be parallel to the plane's normal.

The ellipsoid's surface normal will point along its gradient

$$grad(E) = \frac{2x}{Sx^2}, \frac{2y}{Sy^2}, \frac{2z}{Sz^2}$$

Hence, for closest and farthest points, you would have

$$\frac{2x}{Sx^2} = ka, \frac{2y}{Sy^2} = kb, \frac{2z}{Sz^2} = kc$$

for some scalar **k**, or,

$$x = \frac{kaSx^2}{2}, y = \frac{kbSy^2}{2}, z = \frac{kcSz^2}{2} \qquad\qquad \text{equation (1)}$$

Substituting this in the equation of the ellipsoid gives you

$$\frac{k^2}{4}\{a^2Sx^2 + b^2Sy^2 + c^2Sz^2\} = rad^2$$

or

$$k = \frac{\pm 2rad}{\left\{ a^2 Sx^2 + b^2 Sy^2 + c^2 Sz^2 \right\}^{1/2}}$$

Substituting the two values for **k** in equation {1} will give you the closest and farthest points on the ellipsoid.

Appendix B: Point-in-Triangle Test

Given a triangle with three vertices **V0**, **V1**, and **V2**, you need to determine if point **P** lies inside the triangle (see Figure 15.6).

Let **E0** = **V1** − **V0** and **E1** = **V2** − **V0** represent two edges of the triangle. Any point **P** lying in the plane of the triangle can be represented by

P = V0 + s0 * E0 + s1 * E1

for some scalars s0 and s1.

This formulation uses the Barycentric coordinates or, put simply, the parallelogram law (notice the parallelogram in Figure 15.6).

Substituting **Q** = **P** − **V0** in the preceding equation gives you

Q = s0 * E0 + s1 * E1

In this equation, you have two unknowns: s0 and s1 (**Q** is known, as **P** is the point that you are testing). To solve for two unknowns, you need to have two equations.

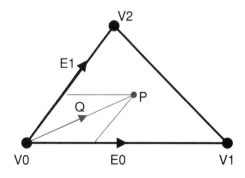

Figure 15.6

Multiplying the previous equation first by **E0** and then **E1** yields two equations that can be solved for the two unknowns:

$$Q \cdot E0 = s0 * E0 \cdot E0 + s1 * E1 \cdot E0$$

$$Q \cdot E1 = s0 * E0 \cdot E1 + s1 * E1 \cdot E1$$

Substituting as follows

$$q0 = \mathbf{Q} \cdot \mathbf{E0}$$

$$q1 = \mathbf{Q} \cdot \mathbf{E1}$$

$$e00 = \mathbf{E0} \cdot \mathbf{E0}$$

$$e01 = \mathbf{E0} \cdot \mathbf{E1}$$

$$e11 = \mathbf{E1} \cdot \mathbf{E1}$$

gives you

$$q0 = s0 * e00 + s1 * e01 \text{ and } q1 = s0 * e01 + s1 * e11$$

Let

$$z0 = e11{}^*q0 - e01{}^*q1$$

$$z1 = e00{}^*q1 - e01{}^*q0$$

$$det = e00{}^*e11 - e01{}^*e01$$

Then, $s0 = z0 / det$ and $s1 = z1 / det$.

P will be inside triangle if

$$0 \leq s0 \leq 1$$

$$0 \leq s1 \leq 1$$

$$s0 + s1 \leq 1$$

or if

$$0 \leq z0 \leq det$$

$$0 \leq z1 \leq det$$

$$z0 + z1 \leq det$$

Appendix C: Distance Between Point and Line Segment

Let a line segment be defined by two points P_1 and P_2. You need to determine the shortest distance (dist) between an arbitrary point V and this line segment (see Figure 15.7).

Direction along P_1 to P_2 is given by $\mathbf{Dir} = \mathbf{Edge} / len$, where $\mathbf{Edge} = P_2 - P_1$ and len = magnitude of $\mathbf{Edge}$.

A point along the line segment is given by

$$P = P_1 + s^*Edge \qquad\qquad\qquad \text{equation (2)}$$

where $0 \leq s \leq 1$, for all other values of s, P lies outside the line segment. Let $VP_1 = V - P_1$ and $V'P_1 = V' - P_1$

The length of $\mathbf{V'P_1}$ is given by $V'P_1 = \mathbf{VP_1} \cdot \mathbf{Dir}$

Then $\mathbf{V'}$ is given by $\mathbf{V'} = \mathbf{P_1} + V'P_1 {}^* \mathbf{Dir}$, where $V'P_1$ is length of $\mathbf{V'P_1}$

Or,

$$\mathbf{V'} = \mathbf{P_1} + V'P_1 * \mathbf{Edge}/len \qquad\qquad \text{equation (3)}$$

Comparing equations {2} and {3} you have

$$s = V'P_1/len$$

If s < 0, then the closest point ($\mathbf{ClsPt}$) is P_1. If s > 1, the closest point is P_2.

For all other cases the closest point will be $\mathbf{V'}$.

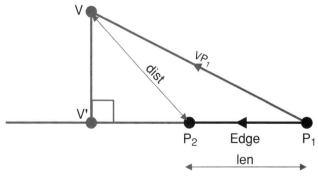

Figure 15.7

The closest distance is then

$$\text{dist} = \parallel \mathbf{V} - \mathbf{ClsPt} \parallel$$

Appendix D: Ray-Ellipsoid Intersection

By transforming the ray to the ellipsoidal space (where the ellipsoid becomes a sphere), the problem reduces to a ray sphere intersection check.

The equation of a sphere of radius r and centered at the origin is given by

$$x^2 + y^2 + z^2 = r^2$$

That is, a point **P** on the sphere satisfies the equation

$$\mathbf{P} \cdot \mathbf{P} = r^2 \qquad\qquad \text{equation (4)}$$

Let the ray originate from **O** and travel along a displacement vector given by **D**. Then a point along the ray is given by

$$\mathbf{P} = \mathbf{O} + t * \mathbf{D} \qquad\qquad \text{equation (5)}$$

where t is some scalar.

At the point of intersection, both the equations are satisfied—that is,

$$r^2 = (\mathbf{O} + t * \mathbf{D}) \cdot (\mathbf{O} + t * \mathbf{D}) \ .$$

or

$$r^2 = \mathbf{O} \cdot \mathbf{O} + t^2 * \mathbf{D} \cdot \mathbf{D} + 2\,t * \mathbf{O} \cdot \mathbf{D}$$

or

$$\mathbf{D} \cdot \mathbf{D} * t^2 + 2\,\mathbf{O} \cdot \mathbf{D} * t + \mathbf{O} \cdot \mathbf{O} - r^2 = 0$$

If you substitute

$$a = \mathbf{D} \cdot \mathbf{D}$$
$$b = 2\,\mathbf{O} \cdot \mathbf{D}$$
$$c = \mathbf{O} \cdot \mathbf{O} - r^2$$

you have a quadratic equation of the form $at^2 + bt + c = 0$, whose solution is given by $t = (-b +/- \text{ Disc }) / 2a$, where discriminant $\text{Disc} = (b^2 - 4ac)^{1/2}$.

There are two possible solutions because a ray can intersect a sphere at two different places. If the discriminant is zero, there is only one solution, and the ray will be tangent to the sphere. If the discriminant is −ve, there is no solution, and the ray will not intersect the sphere.

Since you are interested in the closest intersection (smallest t) only,

$$t = (-b - \text{ Disc }) / 2a$$

Note if $t > 1$, ray displacement **D** is not sufficient to intersect with the sphere.

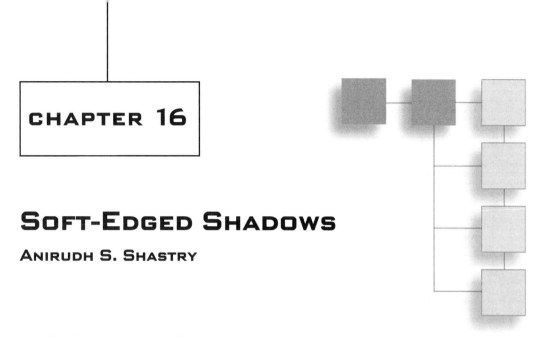

CHAPTER 16

SOFT-EDGED SHADOWS

ANIRUDH S. SHASTRY

Originally, dynamic shadowing techniques were possible only in a limited way. But with the advent of powerful programmable graphics hardware, dynamic shadow techniques have almost completely replaced static techniques, like light mapping, and semi-dynamic techniques, like projected shadows. Two popular dynamic shadowing techniques are shadow volumes and shadow mapping.

A Closer Look

Shadow volumes is a geometry-based technique that requires the extrusion of the geometry in the direction of the light to generate a closed volume. Then, via raycasting, the shadowed portions of the scene can be determined (usually, the stencil buffer is used to simulate raycasting). This technique is pixel-accurate and doesn't suffer from any aliasing problems; but as with any technique, it suffers from its share of disadvantages. Two major problems with this technique are that it is heavily geometry-dependent and fill-rate intensive. Because of this, shadow mapping is slowly becoming more popular.

Shadow mapping, on the other hand, is an image space technique that involves rendering the scene depth from the light's point of view and using this depth information to determine which portions of the scene are in shadow. Though this technique has several advantages, it suffers from aliasing artifacts and z-fighting. But there are solutions to this, and since the advantages outweigh the disadvantages, this will be my technique of choice in this article.

Soft Shadows

Hard shadows destroy the realism of a scene. Hence, you need to fake soft shadows in order to improve the scene's visual quality (Figure 16.1). A lot of over-zealous Ph.D. students have come up with papers describing soft shadowing techniques, but in reality, most of these techniques are not viable in real time, at least when considering complex scenes. Until we have hardware that can overcome some of the limitations of these techniques, we will need to stick to more down-to-earth methods.

Figure 16.1

In this article, I present an image space method to generate soft-edged shadows using shadow maps. This method doesn't generate perfectly soft shadows (no umbra-penumbra). But it not only solves the aliasing problems of shadow mapping, it also improves the visual quality by achieving aesthetically pleasing soft-edged shadows.

So How Does It Work?

First, you generate the shadow map as usual by rendering the scene depth from the light's point of view into a floating-point buffer. Then, instead of rendering the scene with shadows, you render the shadowed regions into a screen-sized buffer. Now, you can blur this using a bloom filter and project it back onto the scene in screen space. Sounds simple, right?

In this article, I'll only deal with spot lights, but this technique can easily be extended to handle point lights as well. Here are the steps:

1. Generate the shadow map as usual by writing the scene depth into a floating-point buffer.

2. Render the shadowed portions of the scene after depth comparison into fixed-point texture, without any lighting.

3. Blur the buffer using a bloom filter. (Though I use a separable Gaussian filter in this article, any filter can be used.)

4. Project the blurred buffer onto the scene in screen space to get cool soft-edged shadows, along with full lighting.

Step 1: Rendering the Shadow Map

First, you need to create a texture that can hold the scene depth. Since you need to use this as a render target, you will also need to create a surface that holds the texture's surface data. The texture must be a floating-point one because of the large range of depth values. The R32F format has sufficient precision, so I'll use it. Here's the codelet used to create the texture:

```
// Create the shadow map
if( FAILED( g_pd3dDevice->CreateTexture( SHADOW_MAP_SIZE,
SHADOW_MAP_SIZE, 1, D3DUSAGE_RENDERTARGET, D3DFMT_R32F,
D3DPOOL_DEFAULT, &g_pShadowMap, NULL ) ) )
{
   MessageBox(g_hWnd, "Unable to create shadow map!",
             "Error", MB_OK | MB_ICONERROR);
   return E_FAIL;
}

// Grab the texture's surface
g_pShadowMap->GetSurfaceLevel( 0, &g_pShadowSurf );
```

Now to generate the shadow map, you need to render the scene's depth to the shadow map. To do this, you must render the scene with the light's world-view projection matrix. Here's how you build that matrix:

```
// Ordinary view matrix
D3DXMatrixLookAtLH( &matView, &vLightPos, &vLightAim, &g_vUp );
// Projection matrix for the light
D3DXMatrixPerspectiveFovLH( &matProj, D3DXToRadian(30.0f), 1.0f, 1.0f,
  1024.0f );
// Concatenate the world matrix with the above two
// to get the required matrix
matLightViewProj = matWorld * matView * matProj;
```

Here are vertex and pixel shaders for rendering the scene depth:

```
// Shadow generation vertex shader
struct VSOUTPUT_SHADOW
{
    float4 vPosition    : POSITION;
    float  fDepth       : TEXCOORD0;
};

VSOUTPUT_SHADOW VS_Shadow( float4 inPosition : POSITION )
{   // Output struct
    VSOUTPUT_SHADOW OUT = (VSOUTPUT_SHADOW)0;
    // Output the transformed position
    OUT.vPosition = mul( inPosition, g_matLightViewProj );
    // Output the scene depth
    OUT.fDepth = OUT.vPosition.z;
    return OUT;
}
```

Here, you multiply the position by the light's world-view projection matrix (g_matLightViewProj) and use the transformed position's z value as the depth. In the pixel shader, you output the depth as the color:

```
float4  PS_Shadow( VSOUTPUT_SHADOW IN ) : COLOR0
{   // Output the scene depth
    return float4( IN.fDepth, IN.fDepth, IN.fDepth, 1.0f );
}
```

Voilà! You have the shadow map. Figure 16.2 is a grayscale version of the shadow map: dark indicates smaller depth values, whereas light indicates larger depth values.

Figure 16.2

Step 2: Rendering the Shadowed Scene into a Buffer

Next, you need to render the shadowed portions of the scene to an off-screen buffer so that you can blur it and project it back onto the scene. To do that, you first render the shadowed portions of the scene into a screen-sized fixed-point texture:

```
// Create the screen-sized buffer map
if( FAILED( g_pd3dDevice->CreateTexture( SCREEN_WIDTH,
SCREEN_HEIGHT, 1, D3DUSAGE_RENDERTARGET, D3DFMT_A8R8G8B8,
D3DPOOL_DEFAULT, &g_pScreenMap, NULL ) ) )
{
    MessageBox( g_hWnd, "Unable to create screen map!",
                "Error", MB_OK | MB_ICONERROR );
    return E_FAIL;
}
// Grab the texture's surface
g_pScreenMap->GetSurfaceLevel( 0, & g_pScreenSurf );
```

To get the projective texture coordinates, you need a "texture" matrix that will map the position from projection space to texture space:

```
// Generate the texture matrix
float fTexOffs = 0.5 + (0.5 / (float)SHADOW_MAP_SIZE);
D3DXMATRIX matTexAdj( 0.5f,      0.0f,      0.0f,      0.0f,
                      0.0f,     -0.5f,      0.0f,      0.0f,
```

```
                              0.0f,        0.0f,      1.0f,   0.0f,
                              fTexOffs,    fTexOffs,  0.0f,   1.0f );
```

```
matTexture = matLightViewProj * matTexAdj;
```

You get the shadow factor as usual by depth comparison, but instead of outputting the completely lit scene, you output only the shadow factor. Here are the vertex and pixel shaders that do the job:

```
// Shadow mapping vertex shader
struct VSOUTPUT_UNLIT
{
    float4 vPosition    : POSITION;
    float4 vTexCoord    : TEXCOORD0;
    float  fDepth       : TEXCOORD1;
};

VSOUTPUT_UNLIT VS_Unlit( float4 inPosition : POSITION )
{   // Output struct
    VSOUTPUT_UNLIT OUT = (VSOUTPUT_UNLIT)0;

    // Output the transformed position
    OUT.vPosition = mul( inPosition, g_matWorldViewProj );

    // Output the projective texture coordinates
    OUT.vTexCoord = mul( inPosition, g_matTexture );

    // Output the scene depth
    OUT.fDepth = mul( inPosition, g_matLightViewProj ).z;

    return OUT;
}
```

You use percentage closer filtering (PCF) to smooth out the jagged edges. To "do" PCF, you simply sample the eight (I'm using a 3×3 PCF kernel here) surrounding texels along with the center texel and take the average of all the depth comparisons:

```
// Shadow mapping pixel shader
float4  PS_Unlit( VSOUTPUT_UNLIT IN ) : COLOR0
{   // Generate the 9 texture co-ordinates for a 3x3 PCF kernel
    float4 vTexCoords[9];
```

```
// Texel size
float fTexelSize = 1.0f / 1024.0f;

// Generate the texture co-ordinates for the
// specified depth-map size
// 4 3 5
// 1 0 2
// 7 6 8
vTexCoords[0] = IN.vTexCoord;
vTexCoords[1] = IN.vTexCoord + float4( -fTexelSize, 0.0f, 0.0f, 0.0f );
vTexCoords[2] = IN.vTexCoord + float4(  fTexelSize, 0.0f, 0.0f, 0.0f );
vTexCoords[3] = IN.vTexCoord + float4( 0.0f, -fTexelSize, 0.0f, 0.0f );
vTexCoords[6] = IN.vTexCoord + float4( 0.0f,  fTexelSize, 0.0f, 0.0f );
vTexCoords[4] = IN.vTexCoord + float4( -fTexelSize, -fTexelSize, 0.0f, 0.0f );
vTexCoords[5] = IN.vTexCoord + float4(  fTexelSize, -fTexelSize, 0.0f, 0.0f );
vTexCoords[7] = IN.vTexCoord + float4( -fTexelSize,  fTexelSize, 0.0f, 0.0f );
vTexCoords[8] = IN.vTexCoord + float4(  fTexelSize,  fTexelSize, 0.0f, 0.0f );
// Sample each of them, checking whether the pixel
// under test is shadowed or not
float fShadowTerms[9];
float fShadowTerm = 0.0f;
for( int i = 0; i < 9; i++ )
{
    float A = tex2Dproj( ShadowSampler, vTexCoords[i] ).r;
    float B = (IN.fDepth - 0.1f);

    // Texel is shadowed
    fShadowTerms[i] = A < B ? 0.0f : 1.0f;
    fShadowTerm     += fShadowTerms[i];

}
// Get the average
fShadowTerm /= 9.0f;
return fShadowTerm;
}
```

The screen buffer is good to go (see Figure 16.3)! Now all you need to do is blur this and project it back onto the scene in screen space.

Step 3: Blurring the Screen Buffer

You use a separable Gaussian filter to blur the screen buffer, but you could also use a Poisson filter. The render targets this time are A8R8G8B8 textures

Figure 16.3

accompanied by corresponding surfaces. You need two render targets, one for the horizontal pass and the other for the vertical pass:

```
// Create the blur maps
for( int i = 0; i < 2; i++ )
{
    if( FAILED( g_pd3dDevice->CreateTexture( SCREEN_WIDTH, SCREEN_HEIGHT,
    1, D3DUSAGE_RENDERTARGET, D3DFMT_A8R8G8B8, D3DPOOL_DEFAULT,
    &g_pBlurMap[i],
    NULL ) ) )
    {
        MessageBox( g_hWnd, "Unable to create blur map!",
                    "Error", MB_OK | MB_ICONERROR );
        return E_FAIL;
    }
    // Grab the texture's surface
    g_pBlurMap[i]->GetSurfaceLevel( 0, & g_pBlurSurf[i] );
}
```

You generate 15 Gaussian offsets and their corresponding weights using the following functions:

```
float GetGaussianDistribution( float x, float y, float rho )
{
```

```
    float g = 1.0f / sqrt( 2.0f * 3.141592654f * rho * rho );
    return g * exp( -(x * x + y * y) / (2 * rho * rho) );
}


void GetGaussianOffsets( bool bHorizontal, D3DXVECTOR2 vViewportTexelSize,
D3DXVECTOR2* vSampleOffsets, float* fSampleWeights)
{   // Get the center texel offset and weight
    fSampleWeights[0] = 1.0f * GetGaussianDistribution( 0, 0, 2.0f );
    vSampleOffsets[0] = D3DXVECTOR2( 0.0f, 0.0f );
    // Get the offsets and weights for the remaining taps
    if( bHorizontal )
    {
        for( int i = 1; i < 15; i += 2 )
        {
            vSampleOffsets[i + 0] = D3DXVECTOR2( i * vViewportTexelSize.x, 0.0f );
            vSampleOffsets[i + 1] = D3DXVECTOR2( -i * vViewportTexelSize.x, 0.0f );
            fSampleWeights[i + 0] = 2.0f * GetGaussianDistribution( float(i + 0),
              0.0f, 3.0f );
            fSampleWeights[i + 1] = 2.0f * GetGaussianDistribution( float(i + 1),
              0.0f, 3.0f );
        }
    }
    else
    {
        for( int i = 1; i < 15; i += 2 )
        {
            vSampleOffsets[i + 0] = D3DXVECTOR2( 0.0f,
            i * vViewportTexelSize.y );
            vSampleOffsets[i + 1] = D3DXVECTOR2( 0.0f,
            -i * vViewportTexelSize.y );
            fSampleWeights[i + 0] = 2.0f * GetGaussianDistribution
            ( 0.0f, float(i + 0), 3.0f );
            fSampleWeights[i + 1] = 2.0f * GetGaussianDistribution
            ( 0.0f, float(i + 1), 3.0f );
        }
    }
}
```

To blur the screen buffer, you set the blur map as the render target and render a screen-sized quad with the following vertex and pixel shaders:

```
// Gaussian filter vertex shader
struct VSOUTPUT_BLUR
```

```
{
    float4 vPosition    : POSITION;
    float2 vTexCoord    : TEXCOORD0;
};

VSOUTPUT_BLUR VS_Blur( float4 inPosition : POSITION, float2 inTexCoord :
TEXCOORD0 )
{   // Output struct
    VSOUTPUT_BLUR OUT = (VSOUTPUT_BLUR)0;
    // Output the position
    OUT.vPosition = inPosition;
    // Output the texture coordinates
    OUT.vTexCoord = inTexCoord;
    return OUT;
}


// Horizontal blur pixel shader
float4 PS_BlurH( VSOUTPUT_BLUR IN ): COLOR0
{   // Accumulated color
    float4 vAccum = float4( 0.0f, 0.0f, 0.0f, 0.0f );
    // Sample the taps (g_vSampleOffsets holds the texel offsets
    // and g_fSampleWeights holds the texel weights)
    for(int i = 0; i < 15; i++ )
    {
        vAccum += tex2D( ScreenSampler, IN.vTexCoord + g_vSampleOffsets[i] )
        * g_fSampleWeights[i];
    }
    return vAccum;
}


// Vertical blur pixel shader
float4 PS_BlurV( VSOUTPUT_BLUR IN ): COLOR0
{   // Accumulated color
    float4 vAccum = float4( 0.0f, 0.0f, 0.0f, 0.0f );
    // Sample the taps (g_vSampleOffsets holds the texel offsets and
    // g_fSampleWeights holds the texel weights)
    for( int i = 0; i < 15; i++ )
    {
        vAccum += tex2D( BlurHSampler, IN.vTexCoord + g_vSampleOffsets[i] )
        * g_fSampleWeights[i];
    }
    return vAccum;
}
```

There, the blur maps are ready. To increase the blurriness of the shadows, increase the texel sampling distance. The last step, of course, is to project the blurred map back onto the scene in screen space. The first Gaussian pass is shown in Figure 16.4, and the second Gaussian pass is shown in Figure 16.5.

Figure 16.4

Figure 16.5

Step 4: Rendering the Shadowed Scene

To project the blur map onto the scene, you render the scene as usual but project the blur map using screen-space coordinates. You use the clip space position with some hard-coded math to generate the screen-space coordinates. The following vertex and pixel shaders render the scene with per-pixel lighting along with shadows:

```
struct VSOUTPUT_SCENE
{
    float4 vPosition      : POSITION;
    float2 vTexCoord      : TEXCOORD0;
    float4 vProjCoord     : TEXCOORD1;
    float4 vScreenCoord   : TEXCOORD2;
    float3 vNormal        : TEXCOORD3;
    float3 vLightVec      : TEXCOORD4;
    float3 vEyeVec        : TEXCOORD5;
};
// Scene vertex shader
VSOUTPUT_SCENE VS_Scene( float4 inPosition : POSITION, float3 inNormal :
NORMAL, float2 inTexCoord : TEXCOORD0 )
{
    VSOUTPUT_SCENE OUT = (VSOUTPUT_SCENE)0;
    // Output the transformed position
    OUT.vPosition = mul( inPosition, g_matWorldViewProj );
    // Output the texture coordinates
    OUT.vTexCoord = inTexCoord;
    // Output the projective texture coordinates
    // (you use this to project the spot texture down onto the scene)
    OUT.vProjCoord = mul( inPosition, g_matTexture );
    // Output the screen-space texture coordinates
    OUT.vScreenCoord.x = ( OUT.vPosition.x * 0.5 + OUT.vPosition.w * 0.5 );
    OUT.vScreenCoord.y = ( OUT.vPosition.w * 0.5 - OUT.vPosition.y * 0.5 );
    OUT.vScreenCoord.z = OUT.vPosition.w;
    OUT.vScreenCoord.w = OUT.vPosition.w;
    // Get the world space vertex position
    float4 vWorldPos = mul( inPosition, g_matWorld );
    // Output the world space normal
    OUT.vNormal = mul( inNormal, g_matWorldIT );
    // Move the light vector into tangent space
    OUT.vLightVec = g_vLightPos.xyz - vWorldPos.xyz;
    // Move the eye vector into tangent space
    OUT.vEyeVec = g_vEyePos.xyz - vWorldPos.xyz;
    return OUT;
}
```

You add an additional spot term by projecting down a spot texture from the light. This not only simulates a spot lighting effect, but it also cuts out parts of the scene outside the shadow map. The spot map is projected down using standard projective texturing:

```
float4 PS_Scene( VSOUTPUT_SCENE IN ) : COLOR0
{   // Normalize the normal, light and eye vectors
    IN.vNormal   = normalize( IN.vNormal );
    IN.vLightVec = normalize( IN.vLightVec );
    IN.vEyeVec   = normalize( IN.vEyeVec );
    // Sample the color and normal maps
    float4 vColor  = tex2D( ColorSampler, IN.vTexCoord );
    // Compute the ambient, diffuse and specular lighting terms
    float ambient  = 0.0f;
    float diffuse  = max( dot( IN.vNormal, IN.vLightVec ), 0 );
    float specular = pow(max(dot( 2 * dot( IN.vNormal, IN.vLightVec )
                   * IN.vNormal - IN.vLightVec, IN.vEyeVec ), 0 ), 8 );
    if( diffuse == 0 ) specular = 0;
    // Grab the shadow term
    float fShadowTerm = tex2Dproj( BlurVSampler, IN.vScreenCoord );
    // Grab the spot term
    float fSpotTerm = tex2Dproj( SpotSampler, IN.vProjCoord );
    // Compute the final color
    return (ambient * vColor) +
        (diffuse * vColor * g_vLightColor *
    fShadowTerm * fSpotTerm)
        + (specular * vColor * g_vLightColor.a *
    fShadowTerm
        * fSpotTerm);
}
```

That's it! You have soft-edged shadows that look quite nice! The advantage of this technique is that it completely removes edge-aliasing artifacts that the shadow mapping technique suffers from. Another advantage is that you can generate soft shadows for multiple lights with a small memory overhead. When dealing with multiple lights, all you need is one shadow map per light, whereas the screen and blur buffers can be common to all the lights! Finally, this technique can be applied to both shadow maps and shadow volumes, so irrespective of the shadowing technique, you can generate soft-edged shadows with this method. One disadvantage is that this method is a wee bit fill-rate intensive due to the Gaussian filter. This can be minimized by using smaller blur buffers and slightly sacrificing the visual quality.

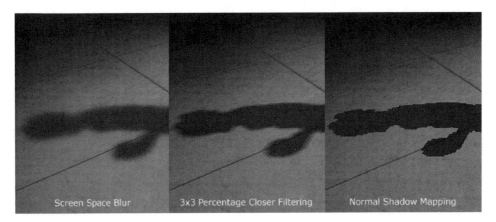

Figure 16.6

Figure 16.6 shows a comparison between the approach mentioned here, 3x3 percentage closer filtering, and normal shadow mapping.

If you have any doubts, questions, or comments, please feel free to e-mail me at anidex@yahoo.com. The source code for these examples is available on the book's companion web site at www.courseptr.com/downloads.

References

Brabec, Stefan and Hans-Peter Seidel. "Hardware-Accelerated Rendering of Antialiased Shadows with Shadow Maps." Computer Graphics Group, Max-Planck-Institut fur Infomatik (www.mpi-inf.mpg.de/∼brabec/doc/brabec_cgi01.pdf).

Everitt, Cass, Ashu Rege, and Cem Cebenoyan. "Hardware Shadow Mapping." (http://developer.nvidia.com/object/hwshadowmap_paper.html).

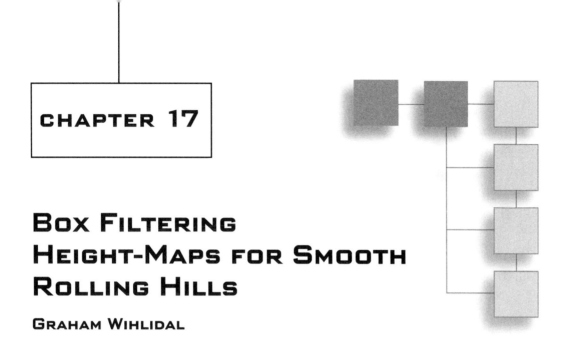

CHAPTER 17

Box Filtering
Height-Maps for Smooth
Rolling Hills

Graham Wihlidal

Real-time terrain is an extremely common element within most 3D engines and generally serves as the building block for outdoor scenes. One of the most common methods of terrain rendering is using height values to perform displacement mapping on a flat mesh grid—a method of visualizing geometry based on a source image and scaling factors for vertex positioning. Using this technique for terrain results in sharp edges, and it is generally something to avoid when developing the visuals for a cutting-edge game, especially if the environment for the game is best suited with smooth hills.

The sharp edges produced when working with height-maps generally result from noise in the source image, and they can be removed using one of many convolution filters. The easiest type of convolution filter to implement is box filtering, and will be utilized in this article to remove noise present in terrain height-maps prior to rendering.

Box Filtering Technique

Box filtering, also known as *average* or *mean filtering*, is a method of reducing the intensity variation between pixels in an image and is commonly used to reduce noise. This type of filtering is accomplished by replacing each pixel value with the average value of its surrounding neighbors, including itself. Doing so removes large intensity variations between pixels and produces a much smoother displacement map.

A *convolution filter* is a simple mathematical operation commonly used in image processing operations. Convolution filters provide a way of multiplying two numerical arrays together, generally of different sizes but of the same dimensionality, to produce a third numerical array, which is the result of the filter operation. Of the two input arrays, one is generally the source image to process, and the second array is commonly referred to as a filtering or convolution kernel. The resultant array has the same dimensionality as the source image array.

The convolution is performed by sliding the filtering kernel over the image through all positions where the kernel fits within the boundaries of the image. This is not always the case in regard to edge smoothing though, as some implementations handle bounds checking so that the edges may be filtered as well.

Box filtering can be thought of as a convolution filter because it too is based around a filtering kernel. This kernel represents the size of the surrounding area that will be sampled. The most common convolution filter for the box technique is a 3x3 cell size, as shown in Figure 17.1. A larger kernel can be used for severe smoothing, or several iterations of a smaller kernel can be used to achieve similar results.

$\dfrac{1}{9}$	$\dfrac{1}{9}$	$\dfrac{1}{9}$
$\dfrac{1}{9}$	$\dfrac{1}{9}$	$\dfrac{1}{9}$
$\dfrac{1}{9}$	$\dfrac{1}{9}$	$\dfrac{1}{9}$

Simple 3×3 Filter Kernel

Figure 17.1
A 3x3 cell for a convolution filter.

Using this technique, you can box filter any terrain height-map and produce smooth rolling hills with hardly any noticeable edges.

Algorithm Example

```
void BoxFilterHeightMap(unsigned long width, unsigned long height,
                        float*& heightMap, bool smoothEdges)
{ //      width: Width of the height map in bytes
  //     height: Height of the height map in bytes
  // heightMap: Pointer to your height map data

  // Temporary values for traversing single dimensional arrays
  long x = 0;
  long z = 0;

  long  widthClamp = (smoothEdges) ?  width : width  - 1;
  long heightClamp = (smoothEdges) ? height : height - 1;

  // [Optimization] Calculate bounds ahead of time
  unsigned int bounds = width * height;

  // Validate requirements
  if (!heightMap)
    return;

  // Allocate the result
  float* result = new float[bounds];

  // Make sure memory was allocated
  if (!result)
    return;

  for (z = (smoothEdges) ? 0 : 1; z < heightClamp; ++z)
  {
    for (x = (smoothEdges) ? 0 : 1; x < widthClamp; ++x)
    { // Sample a 3x3 filtering grid based on surrounding neighbors
      float value = heightMap[x + z * width];
      float cellAverage = 1.0f;

      // Sample top row
      if (((x - 1) + (z - 1) * width) >= 0 &&
          ((x - 1) + (z - 1) * width) < bounds)
      {
        value += heightMap[(x - 1) + (z - 1) * width];
        ++cellAverage;
      }
      if (((x - 0) + (z - 1) * width) > = 0 &&
```

```
      ((x - 0) + (z - 1) * width) < bounds)
{
  value + = heightMap[(x     ) + (z - 1) * width];
  ++cellAverage;
}


if (((x + 1) + (z - 1) * width) >= 0 &&
    ((x + 1) + (z - 1) * width) < bounds)
{
  value + = heightMap[(x + 1) + (z - 1) * width];
  ++cellAverage;
}
// Sample middle row

if (((x - 1) + (z - 0) * width) >= 0 &&
    ((x - 1) + (z - 0) * width) < bounds)
{
  value + = heightMap[(x - 1) + (z     ) * width];
  ++cellAverage;
}


// Sample center point (will always be in bounds)
value + = heightMap[x + z * width];

if (((x + 1) + (z - 0) * width) >= 0 &&
    ((x + 1) + (z - 0) * width) < bounds)
{
  value + = heightMap[(x + 1) + (z     ) * width];
  ++cellAverage;
}


// Sample bottom row
if (((x - 1) + (z + 1) * width) >= 0 &&
    ((x - 1) + (z + 1) * width) < bounds)
{
  value + = heightMap[(x - 1) + (z + 1) * width];
  ++cellAverage;
}


if (((x - 0) + (z + 1) * width) >= 0 &&
    ((x - 0) + (z + 1) * width) < bounds)
{
  value + = heightMap[(x     ) + (z + 1) * width];
```

```
        ++cellAverage;
    }

    if (((x + 1) + (z + 1) * width) >= 0 &&
        ((x + 1) + (z + 1) * width) < bounds)
    {
      value + = heightMap[(x + 1) + (z + 1) * width];
      ++cellAverage;
    }

    // Store the result
    result[x + z * width] = value / cellAverage;
  }
}

// Release the old array
delete [] heightMap;

// Store the new one
heightMap = result;
}
```

Screenshots

Figure 17.2
Unfiltered.

Figure 17.3
Filtered.

Conclusion

I would like to point out that box filtering is not the only solution to smoothing sharp edges in terrain and generally will not be a decent convolution filter to use in certain situations. For example, if you want to have sharp cliffs and canyons, box filtering will smooth your cliffs into a gentle slope. In this case, what you would want to add to your filtering operation is edge detection, also known as a *smart blur*, which smoothes noise patterns without adversely affecting sharpness or fine details in the height-map. Using this filter method will smooth noise but leave your cliffs and canyons recognizable as such.

The example provided in this article is simplistic, and even though the algorithm is fairly optimized, a couple of optimizations were neglected to preserve readability. The out-of-bounds testing could be simplified further, and the loop conditionals could also be evaluated prior to processing.

The ability to specify whether or not to perform edge smoothing is dependent upon your implementation. Having the option to disable edge smoothing will allow terrain blocks to be tile-able, as long as the height-map was designed properly. With edge smoothing and multiple blocks of terrain, cracks would appear between the blocks and skirting would be required to remove them.

Terrain rendering is a popular and important topic for 3D graphics, and height-mapping is just one method of visualizing terrain geometry. It is my intent with this article to help improve the quality of your terrain engine using box filtering as a simple yet effective way of removing sharp edges.

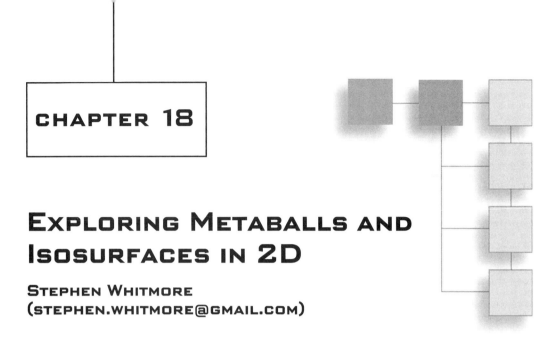

CHAPTER 18

Exploring Metaballs and Isosurfaces in 2D

Stephen Whitmore
(stephen.whitmore@gmail.com)

In the history of game development, there has always been a "standard" means to represent data in the game world. During the 2D era the world and its components were shown by using sprites—collections of pixels to form an image. As the industry moved into three dimensions, this standard format became the 3D model—models representing the world, characters, and objects as collections of vertices in 3D space.

Both (arguably) represent the most basic element that can be used in the given number of dimensions, but still allow for the greatest amount of speed. Making things run as fast as possible has always been a critical element in the game industry.

But what about other data representations? Aren't there other means of storing information about a given "thing" in the game world aside from sprites and models? They exist but generally don't succeed in quite reaching into the industry of game development. The premise of this article is to show that metaballs and isosurfaces in particular are a feasible data representation for game developers to consider.

Overview

The goals of this article are three-fold:

- To discuss the history, concept, and implementation of metaballs and isosurfaces.

- To examine the current applications of isosurfaces in the game and graphics industries and their possible future.

▪ To investigate the performance issues involved with isosurfaces and some existing optimizations/approximations.

What Are Metaballs?

Metaballs largely made their introduction in the 1990s through the *demoscene*: groups of enthusiastic programmers and artists that aimed to create graphical/musical effects that pushed the known limits of older hardware, such as the Commodore 64 and Amiga. The goal of demosceners was to create audio-visual effects in real time that would impress viewers and confound other demoscene programmers with how the effect was implemented. One such effect that gained popularity was metaballs: squishy circular objects that had an organic look and feel to them (see Figure 18.1).

The main allure to metaballs is their tendency to meld into other metaballs nearby, thus creating smoothly formed shapes. Well, how are these objects represented, and why aren't they being used in real time more often? To discuss this, I will have to talk about the subset of which metaballs is a member: isosurfaces.

What is an isosurface? Although an isosurface generally refers to 3D space, it will be seen that it is very easily adapted to two dimensions. This article will focus entirely on 2D metaballs and isosurfaces. Simply put, an *isosurface* is a surface created by applying one or more functions—whose domain is the entire real 2D plane—onto the screen (or game map). An isosurface is a level set of this function.

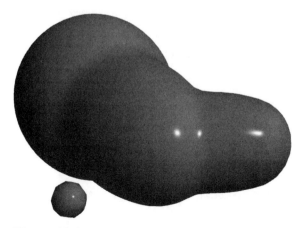

Figure 18.1
Metaballs—note how they have a tendency to "merge" with nearby metaballs.

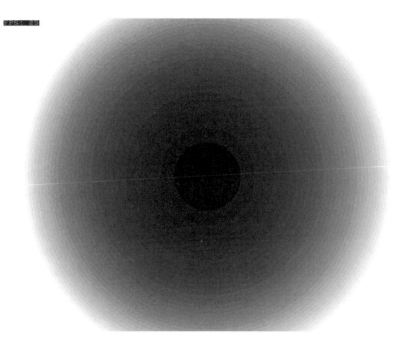

Figure 18.2
An image where pixel brightness corresponds to distance from the center of the screen.

For those of you who are not already familiar with the subject, just what does this mean? Pretend you had a function over the 2D plane (read: a function that has a certain resulting value, given any X and Y) that looked like this:

```
F(x,y) = (x - x0) ^2 + (y - y0) ^2
```

You might recognize this as looking similar to the equation for distance from the point (x0,y0). Well, what would this function look like if you drew it on the 2D plane at some arbitrary point? It might look something like Figure 18.2, if distances are highlighted.

From this it is clear that any given X and Y coordinate will have a value corresponding to it, with said value becoming larger and larger as it gets farther from the center (x0,y0). It's sort of pretty, but how is this useful? It's not really an isosurface after all. As I said above, an isosurface is a level set of this function.

What the heck does that mean? It means that the surface is composed of all points on your screen/world that are equal to a certain constant value. To make that a little more clear, let's look at a modification to the previous function:

```
F(x,y) = (x - x0)^2 + (y - y0)^2 = R^2
```

Figure 18.3
Circle generated by a metaball-like function.

This is starting to look very familiar as the equation for a circle in 2D space. As shown in Figure 18.3, it shouldn't be a surprise what you get if you were to draw this equation over the 2D plane. It's a plain circle, nothing more. I said that an isosurface is made up of all of the points that are equal to a certain value across the 2D plane. This circle is a simple isosurface, which is composed of just that: every single point in the 2D plane has a distance of exactly R units from the center of the circle. After all of that talk of level sets, it turns out that these isosurfaces really aren't that complicated after all.

In fact, breaking down the word "isosurface," you see "iso," meaning "the same," and "surface," referring to something that is solid and flat. By taking the set of all points in the 2D plane that exactly meet the radius of the circle, you see just that: a surface created by all of the values in X and Y that meet the same value required by the function. Hardly rocket science!

But surely you're now wondering, "If an isosurface is just something simple like a circle, then how do I use this information to make something that looks neat, like that 3D image?"

Creating Meta-Things

Let's take a look at a simple implementation for metaballs.

A Simple 2D Implementation

Before stepping into more explanations and equations, here is the basic algorithm that I will be using for rendering metaballs to the screen:

1. Iterate through every pixel on the screen.

2. Iterate through every metaball in the world.

3. Calculate that metaball's function for the current pixel, and add it to that coordinate's current value.

So for every frame you want to render featuring metaballs, you want to examine every pixel, and then do a summation of all of the metaballs' functions on each of these pixels. What do I mean by a summation and the metaballs' functions? Each metaball (or "meta-thing") is defined by a function over the X/Y plane. As I said in the previous example, you create a circular isosurface with the following function:

```
F(x,y) = (x - x0)^2 + (y - y0)^2 = R^2
```

In order to have metaballs influence other metaballs that are nearby (thus creating that gooey effect), you need to add a little more complexity to the equation in order to achieve the effect.

Equation of a Metaball

As an end result, you want to eventually achieve something like what's shown in Figure 18.4. As you can see, the circles are contributing to each other directly, creating a unique isosurface in the end that is more complex—and much more interesting—than just one plain circle. However, how is this creating the gooey effect? It seems like the metaballs tend to attract each other more strongly, depending on how close they are to one another.

The typical equation for a metaball is as follows:

```
M(x,y) = R / sqrt( (x-x0)^2 + (y-y0)^2 )
```

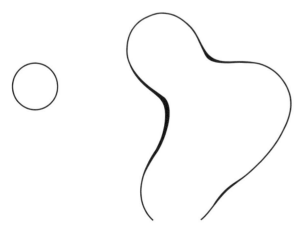

Figure 18.4
Four metaballs, all influencing each other's overall shape. Metaballs that are closer to each other provide greater attraction.

FPS: 17

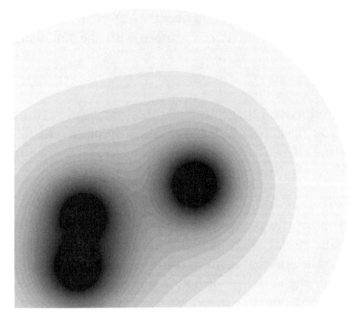

Figure 18.5
Notice the banding that occurs around each of the metaballs and the way they combine to form layers of meta-things.

It seems to vaguely resemble the equation for a circle, but you are instead dividing the radius of the metaball by the distance the point is from its center. This equation is based on the equation for calculating the strength of an electrical field in science, which is why this function will provide the largest value in the center of the metaball (positive infinity) and then drop off quickly, approaching zero as the distance from the metaball grows larger and larger. If you were to look at what these values look like on the 2D plane, it would resemble Figure 18.5.

In order to define the curves shown, you need to also define a threshold value (with a minimum and maximum) to have the pixels appear along the perimeter of your newly created isosurface. You need to use this minimum and maximum threshold because the screen, unlike a mathematical real-valued 2D plane, only has a finite amount of accuracy and a finite number of points. If you only used a single value for your threshold [e.g., $F(x,y) = C$], many points would be missed by the algorithm, resulting in a much less accurate image (see Figure 18.6).

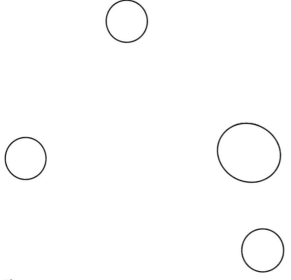

Figure 18.6
Badly chosen `MAX` and `MIN` threshold values can result in very thick metaballs, or ones that are thin and flicker as they move.

An ideal threshold is usually found by trial-and-error, based on the average size of the metaballs in the game world.

Writing a 2D Implementation

Now that you're familiar with the ideas, equations, and algorithm behind metaballs, let's examine some code that will provide you with a 2D implementation to work with. I'll start by defining a structure for a `Metaball` object and an array to hold all of the metaballs in:

```
struct METABALL
{
  float _x, _y;
  float _radius;
  METABALL(float startx, float starty, float radius)
  {
    _x = startx;
    _y = starty;
    _radius = radius;
  }
  float Equation(float x, float y)
```

```
  {
    return (_radius / sqrt( (x-_x)*(x-_x) + (y-_y)*(y-_y) ) ) );
  }
};
const MAX_METABALLS = 15;
METABALL *ballList[MAX_METABALLS]; // A list of metaballs
                                  // in our world
```

Now, assuming that you already have your graphics library of choice up and running, you'll jump straight into the core of the implementation, which is just as simple as applying the algorithm discussed:

```
const float MIN_THRESHOLD = 0.99f;
const float MAX_THRESHOLD = 1.01f; // Min and max threshold
                                   // for an isosurface
...
void draw_metaballs()
{
  // Value to act as a summation of all Metaballs fields
  // applied to this particular pixel
  float sum;
  // Iterate over every pixel on the screen
  for(int y = 0; y < SCREEN_HEIGHT; y++)
  {
    for(int x = 0; x < SCREEN_WIDTH; x++)
    {
      // Reset the summation
      sum = 0;
      // Iterate through every Metaball in the world
      for(int i = 0; i < MAX_METABALLS && ballList[i] != NULL; i++)
      {
        sum += ballList[i]->Equation(x,y);
      }
      // Decide whether to draw a pixel
      if(sum >= MIN_THRESHOLD && sum <= MAX_THRESHOLD)
        draw_pixel(x, y, COLOR_WHITE);
    }
  }
}
```

This is the real workhorse of the entire metaballs implementation. With this, you can easily create and tinker with your own metaballs. If you'd like to see the full source code of a working implementation, you can download several examples and demos from the "References" section at the end of this article.

Other Meta-Shapes

Balls are certainly the most popular shape to apply this effect to, largely due to the simple nature of the equation of a circle; but it's not hard to modify the original equation to form other interesting blobby shapes.

Ellipses

An ellipse isn't really a far cry from a circle, so its equation might be the easiest to fathom. The equation for an elliptical metaball is much the same as our original equation, but with floating-point multipliers (Xm and Ym, respectively) applied to the X and Y squares (see Figure 18.7):

```
M(x,y) = R / sqrt( Xm*(x-x0)^2 + Ym*(y-y0)^2 )
```

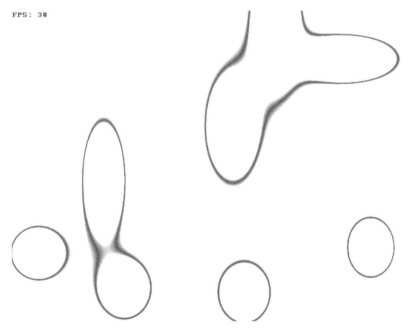

Figure 18.7
An elliptical shape generated from a metaball.

Figure 18.8
A simple diamond shape generated from a metaball.

When Xm and Ym are both 1, it will be identical to a regular metaball; but supplying numbers between zero and 1 will stretch the meta-ellipse, while numbers greater than 1 will shrink it.

Diamonds

The equation for a meta-diamond is as follows (see Figure 18.8):

```
M(x,y) = R / ( |x-x0| + |y-y0| )
```

There is a much simpler formula here, where you are simply dividing the radius (or size) by the sum of the X distance from the center and the Y distance from the center, via the absolute value (|) symbols. These shapes are particularly fast to render compared to metaballs, since they only consist of a few relatively inexpensive operators and functions.

Donuts

You can define a donut-like shape by considering a function that passes your threshold value twice: once near the center and again farther away. You can accomplish this by introducing an offset to the distance calculated (i.e., the value

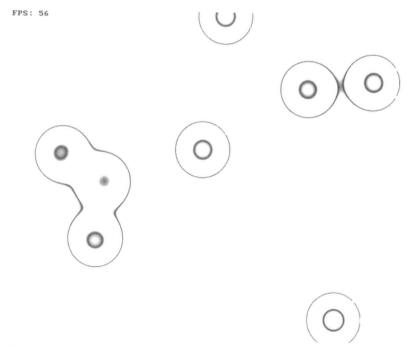

FPS: 56

Figure 18.9
A donut shape generated from a metaball.

in the denominator) to make the meta-shape cross your threshold more than once. Consider the following equation:

```
M(x,y) = Radius_1 / |Radius_2 - sqrt( (x-x0)^2 + (y-y0)^2 )|
```

Given two radius values, somewhat alike to an inner- and outer-radius, the threshold for your points to draw will become both `Radius_2` units toward the center of the shape and `Radius_2` units away from the center of the shape, thus producing a donut-like shape (see Figure 18.9). Note that these are a little slower to draw, since the equation requires an additional subtraction and absolute value compared to regular metaballs.

Optimizations and Improvements

With all of the practical uses for clearly high-demand areas like medicine and engineering, why is it that they aren't particularly prominent in the world of game development? If you've taken a try at implementing the algorithm discussed in this article, you'll know the answer in a heartbeat: *they're slow.*

Or rather, rendering isosurfaces is slow in the naive implementation of performing a summation of each meta-shape on every pixel. There are several immediately noticeable optimizations that you can apply to speed up your metaballs, depending on what result exactly you want to end up with. Following are several optimizations that you can implement that are not too challenging to add into your own metaballs rendering routine, or you may find them generally useful.

Uniform Box Division

As you may have noticed, in many of the images shown in this article, only a small amount of the screen is actually being drawn. The majority of the pixels (in most situations) remain black and unaffected by the metaballs. Thus a fairly easy-to-implement optimization is to compute only the portions of the screen that will actually be drawn. Imagine the screen divided into uniformly sized grid boxes. The idea is to sample one or more points within that box to determine if it is worth drawing the contents of it.

Recall that the equation for a metaball is much like the equation of an electrical field, where the "charge" of the metaball grows gradually smaller and smaller the farther from the center of the metaball that you go. This means that you can check for another threshold value every time you sample from the grid to determine whether the grid box is worth drawing. If it is above the threshold, then there must be a metaball nearby. To make it easier to visualize, the end result should look something like what's shown in Figure 18.10.

In terms of how useful the optimization is, I receive a speed increase of between 200% and 300% on my machine, but your mileage may vary. The increase you receive is proportional to the size of the grid boxes, how large most metaballs are, and how many metaballs are in the game world. This requires a bit of experimentation to find values that fit nicely for your purposes.

A possible further improvement to this would be to implement something like a quadtree, which would allow for quicker sampling and culling of unneeded areas.

Equation Simplification (Square Root)

The original equation for a metaball was given as follows:

```
M(x,y) = R / sqrt( (x-x0)^2 + (y-y0)^2 )
```

In general, square root is a rather expensive function, especially when it is being used for every metaball and for every pixel on the screen. By dropping the square

FPS: 46

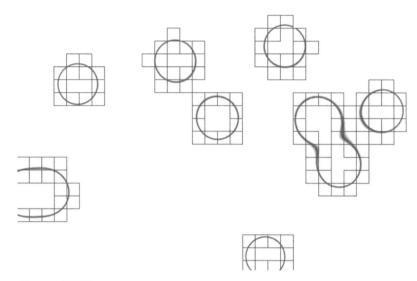

Figure 18.10
Filling the map with fixed-sized boxes, which are sampled to determine their viability to be drawn.

root operation, the speed can increase by an additional 300% or more, but at the cost of making the radius for the metaballs a little more awkward to work with. Since square root is no longer being applied to make the denominator much smaller, the radius has to be made much larger to compensate. The result is metaballs that are processed much faster, at the cost of using radius values for the metaballs which are much larger, and so less intuitive to work with, than before—a small trade-off for a significant speed gain.

More Optimizations and Techniques

The two previous optimizations only scratch the surface of what is possible. There really is a lot that can be done from the original naive equation of a metaball to something that allows dozens of metaballs to be rendered quickly and efficiently.

In the "References" section are links to other resources and papers on metaballs and isosurfaces, which explore other techniques and optimizations in regard to metaballs.

Above and Beyond
3D Isosurfaces

Once you have a firm grasp on the algorithm and idea behind metaballs, applying the information acquired here is not too difficult to expand into the third dimension. New difficulties are introduced, however, such as working with a space that you cannot practically draw on a per-pixel basis in (i.e., you must use polygons/triangles), you need to define surface normals for, and other irksome challenges.

This unfortunately goes beyond the scope of this article, but several helpful web sites detailing some insights into 3D metaballs are listed in the "References" section.

Isosurfaces in the Real World

As a brief aside, it's worth talking a little about where isosurfaces are outside of the numerous demos that showcase metaballs. One prominent use is that a metaball primitive is included as a tool or plug-in in many 3D modeling software packages, like Maya or 3D Studio Max. Ray tracers like POV-Ray also include functionality to render flexible isosurfaces.

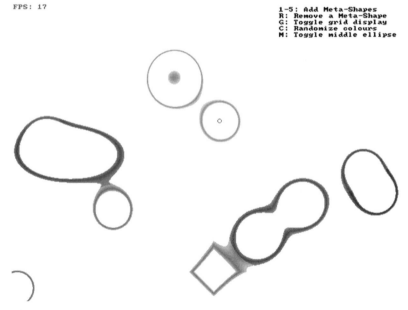

FPS: 17

```
1-5: Add Meta-Shapes
R: Remove a Meta-Shape
G: Toggle grid display
C: Randomize colours
M: Toggle middle ellipse
```

Figure 18.11
Playing with several meta-shapes.

Medical imaging is another area where isosurfaces are heavily used, as they can be an efficient means of volume visualization (e.g., MRI scans). Engineering also uses isosurfaces as a means of visualizing things like air pressure or fluid flow in simulations.

The Meta Playground

Available for download is my Meta Playground, which allows for the manipulation and viewing of all of the meta-shapes covered in this article, plus a few extra aesthetic features (see Figure 18.11). Source code is available on the book's companion web site (www.courseptr.com/downloads), and should compile on all major platforms.

References

The following web sites were used for ideas and/or understanding of the theory behind metaballs, isosurfaces, and level sets, as well as some of their applications.

Geiss, Ryan. "Metaballs" (www.geisswerks.com/ryan/BLOBS/blobs.html).

Hannu's Plaza. "Metaball Math" (www.niksula.cs.hut.fi/~hkankaan/Homepages/metaballs.html).

Paul's Projects (www.paulsprojects.net).

Wikipedia.org ("Metaballs," "Isosurface," "Level Set").

Thanks to Adam Stanton for helping to get the source code running under UNIX.

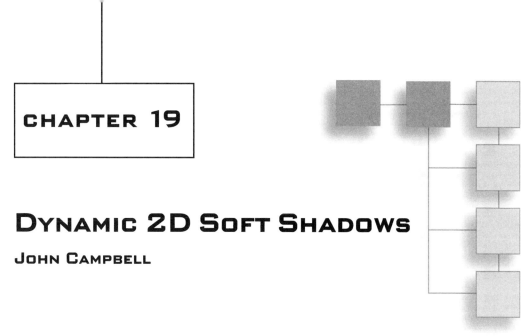

CHAPTER 19

Dynamic 2D Soft Shadows

John Campbell

The aim of this article is to describe an accurate method of generating soft shadows in a 2D environment. The shadows are created on the fly via geometry as opposed to traditional 2D shadow methods, which typically use shadow sprites or other image-based methods. This method takes advantage of several features available in the core OpenGL API, but is by no means restricted to this platform. Direct3D would also be a suitable rendering API, and the concepts and reasoning behind the various rendering stages should hopefully be clear enough that a reader can make the conversion without too much hassle.

Overview

I will start by defining a few terms that you will use frequently, along with a brief explanation of the phenomena that you will reproduce on your digital canvas.

Light Source

An obvious place to start—in this implementation I will discuss a point light source, although extending the method to include directional lights as well could be easily done, as is adding ambient lighting into the system. I use a point light source with a user-defined radius to generate the soft shadows accurately.

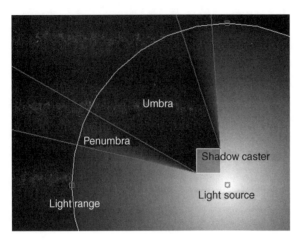

Figure 19.1
Overview of terms.

Shadow Caster

A *shadow caster* is any object that blocks the light emitted from the source. In this article, I present implementation details for using convex hulls as shadow casters. Convex hulls have several useful properties and provide a flexible primitive from which to construct more complex objects. Details of the hulls are discussed in just a bit.

Light Range

In reality, light intensity over a distance is subject to the inverse square relationship and so can never really reach zero. In games, however, linear light fall-off often looks as good or better, depending on the circumstances. In Figure 19.1, a linear fall-off in the intensity is used, dropping to zero at the edge of the light range.

Umbra

The *umbra* region of a shadow is the area completely hidden from the light source and, as such, is a single color. (Figure 19.1 shows the umbra region in black, since there is no other light source to illuminate this region.)

Penumbra

The *penumbra* region of a shadow is what creates the soft edges. This is cast in any area that is partially hidden from the light—neither in full view or totally hidden.

The size and shape of the penumbra region are related to the light's position and physical size (not its range).

Core Classes

First, you'll have a look at a couple of classes that are at the core of the system: the Light and ConvexHull classes.: The Light class is fairly self-explanatory, holding all the information needed to represent a light source in your world. It contains the following:

- **Position and depth**. Fairly obvious, these are the location in the world. Although the system is 2D, you still use a depth for correctly defining which objects to draw in front of others. Since you'll be using 3D hardware to get fast rendering, you'll take advantage of the depth buffer for this.

- **Physical size and range**. Both stored as a simple radial distance, these control how the light influences its surroundings.

- **Color and intensity**. Lights have a color value stored in the standard RGB form and an intensity value, which is the intensity at the center of the light.

The ConvexHull class is the primitive shape from which you will construct your world. By using these primitives, you are able to construct more complex geometry. It contains the following:

- **List of points**. A simple list is maintained of all the points that make up the edges of the hull. This is calculated from a collection of points, and the gift-wrapping algorithm is used to discard unneeded points. The gift-wrapping method is useful, since the output geometry typically has a low number of edges. You may want to look into the QuickHull method as an alternative.

- **Depth**. As for the light, a single depth value is used for the proper display of overlapping objects.

- **Shadow depth offset**. The importance of this is described later.

- **Center position**. The center of the hull is approximated by averaging all the points on the edge of the hull. While not an exact geometric center, it is close enough for our needs.

■ **Vertex data**. Other data associated with the vertex positions. Currently only per-vertex colors, but texture cords could be added without requiring any major changes.

Rendering Overview

The basic rendering process for a single frame goes like this:

1. Clear screen, and initialize camera matrix.

2. Fill z buffer with all visible objects.

3. For every light:
   a. Clear alpha buffer.
   b. Load alpha buffer with light intensity.
   c. Mask away shadow regions with shadow geometry.
   d. Render geometry with full detail (colors, textures, and so on) modulated by the light intensity.

The essential point from the list is that a rendering pass is performed for every visible light, during which the alpha buffer is used to accumulate the light's intensity. Once the final intensity values for the light have been created in the alpha buffer, you render all the geometry modulated by the values in the alpha buffer.

Simple Light Attenuation

First, you'll set up the foundation for the lighting—converting the previous pseudo code into actual code but without the shadow generation for now.

```
public void render(Scene scene, GLDrawable canvas)
{
  GL gl = canvas.getGL();
  gl.glDepthMask(true);
  gl.glClearDepth(1f);
  gl.glClearColor(0.0f, 0.0f, 0.0f, 0.0f);
  gl.glClear(GL.GL_COLOR_BUFFER_BIT |
             GL.GL_DEPTH_BUFFER_BIT |
             GL.GL_STENCIL_BUFFER_BIT);
  gl.glMatrixMode(GL.GL_PROJECTION);
  gl.glLoadIdentity();
  gl.glMatrixMode(GL.GL_MODELVIEW);
```

```
gl.glLoadIdentity();
gl.glMatrixMode(GL.GL_TEXTURE);
gl.glLoadIdentity();
gl.glDisable(GL.GL_CULL_FACE);
findVisibleLights(scene);
Camera activeCamera = scene.getActiveCamera();
activeCamera.preRender(canvas);
{
  // First you need to fill the z buffer
  findVisibleObjects(scene, null);
  fillZBuffer(canvas);
  // For every light
  for (int lightIndex=0; lightIndex<visibleLights.size();
  lightIndex++)
  {
    Light currentLight = (Light)visibleLights.get(lightIndex);
    // Clear current alpha
    clearFramebufferAlpha(scene, currentLight, canvas);
    // Load new alpha
    writeFramebufferAlpha(currentLight, canvas);
    // Mask off shadow regions
    mergeShadowHulls(scene, currentLight, canvas);
    // Draw geometry pass
    drawGeometryPass(currentLight, canvas);
  }
  // Emissive/self-illumination pass
  // ..
  // Wireframe editor handles
  drawEditControls(canvas);
}
activeCamera.postRender(canvas);
}
```

Note that code here is written in Java, using the Jogl set of bindings to OpenGL. For C++ programmers, you simply have to remember that primitives such as int, float, Boolean, and so on are always passed by value, and objects are always passed by reference. OpenGL commands and enumerations are scoped to a GL object, which leads to the slightly extended notation from the straight C style.

First, you reset the GL state ready for the next frame, collect all the lights that you will need to render for this frame, and retrieve the currently active camera from the scene. Camera.preRender() and .postRender() are used to set the modelview and projection matrices to that needed for the view position.

Once this initialization is complete, you need to fill the z buffer for the whole scene. Although not discussed here, this would be the perfect place to take advantage of your favorite type of spatial tree. A quadtree or AABB tree would make a good choice for inclusion within the scene and would be used for all testing of objects against the view frustum. To fill the depth buffer, you simply enable z buffer reading and writing, but with color writing disabled to leave the color buffer untouched. This creates a perfect depth buffer for you to use and stops later stages blending pixels hidden from view. It is worth noting that by enabling color writing, an ambient lighting pass can be added here to do both jobs at the same time. From this point onward, you can disable depth writing, as it no longer needs to be updated.

Now you perform a rendering pass for every light. First, the alpha buffer is cleared in preparation for its use. This is simply a full screen quad drawn without blending, depth testing, or color writing to reset the alpha channel in the frame buffer to 0f. Since you don't want to disturb the current camera matrices that have been set up, you create this quad by using the current camera position to determine the quad's coordinates.

Next you need to load the light's intensity into the alpha buffer. This does not need any blending, but depth testing is enabled this time to allow lights to be restricted to illuminating only the objects beneath them. Again, color writing is left disabled because you are not ready to render any visible geometry yet. The following function is used to create the geometry for a single light:

```
public void renderLightAlpha(float intensity, GLDrawable canvas)
{
  assert (intensity > 0f && intensity <= 1f);
  GL gl = canvas.getGL();
  int numSubdivisions = 32;
  gl.glBegin(GL.GL_TRIANGLE_FAN);
  {
    gl.glColor4f(0f, 0f, 0f, intensity);
    gl.glVertex3f(center.x, center.y, depth);
    // Set edge colour for rest of shape
    gl.glColor4f(0f, 0f, 0f, 0f);
    for (float angle=0; angle<=Math.PI*2;
        angle+=((Math.PI*2)/numSubdivisions) )
    {
      gl.glVertex3f( radius*(float)Math.cos(angle) + center.x,
                radius*(float)Math.sin(angle) + center.y, depth);
```

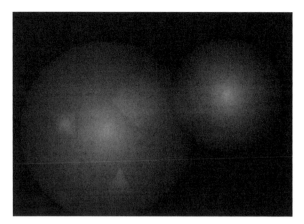

Figure 19.2
Per-pixel lighting with intensities accumulated in the alpha buffer.

```
    }
    gl.glVertex3f(center.x+radius, center.y, depth);
  }
  gl.glEnd();
}
```

What happens is, you create a triangle fan rooted at the center position of the light, then loop around in a circle, creating additional vertices as you go. The alpha value of the center point is your light intensity, fading linearly to zero on the edges of the circle. This creates the smooth light fall-off seen in Figure 19.2. If other methods of light attenuation are needed, they can be generated here. An interesting alternative would be to use an alpha texture instead of vertex colors; a 1D texture could happily represent a non-linear set of light intensities. Other unusual effects could be achieved by animating the texture coordinates over a 2D texture, such as flickering candlelight or a pulsing light source.

So now that you have your light intensity values in the alpha buffer, I will skip the generation of shadow hulls for the moment and move on to getting your level geometry up on the screen.

The geometry pass is where you really start to see things coming together, using the results you have carefully composed in the alpha of the frame buffer. First, you need to make sure you have depth testing enabled (using less-than-or-equal-to, as before), and then enable and set up your blending equation correctly:

```
gl.glEnable(GL.GL_BLEND);
gl.glBlendFunc(GL.GL_DST_ALPHA, GL.GL_ONE);
```

Simple, yes? What you're doing here is multiplying the incoming fragments (from the geometry you're about to draw) by the alpha values already sitting in the frame buffer. This means any alpha values of one will now be drawn at full intensity, with values of 0 being unchanged. This is then added to the current frame buffer color multiplied by one. This addition to the existing color means you slowly accumulate your results from previous passes. With your blend equation set up, you simply render your geometry as normal, using whatever vertex colors and textures that strike your fancy.

If you take another look at the render() function near the top, you'll see you've almost finished composing your frame. Once you've looped over all the lights, you've practically finished, but you'll insert a couple of extra stages. First, there's an emissive or self-illumination pass (which is discussed near the end of the article). After this is a simple wireframe rendering, which draws object outlines, such as seen in Figure 19.2.

Colored Lighting

What was once seen as "the next big thing" in the *Quake II* and *Unreal* era, colored lighting is pretty much standard by now and a powerful tool for level designers to add atmosphere to a scene. Now since you've already got your light intensity ready and waiting for your geometry in the alpha buffer, all you need to do is modulate the geometry color by the current light color while drawing. That's a whole lot of multiplication if you want to do it yourself; but on TnL hardware, you can get it practically for free with a simple trick. You enable lighting while drawing your geometry, yet define no normals because you have no need of them. Instead, you just enable a single light and set its ambient color to the color of your current light. The graphics card will calculate the effect of the light color on your geometry for you—you need barely lift a finger. Note that because you're accumulating light intensities over multiple lights in the frame buffer, you get accurate over-brightening effects when lights overlap, and multiple colored lights will merge and produce white illumination of your objects.

Hard-Edged Shadow Casting

Now that you have your lights correctly illuminating their surroundings, you can start thinking about correctly limiting their light to add shadows into the scene. First, you will cast hard-edged shadows from shadow casters, and then you will extend this to cover soft-edged shadows with correct umbra and penumbra. This is done in the function you previously skipped, mergeShadowHulls().

You will remember that at this point in the rendering you have the light intensity stored in the alpha buffer. Now what you will do is create geometry to represent the shadow from each shadow caster, then merge this into the alpha buffer. This is done inside the ConvexHull class.

Finding the Boundary Points

Your first step is to determine which points your shadow should be cast from. The list of points that make up the ConvexHull is looped, though, and each edge is classified in regard to the light position. Here it is in pseudo code:

- For every edge:
    - Find normal for edge<.
    - Classify edge as front facing or back facing.
    - Determine if either edge points are boundary points or not.

The normal for the edge is found by the following:

```
float nx = currentPoint.y - prevPoint.y;
float ny = currentPoint.x - prevPoint.x;
```

Then a dot product is performed with this vector and the vector to the light. If this is greater than zero, the edge is front facing. Once an edge has been classified, it is compared against the previous edge. If one is front facing and the other back facing, then the shared vertex is a boundary point. As you walk around the edge of the hull (in a counter-clockwise direction), the boundary point from light to shadow is the start shadow point. The boundary from shadow to light is the end shadow point.

Creating the Shadow Geometry

Once you have these positions, you can generate your shadow geometry. Since you are only generating hard-edged shadows at the moment, you will be ignoring the physical size of your light source. Figure 19.3 shows how the shadow geometry is built.

As shown in the image, the shadow geometry is a single triangle strip projected outward from the back-facing edges of the shadow caster. You start at the first boundary point (marked with an X) and work your way counter-clockwise. The

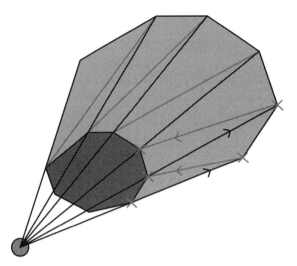

Figure 19.3
Hard-edged shadow generation.

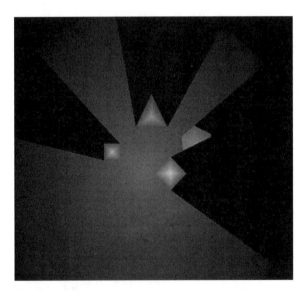

Figure 19.4
Hard-edged shadows.

second point is established by finding the vector from the light to the point and using this to project the point away from the light. A projection scale amount is used to ensure that the edges of the shadow geometry are always off screen. For now you can simply set this to a sufficiently large number, but later it will be advantageous to calculate this every frame depending on how far zoomed in or out the camera is.

You render the shadow geometry with depth testing enabled to properly layer the shadow between various other objects in the world; but with color writing disabled, only the alpha in the frame buffer is changed. You may remember that the final geometry pass is modulated (multiplied) by the existing alpha values, which means you need to set the shadow to have an alpha value of zero. Because the frame buffer will clamp the values to between one and zero, overlapping shadows will not make an affected area too dark, but instead will merge correctly. Notice in Figure 19.4 how the shadow from the diamond correctly obscures the right-most object and that their shadows are correctly merged where they overlap.

Soft-Edged Shadow Casting

Now that you can properly construct hard-edged shadows, it is time to extend this to cover soft shadows—note that you cannot simply add faded edges to the existing shadow geometry, since this would result in inaccurate penumbra and umbra regions. First, you start by defining a physical radius for the light source to generate the correct penumbra regions. Then you need to create the penumbra geometry and modify the creation of the umbra region that you used for the hard-edged shadows.

Shadow Fins

Each penumbra region will be created by one or more shadow fins via the ConvexHull and ShadowFin classes. The ShadowFin class is an object that encompasses all or part of a penumbra region. It contains the following:

- **Root position**. This is the position that the fin protrudes from.

- **Penumbra vector**. This is a vector from the root position that lies on the outer edge of the fin (the highest light intensity).

- **Umbra vector**. This vector from the root position lies on the inner edge of the fin (lowest light intensity).

- **Penumbra and umbra intensities**. These are the light intensities of their relative edges for the fin. If the fin makes up an entire penumbra region, these are one and zero, respectively.

You create a ShadowFin from the first boundary point. The root position becomes the boundary point, and the penumbra and umbra intensities are initially one

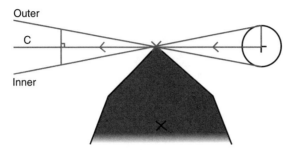

Figure 19.5
Shadow fin generation.

and zero. The difficult parts of the fin—the penumbra and umbra vectors—are done by the getUmbraVector and getPenumbraVector methods within your Light object (see Figure 19.5).

If you look at the vector that lies along the outer penumbra edge, you can imagine it as the vector from the light through the boundary point (C, the center vector) displaced by the light radius, so you must find this displacement.

First, note that the displacement is at right angles to the center vector. So you take C and find this perpendicular vector in the same way you did to find the normals for the hull edges. Although looking at Figure 19.5 you know which way you want this to point, when you're dealing with boundary points and light positions at all sorts of funny angles to each other, you may end up with it pointing in the opposite direction to what you expect. To solve this, you find the vector from the center of the hull to the boundary point (between the two Xs in Figure 19.5), and take the dot product of this and the perpendicular vector. If this is less than zero, your vector is pointing in the wrong direction and you need to invert it.

Armed with this new vector, you normalize it and the center vector, then add them together, and you've found your crucial outer penumbra vector. Finding the inner vector requires that you repeat the process; but this time you invert the logic for the dot product test to displace the center vector in the opposite direction. You now have a fully calculated shadow fin to send to your renderer!

Non-Linear Shading

Although you have all the numbers you need to render your shadow fin, you'll soon hit a major snag—you can't use regular old vertex colors this time to write to the alpha buffer. You need the inner edge of the penumbra to be zero intensity (zero alpha) and your outer edge to be fully bright (alpha of one). While you can probably visualize that easily, getting your graphics card to actually render a triangle with the colors like this just isn't possible. Try it yourself if you're not sure; you'll soon see how it's the root point that causes the problems—it lies on both edges, so it needs to be *both* zero and one at the same time.

The solution to this (and indeed most cases when you need non-linear shading) is to abandon vertex colors for the fins and instead use a texture to hold the information. Figure 19.6 shows a copy of the texture I used.

You can clearly see how the shadow fin will be rooted at the bottom left, while the two edges run vertically and diagonally to the top edge. Since you don't want texels from the right edge bleeding into the left, you set the texture wrapping mode to clamp to the edge values (using glTexParameteri and GL_CLAMP_TO_EDGE). The bottom-right half of the texture is unused, although if you really wanted to, you could pack something else in there as long as you're careful not to bleed over the edge.

So you load this texture and bind it for use before drawing your shadow fins, and then set the vertex color to white to leave the texture unchanged by it. Other than that, rendering the fins is no different from the shadow hull. The only other thing you need to watch out for is how far back you project your points by the umbra/

Figure 19.6
Penumbra texture.

penumbra vectors, as the limited resolution of the penumbra texture will show if these are moved too far away. Ideally, they will be projected to just off screen.

Modifying the Umbra Generation

Now that you've got the fins drawn, you can fill in the umbra between them. This is done in almost exactly the same way as with hard shadows, except you must use the fins' inner edges to start and finish from instead of directly projecting away from the center of the light source. As you move across the back of the shadow caster, you perform a weighted average between these two edge vectors to properly fill in the umbra region. When done correctly, you should see no gaps between the fins and the umbra geometry, giving you one consistent, accurate shadow cast into the alpha buffer.

Making It Robust

Self-Intersection

Now that you have this implemented, the shadows will be looking quite nice—when static. However, problems will become apparent when moving the light sources around. The most glaring is that of *self-intersection* (see Figure 19.7).

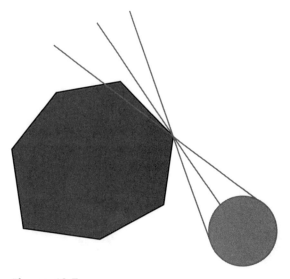

Figure 19.7
Self-intersection of shadow fin.

If the light source is too large in relation to the object or too near, the inner penumbra edge will intersect the hull. First, you need to detect this case. You find the vector from the boundary point to the next edge point in the shadow (moving counter-clockwise here, since you're on the shadow start boundary point). Then you compare the angle between the outer penumbra edge and your newly found hull edge, and the angle between the outer and inner penumbra edges. If the angle to the boundary edge is smaller, then you've got an intersection case you need to fix.

First, you snap the current fin to the boundary edge and calculate the new intensity for the inner edge via the ratio of the angles. Then you create a new shadow fin at the next point on the hull. This has an outer edge set to the same vector and intensity as the existing fin's inner edge, while the new fin's inner edge is calculated as before. By gluing these two fins together, you create a single smooth shadow edge. Technically, you should repeat the self-intersection test and keep adding more fins as needed; however, I've not found that this is needed in practice.

Eliminating "Popping"

You will also notice one other problem with this as it stands: the shadow fins will "pop" along the edges of the hull as a light rotates. This is because you're still using an infinitely small point light to find the boundary points. To solve this, you should take the physical radius into account when finding them. A robust way of doing this is to shift the light source position toward the hull by the radius distance before you find your boundary points. With these two fixes in place, the fins will be visually stable as either the light or the hull moves (or both!).

Depth Offset

Depending on the style of game and the view used (such as a side-scrolling platformer as opposed to a top-down shooter), the way light and shadow interacts with the various level objects will be different. What seems sensible for one may appear wrong in another. Most obviously, this happens with objects casting shadows onto objects at the same depth.

Figure 19.8 shows the same scene with different shadow offsets. Imagine that the scene is a top-down viewpoint: the light gray areas are impassable walls surrounding the floor showing a T junction (imagine hard!). Now the image on the left seems slightly out of place—the shadows are being projected on top of the walls, yet these are much higher than the light source. Realistically, they shouldn't be lit at all, but

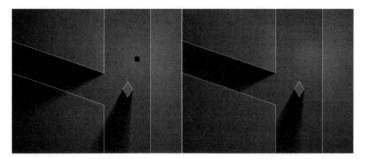

Figure 19.8
The effect of shadow offset.

solid black walls aren't very visually appealing. The image on the right shows the shadows being offset and only obscuring the floor and any objects on it.

Now if you were to imagine the same scene as a 2D platformer, you might prefer the left image. Here it seems to make more sense that the objects should shadow those on the same level. This decision is usually very dependent on the geometry and art direction of the level itself, so no hard and fast rules seem to apply. The best option seems to be to experiment and see which looks best.

Adding control over this is a small modification. At the moment, the scene on the right is the common case, and by generating shadow volumes that are a close fit to the edge of the shadow caster, you've already done all the hard work; all you need to do is store a shadow depth offset in your `ConvexHull` and apply it to the depth of the shadow geometry. The existing depth testing will reject fragments drawn behind other objects and leave them at the original intensity.

Emissive/Self-Illumination Pass

This is a simple addition that can produce some neat effects and can be seen as a generalization of the wireframe "full-bright" pass. After the lights have been drawn, you clear the alpha buffer again as before, but instead of writing light intensities into it, you render your scene geometry with their associated emissive surface. This is an alpha texture used to control light intensities, as before, and can be used for glowing objects, such as a computer display or a piece of hardware with a bank of LEDs—everything that has its own light source but is too small to require an individual light of its own. Because these are so small, you skip the shadow generation and can do them all in one go. Then you modulate the scene geometry by this alpha intensity as before. Unusual effects are possible with this, such as particles that light up their immediate surroundings or the bright local illumination provided by a neon sign (with one or two associated lights to provide the lighting at medium and long range).

Scissor Testing

You are extending the shadow geometry until it's off the edge of the screen, but often the area a light affects is much smaller than this. The scissor test (`glScissor` in OpenGL) allows you to restrict rendering to a rectangle within your window and avoid drawing pixels that have no effect. You just have to project the light's bounds to screen space and set the scissor area before drawing the shadow geometry. This can increase the frame rate considerably.

Conclusion

After a lot of work, much math, and a few sneaky tricks, you've finally got a shadow system that's both physically accurate and robust. The hardware requirements are modest indeed: a frame buffer with an alpha component is about all that's required. You don't even need to stray into extensions to get the correct effect. There is a whole heap of possible optimizations and areas for improvement, notably caching the calculated shadow geometry when neither the light nor the caster has changed and including some sort of spatial tree so that only the shadow casters that are actually needed are used for each light (see Figure 19.9).

Figure 19.9
The final system in action! A total of seven lights are used here.

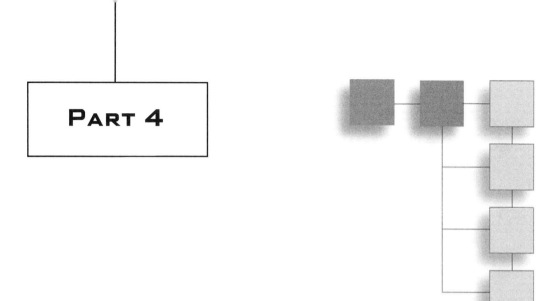

PART 4

NETWORKING

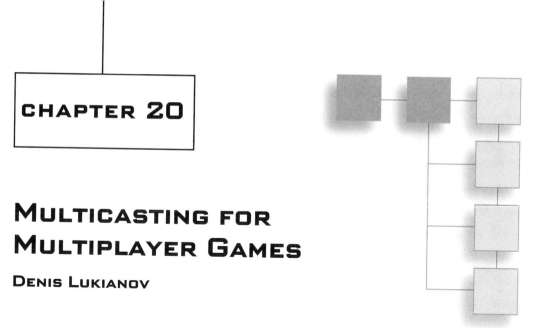

CHAPTER 20

Multicasting for Multiplayer Games

Denis Lukianov

Combating latency is a major problem in multiplayer network game development. As multiplayer game developers, we always strive to make things faster, leaner, and meaner to reduce lag and bandwidth requirements. This is why we often forsake the reliability of TCP for the speed that UDP provides. On the other hand, we aim to send as much information as possible to enrich the player interaction. This is why network engines often include a layer for data compression.

Multicasting is yet another step in the fight against latency, carrying many promises, including the streaming of very high-quality digital TV over the Internet. What is the magic behind multicasting and how can it be used in your games? In short, it not only reduces server workload, but also solves the age-old problem of server discovery without dedicated master servers. Some application interfaces, such as DirectPlay, have used multicasting internally.

The Idea Behind Multicasting

The theory goes something like this. In the most commonly used networking client-server model, when a client sends input to the server, this input updates the game state, and then the server tells all the other clients about what has happened by sending the same information to all the clients (see Figure 20.1). This is the unicast model. As you can see, there is a traffic problem on the server's

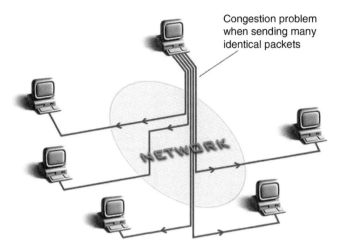

Congestion problem when sending many identical packets

Figure 20.1

network connection. If, say, there were 32 players connected to the server at the time, then the same information would be sent 32 times (once to each player). If there were 20 bytes of data to be sent to each of the 32 players, then 640 bytes would have to be sent through the server's network connection. If that were to happen, every time any of the 32 players pressed a key or moved the mouse, a huge amount of traffic is generated. This can exceed the server's available bandwidth, pushing messages into a queue and thereby ruining the latency. It goes without saying that only the data that is needed should be sent.

So how can multicasting help? Well, it can dramatically reduce the amount of data that needs to be sent by taking the task of packet replication away from the game server and handing it over to the network infrastructure. In multicasting, packets can be sent to groups of network addresses instead of individual addresses. The routing equipment does the rest.

This is similar to the way e-mail works. When you want to send the same e-mail message to multiple e-mail addresses, you don't send the message to every recipient address from your computer. Instead, you send the message once, telling the server to carbon-copy the message to the other addresses (see Figure 20.2).

How Multicasting Works

You may have heard of *broadcasting*. A broadcast packet is received by every node on the network. There is only a single packet that is transmitted on the physical wire, to which many computers are connected. Unlike a broadcast, a

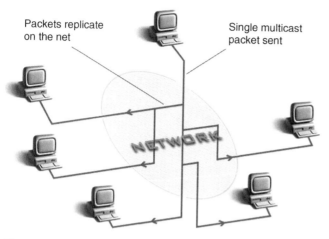

Packets replicate
on the net

Single multicast
packet sent

NETWORK

Figure 20.2

multicast is only processed by those nodes that have explicitly registered interest in the data.

On an IP network that supports multicasting, there are special addresses reserved for multicast groups. If you want to receive multicast data packets, you must join a multicast group. It is possible to send data packets to the multicast group address, regardless of membership. If you are a member of a group to which you are sending multicast data packets, you will receive a copy of all the data packets you send. This can be useful for testing and capability determination. Note that a group member will not indiscriminately receive all data packets from a multicast group, but only those that are sent to the port that their socket is bound to.

So a sensible strategy is for all the game clients to join a multicast group and wait for data on the same port. Then the server, by sending a single packet of data to that multicast group, would be sending to all the clients as the packets are replicated somewhere along the way (see Figure 20.3).

Player Discovery

Here is a typical discovery scenario. There are several people on a large local area network running the same game who want to play together, but they don't know each other's IP addresses, let alone that potential opponents exist. The common ways for connecting the players are as follows:

- The players send out a broadcast message to the entire network; however, this would probably be restricted to sub-networks. Broadcasting on the

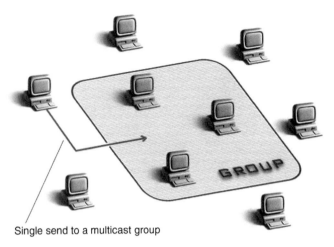

Single send to a multicast group

Figure 20.3

Internet would create an impossible amount of traffic to handle, so it is not allowed.

▪ The players connect to an intermediate, "known" master server IP, which tells them of each other's existence. These servers are costly to run, and their uptime is often undependable. Moreover, the local area network might lack an Internet connection.

Multicasting groups always have the same address—a "known" global address, as in the case of a dedicated server. However, they have unlimited uptime, and they don't cost anything to run. Game clients can join the game's multicast group, then send and receive "I want to play" multicasts, advertising their availability directly to all clients who are members of the same group. The idea is cool enough, but ISP support remains the big problem. This will work on the vast majority of local area networks, but it does not currently work on the Internet.

The Darker Side

Of course, there are reasons not to use multicasting as well. Realistically, it is only worth the effort when you want support for more than four players. Few Internet service providers support IPv4 multicasting. So massively multiplayer online games, which would be the primary beneficiary of this technology, are left out in the cold. I hope this will change with IPv6. But for now, if you want to implement multicasting in a game, you'd better add it as an option.

It is not a cure-all for bandwidth problems. Multicasting only makes a worth-while gain in performance when network data is replicated exactly. There may be better ways of reducing the amount of information sent, such as only sending information about players who are near to the receiving client.

Multicasting requires a little bit more code and a lot of extra testing. I will demonstrate the most important aspects. It is simple in essence, but it can easily balloon. For example, you might want to test IPv4 and IPv6 interfaces on Linux, Windows, and Mac for both the case where multicasting is supported and not—that means you have to do 12 tests! Handling lost multicast packets can be achieved via unicast, but it is not a trivial problem to solve.

The openness of multicast groups may make your packets easier to sniff. Usually, UDP packets can only be intercepted between their source and destination. But now they can be captured anywhere on the network. By joining the right group, anyone can get a carbon-copy!

Receiving Multicasts (IPv4)

I have covered the pros and cons, so lets delve into the code. I will assume you know how to create a UDP socket in order to send and receive unicast packets. Here I am using the API for Windows, but the Linux code would be almost the same.

To receive multicast packets sent to a multicast group, your socket will need to join or become a member of that multicast group. To request becoming a member of a multicast group, you need to first bind() your UDP socket to a local port (elementary, my dear friend):

```
SOCKADDR_IN addrLocal;
// We want to use the Internet address family
addrLocal.sin_family = AF_INET;
// Use any local address
addrLocal.sin_addr.s_addr = INADDR_ANY;
// Use arbitrary port - but the same as on other clients/servers
addrLocal.sin_port = htons(uiPort);
// Bind socket to our address
if(SOCKET_ERROR == bind(UDPSocket, (LPSOCKADDR)&addrLocal,
sizeof(struct sockaddr)))
{
   cout << "Euston, we have a problem";
}
// Ready to switch to multicasting mode
```

Then just make a call to setsockopt(). Here's a prototype for your convenience:

```
int WSAAPI setsockopt(SOCKET s, int level, int optname,
                      const char FAR * optval, int optlen);
```

If you thought you were getting away with just one new line of code to learn, you were wrong—you're only getting away with four new lines! There are special parameters to prepare for this call: s is your socket handle, level should be set to IPPROTO_IP, optname should be set to IP_ADD_MEMBERSHIP and a pointer to the ip_mreq structure passed as optval, with its length in optlen. This is what the ip_mreq structure looks like:

```
struct ip_mreq
{
   struct in_addr imr_multiaddr;   /* multicast group to join */
   struct in_addr imr_interface;   /* interface to join on    */
}
```

It has two fields—both of them are in_add r structures: imr_multiaddr specifies the address of the multicast group to join, and imr_interface specifies the local address INADDR_ANY.

There are special (class D) addresses allocated for multicast groups. These are in the range from 224.0.1.0 to 239.255.255.255. You can choose an address from the range as the target multicast group to join, and then set the imr_multiaddr to this address. The full setsockopt() call would look something like this:

```
struct ip_mreq mreq;
mreq.imr_multiaddr.s_addr = inet_addr("234.5.6.7");
mreq.imr_interface.s_addr = INADDR_ANY;
nRet = setsockopt(UDPSocket, IPPROTO_IP, IP_ADD_MEMBERSHIP,
                  (char*)&mreq, sizeof(mreq));
```

And that's all there is to it, apart from a lot of error checking, which I have omitted for clarity. The socket will now receive data packets sent to the multicast group on the specified port with calls to recvfrom():

```
SOCKADDR_IN addrSrc;
nRet = recvfrom(UDPSocket, (char *)&Data, sizeof(Data), 0,
                (struct sockaddr*)&addrSrc, sizeof(addrSrc));
```

When you're finished with the group and want to leave, just repeat the call with identical parameters apart from IP_ADD_MEMBERSHIP, which should be replaced with IP_DROP_MEMBERSHIP.

```
nRet = setsockopt(UDPSocket, IPPROTO_IP, IP_DROP_MEMBERSHIP,
                  (char*)&mreq, sizeof(mreq));
```

Now that you can join a multicast group and receive packets sent to it, the logical thing to do is to send packets to the group.

Sending Multicasts (IPv4)

Sending multicast data packets is accomplished with a call to sendto(), specifying a multicast group address as the destination IP address and the wanted port (on which your clients are tuned to listen for data).

All IP packets carry a TTL value to make sure that they are discarded if they don't reach a destination so they don't clog up the network. In a multicast data packet, TTL specifies how far a multicast data packet can travel. Although this is in terms of the number of routers the packet is forwarded by before it is discarded, MSDN provides a very rough interpretation:

TTL Threshold	Description
0	Restricted to the same host
1	Restricted to the same subnet
32	Restricted to the same site
64	Restricted to the same region
128	Restricted to the same continent
255	Unrestricted in scope

Multicasting is nowhere near as dangerous as broadcasting in terms of unwanted traffic that it can produce, but caution is advised when using some of the higher TTL values. To set a socket's multicast TTL value, setsockopt() can be used with IPPROTO_IP as the protocol level and IP_MULTICAST_TTL as the socket option:

```
char TTL = 32 ; // Restrict to our school network, for example
setsockopt(UDPSocket, IPPROTO_IP, IP_MULTICAST_TTL,
           (char *)&TTL, sizeof(TTL));
```

You must also tell the system exactly which local network interface you would like to multicast on. Note that this has to be a real IP address that is connected with the network you wish to send across. The loopback address, ''127.0.0.1'', is only connected to itself and nothing else.

```
// Set the local interface from which multicast is to be transmitted
unsigned long addr = inet_addr(YOUR_IP_ADDRESS_STRING);
setsockopt(UDPSocket, IPPROTO_IP, IP_MULTICAST_IF, (char *)&addr,
          sizeof(addr));
```

Once the TTL and multicast interface are set, just sendto() away:

```
SOCKADDR_IN  addrDest;
char         szHi[50];
addrDest.sin_family      = AF_INET;
// Target multicast group address
addrDest.sin_addr.s_addr = inet_addr("234.5.6.7");
// Port on which client is set to receive data packets
addrDest.sin_port        = htons(uiPort);
// Something unoriginal to send
strcpy(szHi,"Hello Multicast Group!");
nRet = sendto(UDPSocket, (char *)szHi, strlen(szHi), 0,
              (struct sockaddr*)&addrDest, sizeof(addrDest));
```

Receiving Multicasts (IPv6)

Multicasting is integral to the design of IPv6. In fact, IPv6 has the ability to support multicasting on disparate networks, even if the intermediate link between them does not. As with IPv4, to receive multicasts, you must create a socket and join a multicast group. However, addresses are 128 bits long, and the multicast address can be derived from the unicast address of the host. The first byte determines the type of address—for a multicast address, this is 256. The next byte determines the scope of the address. This is not defined in terms of the number of hops but has a more concrete meaning:

Value	Scope
1	Node local
2	Link local
3	Administrative local
5	Site local
8	Organization local
14	Global (Internet)

At the time of this writing, the higher bits of the second byte can also contain transience and prefix flags. As the IPv6 protocol continues to evolve, you will need to consult the latest documentation regarding these flags.

Assuming you have created an IPv6 UDP socket, it needs to be bound to a local port. You can work out the local address using the getaddrinfo() function, which, with some hints about the address you want, will figure out the appropriate one:

```
struct sockaddr_in6 addrLocal;
struct addrinfo hints, *result;
memset(&hints, 0, sizeof (hints));
hints.ai_family = AF_INET6;
hints.ai_socktype = SOCK_DGRAM;
hints.ai_flags = AI_NUMERICHOST | AI_PASSIVE;
const char *HOST = "::";    // any local ipv6 interface, e.g. loopback
const char *PORT = "12345"; // specific game port
int ret = getaddrinfo(HOST, PORT, &hints, &result);
memcpy(&addrLocal.sin6_addr, &((struct sockaddr_in6 *)
result->ai_addr)- >sin6_ad dr,
      result->ai_addrlen);
ret = bind(UDP6Socket, (struct sockaddr *)&addrLocal, sizeof(addrLocal)
```

Then you can construct a multicast address based on the unicast address by overriding the first two bytes:

```
struct sockaddr_in6 addrGroup;
ret = getaddrinfo(HOST, PORT, &hints, &result);
memcpy(&addrGroup, &((struct sockaddr_in6 *)result->ai_addr)- >sin6_ad dr,
      result->ai_addrlen);
// Derive the multicast address
addrGroup.sin6_addr.s6_addr[0] = 0xFF; // Multicast
addrGroup.sin6_addr.s6_addr[1] = 0x0E; // Global, Internet
```

We can use the address to join the group. The structure ipv6_mreq is used instead of ip_mreq to accommodate the longer address with the IPV6_JOIN_GROUP option:

```
struct ipv6_mreq mreq6;
mreq6.ipv6mr_multiaddr = addrGroup.sin6_addr;
mreq6.ipv6mr_interface = 0;
ret = setsockopt(UDP6Socket, IPPROTO_IPV6, IPV6_JOIN_GROUP, (char *)&mreq6,
                sizeof(mreq6));
```

Once the group has been joined, recvfrom() will receive the group's IPv6 multicasts for the bound port. You can enable or disable receiving your own multicasts with the IPV6_MULTICAST_LOOP option. To leave the group, use the IPV6_LEAVE_GROUP option:

```
ret = setsockopt(UDP6Socket, IPPROTO_IPV6, IPV6_LEAVE_GROUP, (char *)&mreq6,
                 sizeof(mreq6));
```

Sending Multicasts (IPv6)

As in the receive example, you will first look up the unicast host address and override the first two bytes of the destination unicast address to derive the group address. To set an IPv6 socket's multicast TTL value, setsockopt() can be used with IPPROTO_IPV6 as the protocol level and IP_MULTICAST_HOPS as the socket option:

```
unsigned long HTL = 32 ; // Hops to live
setsockopt(UDP6Socket, IPPROTO_IPV6, IPV6_MULTICAST_HOPS,
           (char *)&HTL, sizeof(HTL));
```

You could also tell the system exactly which local network interface you would like to multicast on with the IPV6_MULTICAST_IF option, but this is optional in IPv6, and a default interface is used. Once the options have been set, use sendto() to send to the group as before:

```
// Something unoriginal to send
char szHi[50];
strcpy(szHi,"Hello IPv6 Multicast Group!");
ret = sendto(UDP6Socket, (char *)szHi, strlen(szHi), 0,
             (struct sockaddr*)&addrGroup, sizeof(addrGroup));
```

You can now join multicast groups and send and receive data from them in both the current- and the next-generation Internet protocols. But how would you implement multicasting as an option in your games?

Integrating Multicast Support into a Game

I won't even try to explain how to integrate multicasting into every different type of game. Instead, I'll give you some ideas about using it in a client-server relationship. First of all, the network code must be backward-compatible. When you add multicast support, make sure you do not remove any existing code unless you really think it is necessary.

When adding multicast support, you can either do a parallel integration where multicasting runs along with existing code, or you could write two separate sets of network code and add a multicast on/off switch for the user. The on/off switch would isolate servers using the other network code and add one more daunting and mysterious switch for the average newbie to get wrong. Parallel integration is my favorite, as it will transparently use multicasting only if it is available.

So let's stick with parallel integration. In this case, the normal network code always runs, but the multicasting code only runs if multicasting is supported. How do you determine if multicasting is supported? Just read the error setsockopt() gives you when trying to join a group. The function will return zero if it succeeds and SOCKET_ERROR if it fails:

```
BOOL ServerSupportMulticast = TRUE;
int nRet = setsockopt(UDPSocket, IPPROTO_IP, IP_ADD_MEMBERSHIP,
                      (char*)&mreq, sizeof(mreq));
if(nRet == SOCKET_ERROR)
{
  // Multicasting not supported. Damn.
  ServerSupportMulticast = FALSE;
}
```

The client-server relationship is a game of two halves. Even if the server supports multicasting, the client might not. How does the server know which clients would be covered with a single send to the multicast group and which would not? The client first determines whether it supports multicasting, and tells the server in a unicast. The server usually keeps a list or an array of clients to which it is easy to add an extra Boolean flag:

```
struct Client
{
  SOCKADDR_IN addrRemote;
  /* ... Game specific info here ...*/
  BOOL SupportMulticast;
};
```

The server's data-sending function must send a multicast to clients that support multicasting and a unicast to those that do not. If, however, the server itself does not support multicasting, then it sends a unicast to every client. Here's a useful pseudo code snippet to illustrate this:

```
int SendToAll(char *Data)
```

```
{
  if(ServerSupportMulticast)
  {
    // First send one multicast, then send individually
    // to those who don't support it
    for(int index = 0; index < MAX_CLIENTS; index++)
    {
      if(Clients[index].Exist && Clients[index].SupportMulticast)
      {
        // At least one client supports multicasting, so use it
        SendMulticast(Data, addrMulticast);
        break;
      }
    }
    for(int index = 0; index < MAX_CLIENTS; index++)
    {
      if(Clients[index].Exist && !Clients[index].SupportMulticast)
      {
        // Only send unicast to clients which do not support multicast
        SendUnicast(Data, Clients[index].addrRemote);
      }
    }
  }
  else
  {
    // Use the old method all the way regardless of client support
    // as we ourselves don't support it
    for(int index = 0; index < MAX_CLIENTS; index++)
    {
      if(Clients[index].Exist)
      {
        SendUnicast(Data, Clients[index].addrRemote);
      }
    }
  }
}
```

I hope I've shed some light on multicasting and its possible uses in games—so for now, happy multicasting!

Thanks to Jan "Riva" Halfar for the wonderful diagrams.

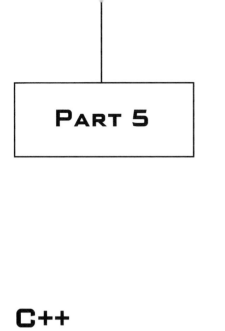

PART 5

C++

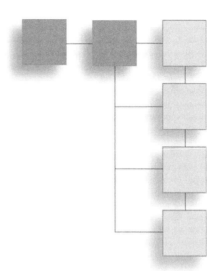

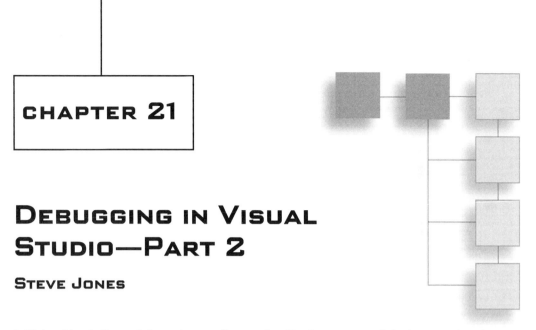

CHAPTER 21

Debugging in Visual Studio—Part 2

Steve Jones

Wikipedia defines debugging as "a methodical process of finding and reducing the number of bugs, or defects, in a computer program or a piece of electronic hardware, thus making it behave as expected." It goes on to explain where the term "bug" came from in the first place. Well regardless of its origin, a bug is widely known in software development to mean an error in the code.

What Are "Bugs"?

In computer software, you can categorize all bugs into a few categories such as *syntax*, *logical*, and *design*. Although it is less common to think of design flaws in programs as "bugs," they can still be considered as such. This article will not spend any time on design bugs, as they can be very, very specific to the software being developed. A syntax bug is an error like forgetting to add the semicolon at the end of a C or C++ statement or a misspelled keyword. Because today's compilers are much more advanced than in earlier days, they will catch most if not all syntax bugs. Much of the time, the Output statements resulting from the errors will give the reasons and the exact locations in source code for the error. In the Visual Studio Integrated Development Environment (IDE), you can simply double-click on the error statement in the Output window, and you will be sent to the line in the problem source code (see Figure 21.1).

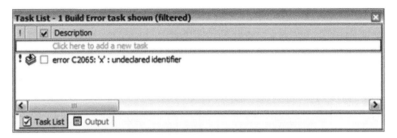

Figure 21.1
Example of a syntax error shown in the Visual Studio Task List window.

Logical bugs (also called *semantic errors*) are those where the source code compiles and perhaps even runs or seems to run fine, yet at some point will fail. Examples of logical bugs are incorrect usage of conditional statements - if (x < 0) instead of if (x > 0) -, which causes unexpected results in the program. Another common example is an uninitialized pointer variable:

```
Monster* pMonster;
pMonster->Attack(); // you will get a run-time error here because
                    // pMonster is uninitialized.
```

This example is pretty blatant, and a good programmer would most likely catch this error before even compiling. Yet an uninitialized pointer variable is still a common bug that finds its way into many programs. Logic errors are the bugs you will be spending most of your time finding and fixing.

So does every programmer know how to debug? Again the answer is sadly, no. While the typical programmer has normally taken courses or has read books on learning software language syntax and software design and construction, it is not so common to see courses devoted to debugging. Yet debugging can be one of the more time-consuming parts of developing good, robust software. Is debugging required for all types of software development? Well, technically speaking, no. If you develop high-quality software from the beginning, then there will not be any errors in the first place. Since most of us live in the real world, we will tend to enter errors into our code mostly by accident.

This article will attempt to explain the more common steps required to successfully debug all types of software programs. The process of debugging is not actually specific to programming. These same principles have been applied to many other types of problem solving as well, yet this article will focus the details on detecting and fixing software bugs.

Simple Debugging Steps Defined

You could call these steps the debugging strategy. Later, I will be discussing more of the tactics of debugging, which include tools to better help the debugger or the one actively involved in finding and solving bugs.

- Identify and stabilize

- Gather behavioral data

- Analyze the data and form hypothesis

- Design experiments to prove or disprove the hypothesis

- Fix the bug

- Verify the fix

- Search for similar bugs

Well there it is—the scientific method of debugging. You may have done most if not all of these steps before. Sometimes a particular step could be very short in duration—for example, you have an integer class variable that you use for counting. Let's also say that you forgot to initialize it during construction of the class object, and its value was supposed to be zero but it was a very large value instead. It may be easy for you to gather the data, analyze it, form a hypothesis, and even suggest a fix all in one step. You basically completed steps 1 through 5 very quickly and in your head. You didn't require any formalized propagation through each debugging step because this error was fairly self-evident. Not all debugging attempts are as simple as the preceding example, so let's take a look at each step in detail.

Identify and Stabilize

If the error is obvious when running the game, then you have at least done the discovery part of this step. This part of debugging requires you to understand how your program works or at least how your program is supposed to work. Perhaps you have run the code in its normal state, and you haven't identified any errors yet. It is a good idea to create *unit tests*. A unit test is a small chunk of code that tests only small parts of your code in a very predictable way. Newer versions of Visual Studio have unit tests built right into the IDE, and they are very easy to construct and execute. When writing units tests, you are specifying how your program ought to behave, therefore, you need to know what to expect as the outcome of the test. Even if you do not write formalized unit tests, you should always perform some sort of testing on your program in order to force unexpected behavior.

Once you have discovered the bug, the next thing you need to do is try to duplicate it. It is much easier to debug when you can predictably reproduce the issue at will. Repeating the bug means you are stabilizing the error. You may need to narrow down a test case so that by changing any aspect of it, it will change the behavior of the error. Then by changing the behavior under your controlled conditions, you can effectively diagnose the problem. This leads us into data gathering.

Gather Behavioral Data

Typically this is the step where you will spend most of your time. So where do you find or detect these behavioral data? If you are one of those programmers who like to use printf or message box instructions, then you probably start adding "I'm here" or variable printouts all over your code so you can gather more detailed information, such as program flow and program state data. Thankfully, there is a better way, which is to use a common tool called a *debugger*. Using a debugger, you can examine the content of variables in your program without having to insert additional calls to output the values. You will be able to control the flow of execution of your program on a very finite level. At the same time, you will be able to watch the state of the variables at deterministic points in time while you are stepping through the code.

Included in most of the Microsoft Visual Studio IDEs is an integrated debugger. Since Visual Studio is one of the most popular compiling environments for Windows, I will discuss using its debugger. For simplicity, I will be covering the tools found in Visual Studio 2005. If you have any of the versions of 2005, including VC++ Express 2005, the same information will apply. In fact, even newer (Visual Studio 2008) and some earlier versions of Visual Studio have the same features, yet they may be found under slightly different menus.

Assertions

What is an assertion? An assertion is a Boolean statement specifying a condition that you expect to get a true result. If the condition is false, then the application discontinues to run at that point and the Assertion Failed dialog appears.

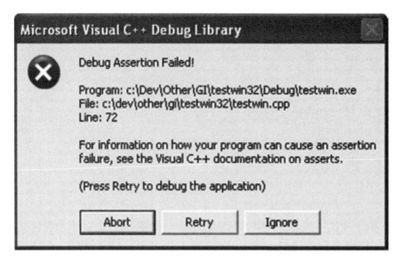

Figure 21.2
Typical Assertion dialog.

Unfortunately, the message found in the dialog isn't always the most informative one.

A screenshot of an Assertion dialog is shown in Figure 21.2. Notice the lack of much useful information. If you look at the message text, you will see that the assert failed in file testwin.cpp at line 72. For a user who may be running your application, this message is next to useless. But as the developer, you have access to that source file and that line of source code so you can go fix the issue.

Asserts are typically used for catching logical errors of operations, validating return codes from function calls, and checking the results from operations.

You might use an assert that checks to see that a string input is not null before performing any actions on it, or verifies the length of a static array before accessing it. Assertions are good for debugging because they can alert the programmer of potentially bad situations that may end up crashing the program later. They highlight buggy areas of code so that they can inject more robust code to prohibit crashes in released code.

In a win32 application, you can use the C runtime (CRT) libraries to help you with asserting. To use them, you need to simply include the header file and the runtime library will automatically be linked for you:

```
#include "crtdbg.h"
```

Here are some examples of using assert:

```
FILE* f = fopen("myfile.txt", "r+");
    assert ( f );
```
or,
```
void MyClass::MyFunction(LPCTSTR szMyStringPtr)
{
  _ASSERT(szMyStringPtr); // asserts here is NULL string
  if (*szMyStringPtr == "whatever")
    DoThis();
}
```

One of the downsides of using asserts is they are not produced in release code. In other words, when compiling released versions of the project, the assert conditions are not tested; therefore, they will not stop potentially bad code from crashing. It is very important that you do not put conditions inside the assertion statement that would not execute in release mode. For example taking one of the previous examples of the right way to use an assert, you can modify it only a little and come up with a wrong way to do it. Do not do this:

```
FILE* f = 0;
assert( f = fopen("myfile.txt", "r+") ); // this line
```

In release builds, the line marked this line will not be compiled; therefore, it will not get executed. This unexpected result will definitely cause you to scratch your head. The point in the preceding code is to detect a null FILE handle before trying to use it further in the program. Since the file is hard-coded in this example you, as the developer, have control over the results. If you are prompting the user for a file to input, using an assertion would not be the best choice. You would want to simply check the FILE pointer and either do nothing and disallow the actions on the file to occur or notify the user with a message or prompt. Or you could do nothing and simply log the error in some log file.

Here's one more example of how *not* to use assert because there will be side effects you may not want:

```
assert(m_nCount++ > 0); // do not do this!
```

Typically, you want to use assert to test for coding and design errors. If the assertion is false, the program terminates and the code must be fixed. Assertions do tend to cloud the code if you sprinkle too many of them throughout your program. It may be better to use asserts wisely in areas you are unsure of in your code to help expose problems.

Exceptions

Exceptions are abnormal situations that happen in your application while it is running. When an exception is thrown, it can either be "handled" or "unhandled." Handling the exception means you are providing a `try`/`catch`, which catches the exceptions you have specified to be caught. If you do not catch the exception, then it is passed up the call stack until it is handled. If it is never handled, then it is called an "unhandled exception" in which the application will crash.

One of the downsides of using exceptions is that when they happen, they do incur some execution-time overhead, which means it can affect the performance of the application. On the flip side, when there is no exception occurring, there is little or no overhead for the application.

Exceptions are different from assertions in that they can have exception handlers associated with them. This feature helps with "fault tolerance," which means you can trap the exception and deal with it gracefully as opposed to the ungraceful application halt with assertions. Trapping or catching the exception allows you to disallow any further action to happen and log the error while moving on. Also in contrast to assertions, exceptions appear in both debug and release builds.

The Visual Studio debugger has a nice feature with exceptions. The feature allows you to break the execution of the application on unhandled exceptions. If you select the menu item Debug > Exceptions, the dialog box shown in Figure 21.3 will pop up, giving you control over the types of exceptions you want the debugger to handle. By default, the Exceptions dialog box lists the most common

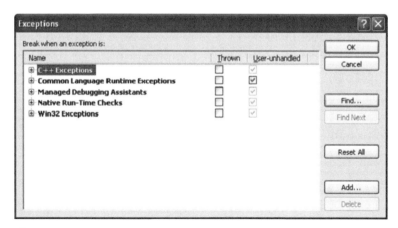

Figure 21.3
Visual Studio's Exceptions dialog box.

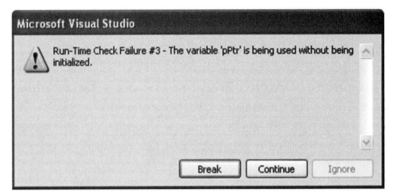

Figure 21.4
Exception Assistant dialog box.

exceptions in each category. When an exception occurs in the application, the debugger kicks in and handles it even before your handler sees it if you have defined one. This gives you the chance to debug the exception before a handler is invoked. If the exception is completely unhandled, then the debugger will always break.

For C++ or native applications, when the debugger breaks due to an exception, the dialog box shown in Figure 21.4 will appear. You have two choices. You can choose Break to try and fix the problem. (Break mode in Visual Studio will be discussed later.) Suffice it to know that you will be taken directly to the problem in your source code. You can also choose to continue the execution of your application without trying to fix the problem, but realize that the Exception dialog box may reappear, since you have not done anything to fix the problem.

Exceptions provide you with the opportunity to handle an error condition, clean up resources, and shut down gracefully if needed. Exceptions work in both debug and release builds of your application. For released applications, your user has come to expect the program to behave properly when an unexpected condition occurs. Using exceptions forces the caller to do something with it—either handle it or not. If not handled, it will "percolate" up the call chain to the next recipient, who then has a chance to handle it.

Visual Studio Debugging

Microsoft Visual Studio is one of the *de facto* IDE compilers out there for making programs that run in Windows. It has an integrated debugger that is very powerful. In a 1000-foot view, the debugger gives you execution control and state inspection tools in the form of windows used for displaying variables and other objects. Having these will allow you to gather behavioral data, which I discussed earlier. Execution control is like aiming a magnifying glass around in your code while the application is running. After you control where the "magnifying glass" points, you can look through it to discover the state of variables. These are necessary data-gathering techniques.

If you don't use a debugger inside an IDE, then in order to trace your program execution, you are left to print statements. But that litters your program with non-essential pieces of code that you either leave in or have to find and remove later. The built-in debugger makes the `print` statement almost obsolete.

Stepping Through Code

You can start and pause/resume, single step your code, pause at specific locations, and jump to specific locations in code at runtime.

Pause/Resume/Stop

You start debugging by either hitting F5 (if your keyboard setting is configured for C++) or clicking on the toolbar button (see Figure 21.5).

In the "paused" mode, the place where you are currently paused is shown by a small, yellow arrow in the left margin of the editor. You always know exactly where you are in the program by this symbol (see Figure 21.6).

Step Into/Step Over/Step Out

Once you pause execution, you have the ability to step through your code line by line, in other words, execute your code one line at a time. From the Debug menu, there is a Step Into command (F11). If you are currently in break mode on a line of code that contains a method call, the Step Into command will enter the method and break again on the first line of code inside the method. In contrast, the Step Over command will execute the entire method call and break on the next

Figure 21.5
Toolbar buttons.

```
TestDebugWindows.cpp
(Global Scope)

 int _tmain(int argc, _TCHAR* argv[])
 {
     CMyClass myclass;
     myclass.Method1();
     int ary[3] = {3,6, 9};

     while(true);

     myclass.Method2(ary);

     return 0;
 }
```

Figure 21.6
The arrow on the left shows where you are currently paused.

Figure 21.7
Step Into, Step Over, and Step Out buttons.

line of code in the current method. Use Step Into if you want to see what happens inside a method call; use Step Over if you only want to execute the entire method and continue in the current code block. See Figure 21.7.

If you are currently inside a method call, you can use Step Out (Shift+F11) to execute all of the remaining lines of code in the method and break again on the first line of code just outside the method call back in the calling routine.

Set Next Statement

Set Next Statement allows you to jump the yellow arrow to anywhere you want to go in your program. All you need to do is position the cursor where you want to skip to and click Set Next Statement on the Debug menu or toolbar button (see Figure 21.8). This may not always give you the results you expect, but for short forward jumps it works better. Alternatively, you can drag the yellow arrow to the line you want, which gives the same effect as if you put the cursor in a new location and selected Set Next Statement.

➡ Set Next Statement

Figure 21.8
Set Next Statement.

➡ Show Next Statement

Figure 21.9
Show Next Statement.

➡☰ Run To Cursor

Figure 21.10
Run to Cursor.

Show Next Statement

To return to the line where the yellow arrow is, just click Show Next Statement on the Debug menu or toolbar button (see Figure 21.9). This is handy if you are in a different file and lost the line where the current program is paused. It is like a homing beacon.

Run to Cursor

This feature allows you to run to a specific insertion point, whether you are in a break or pause mode or not (see Figure 21.10). This is useful as a one-off way to start debugging and pause at a location without having to add a breakpoint there. You can also do this if you are paused already and need to jump to a new location, again not having to insert a breakpoint manually.

Breakpoints

This feature will be one of the most useful things for controlling program execution. Get to know how to use them and use them effectively because they are invaluable. I use breakpoints to tell the debugger where and when I want to pause the execution of the application.

A common method for setting a breakpoint is to press F9 while the cursor is on the line of code you want to break on. When a breakpoint is set, a round, red dot will appear in the left margin of the editor (see Figure 21.11). You can also click in this area of the editor to add a breakpoint. Right-click on an existing breakpoint glyph to set properties, disable, or delete the breakpoint.

```
HRESULT CGame::InitializeD3D( )
{
    HRESULT hr;

    // Create a direct 3D interface object
    m_pD3D9 = Direct3DCreate9( D3D_SDK_VERSION );

    if( m_pD3D9 == NULL )
    {
        // TO DO: Respond to failure of Direct3DCreate9
        return E_FAIL;
    }
}
```

Figure 21.11
A breakpoint set in the left margin.

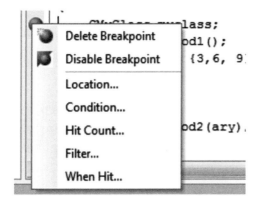

Figure 21.12
The breakpoint context menu showing the types of breakpoints available.

When execution reaches a breakpoint, the debugger pauses all of the application's threads and allows you to inspect the state of your application. You can tell at which breakpoint the pause occurred by noticing which one has the yellow arrow over it, as shown in Figure 21.11. However, you might not want the debugger to pause the application every time you hit the breakpoint, so there are conditions you set for each breakpoint.

Conditional Breakpoints

As you can imagine, these types of breakpoints have some sort of conditions assigned to them. Basically, conditional breakpoints are normal breakpoints, but you continue to add a condition to them. In the Visual Studio 2005 context menu, you can change the Hit Count and Condition of the breakpoint (see Figure 21.12). You need to right-click on the breakpoint dot to bring up the menu.

Conditions and hit counts are useful when setting breakpoints inside of a loop or where code repeats at some frequency, like the main game loop. For example, if something bad happens only when the game mouse cursor in a menu has passed a certain screen location, you can select Condition from the menu, and enter the expression `point.x > 500` into the Condition text box (see Figure 21.13). Instead of breaking on a true condition, you can choose to break when some variable has changed.

For hit count, you can select one of four frequencies when the program encounters the breakpoint. A normal breakpoint is set to break always (see Figure 21.14). For example, you can have a breakpoint only break on the tenth time or break only after skipping the first five times, then break every time thereafter. There is a lot of flexibility when setting conditions on breakpoints.

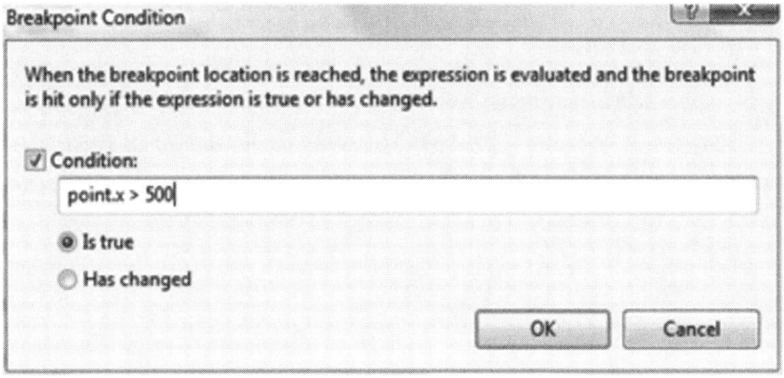

Figure 21.13
A conditional breakpoint.

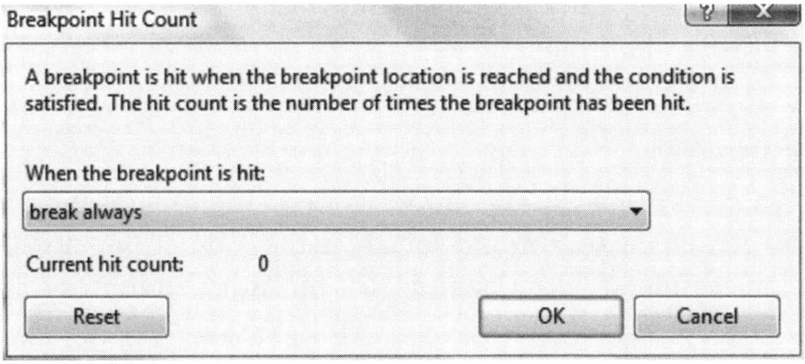

Figure 21.14
A breakpoint set to break on a hit count.

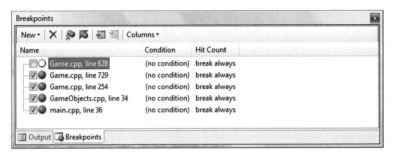

Figure 21.15
The list of breakpoints.

There is a window called Breakpoints found in the Debug > Windows menu selection (see Figure 21.15). This window gives you full control over all the breakpoints currently set in the application. You have control over creating new ones if you know the source file name and line number of where you want it to go. Or you can delete or disable existing ones by selecting them in the window and choosing the appropriate action.

Disabling breakpoints is very advantageous when you want to keep the break-point around but only temporarily take it out of the way. All of the breakpoint settings remain persistent when you shut down and reopen your project's solution file.

Viewing the State of Code

So I have covered the tools in Visual Studio that give you full control over your application in a debugger atmosphere; you have the ability to control where the program goes. Now I need to cover the equally important set of tools that allow you to view the state of your code. Luckily, Visual Studio offers myriad ways to view and analyze data in your application.

State Monitor Windows

The Autos and Locals windows display similar information. If they do not appear automatically, while in a debugging session and you are in break mode or paused, go to the Debug > Windows menu selection and click on Autos and/or Locals submenu (see Figure 21.16).

With each window you get three columns that show you the name, current value, and type of the variable. This is common for all of the windows where you will be

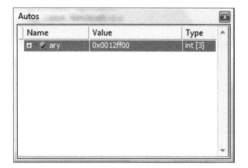
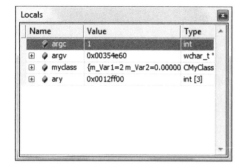

Figure 21.16
Clicking on the plus sign (+) allows you to expand variable types, such as static arrays, classes, and structures.

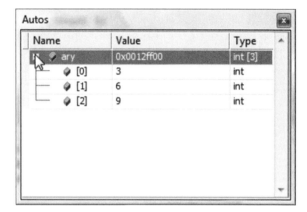

Figure 21.17
The Autos window as a type of "sliding magnifying glass."

watching variables. When a variable changes while single-stepping, it will turn red. That is very handy in situations where you are watching many variables at once.

The Locals window automatically shows all the variables in the current block of code. Inside functions you will see all of the variables that are local to that function. It will show function parameters as well. When the variables go out of scope, they leave the window. The Autos window is similar in that it automatically displays variables, but the variables that show up are only from the current and previous statements (see Figure 21.17). You should consider this window as a type of "sliding magnifying glass" that moves along with you as you step through the code.

There is another highly used window called the Watch window. Like the Autos and Locals windows, it shows you the names, values, and types of variables. In contrast, you need to explicitly put variables you want to watch in the window. This can be done by mouse dragging the variable into the window or by right-clicking and selecting Add Watch from the context menu. To remove variables, you need to manually delete them or drag them outside the window.

For all of these windows mentioned, not only can you view variables, but you are also given another powerful technique that allows you to change things. You are allowed to change the values of variables and the variable names into expressions. In Figure 21.18, ary[1] was changed to 12 by double-clicking on the Value field and typing in the new value. At this point, the program can be continued, and the new value will be in effect. Note that you are only changing the variable's value in memory, not in source code.

You get four independent Watch windows in Visual Studio to use as you need (see Figure 21.19). Each one is identical in function. The state of the Watch

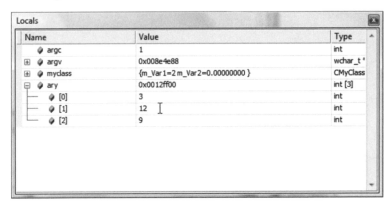

Figure 21.18
Double-click to type in a new value.

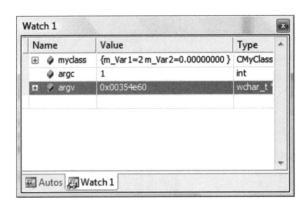

Figure 21.19
A Watch window in Visual Studio.

windows stays persistent when you close down and reopen your solution file, so you don't have to worry about "rebuilding" all of the variables that went into them. That is a nice feature.

Summary

When your program is "buggy," that most likely means you have logical or semantic errors in your code. You need to use a good strategy to repeat, isolate, locate, and fix them. Use asserts and exceptions wisely in order to locate bugs at development time before ever releasing your code. Gathering data is where you will spend most of your time when debugging. There are many ways to gather data, from simple `printf` statements throughout your code to utilizing very powerful debuggers. Visual Studio is one of the more prominent debuggers. A visual debugger gives you many tools used for pinpointing where your code may be going astray. Use the program execution tools to step through the code at the same time that you are using the state visualization tools to watch objects and variables.

Debugging is something you should, and most likely will, be doing; however, you should always avoid having to do it in the first place. You should always be trying to develop code in such a way that those nasty bugs do not creep in. Learn from your usage of the debugger, and put those things in each future project.

References

Deitel, Harvey M. and Paul J. Deitel. *C++ How to Program*. 3rd Ed. Upper Saddle River, NJ: Prentice-Hall, 2001.

Fine, Richard. "Introduction to Debugging" (www.gamedev.net/reference/articles/article2322.asp).

Wikipedia. "Debugging" (http://en.wikipedia.org/wiki/Debugging).

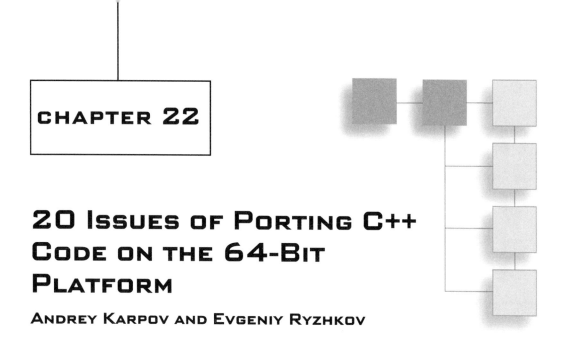

CHAPTER 22

20 Issues of Porting C++ Code on the 64-Bit Platform

Andrey Karpov and Evgeniy Ryzhkov

Program errors can occur while porting C++ code from 32-bit platforms to 64-bit. Examples of the incorrect code and the ways to correct it are given. Methods and means of the code analysis that allow you to diagnose the errors discussed are listed.

Introduction

This article describes the process of porting a 32-bit application to 64-bit systems. The article is written for programmers who use C++, but it may also be useful for all who face the problem of porting applications on other platforms.

You should understand that the new class of errors, which appear while developing 64-bit programs, are not just some new incorrect constructions among thousands of others. These are inevitable difficulties that the developers of any developing program will face. This article will help you to prepare for these difficulties and will show ways to overcome them. Besides advantages, any new technology (in programming and other spheres as well) carries some limitations and even problems. The same situation can be observed in the sphere of 64-bit software development. We all know that 64-bit software is the next step of information technologies development. But in reality, only a few programmers have faced the nuances of this sphere and developing 64-bit programs in particular. We won't dwell on the advantages that the use of 64-bit architecture provides. There are a lot of publications devoted to this theme, and the reader can find them easily.

The aim of this article is to observe thoroughly the problems that can be faced by a developer of 64-bit programs. In this article you will learn about the following:

- Typical programming errors that occur on 64-bit systems

- Causes of these errors, with corresponding examples

- Methods of error correction

- Review of methods and means of searching errors in 64-bit programs

The given information will allow you to do the following:

- Find out the differences between 32-bit and 64-bit systems

- Avoid errors while writing code for 64-bit systems

- Speed up the process of migration of a 32-bit application to the 64-bit architecture via reducing the amount of time necessary for debugging and testing

- Forecast the amount of time necessary to port the code on the 64-bit system more accurately and seriously

This article contains a lot of examples you should try in your programming environment for better understanding. Going into them will give you more than just a set of separate elements—you will open the door into the world of 64-bit systems. To make the following text easier to understand, here's a reminder of some types you can face (see Table 22.1).

We'll use memsize type in the text. This term means any simple integer type that is capable of holding a pointer and changes its size according to the change platform, from 32-bit to 64-bit. For example, memsize types are size_t, ptrdiff_t, all pointers, intptr_t, INT_PTR, and DWORD_PTR.

We should say some words about the data models that determine the correspondence of the sizes of fundamental types for different systems. Table 22.2 contains data models that interest us.

In this article, we'll assume that the program will be ported from a system with the ILP32 data model to systems with the LP64 or LLP64 data model.

Table 22.1 Description of Some Integer Types

Type Name	Type Size (32-Bit System)	Type Size (64-Bit System)	Description
ptrdiff_t	32	64	Signed integer type that appears after subtraction of two pointers. This type is used to keep memory sizes. Sometimes it is used as the result of function returning size or −1 if an error occurs.
size_t	32	64	Unsigned integer type. Data of this type is returned by the sizeof() operator. This type is used to keep size or number of objects.
intptr_t, uintptr_t, SIZE_T, SSIZE_T, INT_PTR, DWORD_PTR, etc	32	64	Integer types capable of keeping pointer value.
time_t	32	64	Amount of time in seconds.

Table 22.2 32-Bit and 64-Bit Data Models

	ILP32	LP64	LLP64	ILP64
char	8	8	8	8
short	16	16	16	16
int	32	32	32	64
long	32	64	32	64
long long	64	64	64	64
size_t	32	64	64	64
pointer	32	64	64	64

And finally, a 64-bit model in Linux (LP64) differs from that in Windows (LLP64) only in the size of long type. Since it is their only difference, we'll avoid using long, unsigned long types, and will instead use ptrdiff_t, size_t types to generalize the article. Following are the type errors that occur while porting programs on the 64-bit architecture.

Disabled Warnings

All books on high-quality code development recommend you set the level of warnings shown by the compiler to the highest possible value. But there are situations in practice when the diagnosis level is low or even disabled. As a rule, it is very old code that is supported but not modified. Programmers who work on the project are used to the fact that this code works, and they don't take its quality into consideration. Thus you can miss serious warnings produced by the compiler while porting programs to the new 64-bit system.

While porting an application, you should turn on warnings for the entire project. This will help you check the compatibility of the code and analyze the code thoroughly. This approach can help you save a lot of time while debugging the project on the new architecture.

If you won't do this, you will face a variety of simple and even stupid errors. Here is a simple example of overflow that occurs in a 64-bit program if you ignore warnings:

```
unsigned char *array[50];
unsigned char size = sizeof(array);
32-bit system: sizeof(array) = 200
64-bit system: sizeof(array) = 400
```

Use of Functions with a Variable Number of Arguments

The typical example is the incorrect use of printf or sprintf functions and their variants:

```
1) const char *invalidFormat = "%u";
   size_t value = SIZE_MAX;
   printf(invalidFormat, value);
2) char buf[9];
   sprintf(buf, "%p", pointer);
```

In the first case, it is not taken into account that size_t is not equivalent to unsigned on the 64-bit platform. It will print an incorrect result if value > UINT_MAX. In the second case, the developer didn't take into account that the pointer size may become more than 32-bit in the future. As a result, this code will cause buffer overflow on the 64-bit architecture.

Incorrect use of functions with a variable number of arguments is a typical error on all architectures, not only on the 64-bit one. This is related to the fundamental danger of the construct as it is used in C++. The common practice is to prefer safe programming methods. We strongly recommend you modify the code and use safe methods. For example, you may replace `printf` with `cout` and `sprintf` with `boost::format` or `std::stringstream`.

If you have to maintain code that uses functions of `sscanf` type, in the format string you can use special macros that turn into necessary modifiers for different systems. For example:

```
// PR_SIZET on Win64 = "I"
// PR_SIZET on Win32 = ""
// PR_SIZET on Linux64 = "l"
// ...
size_t u;
scanf("%" PR_SIZET "u", &u);
```

Magic Numbers

Low-quality code often contains magic numbers, the mere presence of which is dangerous. During the migration of the code to the 64-bit platform, these magic numbers may make the code inefficient if they involve calculation of address, object size, or bit operations. Table 22.3 contains basic magic numbers that may adversely influence an application on a new platform.

You should study the code thoroughly in search of magic numbers and replace them with safe numbers and expressions. To do so, you can use the `sizeof()`

Table 22.3 Unsafe Magic Numbers

Value	Description
4	Number of bytes in a pointer type.
32	Number of bits in a pointer type.
0x7fffffff	The maximum value of a 32-bit signed variable. Mask for zeroing of the high bit in a 32-bit type.
0x80000000	The minimum value of a 32-bit signed variable. Mask for allocation of the high bit in a 32-bit type.
0xffffffff	The maximum value of a 32-bit variable. An alternative record −1 as an error sign.

operator, special values from <limits.h>, <inttypes.h>, and so on. Let's take a look at some errors related to the use of magic numbers. The most frequent is using numbers to store type sizes:

```
1) size_t ArraySize = N * 4;
   intptr_t *Array = (intptr_t *)malloc(ArraySize);
2) size_t values[ARRAY_SIZE];
   memset(values, ARRAY_SIZE * 4, 0);
3) size_t n, newexp;
   n = n >> (32 - newexp);
```

Let's assume that in all cases the size of the types used is always 4 bytes. To make the code correct, you should use the sizeof() operator:

```
1) size_t ArraySize = N * sizeof(intptr_t);
   intptr_t *Array = (intptr_t *)malloc(ArraySize);
2) size_t values[ARRAY_SIZE];
   memset(values, ARRAY_SIZE * sizeof(size_t), 0);
```

or

```
   memset(values, sizeof(values), 0); //preferred alternative
3) size_t n, newexp;
   n = n >> (CHAR_BIT * sizeof(n) - newexp);
```

Sometimes you may need a specific number. As an example, let's take the size_t where all the bits except four low bits must be filled with ones. In a 32-bit program, this number may be declared in the following way:

```
// constant '1111..110000'
const size_t M = 0xFFFFFFF0u;
```

This code is incorrect for a 64-bit system. Such errors are very unpleasant because recording magic numbers may be done in different ways, and it is not easy to search for them. Unfortunately, there is no other way except to find and correct this code using #ifdef or a special macro.

```
#ifdef _WIN64
  #define CONST3264(a) (a##i64)
#else
  #define CONST3264(a)  (a)
#endif
const size_t M = ~CONST3264(0xFu);
```

Sometimes an error code or other special marker -1 is used as 0xFFFFFFFF. On the 64-bit platform, the recorded expression is incorrect, and you should use the -1 value explicitly. Here is an example of using 0xFFFFFFFF value as an error sign:

```
#define INVALID_RESULT (0xFFFFFFFFu)
size_t MyStrLen(const char *str) {
  if (str == NULL)
    return INVALID_RESULT;

  ...
  return n;
}
size_t len = MyStrLen(str);
if (len == (size_t)(-1))
  ShowError();
```

To be on the safe side, let's make sure that you know clearly what the result of (size_t)(-1) value is on the 64-bit platform. You may make a mistake saying the value 0x00000000FFFFFFFFu. According to C++ rules, a −1 value turns into a signed equivalent of a higher type and then into an unsigned value:

```
int a = -1;          // 0xFFFFFFFFi32
ptrdiff_t b = a;     // 0xFFFFFFFFFFFFFFFFi64
size_t c = size_t(b); // 0xFFFFFFFFFFFFFFFFui64
```

Thus (size_t)(-1) on the 64-bit architecture is represented by the 0xFFFFFFFFFFFFFFFFui64 value, which is the highest value for the 64-bit size_t type.

Let's return to the error with INVALID_RESULT. Using the number 0xFFFFFFFFu causes an execution failure of len == (size_t)(-1) in a 64-bit program. The best solution is to change the code in such a way that it doesn't need special marker values. If you need to use them for some reason or consider this suggestion unreasonable, just use value -1:

```
#define INVALID_RESULT (size_t(-1))
...
```

Storing Integers in double Type

double type as a rule has 64 bits size and is compatible with IEEE-754 standard on 32-bit and 64-bit systems. Some programmers use double type for storing of and working with integer types.

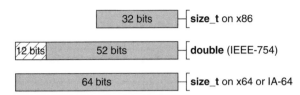

Figure 22.1
The number of significant bits in `size_t` and `double` types.

```
size_t a = size_t(-1);
double b = a;
--a;
--b;
size_t c = b; // x86: a == c
             // x64: a != c
```

The preceding example can be justified on a 32-bit system, for `double` type has 52 significant bits and is capable of storing a 32-bit integer value without a loss. But while trying to store a 64-bit integer in `double`, the exact value can be lost (see Figure 22.1).

It is possible that an approximate value can be used in your program, but to be on the safe side, we'd like to warn you about possible effects on the new architecture. And in any case, it is not recommended to mix integer arithmetic with floating-point arithmetic.

Bit-Shifting Operations

Bit-shifting operations can cause a lot of problems during the port from the 32-bit system on a 64-bit one if used carelessly. Let's begin with an example of a function that defines the bit you've chosen as 1 in a variable of `memsize` type:

```
ptrdiff_t SetBitN(ptrdiff_t value, unsigned bitNum) {
  ptrdiff_t mask = 1 << bitNum;
  return value | mask;
}
```

The given code works only on the 32-bit architecture and works with bits with numbers from 0 to 31. After the program is ported to a 64-bit platform, it becomes necessary to define bits from 0 to 63. What value will the `SetBitN(0, 32)` call return? If you think that the value is `0x100000000`, then this article has not been prepared in vain. You'll get 0.

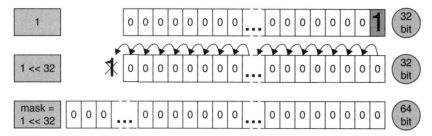

Figure 22.2
Mask value calculation.

Pay attention that 1 has `int` type, and during the shift on 32 positions, an overflow will occur, as shown in Figure 22.2.

To correct the code, it is necessary to make the constant 1 of the same type as the variable `mask`:

```
ptrdiff_t mask = ptrdiff_t(1) << bitNum;
```

or

```
ptrdiff_t mask = CONST3264(1) << bitNum;
```

One more question. What will be the result of the uncorrected function `SetBitN(0, 31)`? The right answer is `0xffffffff80000000`. The result of `1 << 31` expression is the negative number –2147483648. This number is formed in a 64-bit integer variable as `0xffffffff80000000`. You should keep in mind and take into consideration the effects of the shift of values of different types. To help you understand better, Table 22.4 contains interesting expressions with shifts on the 64-bit system.

Table 22.4 Expressions on a 64-Bit System

Expression	Result (Dec)	Result (Hex)
ptrdiff_t Result; Result = 1 << 31;	-2147483648	0xffffffff80000000
Result = ptrdiff_t(1) << 31;	2147483648	0x0000000080000000
Result = 1U << 31;	2147483648	0x0000000080000000
Result = 1 << 32;	0	0x0000000000000000
Result = ptrdiff_t(1) << 32;	4294967296	0x0000000100000000

Storing Pointer Addresses

Many errors during migration to 64-bit systems are related to the change of pointer size in relation to the size of standard integers. Integers and pointers have the same size in an environment with the ILP32 data model. Unfortunately, lots of 32-bit code assumes this everywhere. Pointers are often cast to int, unsigned int, and other improper types for address calculations.

You should use only memsize types for the integer form of pointers. The uintptr_t type is preferable because it clearly shows a programmer's intentions and makes the code more portable, saving it from future changes. Let's take a look at two small examples:

```
1) char *p;
     p = (char *) ((int)p & PAGEOFFSET);
2) DWORD tmp = (DWORD)malloc(ArraySize);

   . . .
     int *ptr = (int *)tmp;
```

Neither example takes into account that the pointer size may differ from 32 bits. They use explicit type conversion, which truncates high bits in the pointer, and this is an error on the 64-bit system. Here are the corrected versions, which use integer memsize types intptr_t and DWORD_PTR to store pointer addresses:

```
1) char *p;
     p = (char *) ((intptr_t)p & PAGEOFFSET);
2) DWORD_PTR tmp = (DWORD_PTR)malloc(ArraySize);

   . . .
     int *ptr = (int *)tmp;
```

The two examples studied are dangerous because their failure might not be found until much later. The program may work correctly with small amounts of data on a 64-bit system, while the truncated addresses are located in the first 4GB of memory. Upon launching the program in a large production environment, there will be memory allocation out of the first 4GB. The code given in the examples will cause undefined behavior of the program on the object out of the first 4GB while processing the pointer. The following code won't hide and will show up at the first execution:

```
void GetBufferAddr(void **retPtr) {

   . . .
   // Access violation on 64-bit system
```

```
  *retPtr = p;
}
unsigned bufAddress;
GetBufferAddr((void **)&bufAddress);
```

The correction is also in the choice of the type capable of storing the pointer:

```
uintptr_t bufAddress;
GetBufferAddr((void **)&bufAddress); //OK
```

There are situations when storing a pointer address into a 32-bit type is just necessary. Mostly such situations appear when it is necessary to work with old API functions. For such cases, you should resort to special functions like Long-ToIntPtr, PtrToUlong, and so on.

In the end, we'd like to mention that it is bad style to store a pointer address into types that are always equal to 64 bits. You will have to correct the code again when 128-bit systems appear:

```
PVOID p;
// Bad style. The 128-bit time will come.
__int64 n = __int64(p);
p = PVOID(n);
```

memsize Types in Unions

The peculiarity of a union is that for all members of the union, the same memory area is allocated—they overlap. Although access to this memory is possible with the use of any of the elements, the element should be chosen so that the result won't be meaningless. You should pay attention to the unions that contain pointers and other members of memsize type.

When it is necessary to work with a pointer as an integer, sometimes it is convenient to use the union as it is shown in the following example and work with the numeric form of the type without using explicit conversions:

```
union PtrNumUnion {
  char *m_p;
  unsigned m_n;
} u;
u.m_p = str;
u.m_n += delta;
```

This code is correct on 32-bit systems but is incorrect on 64-bit ones. When changing the m_n member on a 64-bit system, you work with only a part of the m_p. You should use the type that corresponds to the pointer size:

```
union PtrNumUnion {
  char *m_p;
  size_t m_n; //type fixed
} u;
```

Another frequent use of the union is the presentation of one member as a set of other smaller ones. For example, you may need to split a value of size_t type into bytes to carry out the table algorithm to calculate the number of zero bits in a byte:

```
union SizetToBytesUnion {
  size_t value;
  struct {
    unsigned char b0, b1, b2, b3;
  } bytes;
} u;
SizetToBytesUnion u;
u.value = value;
size_t zeroBitsN = TranslateTable[u.bytes.b0] +
                   TranslateTable[u.bytes.b1] +
                   TranslateTable[u.bytes.b2] +
                   TranslateTable[u.bytes.b3];
```

Following is a fundamental algorithmic error that works with the supposition that size_t type consists of 4 bytes. The possibility of an automatic search of algorithmic errors is hardly possible, but you can search all the unions and check the presence of memsize types in them. Having found such a union, you can find an algorithmic error and rewrite the code in the following way:

```
union SizetToBytesUnion {
  size_t value;
  unsigned char bytes[sizeof(value)];
} u;
SizetToBytesUnion u;
u.value = value;
size_t zeroBitsN = 0;
for (size_t i = 0; i != sizeof(bytes); ++i)
  zeroBitsN += TranslateTable[bytes[i]];
```

Changing an Array Type

Sometimes it is necessary (or just convenient) to present array items as elements of a different type. Dangerous and safe type conversions are shown in the following code:

```
int array[4] = { 1, 2, 3, 4 };
enum ENumbers { ZERO, ONE, TWO, THREE, FOUR };
//safe cast (for MSVC2005)
ENumbers *enumPtr = (ENumbers *)(array);
cout << enumPtr[1] << " ";
//unsafe cast
size_t *sizetPtr = (size_t *)(array);
cout << sizetPtr[1] << endl;
//Output on 32-bit system: 2 2
//Output on 64 bit system: 2 17179869187
```

As you can see, the program output is different in 32-bit and 64-bit systems. On the 32-bit system, the access to the array items is correct because sizes of size_t and int coincide and you see 2 2.

On a 64-bit system, we got 2 17179869187 in the output because the 17179869187 value is located in the first item of sizetPtr array (see Figure 22.3). In some cases, you need this very behavior, but usually it is an error.

The fix for this situation is rejecting dangerous type conversions by modernizing the program. Or create a new array and copy values of the original one into it.

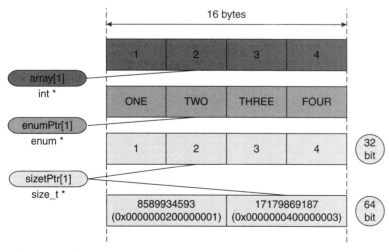

Figure 22.3
Arrangement of array items in memory.

Virtual Functions with Arguments of memsize Type

If there are big derived class graphs with virtual functions in your program, there is a risk of using arguments of different types carelessly. However, these types actually coincide on the 32-bit system. For example, in the base class you use size_t type as an argument of a virtual function, and in the derived class you use the unsigned type. This code will be incorrect on a 64-bit system. But an error like this doesn't necessarily hide in big derived class graphs. Here is one of the examples:

```
class CWinApp {
  ...
  virtual void WinHelp(DWORD_PTR dwData, UINT nCmd);
};
class CSampleApp : public CWinApp {
  ...
  virtual void WinHelp(DWORD dwData, UINT nCmd);
};
```

Let's follow the development life cycle of some applications. Imagine that first it was being developed for Microsoft Visual C++ 6.0 when the WinHelp function in CWinApp class had the following prototype:

```
virtual void WinHelp(DWORD dwData, UINT nCmd = HELP_CONTEXT);
```

It was absolutely correct to overlap the virtual function in CSampleApp class as it is shown in the example. Then the project was ported into Microsoft Visual C++ 2005 where the function prototype in the CWinApp class had undergone some changes, which consisted of replacing the DWORD type with the DWORD_PTR type. On the 32-bit system, the program will work correctly since DWORD and DWORD_PTR types are the same size. There will be trouble during the compilation of the given code for a 64-bit platform. You'll get two functions with the same name but different parameters and, as a result, the user's code won't be executed. The correction is to use the same types in the corresponding virtual functions:

```
class CSampleApp : public CWinApp {
  ...
  virtual void WinHelp(DWORD_PTR dwData, UINT nCmd);
};
```

Serialization and Data Exchange

An important point when porting a software solution to a new platform is the successor to the existing data exchange protocol. It is necessary to read existing project formats, to carry out the data exchange between 32-bit and 64-bit processes, and so on. Mostly, the errors of this kind are in the serialization of memsize types and the data exchange operations using them:

```
1) size_t PixelCount;
   fread(&PixelCount, sizeof(PixelCount), 1, inFile);
2) __int32 value_1;
   SSIZE_T value_2;
   inputStream >> value_1 >> value_2;
3) time_t time;
   PackToBuffer(MemoryBuf, &time, sizeof(time));
```

In all the given examples, there are two kinds of errors: using types of volatile size in binary interfaces and ignoring the byte order.

Using Types of Volatile Size

It is unacceptable to use types that change their size depending on the development environment in binary data exchange interfaces. In C++, none of the types has distinct sizes and, consequently, it is not possible to use them all for these purposes. That's why the developers of the development environments and programmers themselves create data types that have an exact size, such as __int8, __int16, INT32, word64, and so forth.

The usage of such types provides data portability between programs on different platforms, although it needs the usage of odd ones. The following three examples are written inaccurately, and this will show up when changing from 32-bit to 64-bit. Taking into account the necessity to support old data formats, the correction may look as follows:

```
1) size_t PixelCount;
   __uint32 tmp;
   fread(&tmp, sizeof(tmp), 1, inFile);
   PixelCount = static_cast<size_t>(tmp);
2) __int32 value_1;
   __int32 value_2;
   inputStream >> value_1 >> value_2;
3) time_t time;
   __uint32 tmp = static_cast<__uint32>(time);
   PackToBuffer(MemoryBuf, &tmp, sizeof(tmp));
```

But the given correction is not the best. During the port to 64-bit, the program may process large numbers of data, and the use of 32-bit types in the data may become a serious problem. In this case, you may leave the old code for compatibility with the old data format, having corrected the incorrect types, and fulfill the new binary data format taking the errors into account. One more variant is to refuse binary formats and use text format or other formats provided by various libraries.

Ignoring the Byte Order

Even after correcting volatile type sizes, you may face incompatible binary formats. The reason is different data presentation. Most frequently it is related to a different byte order.

The byte order is a method of recording of bytes of multibyte numbers (see Figure 22.4). The little-endian order means that the recording starts with the lowest byte and ends with the highest one. This recording order was acceptable for the memory of x86 PCs. With the big-endian order, the recording starts with the highest byte and ends with the lowest one. This order is a standard for TCP/IP protocols. That's why the big-endian byte order is often called the *network* byte order. This byte order is used by the Motorola 68000 and SPARC processors.

While developing the binary interface or data format, you should keep the byte order in mind. If the 64-bit system on which you are porting a 32-bit application has a different byte order, you'll just have to take it into account in your code. For conversion between the big-endian and the little-endian byte orders, you may use functions like `htonl()`, `htons()`, `bswap_64`, and so on.

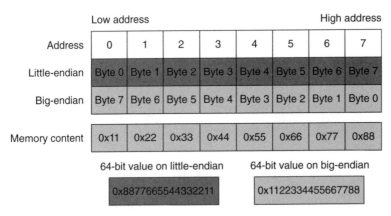

Figure 22.4
Byte order in a 64-bit type on little-endian and big-endian systems.

Bit Fields

If you use bit fields, you should keep in mind that the use of memsize types will change sizes of structures and alignment. For example, the following structure has 4 bytes size on the 32-bit system and 8 bytes size on a 64-bit one:

```
struct MyStruct {
  size_t r : 5;
};
```

But our attention to bit fields is not limited by that. Let's take a delicate example:

```
struct BitFieldStruct {
  unsigned short a:15;
  unsigned short b:13;
};
BitFieldStruct obj;
obj.a = 0x4000;
size_t addr = obj.a << 17; //Sign Extension
printf("addr 0x%Ix\n", addr);
//Output on 32-bit system: 0x80000000
//Output on 64-bit system: 0xffffffff80000000
```

Note that if you compile the example for a 64-bit system, there is a sign extension in the addr = obj.a << 17; expression, despite the fact that both variables, addr and obj.a, are unsigned. This sign extension is caused by the rules of type conversion, which are used in the following way (see also Figure 22.5):

- A member of obj.a is converted from a bit field of unsigned short type into int. You get int type and not unsigned int because the 15-bit field can be located in the 32-bit signed integer.

- obj.a << 17; expression has int type, but it is converted into ptrdiff_t and then into size_t before it will be assigned to variable addr. The sign extension occurs during the conversion from int into ptrdiff_t.

Therefore, you should be attentive while working with bit fields. To avoid the described effect in our example, you can simply use explicit conversion from obj.a type to size_t type.

```
...
size_t addr = size_t(obj.a) << 17;
printf("addr 0x%Ix\n", addr);
//Output on 32-bit system: 0x80000000
//Output on 64-bit system: 0x80000000
```

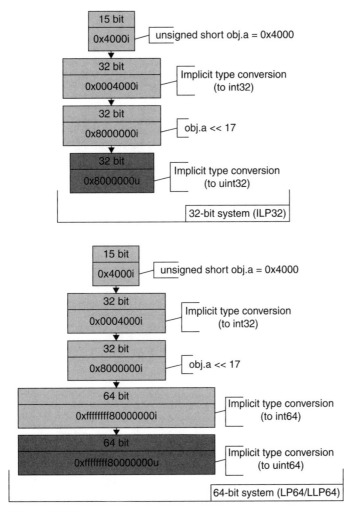

Figure 22.5
Expression calculation on different systems.

Pointer Address Arithmetic

The first example:

```
unsigned short a16, b16, c16;
char *pointer;
...
pointer += a16 * b16 * c16;
```

This example works correctly with pointers if the value of the a16 * b16 * c16 expression does not exceed UINT_MAX (4GB). Such code could always work correctly on the 32-bit platform, for the program does not have large unallocated arrays. On the 64-bit architecture, the size of the array exceeded UINT_MAX items. Suppose you would like to shift the pointer value 6,000,000,000 bytes, and that's why variables a16, b16, and c16 have values 3000, 2000, and 1000, correspondingly. While calculating a16 * b16 * c16, all the variables according to C++ rules will be converted to int type, and only then their multiplication will occur. During multiplication, an overflow will occur. The incorrect expression result will be extended to ptrdiff_t type, and the calculation of the pointer will be incorrect.

One should take care to avoid possible overflows in pointer arithmetic. For this purpose, it's better to use memsize types or explicit type conversion in expressions that carry pointers. You can rewrite the code in the following way using explicit type conversion:

```
short a16, b16, c16;
char *pointer;
...
pointer += static_cast<ptrdiff_t>(a16) *
           static_cast<ptrdiff_t>(b16) *
           static_cast<ptrdiff_t>(c16);
```

If you think that only programs that work on larger data sizes face problems, we have to disappoint you. Let's take a look at some interesting code for working with an array containing only five items. The second example works in the 32-bit version but does not work in the 64-bit one.

```
int A = -2;
unsigned B = 1;
int array[5] = { 1, 2, 3, 4, 5 };
int *ptr = array + 3;
ptr = ptr + (A + B); //Invalid pointer value on 64-bit platform
printf("%i\n", *ptr); //Access violation on 64-bit platform
```

Let's follow the calculation flow of the ptr + (A + B) expression:

- According to C++ rules, variable A of int type is converted to unsigned type.

- Addition of A and B occurs. The result you get is value 0xFFFFFFFF of unsigned type.

Then calculation of ptr + 0xFFFFFFFFu takes place, but the result of it depends on the pointer size on the particular architecture. If the addition will take place in a

32-bit program, the given expression will be an equivalent of ptr - 1, and we'll successfully print number 3.

In a 64-bit program, 0xFFFFFFFFu value will be added properly to the pointer, and the result will be that the pointer will be outside the array bounds. And we'll face problems while getting access to the item of this pointer. To avoid the shown situation, as well as in the first case, we advise you to use only memsize types in pointer arithmetic. Here are two variants of the code correction:

```
ptr = ptr + (ptrdiff_t(A) + ptrdiff_t(B));
ptrdiff_t A = -2;
size_t B = 1;
...
ptr = ptr + (A + B);
```

You may object and offer the following variant of the correction:

```
int A = -2;
int B = 1;
...
ptr = ptr + (A + B);
```

Yes, this code will work, but it is bad for the following reasons:

1. It will teach you inaccurate pointer arithmetic. After a while, you may forget nuances and make a mistake by making one of the variables of unsigned type.

2. Use of non-memsize types along with pointers is potentially dangerous. Suppose variable Delta of int type participates in an expression with a pointer. This expression is absolutely correct. But the error may hide in the calculation of the variable Delta itself, for 32-bit may not be enough to make the necessary calculations while working with large data arrays. The use of memsize type for variable Delta liquidates the problem automatically.

Array Indexing

These errors are separated from the others because indexing in arrays with square brackets is just a different method of address arithmetic observed before. Programming in C and then C++ has made a custom of using variables of int/ unsigned types in the following way:

```
signed Index = 0;
```

```
while (MyBigNumberField[Index] != id)
  Index++;
```

But time passes, and everything changes. And now it's time to say—do not do this anymore! Use `memsize` types for indexing (large) arrays.

The given code won't process an array containing more than `UINT_MAX` items in a 64-bit program. After accessing an item with an index of `UNIT_MAX`, an overflow of the `Index` variable will occur, and you'll get an infinite loop. To persuade you of the necessity of using only `memsize` types for indexing and in the expressions of address arithmetic, we'll give the last example:

```
class Region {
  float *array;
  int Width, Height, Depth;
  float Region::GetCell(int x, int y, int z) const;
  ...
};
float Region::GetCell(int x, int y, int z) const {
  return array[x + y * Width + z * Width * Height];
}
```

The given code is taken from a real mathematics simulation program in which the size of RAM is an important resource, and the possibility to use more than 4GB of memory on the 64-bit architecture improves the calculation speed greatly. In the programs of this class, one-dimensional arrays are often used to save memory while they act as three-dimensional arrays. For this purpose, there are functions like `GetCell`, which provide access to the necessary items. But the given code will work correctly only with the arrays containing less than `INT_MAX` items. The reason for that is the use of 32-bit `int` types for calculation of the item's index.

Programmers often make a mistake trying to correct the code in the following way:

```
float Region::GetCell(int x, int y, int z) const {
  return array[static_cast<ptrdiff_t>(x) + y * Width +
               z * Width * Height];
}
```

They know that according to C++, rules the expression for calculation of the index will have `ptrdiff_t` type and hope to avoid the overflow with its help. But the overflow may occur inside the subexpression y * Width or z * Width * Height because the int type is still used to calculate them.

If you want to correct the code without changing variables' types in the expression, you may use explicit type conversion of every variable to memsize type:

```
float Region::GetCell(int x, int y, int z) const {
  return array[ptrdiff_t(x) +
            ptrdiff_t(y) * ptrdiff_t(Width) +
            ptrdiff_t(z) * ptrdiff_t(Width) *
            ptrdiff_t(Height)];
}
```

Another solution is to replace types of variables with memsize type:

```
typedef ptrdiff_t TCoord;
class Region {
  float *array;
  TCoord Width, Height, Depth;
  float Region::GetCell(TCoord x, TCoord y, TCoord z) const;
  ...
};
float Region::GetCell(TCoord x, TCoord y, TCoord z) const {
  return array[x + y * Width + z * Width * Height];
}
```

Mixed Use of Simple Integer Types and memsize Types

Mixed use of memsize and non-memsize types in expressions may cause incorrect results on 64-bit systems and can be related to the change of the input value's rate. Let's study some examples.

```
size_t Count = BigValue;
for (unsigned Index = 0; Index != Count; ++Index)
{ ... }
```

The preceding is an example of an infinite loop if Count > UINT_MAX. Suppose this code worked on 32-bit systems with the range less than UINT_MAX iterations. But a 64-bit variant of the program may process more data, and it may need more iterations. As long as the values of the Index variable lie in the [0..UINT_MAX] range, the `Index != Count` condition will never be executed and this will cause the infinite loop.

Another frequent error is recording expressions in the following form:

```
int x, y, z;
intptr_t SizeValue = x * y * z;
```

Similar examples were discussed earlier when, during the calculation of values with the use of non-`memsize` types, an arithmetic overflow occurred and the last result was incorrect. Search and correction of the given code is made more difficult because compilers do not show any warning messages as a rule. This construction is absolutely correct for the C++ language. Several variables of `int` type are multiplied, and after that the result is implicitly converted to `intptr_t` type and assignment occurs.

We'll provide an example of a small code fragment that shows the danger of inaccurate expressions with mixed types. (The results are retrieved in Microsoft Visual C++ 2005, 64-bit compilation mode.)

```
int x = 100000;
int y = 100000;
int z = 100000;
intptr_t size = 1;                    // Result:
intptr_t v1 = x * y * z;         // -1530494976
intptr_t v2 = intptr_t(x) * y * z;   // 1000000000000000
intptr_t v3 = x * y * intptr_t(z);   // 141006540800000
intptr_t v4 = size * x * y * z;      // 1000000000000000
intptr_t v5 = x * y * z * size;      // -1530494976
intptr_t v6 = size * (x * y * z);    // -1530494976
intptr_t v7 = size * (x * y) * z;    // 141006540800000
intptr_t v8 = ((size * x) * y) * z;  // 1000000000000000
intptr_t v9 = size * (x * (y * z));  // -1530494976
```

It is necessary that all the operands in such expressions have been converted to the type of larger capacity in time. Remember that the expression of the following kind

```
intptr_t v2 = intptr_t(x) * y * z;
```

does not promise the right result. It promises only that the intptr_t(x) * y * z expression will have `intptr_t` type. The right result shown by this expression in the example is good fortune caused by a particular compiler version and occasional process.

The calculation order of an expression with operators of the same priority is not defined. To be more exact, the compiler can calculate subexpressions in such an order that it considers to be more efficient, even if subexpressions have side effects. The order of the side effects is not defined. Expressions including commutative and associative operations (∗, +, &, |, ^) may be converted in a free way even if there are brackets. To assign strict order to the calculation of the expression, it is necessary to use an explicit temporary variable. That's why if the result of the expression should be of memsize type, only memsize types must participate in the expression. Here is the right variant:

```
intptr_t v2 = intptr_t(x) * intptr_t(y) * intptr_t(z); // OK!
```

Note

> If you have a lot of integer calculations and overflow-control is an important task for you, we suggest you pay attention to the SafeInt class, the description of which can be found in the MSDN library.

Mixed use of types may cause changes in program logic:

```
ptrdiff_t val_1 = -1;
unsigned int val_2 = 1;
if (val_1 > val_2)
  printf ("val_1 is greater than val_2\n");
else
  printf ("val_1 is not greater than val_2\n");
//Output on 32-bit system: "val_1 is greater than val_2"
//Output on 64-bit system: "val_1 is not greater than val_2"
```

On the 32-bit system, the variable val_1 according to C++ rules was extended to unsigned int and became value 0xFFFFFFFFu. As a result, the condition 0xFFFFFFFFu > 1 was executed. On the 64-bit system, it's just the other way round: the variable val_2 is extended to ptrdiff_t type. In this case, the expression -1 > 1 is checked. Figure 22.6 shows the changes.

If you need to return the previous behavior, you should change the val_2 variable type.

```
ptrdiff_t val_1 = -1;
size_t val_2 = 1;
if (val_1 > val_2)
  printf ("val_1 is greater than val_2\n");
else
  printf ("val_1 is not greater than val_2\n");
```

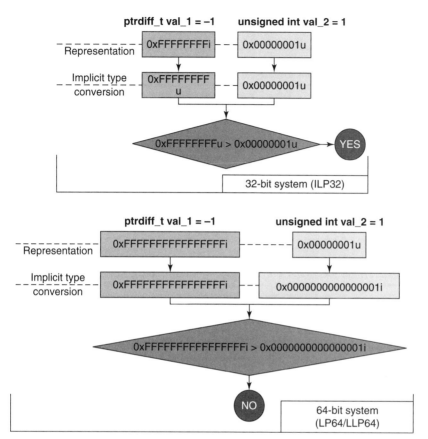

Figure 22.6
Changes occurring in the expression.

Implicit Type Conversions in Functions

Observing the previous kinds of errors related to mixing simple integer types and memsize types, we have examined only simple expressions. But similar problems may occur while using other C++ constructions, too.

```
extern int Width, Height, Depth;
size_t GetIndex(int x, int y, int z) {
  return x + y * Width + z * Width * Height;
}
...
MyArray[GetIndex(x, y, z)] = 0.0f;
```

If you work with large arrays (more than INT_MAX items), the given code may behave incorrectly, and we will not address the items of MyArray that we wanted.

Despite returning the `size_t` type, the `x + y * Width + z * Width * Height` expression is calculated by using the `int` type. We suppose you have already guessed that the corrected code will look as follows:

```
extern int Width, Height, Depth;
size_t GetIndex(int x, int y, int z) {
  return (size_t)(x) +
         (size_t)(y) * (size_t)(Width) +
         (size_t)(z) * (size_t)(Width) * (size_t)(Height);
}
```

In the next example, we also have `memsize` type (pointer) and simple `unsigned` type mixed:

```
extern char *begin, *end;
unsigned GetSize() {
  return end - begin;
}
```

The result of the `end - begin` expression has the `ptrdiff_t` type. As far as the function returns `unsigned` type, implicit type conversion will lose high bits. Thus if the `begin` and `end` pointers address the beginning and the end of an array whose size is larger than `UINT_MAX` (4GB), the function will return an incorrect value.

Here is one more example, but now observe not the returned value but the formal function argument:

```
void foo(ptrdiff_t delta);
int i = -2;
unsigned k = 1;
foo(i + k);
```

Does this code remind you of the incorrect pointer arithmetic example discussed earlier? Yes, we find the same situation here. The incorrect result appears during the implicit type conversion of the actual argument, which has the `0xFFFFFFFF` value from the `unsigned` type to the `ptrdiff_t` type.

Overloaded Functions

During the port of 32-bit programs to a 64-bit platform, there may be a change of logic related to the use of overloaded functions. If the function is overlapped for 32-bit and 64-bit values, access to it with arguments of type `memsize` will be compiled into different calls on different systems. This approach may be useful as, for example, in the following code:

```
static size_t GetBitCount(const unsigned __int32 &) {
  return 32;
}
static size_t GetBitCount(const unsigned __int64 &) {
  return 64;
}
size_t a;
size_t bitCount = GetBitCount(a);
```

But such a change of logic contains a potential danger. Imagine a program in which a class is used for organizing a stack. The peculiarity of this class is that it allows values of different types:

```
class MyStack {
...
public:
  void Push(__int32 &);
  void Push(__int64 &);
  void Pop(__int32 &);
  void Pop(__int64 &);
} stack;
ptrdiff_t value_1;
stack.Push(value_1);
...
int value_2;
stack.Pop(value_2);
```

A careless programmer placed values of different types (ptrdiff_t and int), and then took them from the stack. On the 32-bit system, their sizes coincided and everything worked perfectly. When the size of ptrdiff_t type changes in a 64-bit program, the stack object begins to take more bytes than it retrieves later. You probably understand this class of errors, but you should pay attention to overloaded functions transferring actual arguments of memsize type.

Data Alignment

Processors work more efficiently when they deal with proper data alignment. As a rule, a 32-bit data item must be aligned at the border multiple of 4 bytes and a 64-bit item at the border multiple of 8 bytes. An attempt to work with unaligned data on IA-64 (Itanium) processors will cause an exception, as shown in the following example:

```
#pragma pack (1) // Also set by key /Zp in MSVC
struct AlignSample {
  unsigned size;
  void *pointer;
} object;
void foo(void *p) {
  object.pointer = p; // Alignment fault
}
```

If you have to work with unaligned data on Itanium, you should tell the compiler. For example, you may use a special macro UNALIGNED:

```
#pragma pack (1) // Also set by key /Zp in MSVC
struct AlignSample {
  unsigned size;
  void *pointer;
} object;
void foo(void *p) {
  *(UNALIGNED void *)&object.pointer = p; //Very slow
}
```

This solution is not efficient because access to the unaligned data will be several times slower. A better result may be achieved if you arrange 32-bit, 16-bit, and 8-bit items in 64-bit data items. On the x64 architecture, unaligned data exceptions do not occur, but you should avoid them anyway—first, because of the essential slowdown of access to the data and second, because of the possibility of porting the program to the IA-64 platform in future.

Let's take a look at one more example of code that does not take data alignment into account:

```
struct MyPointersArray {
  DWORD m_n;
  PVOID m_arr[1];
} object;
...
malloc( sizeof(DWORD) + 5 * sizeof(PVOID) );
...
```

If you want to allocate the memory size necessary for storing an object of the MyPointersArray type containing five pointers, you should take into account that

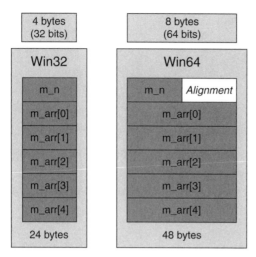

Figure 22.7
Alignment of data in memory on Win32 and Win64 systems.

the beginning of the array m_arr will be aligned at the border of 8 bytes. The order of data in memory on different systems (Win32/Win64) is shown in Figure 22.7.

The correct calculation of the size should look like this:

```
struct MyPointersArray {
  DWORD m_n;
  PVOID m_arr[1];
} object;
...
malloc( FIELD_OFFSET(struct MyPointersArray, m_arr) +
        5 * sizeof(PVOID) );
...
```

In this code, you get the shift of the last structure member and add this shift to the member's size. The shift of a member of the structure or a class may be recognized when the offsetof or FIELD_OFFSET macro is used. Always use these macros to get a shift in the structure without relying on your knowledge of the sizes of types and the alignment. Here is an example of code with the correct calculation of the structure member address:

```
struct TFoo {
  DWORD_PTR whatever;
```

```
    int value;
} object;
int *valuePtr =
  (int *)((size_t)(&object) + offsetof(TFoo, value)); // OK
```

Exceptions

Throwing and handling exceptions using integer types is not good programming practice in C++. You should use more informative types for such purposes—for example, classes derived from the std::exception class. But sometimes you have to work with low-quality code like this:

```
char *ptr1;
char *ptr2;
try {
  try {
    throw ptr2 - ptr1;
  }
  catch (int) {
    std::cout << "catch 1: on x86" << std::endl;
  }
}
catch (ptrdiff_t) {
  std::cout << "catch 2: on x64" << std::endl;
}
```

You should thoroughly avoid throwing or handling exceptions using memsize types, since it may cause a change of program logic. The correction of the given code may consist of replacing catch (int) with catch (ptrdiff_t). A better correction is to use a special class for transferring the information about the error that has occurred.

Using Outdated Functions and Predefined Constants

While developing a 64-bit application, keep in mind the changes in the environment in which it will be performed. Some functions will become outdated, and it will be necessary to replace them with new versions. GetWindowLong is a good example of such a function in Windows. Pay attention to the constants concerning interaction with the environment in which the program is functioning. In Windows, the lines containing system32 or Program Files will be suspicious.

Explicit Type Conversions

Be accurate with explicit type conversions. They may change the logic of the program execution when types change their capacity or cause loss of significant bits. It is difficult to deduce typical examples of errors related to the explicit type conversion, for they are very different and specific for different programs. You should be acquainted with some errors related to the explicit type conversion from earlier in this article.

Error Diagnosis

The diagnosis of the errors occurring while porting 32-bit programs on 64-bit systems is a difficult task. The port of low-quality code written without taking into account peculiarities of other architectures may demand a lot of time and effort. That's why we'll pay some attention to the approach and means that may simplify this task.

Unit Testing

Unit testing earned respect among programmers long ago. Unit tests will help you check the correctness of the program after the port on a new platform. But there is one nuance that you should keep in mind.

Unit testing may not allow you to check the new ranges of input values that have become accessible on 64-bit systems. Unit tests are originally developed in such a way that they can be passed in a short time. And a function that usually works with an array with the size of tens of MB will probably process tens of KB in unit tests. It is justified because this function may be called many times with different sets of input values in tests. But suppose you have a 64-bit version of the program. And now the function we study is processing more than 4GB of data. Of course, it appears necessary to raise the input size of an array in the tests up to sizes greater than 4GB. The problem is that the time to pass the tests will increase greatly in such a case.

That's why, while modifying the sets of tests, keep in mind the compromise between speed of passing unit tests and the fullness of the checks. Fortunately, there are other approaches that can help you make sure your application works correctly.

Code Review

Code review is the best method of searching for errors and improving code. Combined and thorough code review may help you completely get rid of errors that are related to the peculiarities of the development of 64-bit applications. Of course, in the beginning you should learn which errors to search for; otherwise, the review won't give good results. For this purpose, it is necessary to read this and other articles concerning porting programs from 32-bit systems to 64-bit. (Some interesting links concerning this topic can be found in the end of the article in the "References" section.)

But this approach to the analysis of the original code has a significant disadvantage. It demands a lot of time, and because of this, it is actually inapplicable on large projects. The compromise is the use of static analyzers. A *static analyzer* can be considered to be an automated system for code review where a fetch of potentially dangerous places is created for a programmer so that he could carry out the further analysis.

But in any case it is desirable to provide several code reviews for teaching the team to search for new kinds of errors occurring on 64-bit systems.

Built-In Means of Compilers

Compilers can solve some problems with defective code. They often have built-in mechanisms for diagnosing observed errors. For example, in Microsoft Visual C++ 2005, the following keys may be useful: /Wp64, /Wall, and in SunStudio C++, key –xport64.

Unfortunately, the possibilities they provide are often not enough, and you should not rely solely on them. But in any case, it is highly recommended to enable the corresponding options of a compiler for diagnosing errors in the 64-bit code.

Static Analyzers

Static analyzers are a fine means to improve quality and safety of program code. The basic difficulty related to the use of static analyzers is in the fact that they generate quite a lot of false warning messages concerning potential errors. Programmers, being lazy by nature, use this argument to avoid correcting errors that are found. Microsoft solves this problem by including the found errors in the bug tracking system unconditionally. Thus a programmer cannot choose between the correction of the code and an attempt to avoid this.

We think that such strict rules are justified. The profit of quality code justifies the outlay of time for static analysis and corresponding code modification. This profit is achieved by means of simplifying the code support and reducing the time of debugging and testing. Static analyzers may be successfully used for diagnosing many of the errors observed in this article.

We know of three static analyzers that are supposed to have means of diagnosing errors related to porting programs to 64-bit systems. We would like to warn you, however, that we may be mistaken about the possibilities they have. Moreover, these are developing products and new versions may have greater efficiency.

- **Gimpel Software PC-Lint** (www.gimpel.com). This analyzer has a large list of supported platforms and is the static analyzer of general purpose. It catches errors while porting programs to the LP64 data model. The advantage is the possibility to organize strict control over the type conversions. The absence of the environment may be considered a disadvantage, but it may be corrected by using an additional product, Riverblade Visual Lint.

- **Parasoft C++test** (www.parasoft.com). Another well-known general purpose static analyzer, C++test has support for a lot of devices and platforms. It has a built-in environment that greatly simplifies the work process and setting the analysis rules. C++test, like PC-Lint, is intended for the LP64 data model.

- **Viva64** (www.viva64.com). Unlike other analyzers, Viva64 is intended to work with the Windows LLP64 data model. It is integrated into Visual Studio 2005. The analyzer is intended only for diagnosing problems related to porting programs to 64-bit systems, greatly simplifying its setup.

Conclusion

If you read these lines, we are glad that you're interested. We hope the article has been useful for you and will help you simplify the development and debugging of 64-bit applications. We will be glad to receive your opinions, remarks, corrections, and additions and will surely include them in the next version of the article. The more we describe typical errors, the more profitable will be our experience and ability to provide help.

References

Adiga, Harsha S. "Porting Linux Applications to 64-Bit Systems." April 12, 2006 (www.viva64.com/go.php?url=7).

Graegert, Steve. "64-Bit Data Models Explained." (www.viva64.com/go .php?url=10).

Hewlett-Packard. "Porting an Application to 64-bit Linux on HP Integrity Servers." (www.viva64.com/go.php?url=8).

Josey, Andrew. "Data Size Neutrality and 64-Bit Support." *The Open Group* (www.viva64.com/go.php?url = 6).

Murawski, Stan. "Beyond Windows XP: Get Ready Now for the Upcoming 64-Bit Version of Windows." *MSDN Magazine.* November 2001 (www.viva64.com/go.php?url = 9).

Shekar, Chandra. "Extend Your Application's Reach from 32-Bit to 64-Bit Environments: Part 3: Porting Example." October 2006 (www.viva64.com/ go.php?url=4).

Sun Studio Team. "Converting 32-bit Applications into 64-bit Applications: Things to Consider." January 2005 (www.viva64.com/go.php?url=5).

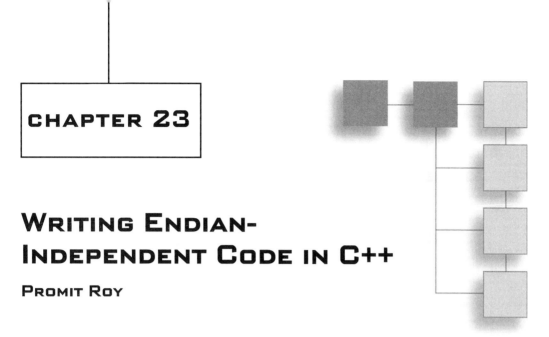

CHAPTER 23

WRITING ENDIAN-
INDEPENDENT CODE IN C++

PROMIT ROY

Endians are a confusing topic for many people. Hopefully, by reading this article you will understand both what endian means and how to write code to deal with it. So I might as well start with the obvious question: what does endian mean?

The actual origin of the term "endian" is a funny story. In *Gulliver's Travels* by Jonathan Swift, one of the places Gulliver visits has two groups of people who are constantly fighting. One group believes that a hard-boiled egg should be eaten from the big, round end (the "big endians"), and the other group believes that it should be eaten from the small, pointy end (the "little endians"). Endian no longer has anything to do with hard-boiled eggs, but in many ways, the essence of the story (two groups fighting over a completely pointless subject) still remains.

Suppose we start with an unsigned 2-byte (16-bit) long number; I'll use 43707. If you look at the hexadecimal version of 43707, it's 0xAABB. Now, hexadecimal notation is convenient because it neatly splits up the number into its component bytes. One byte is AA and the other byte is BB. But how would this number look in the computer's memory (not hard drive space, just regular memory)? Well, the most obvious way to keep this number in memory would be like this:

| AA | BB |

The first byte is the "high" byte of the number, and the second one is the "low" byte of the number. High and low refer to the value of the byte in the number; here, AA is high because it represents the higher digits of the number. This order of keeping things is called MSB (most significant byte) or *big endian*. The most popular processors that use big endian are the PPC family, used by Macs. This family includes the G3, G4, and G5 that you see in most Macs nowadays.

So what is little endian, then? Well, a little endian version of 0xAABB looks like this in memory:

| BB | AA |

Notice that it's the opposite of the other one. This is called LSB (least significant byte) or *little endian*. There are a lot of processors that use little endian; but the most well known are the x86 family, which includes the entire Pentium and Athlon lines of chips, as well as most other Intel and AMD chips. The actual reason for using little endian is a question of CPU architecture and outside the scope of this article; suffice to say that little endian made compatibility with earlier 8-bit processors easier when 16-bit processors came out, and 32-bit processors kept the trend.

It gets a little more complicated than that. If you have a 4-byte (32-bit) long number, it's completely backward, not switched every two bytes. Floating-point numbers are handled a little differently as well. This means you can't arbitrarily change the endian of a file; you have to know what data is in it and what order it's in. The only good news is that if you're reading raw bytes that are only eight bits at a time, you don't have to worry about endians.

When Does the Endian Affect Code?

The short answer is, endians come into play whenever your code assumes that a certain endian is being used. The most frequent time this happens is when you're reading from a file. If you are on a big endian system and write, say, 10 long integers to a file, they will all be written in big endian. If you read them back, the system will assume you're reading big endian numbers. The same is true of little endian systems: everything will work with little endian. This causes problems when you have to use the same file on both little and big endian systems. If you write the file in little endian, big endian systems will get screwed up. If you write it in big endian, little endian systems get screwed up. Sure, you *could* keep two different versions of the file, one big, one small, but that's going to get confusing very quickly, and annoying as well.

The other major time that endians matter is when you use a type cast that depends on a certain endian being in use. I'll show you one example right now (keep in mind that there are many different type casts that can cause problems):

```
unsigned char EndianTest[2] = { 1, 0 };
short x;
x = *(short *) EndianTest;
```

So the question is, what's x? Let's look at what this code is doing. I'm creating an array of two bytes, and then casting that array of two bytes into a single short. What I've done by using an array is basically forced a certain byte order, and you're going to see how the system treats those two bytes. If this is a little endian system, the 0 and 1 will be interpreted backward and will be seen as 0,1. Since the high byte is 0, it doesn't matter and the low byte is 1—x will be equal to 1. On the other hand, if it's a big endian system, the high byte will be 1 and the value of x will be 256. I'll use this trick later to determine what endian the system is using without having to set any conditional compilation flags.

Writing Endian-Independent Code

So we finally get down to the most important part: how do you go about writing code that isn't bound to a certain endian? There are many different ways of doing this. The one I'm going to present was used in *Quake 2*, and most of the code you'll see here is somewhat modified out of the *Quake 2* source code. It's mostly geared toward fixing files that are written in a certain endian, since the type casting problem is much harder to deal with. The best thing to do is to avoid casts that assume a certain byte order.

So the basic idea is this: the files will be written in a certain endian without fail, regardless of what endian the system is. You need to ensure that the file data is in the correct endian when read from or written to file. It would also be nice to avoid having to specify conditional compilation flags; I'll let the code automatically determine the system endian.

Step 1: Switching Endians

The first step is to write functions that will automatically switch the endian of a given parameter. First, ShortSwap:

```
short ShortSwap( short s )
{
  unsigned char b1, b2;
  b1 = s & 255;
  b2 = (s >> 8) & 255;
  return (b1 << 8) + b2;
}
```

This function is fairly straightforward once you wrap your head around the bit math. You take apart the two bytes of the short parameter s with some simple bit math, and then glue them back together in reverse order. If you understand bit shifts and bit ANDs, this should make perfect sense. As a companion to ShortSwap, you'll have ShortNoSwap, which is very simple:

```
short ShortNoSwap( short s )
{
  return s;
}
```

This seems utterly pointless, but you'll see why you need this function in a moment. Next, I want to swap longs:

```
int LongSwap (int i)
{
  unsigned char b1, b2, b3, b4;
  b1 = i & 255;
  b2 = ( i >> 8 ) & 255;
  b3 = ( i>>16 ) & 255;
  b4 = ( i>>24 ) & 255;
  return ((int)b1 << 24) + ((int)b2 << 16) + ((int)b3 << 8) + b4;
}
int LongNoSwap( int i )
{
  return i;
}
```

LongSwap is more or less the same idea as ShortSwap, but it switches around four bytes instead of two. Again, this is straightforward bit math.

Lastly, you need to be able to swap floats:

```
float FloatSwap( float f )
{
  union
  {
    float f;
    unsigned char b[4];
  } dat1, dat2;
  dat1.f = f;
  dat2.b[0] = dat1.b[3];
  dat2.b[1] = dat1.b[2];
```

```
  dat2.b[2] = dat1.b[1];
  dat2.b[3] = dat1.b[0];
  return dat2.f;
}
float FloatNoSwap( float f )
{
  return f;
}
```

This looks a little different than the previous two. There are three major steps here. First, you set one of your unions, dat1, equal to f. The union automatically allows you to split the float into four bytes because of the way unions work. Second, you set each of the bytes in dat2 to be the opposite of the bytes in dat1. Lastly, you return the floating-point component of dat2. This union trick is necessary because of the slightly more complex representation of floats in memory (see the IEEE documentation). The same thing can be done for doubles, but I'm not going to show the code here, as it simply involves adding more bytes, changing to double, and doing the same thing.

Step 2: Set Function Pointers to Use the Correct Swap Function

The next part of the implementation is the clever twist that defines this method of endian independence. I'm going to use function pointers to automatically select the correct endian. I'll put their declarations in a header file:

```
extern short (*BigShort) ( short s );
extern short (*LittleShort) ( short s );
extern int (*BigLong) ( int i );
extern int (*LittleLong) ( int i );
extern float (*BigFloat) ( float f );
extern float (*LittleFloat) ( float f );
```

Remember to put them in a C or C++ file without extern so that they are actually defined, or you'll get link errors. Each one of these functions is going to point to the correct Swap or NoSwap function it needs to invoke. For example, if you are on a little endian system, LittleShort will use ShortNoSwap, since nothing needs to change. But if you are on a big endian system, LittleShort will use ShortSwap. The opposite is true of BigShort.

Step 3: Initialization

In order to initialize all of these function pointers, you'll need a function to detect the endian and set them. This function will make use of the byte array cast I showed you earlier as an example of a byte cast that assumes a certain endian:

```
bool BigEndianSystem;   //you might want to extern this
void InitEndian( void )
{
  byte SwapTest[2] = { 1, 0 };
  if( *(short *) SwapTest == 1 )
  {
    //little endian
    BigEndianSystem = false;
    //set func pointers to correct funcs
    BigShort = ShortSwap;
    LittleShort = ShortNoSwap;
    BigLong = LongSwap;
    LittleLong = LongNoSwap;
    BigFloat = FloatSwap;
    LittleFloat = FloatNoSwap;
  }
  else
  {
    //big endian
    BigEndianSystem = true;
    BigShort = ShortNoSwap;
    LittleShort = ShortSwap;
    BigLong = LongNoSwap;
    LittleLong = LongSwap;
    BigFloat = FloatNoSwap;
    LittleFloat = FloatSwap;
  }
}
```

Let's examine what's going on here. First you use the cast to check your endian. If you get a 1, the system is little endian. All of the Little* functions will point to *NoSwap functions, and all of the Big* functions will point to *Swap functions. The reverse is true if the system is big endian. This way, you don't need to know the endian of the system you're on, only the endian of the file you're reading or writing.

A Practical Demonstration

Okay, let's suppose you have some sort of structure you need to read from file and write to file—maybe a vertex. The structure looks like this:

```
struct Vertex
{
  float Pos[3];
  float Normal[3];
  long Color;
  float TexCoords[2];
};
```

Nothing special here, just a typical vertex structure. Now I'm going to decide that vertices will always be stored to file in little endian. This is an arbitrary choice, but it doesn't matter. What I'm going to do is add a function to this struct that will fix the endian after loading or before saving it:

```
struct Vertex
{
  float Pos[3];
  float Normal[3];
  long Color;
  float TexCoords[2];
  void Endian()
  {
    for(int i = 0; i < 3; ++i) //our compiler will unroll this
    {
      Pos[i]= LittleFloat( Pos[i] );
      Normal[i] = LittleFloat( Pos[i] );
    }
    Color = LittleLong( Color );
    TexCoords[0] = LittleFloat( TexCoords[0] );
    TexCoords[1] = LittleFloat( TexCoords[1] );
  }
};
```

Let's be honest here: it's not exactly the easiest thing ever. You're going to have to write one of those painfully boring functions for each and every structure that goes in and out of files. After those functions are written, though, writing endian-independent code elsewhere is going to be a breeze. Notice that I used Little* functions here because the files are all little endian. If I had decided to use big endian, I could have simply used the Big* functions.

Now what will the actual functions for working with the vertices be like? Well, to read a vertex:

```
void ReadVertex( Vertex* v, FILE* f )
{
  if( v == NULL || f == NULL )
    return;
  fread( v, sizeof(Vertex), 1, f );
  //now, our not quite magical endian fix
  v->Endian();
}
```

Notice the simplicity of correcting the endian; although the structure definitions are slightly messy, the loading code has become very simple. The code to save is equally simple:

```
void WriteVertex( Vertex* v, FILE* f )
{
  if( v == NULL || f == NULL )
    return;
  v->Endian();
  fwrite( v, sizeof(Vertex), 1, f );
}
```

And that's all there is to it. I'm including a sample C++ header/source file pair on the book's companion web site that you're free to use in your own programs (go to www.courseptr.com/downloads). It's GPL code though (since it's actually part of a GPL project I'm working on), so you'll have to write your own if you don't want to release your code.

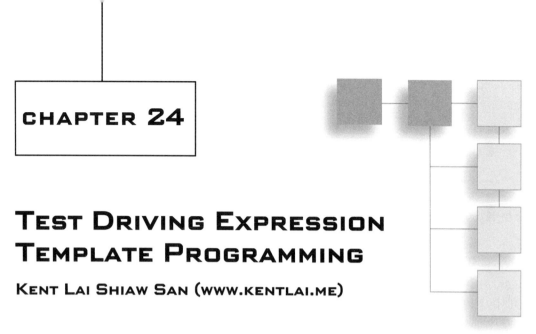

CHAPTER 24

Test Driving Expression Template Programming

Kent Lai Shiaw San (www.kentlai.me)

It's 2 a.m. in the office. All your co-workers left eight hours ago and are currently tucked in their beds, soundly asleep. The only sound that can be heard is your typing and the occasional sipping of coffee. You're about to finally finish a major rewrite of the entire framework of the current project. As you finish typing the last character, you hit the Compile button and cross your fingers. It compiled smoothly. And then you ran the application using the new framework for the first time, and the results make you wish you had never been born. You wish you had not simply gone ahead and made all those changes. You wish you had written tests to verify that the changes did not break any existing functionality. You wish you had made the changes incrementally.

Perhaps that example is a little extreme, but it does demonstrate what most people do—code without testing. They make major changes without a clear and concrete way to verify that the changes did not break existing functionality. This results in a lack of confidence in the code after making the changes, because there are not enough test cases written to cover every possible aspect.

In this article, you will be introduced to the concept of writing unit tests (www.xprogramming.com/Practices/PracUnitTest.html) for your projects, and going a step further, you will begin driving your development process with the *test first, code later* concept. And in order to introduce an interesting project to test drive with, you will be exposed to expression objects in the latter part of the article, where each action of an object does not result in a copy of itself, but merely an object representing that expression.

Note

Sample code for this chapter is available on the book's companion web site at www.courseptr .com/downloads.

Motivational Example

For some obscure reason, imagine there is a need in your application to have arrays of numeric values. The arrays as a whole must be able to perform multiplication by a scalar value, as well as addition and multiplication of two arrays of the same size and type. For even more obscure reasons, your project manager has decided it must be a template class so that it can be reused for other types and sizes. For further obscure reasons, he does not want to use an external library, but rather wants it written by you. (Gotta love the management.) Here's an example of how it should work,

```
array<int, 1000> x, y;
x = 5 * x + x * y;
```

Going through the user story, a list of the following requirements can be quickly generated for the template `array` class:

- Allows different types and sizes

- Allows natural multiplication expression of an array with a scalar value

- Allows natural multiplication expression of an array with other arrays of the same size and type

- Allows natural addition expression of two arrays of same size and type

- Allows assignment between arrays of same size and type

Beginning Development on the New Object

On receiving such a requirement, most programmers' first impulse is to simply fire up their editor and start chunking out code like a factory. However, I would like to restrain you from doing so and instead to take a step back, breathe in, and begin considering how you can test each requirement. "Why?" you may ask. Citing the earlier introductory example, tests for each aspect of functionality is important because they tell you that the code is still working even after the changes you just made. They also tell the customer that your code is still working, serving to boost their confidence in you. Knowing that your code is still working, you can carry on adding more new things, with their corresponding new tests. And the cycle goes on.

Writing test cases that handle each requirement also ensures that you strictly follow the requirements handed to you, and secondly, writing test cases first ensures that you do not write unnecessary code. In most cases, starting work on a class without test cases is too much leeway given to programmers. They soon get creative and start introducing unnecessary features and functions, and what should have been a slim, thin, library class becomes bloatware. Secondly, some who start coding the classes first eventually produce classes that are hard to use and similarly hard to test.

The development platform will be Microsoft Visual C++ 2003, using CPPUnit (http://apps.sourceforge.net/mediawiki/cppunit/index.php?title=Main_Page) as the unit testing tool. To begin with the development, let's begin with a barebones skeleton suite (a collection of related test cases grouped together as a class so that it can also be treated as a test case) for the unit test cases for this project. CPPUnit is not the topic covered here, though, so I will simply provide the code required. Note that for demonstration purposes, namespaces will not be used for the suite of test cases as well as the array class. I would, however, strongly encourage the use of namespaces in your own development.

```cpp
//- - - - - - - - - - - - - -main.cpp- - - - - - - - - - - - - - - -
#include "array_test.hpp"
#include <cppunit/extensions/TestFactoryRegistry.h>
#include <cppunit/ui/text/TestRunner.h>
#include <iostream>
int main(int argc, char** argv)
{
  CppUnit::TextUi::TestRunner runner;
  CppUnit::TestFactoryRegistry &registry =
    CppUnit::TestFactoryRegistry::getRegistry();
  runner.addTest(registry.makeTest());
  bool success = runner.run("", false);
  std::cout << "Press enter to continue..." << std::endl;
  std::cin.get();
  return 0;
}
```

```
//-------------array_test.hpp----------------
#ifndef __array_test
#define __array_test
#include <cppunit/extensions/HelperMacros.h>
class array_test : public CppUnit::TestFixture
{
  public:
  private:
    CPPUNIT_TEST_SUITE(array_test);
    CPPUNIT_TEST_SUITE_END();
};
CPPUNIT_TEST_SUITE_REGISTRATION( ArrayTest );
#endif // __array_test
```

After creation of the preceding two files, running the resulting application (after linking to the cppunit library you built with the source from the cppunit download) would show a console screen saying "OK (0 test)."

First Test Case

Let's see how you can start implementing the first requirement—oops, I mean the test for the first requirement:

■ **Allows different types and sizes**

That's actually pretty easy to write a test case for. To fulfill the requirement, you simply need to be able to declare a template array class for different types and sizes.

```
void test_declaration()
{
  array<int, 100> a;
  array<double, 5> b;
}
```

Due to the lack of full-fledged reflection in C++, you would need to, after adding this test case to the `array_test` class, manually add an entry to the `CPPUNIT_TEST_SUITE` section. The resulting `CPPUNIT_TEST_SUITE` section should look as follows:

```
CPPUNIT_TEST_SUITE(array_test);
  CPPUNIT_TEST(test_declaration);
CPPUNIT_TEST_SUITE_END();
```

Note that in languages that support a more powerful version of reflection methods, like Java and C#, there is no need for this manual creation of `CPPUNIT_TEST_SUITE`.

There, you have your first test case. So let's compile it. Compilation fails, as expected. Why did you compile even when you knew you would fail the compilation? The compiler acts as a to-do list for you. Your job is to simply resolve all the errors (and even warnings for those more zealous programmers out there)—no more and no less. Looking at the list of compilation errors, you can simply deduce that they are all due to the missing `array` class. No worries, let's start coding the `array` class.

```
//- - - - - - - - - - - - -array.hpp- - - - - - - - - - - - -
#ifndef __array_hpp
#define __array_hpp
#include <cstddef>
template<typename T, std::size_t Size>
class array
{
};
#endif // __array_hpp
```

You may have noted that this class does nothing. In fact, it is not even an array, but simply an empty shell! It is, however, the perfect class. It does nothing more than it should right now, which is simply to eliminate the compilation error. With the inclusion of this file in your array_test.hpp, you managed to receive zero compilation errors (though you did get two unreferenced local variables warnings). After running the test case, you should get an OK (1 test). Great, you are progressing!

Moving Along

Moving along to the next requirement:

- **Allows multiplication of an array with a scalar value**

So how are you going to test this requirement? It's as easy as the first case, it appears. Remember to add the function to be tested to the `CPPUNIT_TEST_SUITE` section, as with all of the following test functions:

```
void test_scalar_multiplication()
{
  array<int, 100> a;
  a * 5;
}
```

And so you hit the Compile button again, and the compilation error comes as no surprise. It can't find the * operator, which multiplies an array with a scalar, so you go ahead and add the operator in the array class.

```
void operator*(T const& t) const {}
```

Yes, the operator is even more meaningless than the class. It simply does nothing and returns nothing. Yet it serves its purpose for now, as the program compiles fine. Running the suite of test cases gives you the green bar (compiler success). All is well, but you realize the test case is pretty dumb. You need a way to verify that the array is working. How, then, can you verify that the scalar multiplication works? You need to assert it, of course.

```
void test_scalar_multiplication()
{
  array a;
  for (int i = 0; i < a.size(); ++i)
    a[i] = i;
  a = a * 5;
  for (int i = 0; i < a.size(); ++i)
    CPPUNIT_ASSERT(a[i] == i * 5);
}
```

Rethinking the testing, a new test case is developed. As expected, compilation fails. The new test case has forced you to introduce more functions to the class, but they are as you would most likely use them: a size member function and a subscript member operator. You could just introduce them simply, but I would feel safer if I knew that these functions work properly, as well, when tested independently. So, you take a step back, comment out the previous test case, and instead, introduce a new test case for the size function first:

```
void test_size()
{
  array<int, 100> a;
  CPPUNIT_ASSERT(a.size() == 100);
}
```

And you compile again (a repetitive step to reinforce what you are doing here), with the compiler complaining of the lack of the member function size. A typical implementation would be as follows:

```
const std::size_t size() const { return Size; }
```

But that is only when the implementation is crystal clear in your mind. A more TDD (Test-Driven Development) approach would be to simply make it work for your test case. Remember, resolve the errors—no more, no less.

```
const std::size_t size() const { return 100; }
```

After running the test case and getting the expected result, you know you have to make `size` work for different template arrays. So you add in another assertion in the `test_size` function:

```
array<double, 5> b;
CPPUNIT_ASSERT(b.size() == 5);
```

Before you make the change to the `size` function, run the suite of test cases first. Expect it to fail. If it does not, there is something wrong somewhere. Having it run successfully when you expect it to fail is as disconcerting as if you expect it to succeed instead of failing. In any case, you should have gotten a similar error message as this one:

```
!!!FAILURES!!!
Test Results:
Run:   2   Failures: 1   Errors: 0
1) test: array_test.test_size (F) line: 22
e:\development\projects\library\array_test.hpp
"b.size() == 5"
```

To make the code work, you make the obvious change:

```
const std::size_t size() const { return Size; }
```

Compile and run. Green bar. Next you need the subscript operator. It should support reading and writing. An obvious test case would be as follows:

```
void test_subscript_read()
{
  array<int, 100> a;
  for (int i = 0; i < a.size(); ++i)
    CPPUNIT_ASSERT(a[i] == 0);
}
```

Compile and fix the error. You need the subscript operator. Do you actually need to introduce the member array in the class? Not yet, actually. A simple hack would have made the compiler happy.

```
const T operator[](std::size_t i) const { return 0; }
```

Compile and run. Green bar. Now you need to test the writing part of a subscript operator. The test case should basically be a simple write and read and assert:

```
void test_subscript_write()
{
  array<int, 100> a;
  for (int i = 0; i < a.size(); ++i)
    a[i] = 0;
  for (int i = 0; i < a.size(); ++i)
    CPPUNIT_ASSERT(a[i] == 0);
}
```

Compile it, and the compiler complains of ' = ' : left operand must be l-value. Remember you had returned a const T from the subscript operator. So you actually need to have one that returns a value that you can assign to. So do you need the internal array now? Actually, no, not yet. Why, after this long, are you still not introducing the member array variable? The reason is that you must always follow the rule of not introducing new features until you must. That way, you can get away with the smallest/most slim class interface, as well as get the most return on investments on production, since there are cases where you introduce a new feature that will be useful earlier, but not necessary and get no return on investments. So, to resolve the current compiler error:

```
public:
  T& operator[](std::size_t i) { return temp_; }
private:
  T temp_;
```

Compile and run. Red bar! An assertion error!

```
!!!FAILURES!!!
Test Results:
Run:  4   Failures: 1   Errors: 0
1) test: array_test.test_subscript_read (F) line: 28
e:\development\projects\library\array_test.hpp
"a[i] == 0"
```

A quick look would tell you that the non-const version is actually called for both versions, and temp_ has not been properly initialized. It turns out you need a constructor for your array class after all.

```
explicit array():temp_(0) {}
```

Compile and run. Green bar, finally. After you review the implementation and test case, it is obvious that the subscript is not working as intended. You need to further assert the test case.

```
for (int i = 0; i < a.size(); ++i)
  a[i] = i;
for (int i = 0; i < a.size(); ++i)
  CPPUNIT_ASSERT(a[i] == i);
```

Compile and run. Red bar. So, you need the array after all. Let's introduce the variable first, as v_, and remove temp_.

```
T v_[Size];
```

Compile first so you get a list of errors to missing references of temp_. Remove and replace those with v_:

```
explicit array() { std::fill_n(v_, Size, 0); }
T& operator[](std::size_t i) { return v_[i]; }
```

Compile and run. Green bar. You could now move on back to the scalar multiplication. But wait—why did it run properly, when you have a wrong implementation as the const version of the subscript? To get the bug to shout at you, you need to manifest it as a test case. You will add an additional assertion in the test_subscript_write:

```
array const& b = a;
for (int i = 0; i < b.size(); ++i)
  CPPUNIT_ASSERT(b[i] == i);
```

Hooray! Red bar! Let's fix it!

```
const T& operator[](std::size_t i) const { return v_[i]; }
```

Hooray! Green bar! Back to scalar multiplication!

Back to the Scalar Multiplication Test Case and Others

Uncommenting the scalar multiplication test case and compiling the code gives you one compilation error. It is complaining that there's no assignment operator defined that takes in a void, which is the returned type of operator*. So apparently you need to rework that a bit. Under most circumstances, I might generate an assignment operator that takes in a void, but that function would be meaningless in other operations. So I went ahead and let `operator*` return a new array object.

```
array operator*(T const& t) const { return array(); }
```

Compile and run. Red bar. That is expected because no scalar multiplication was actually performed. So you need to rework the implementation of `operator*` to perform a multiplication of 5. Why did I say 5, specifically? Because that is the fix that will make this test case work, so you should do that for now.

```
array operator*(T const& t) const
{
  array tmp;
  for (std::size_t i = 0; i < size(); ++i)
    tmp[i] = operator[](i) * 5;
  return tmp;
}
```

Notice also that the function is expressed in terms of other member functions. In fact, it has given a strong hint that you can create `operator*` not as a member function, but as a free function.

```
template<typename T, std::size_t Size>
inline array<T, Size> operator*(array<T, Size> const& a, T const& t)
{
  array<T, Size> tmp;
  for (std::size_t i = 0; i < tmp.size(); ++i)
    tmp[i] = a[i] * 5;
  return tmp;
}
template<typename T, std::size_t Size>
inline array<T, Size> operator*(T const& t, array<T, Size> const& a)
{
  return operator*(a, t);
}
```

Compile and run. Green bar. But is it working yet? You know it's not, so you need a better assertion test.

```
for (int i = 0; i < a.size(); ++i)
  a[i] = i;
a = 8 * a;
for (int i = 0; i < a.size(); ++i)
  CPPUNIT_ASSERT(a[i] == i * 8);
```

Note the differing expression 8 * a instead of the usual array * scalar format. This is to test and verify that the other `operator*` works. Compile and run. Red bar. Fix the scalar multiplication function to make use of the variable t now:

```
tmp[i] = a[i] * t;
```

Compile and run. Green bar.

Rest of the List

Let's review the list again—the template `array` class:

- Allows different types and sizes

- Allows natural multiplication expression of an array with a scalar value

- Allows natural multiplication expression of an array with other arrays of the same size and type

- Allows natural addition expression of two arrays of same size and type

- Allows assignment between arrays of same size and type

Wait a minute. Didn't you just perform assignments of arrays earlier? Well, it turns out that C++ has synthesized (as it should) the default assignment operator for you (member-wise copy semantics), and it worked for this purpose. So, crossing out the to-do list, you have the following left:

- Allows natural multiplication expression of an array with other arrays of the same size and type

- Allows natural addition expression of two arrays of same size and type

You will go with addition, since it seems the easier to do (funny how the brain always perceives multiplication as harder). The test case for addition would look like the following:

```
void test_array_addition()
{
  array<int, 100> a;
  array<int, 100> b;
  for (int i = 0; i < a.size(); ++i)
    a[i] = i;
  for (int i = 0; i < b.size(); ++i)
```

```
    b[i] = b.size() - i;
  a = a + b;
  for (int i = 0; i < a.size(); ++i)
    CPPUNIT_ASSERT(a[i] == i + (b.size() - i));
}
```

Good—a compile tells you that you need the operator+ definition. Again you will build it as a free function.

```
template<typename T, std::size_t Size>
inline array<T, Size> operator+(array<T, Size> const& a,
                                array<T, Size> const& b)
{
  array<T, Size> tmp;
  for (std::size_t i = 0; i < tmp.size(); ++i)
    tmp[i] = a[i] + b[i];
  return tmp;
}
```

Compile and run. Green bar. Next, onto the multiplication of arrays.

```
void test_array_multiplication()
{
  array<int, 100> a;
  array<int, 100> b;
  for (int i = 0; i < a.size(); ++i)
    a[i] = i + 1;
  for (int i = 0; i < b.size(); ++i)
    b[i] = b.size() - i;
  a = a * b;
  for (int i = 0; i < a.size(); ++i)
    CPPUNIT_ASSERT(a[i] == (i + 1) * (b.size() - i));
}
```

Compile. It complains that you need the operator* for two arrays.

```
template<typename T, std::size_t Size>
inline array<T, Size> operator*(array<T, Size> const& a,
                                array<T, Size> const& b)
{
  array<T, Size> tmp;
  for (std::size_t i = 0; i < tmp.size(); ++i)
    tmp[i] = a[i] * b[i];
  return tmp;
}
```

Compile and run. Green bar! To verify that what the manager cited as an example actually works, let's enter one last test case!

```
void test_example()
{
  array<int, 100> a;
  array<int, 100> b;
  for (int i = 0; i < a.size(); ++i)
    a[i] = i + 1;
  for (int i = 0; i < b.size(); ++i)
    b[i] = b.size() - i;
  array<int, 100> x = 5 * a + a * b;
  for (int i = 0; i < a.size(); ++i)
    CPPUNIT_ASSERT(x[i] == 5 * (i + 1) + (i + 1) * (b.size() - i));
}
```

Compile and run. Green bar! You're all done! Now this can be submitted to your project manager!

More Changes

All was fine and great, until days later, your project manager comes back and tells you that your array class is the performance bottleneck of the project. It creates and utilizes too many temporaries. Your job now is to optimize it.

Reviewing the code, it seems that you could rewrite the array class to provide operators *= and += instead and eliminate temporaries. However, expressions written with *= and += are not as natural as + and *, resulting in unclear code compared to their * and + counterparts. Not to mention such a change would break all existing code that uses the array class. A solution to this problem seems impossible.

Or does it? Apparently the problem here is premature evaluation of expressions even when they are only used as an element in another expression. Reviewing the example given by the project manager, x = 5 * x + x * y, it can be parsed as x = ((5 * x) + (x * y)), where (5 * x) is an expression object and (x * y) is another expression object, and the encompassing ((5 * x) + (x * y)) is yet another expression object, which eventually can be used in a right-hand side assignment of a template array object. So let's review a new list of requirements:

- Expression object representing array multiplication with a scalar

- Expression object representing array multiplication with another array

■ Expression object representing array addition with another array

■ Assignment of expression object to an array

Let's pick addition to work with first.

Addition Expression

An early attempt to introduce an addition expression would be to modify the operator+. But wait! Where's the test case? Well, the test case has already been defined. You are reusing the test case defined in the previous implementation of array. All changes should still result in a green bar with the previous test case, and since you are simply redefining operators previously defined, you can reuse the test case as well.

```
template<typename T, std::size_t Size>
inline array_addition<T, Size operator+(array<T, Size> const& a,
                                        array<T, Size> const& b)
{
  return array_addition<T, Size>(a, b);
}
```

Following the previous steps, you hit compile again. Error. Let's fix it by introducing array_addition:

```
template<typename T, std::size_t Size>
class array_addition
{
};
```

Compile, and you get an error again. You need the assignment operator to accept a type of array_addition. In fact, you do not have an assignment operator. So let's go about defining it.

```
array& operator=(array_addition<T, Size> const& a) { return *this; }
```

Compile, and you get an error again. You need the copy constructor to accept a type of array_addition as well. In fact, you do not have a copy constructor. So let's go about defining it.

```
array(array_addition<T, Size> const& a) {}
```

Compile, and you get an error again. (Does this ever end?) Okay, now it complains that you need an `array_addition` constructor that takes two `array` objects. Fine.

```
explicit array_addition(array<T, Size> const& a, array<T, Size>
const& b) {}
```

Compile, and finally you get no errors. Run (and expect it to fail). Sure enough, you get two failures:

```
!!!FAILURES!!!
Test Results:
Run:  8   Failures: 2   Errors: 0
1) test: array_test.test_array_addition (F) line: 79
e:\development\projects\library\array_test.hpp
  "a[i] == i + (b.size() - i)"
2) test: array_test.test_example (F) line: 109
e:\development\projects\library\array_test.hpp
  "x[i] == 5 * (i + 1) + (i + 1) * (b.size() - i)"
```

There are people who wouldn't mind dealing with two failures, but personally, I prefer to work on one problem at a time. So, in order to concentrate on one problem only, I comment out the second test case:

```
//  CPPUNIT_TEST(test_example);
```

Looking at the code, you see that the error happens because a = a + b is not assigned the proper value (as expected). So let's fix that first failure first. First step, let's do the proper assignment in the assignment operator:

```
array& operator=(array_addition<T, Size> const& a)
{
  for (std::size_t i = 0; i < size(); ++i)
    v_[i] = a[i];
  return *this;
}
```

Compile, and you get an error again because `array_addition` did not define a subscript operator. To fix it, do the following:

```
const T operator[](std::size_t i) const { return 0; }
```

Notice it's one of those small fixes again. The goal is to get the program to compile properly first, then fix the failures as indicated by the test case. In cases where the failure rate is too high, or where you get too many compilation errors, comment out parts of the test cases so you can fix errors bit by bit. Compile, and run. Red bar, as expected again. Now, you are forced to evaluate the addition expression. So let's work from the top down again, from outside to inside, black box to white box.

```
const T operator[](std::size_t i) const { return a_[i] + b_[i]; }
```

Compile, and it complains that a_ and b_ are not defined.

```
private:
  array<T, Size> a_;
  array<T, Size> b_;
```

Small fixes again. Compile, run, red bar again. That's expected because the values of a_ and b_ are not the arrays that were passed in. So you actually need to make them reference the previous array:

```
private:
  array<T, Size> const& a_;
  array<T, Size> const& b_;
```

And the compiler now complains of uninitialized references in constructed array_addition objects, so you fix it:

```
explicit array_addition(array const& a, array const& b):a_(a), b_(b) {}
```

Compile, run. Green bar! Woo hoo! Now let's move on and uncomment the commented out test case. The rule of thumb is to get all test cases running green before you attempt any more new features. Compile, run. Red bar, as expected (yet again). Looking at the code, you see that the copy constructor is not doing what it should be doing. So let's remedy that.

```
array(array_addition<T, Size> const& a)
{
  for (std::size_t i = 0; i < size(); ++i)
    v_[i] = a[i];
}
```

Compile, run. Green bar. Now let's move on to the next feature!

Generalizing the Expression Object

Or should you? Looking at the example code, you see code breaking, for example, as follows:

```
a = a + b + a;
```

To confirm your suspicions, let's add more meat to the `test_array_addition` test case:

```
for (int i = 0; i < a.size(); ++i)
  a[i] = i;
for (int i = 0; i < b.size(); ++i)
  b[i] = b.size() - i;
a = a + b + a;
for (int i = 0; i < a.size(); ++i)
  CPPUNIT_ASSERT(a[i] == i + (b.size() - i) + i);
```

Sure enough, the compiler complains. It seems that you could either come up with an operator that accepts `array_addition`, as well as the other future possible variations, or you could create a generic addition operator. An instinctive first attempt might generate one that looks as follows:

```
template<typename Arg1, typename Arg2>
inline array_addition<Arg1, Arg2> operator+(Arg1 const& a,
                                            Arg2 const& b)
{
  return array_addition<Arg1, Arg2>(a, b);
}
```

Except that it wouldn't work, as it's too generic. What you need is an `operator+` that only works on an array as well as array expressions. Taking advantage of that array and array expression note, it seems you need to introduce another layer of array. However, since array is already in production, you need to abstract the code instead so that existing code is unaffected. Comment out the newly introduced test case first so you can get the changes to compile:

```
template<typename T, std::size_t Size>
class array_impl
{
  public:
    explicit array_impl() { std::fill_n(v_, Size, 0); }
    array_impl(array_addition<T, Size> const& a)
    {
```

```
      for (std::size_t i = 0; i < size(); ++i)
        v_[i] = a[i];
    }
    const std::size_t size() const { return Size; }
    T const& operator[](std::size_t i) const { return v_[i]; }
    T& operator[](std::size_t i) { return v_[i]; }
  private:
    T v_[Size];
};
template<typename T, std::size_t Size, typename Rep = array_impl<T,
Size> >
class array
{
  public:
    explicit array() {}
    array(array_addition<T, Size> const& a):rep_(a) {}
    const std::size_t size() const { return rep_.size(); }
    T const& operator[](std::size_t i) const { return rep_[i]; }
    T& operator[](std::size_t i) { return rep_[i]; }
    array& operator=(array_addition<T, Size> const& a)
    {
      for (std::size_t i = 0; i < size(); ++i)
        rep_[i] = a[i];
      return *this;
    }
  private:
    Rep rep_;
};
```

Compile, and you get more errors. The array_addition has to change as well.
Though you could employ a quick fix here, such a fix would cause too much
problem to undo later on.

```
template<typename T, std::size_t Size, typename Arg1, typename Arg2>
class array_addition
{
  public:
    explicit array_addition(Arg1 const& a, Arg2 const& b):a_(a), b_(b)
{}
    const T operator[](std::size_t i) const { return a_[i] + b_[i]; }
  private:
    Arg1 const& a_;
    Arg2 const& b_;
};
```

Compile, and you get more errors. Let's generalize all the uses of `array_addition`:

```
template<typename T, std::size_t Size, typename Rep = array_impl<T,
Size> >
class array
{
  public:
    explicit array() {}
    array(Rep const& a):rep_(a) {}
    const std::size_t size() const { return rep_.size(); }
    T const& operator[](std::size_t i) const { return rep_[i]; }
    T& operator[](std::size_t i) { return rep_[i]; }
    template<typename Array>
    array& operator=(Array const& a)
    {
      for (std::size_t i = 0; i < size(); ++i)
        rep_[i] = a[i];
      return *this;
    }
  private:
    Rep rep_;
};
template<typename T, std::size_t Size, typename Arg1, typename Arg2>
inline array_addition<T, Size, Arg1, Arg2> operator+
  (array<T, Size, Arg1> const& a, array<T, Size, Arg2> const& b)
{
  return array_addition<T, Size, Arg1, Arg2>(a, b);
}
```

Compile, and you get errors. error C2676: binary '+' : 'array_addition' does not define this operator or a conversion to a type acceptable to the predefined operator. Well, apparently it's because operator+ returned an array_addition, and there are no defined operators working with that. No biggie. Let's just change it so that it returns an array object:

```
template<typename T, std::size_t Size, typename Arg1, typename Arg2>
inline array<T, Size, array_addition<T, Size, array<T, Size, Arg1>,
                       array<T, Size, Arg2> > >
  operator+(array<T, Size, Arg1> const& a, array<T, Size, Arg2>
const& b)
{
  return array<T, Size, array_addition<T, Size, array<T, Size, Arg1>,
            array<T, Size, Arg2> > >
            (array_addition<T, Size, array<T, Size, Arg1>,
```

```
                    array<T, Size, Arg2> >
                    (a, b));
}
```

Compile. Finally you're down to one error. Right now it's complaining that it can't construct an object out of an addition expression. Looking at the copy constructor you have, it seems to be in the wrong form. So let's provide it with a generic expression copy constructor.

```
template<typename Array>
array(Array const& a)
{
  for (std::size_t i = 0; i < size(); ++i)
    rep_[i] = a[i];
}
```

Compile, and woo hoo! Finally, all done! But wait! You get a compiler warning: warning C4172: returning address of local variable or temporary. Whoops, you are doing such a nasty thing? Let's change the definition of array:: operator[](std::size_t) const to not return a reference but a temporary copy.

```
const T operator[](std::size_t i) const { return rep_[i]; }
```

Now let's run the test case. Whoa! Green bar! And it comes after a big refactoring (changes to a body of code to improve its internal structure without changing its external behavior). Don't you feel much more confident continuing, knowing that your changes have resulted in more efficient code, and yet not broken any existing code?

Multiplication of Arrays

Before moving on, let's review the list again:

- Expression object representing array multiplication with a scalar

- Expression object representing array multiplication with another array

- Expression object representing array addition with another array

- Assignment of expression object to an array

Looking at the list, you had unknowingly implemented two requirements because of the need to have a successful 100% compile rate. Nevertheless, that leaves you with two remaining requirements to meet. You will first implement the multiplication of two arrays. As explained, you will need to introduce an array_multiply object. Let's change the definition of operator* to return an array_multiply and let the compiler tell you where the errors to fix are at. Because you have implemented an array_addition successfully, you already have a rough idea how the array_multiply should look. In fact, you can speed things up a bit here because you can be confident that if the test cases break, you know it's when you are adding the array_multiply.

```
template<typename T, std::size_t Size, typename Arg1, typename Arg2>
class array_multiply
{
  public:
    explicit array_multiply(Arg1 const& a, Arg2 const& b):a_(a), b_(b)
    {}
    const T operator[](std::size_t i) const { return a_[i] * b_[i]; }
  private:
    Arg1 const& a_;
    Arg2 const& b_;
};
template<typename T, std::size_t Size, typename Arg1, typename Arg2>
inline array<T, Size, array_multiply<T, Size, array<T, Size, Arg1>,
array<T, Size, Arg2> > >
  operator*(array<T, Size, Arg1> const& a, array<T, Size, Arg2>
const& b)
{
  return array<T, Size, array_multiply<T, Size, array<T, Size, Arg1>,
              array<T, Size, Arg2> > >
              (array_multiply<T, Size, array<T, Size, Arg1>,
              array<T, Size, Arg2> >
              (a, b));
}
```

Compile and run. Green bar. Okay, let's move on to scalar multiplication, the last on the list. You need to create a scalar expression that can perform lazy evaluation (delaying evaluation until the moment it is needed), be able to be performed on another expression object, and be part of another expression object. So that means you need to represent it as an expression object itself. Using the same approach, you change the operator* for scalar multiplication.

```
template<typename T, std::size_t Size, typename Arg1>
inline array<T, Size, array_multiply<T, Size, array<T, Size, Arg1>,
              array_scalar_value<T, Size> > >
  operator*(array<T, Size, Arg1> const& a, T const& t)
{
  return array<T, Size, array_multiply<T, Size, array<T, Size, Arg1>,
```

```
                    array_scalar_value<T, Size> > >
                    (array_multiply<T, Size, array<T, Size, Arg1>,
                    array_scalar_value<T, Size> >(a,
                    array_scalar_value<T, Size>(t)));
}
template<typename T, std::size_t Size, typename Arg1>
inline array<T, Size, array_multiply<T, Size, array<T, Size, Arg1>,
              array_scalar_value<T, Size> > >
  operator*(T const& t, array<T, Size, Arg1> const& a)
{
  return operator*(a, t);
}
```

Upon compiling, the compiler complains of not knowing what array_
scalar_value is. (Actually, as usual, the error messages are much more obscure
and there are more of them, but for the sake of simplicity, I will tell you what the
error message is about.) So let's introduce the array_scalar_value class:

```
template<typename T, std::size_t Size>
class array_scalar_value
{
};
```

Compile and the compiler complains about the lack of a constructor that accepts
a type T for array_scalar_value (as expected). Let's add one in.

```
explicit array_scalar_value(T const& t) {}
```

Compile and the compiler complains about the lack of a subscript operator for
array_scalar_value. Now, an array_scalar_value is not actually an array, so
what should its subscript return? To make array_scalar_value mimic an array, it
should, of course, return the same scalar value regardless of what subscript index
it is passed. I am going to bypass the small fix here again and instead provide the
proper implementation of array_scalar_value:

```
template<typename T, std::size_t Size>
class array_scalar_value
{
  public:
    explicit array_scalar_value(T const& t):t_(t) {}
    const T operator[](std::size_t i) const { return t_; }
  private:
    const T t_;
};
```

All seems to be in good hands, and so you begin to compile and run the test case. Boom! The red bar appears. Why? After much stepping through, the problem appears to be because `multiply` is holding reference to a temporary scalar. Apparently, this would mean that you would run into the same problem elsewhere. So how do you resolve it? Well, you need a smart way to tell the templates to use references for array and expression objects, but to use a copy of the original expression if they are `array_scalar_value`. So, to solve it, you introduce an `array_trait` class.

```
template<typename T>
class array_traits
{
  public:
    typedef T const& reference;
};
template<typename T, std::size_t Size>
class array_scalar_value;
template<typename T, std::size_t Size>
class array_traits<array_scalar_value<T, Size> >
{
  public:
    typedef const array_scalar_value<T, Size> reference;
};
```

Now, to take advantage of the newly introduced `trait` class, you change all instances of `Arg1` and `Arg2` as follows:

```
typename array_traits<Arg1>::reference a_;
typename array_traits<Arg2>::reference b_;
```

Okay, let's compile and run the test case. Green bar! You managed to introduce expression objects into your `array` class without breaking any existing code and functionalities! And you still have a robust suite of test cases to run the next time you make changes.

Afterword

This article introduced TDD (Test-Driven Development). The example in this code is as it should be, simply an example. For instance, in a real scenario, I would simply provide a member operator $*=$ and $+=$, and then build the free function operator * and + with the member operators *= and +=. However, for example purposes, the preceding case suits well enough.

The article also goes at the speed of a turtle crawling. Does employing TDD necessarily mean that you will be programming this slowly? Well, yes and no. For most trivial cases, you don't need to go through those little fixes, like multiply by 5 instead of i first. In fact, for the later stage, I had to skip most of the small fixes and go straight for the actual implementation due to the fact that this is an article, not a book. The little fixes are just a preparation for more complicated implementations. Note that beginners to TDD will find the approach rather daunting and weird. But once adopted, they will produce code of a better quality and that is easier to maintain.

If you have read through the entire article to this very last stage, you probably have appreciated the existence of unit test cases, especially when there is a sudden requirement change or additional requirements are requested. Should a unit test be removed? No. You should only add more test cases and not remove anything. This allows you to create components that only make the code stronger rather than weakening it. Not only that, it allows you to take solid steps one at a time. Seeing green bars frequently can boost your confidence. In fact, there are people who got so addicted to this method of development that others started calling them "test-infected." (Yes, I admit—I am one of them.)

In the second part of the article, in order to introduce a change to show that the test cases are not a waste of time but a helpful toolkit, the concept of expression objects was introduced. I first encountered expression objects in the book *C++ Templates* and was amazed by their implementation. In terms of games, I can see it expressed, primarily, in terms of matrix and vector calculation. However, I would like to stress that expression objects should be presented as food for thought and not the means to all ends. In fact, some can even take it to an extreme to represent actions as commands and stack them up using a runtime mechanism, with the key being delayed computation of actions. The main idea presented here is lazy evaluation, as well as eliminating unnecessary temporaries, yet still using a natural expression form.

All in all, I hope this article has shown you the importance and benefit of driving your project with tests, as well as opening your mind to the possibilities of expression objects in your code.

References and Further Reading

"An Extreme Programming Episode." Dr. Dobb's Portal. February 1, 2001 (www.ddj.com/cpp/184403770).

Beck, Kent. *Test-Driven Development: By Example.* Addison-Wesley Professional, 2002.

The C++ Source. Artima Developer (www.artima.com/cppsource).

Fowler, Martin, Kent Beck, John Brant, William Opdyke, and Don Roberts. *Refactoring: Improving the Design of Existing Code.* Addison-Wesley Professional, 1999.

Vandevoorde, David and Nicolai M. Josuttis. *C++ Templates: The Complete Guide.* Addison-Wesley Professional, 2002.

XP and Agile Methods page. MartinFowler.com (http://martinfowler.com/articles.html#id59482).

CHAPTER 25

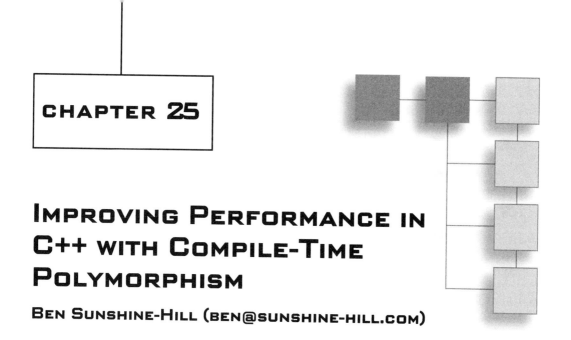

Improving Performance in C++ with Compile-Time Polymorphism

Ben Sunshine-Hill (ben@sunshine-hill.com)

Virtual functions are one of the most interesting and useful features of classes in C++. They allow for thinking of an object in terms of what type it is (Apple) as well as what category of types it belongs with (Fruit). Further, virtual functions allow for operating on objects in ways that respect their actual types while referring to them by category. However, the power and flexibility of virtual functions comes at a price that a good programmer must weigh against the benefits. Let's take a quick look at using virtual functions and abstract base classes and from there examine a way in which you can improve program performance while retaining the power and flexibility of virtual functions.

Along with modeling different kinds of fruit and different kinds of animals, modeling different kinds of shapes accounts for most of the polymorphism examples found in C++ textbooks. More importantly, modeling different kinds of shapes readily lends itself to an area of game programming where improving performance is a high priority, namely graphics rendering. So modeling shapes will make a good basis for this examination. So, let's begin.

```
class Shape
{
public:
  Shape()
```

```cpp
  {
  }

  virtual ~Shape()
  {
  }

  virtual void DrawOutline() const = 0;
  virtual void DrawFill() const = 0;
};

class Rectangle : public Shape
{
public:
  Rectangle()
  {
  }

  virtual ~Rectangle()
  {
  }

  virtual void DrawOutline() const
  {
    ...
  }

  virtual void DrawFill() const
  {
    ...
  }
};

class Circle : public Shape
{
public:
  Circle()
  {
  }

  virtual ~Circle()
  {
  }
```

```
  virtual void DrawOutline() const
  {
    ...
  }

  virtual void DrawFill() const
  {
    ...
  }
};
```

All good so far, right? You can, for example, write...

```
Shape *myShape = new Rectangle;
myShape->DrawOutline();
delete myShape;
```

... and trust C++'s runtime polymorphism to decide that the myShape pointer actually points to a rectangle and that rectangle's DrawOutline() method should be called. If you wanted it to be a circle instead, you could just change new Rectangle to new Circle, and the circle's DrawOutline() method would be called instead.

But wait a second. Thanks, C++, for the runtime polymorphism, but it's pretty obvious from looking at that code that myShape is going to be a rectangle; you don't need fancy vtables to figure that out. Consider this code:

```
void DrawAShapeOverAndOver(Shape* myShape)
{
  for(int i=0; i<10000; i++)
  {
    myShape->DrawOutline();
  }
}
```

```
Shape *myShape = new Rectangle;
DrawAShapeOverAndOver(myShape);
delete myShape;
```

Look at what happens there! The program picks up myShape, inspects it, and says "Hmm, a rectangle. Okay." Then it puts it down. Then it picks it up again. "Hmm. This time, it's a rectangle. Okay. Hmm, and this time it's a ... rectangle. Okay." Repeat 9,997 times. Does all this type inspection eat up CPU cycles? Darn tootin' it does. Although virtual function calls aren't what you'd call slow, even a small delay really starts to add up when you're doing it 10,000 times per object per frame. The real tragedy here is that you *know* that the program doesn't really need to check myShape's type each time through the loop. "It's always going to be the same thing!" you shout at the compiler. "Just have the program look it up the first time!" For that matter, it doesn't really need to be looked up the first time. Because you are calling it on a rectangle that you have just created, the object type is still going to be a rectangle when DrawAShapeOverAndOver() gets to it.

Let's see if you can rewrite this function in a way that doesn't require runtime lookups. You will make it specifically for rectangles, so you can just flat-out *tell* the dumb compiler what it is and forego the lookup code.

```
void DrawAShapeWhichIsARectangleOverAndOver(Shape* myShape)
{
  for(int i=0; i<10000; i++)
  {
    static_cast<Rectangle*>(myShape)->DrawOutline();
  }
}
```

Unfortunately, this doesn't help one bit. Telling the compiler that the object is a rectangle isn't enough. For all the compiler knows, the object could be a subclass of Rectangle. You still haven't prevented the compiler from inserting runtime lookup code. To do that, you must remove the virtual keyword from the declaration of DrawOutline() and thereby change it into a non-virtual function. That means in turn, however, that you have to declare a separate DrawAShapeOverAndOver() for each and every subclass of Shape that you might want to draw. Alas, pursuing the desire for efficiency has driven you farther and farther away from your goal, to the point where there is barely any polymorphism left at all. So sad.

Thanks but No Thanks, C++

Reading over the last few paragraphs, the astute programmer will notice an interesting point: at no time did you actually *need* runtime polymorphism. It helped you write the DrawAShapeOverAndOver() function by letting you write a single function that would work for all classes derived from Shape, but in each case the runtime lookup could have been done at compile time.

Bearing this in mind, let's approach polymorphism again, but this time with more caution. You won't be making the DrawOutline() method virtual again, since so far that has done no good at all. Instead, let's rewrite DrawAShapeOverAndOver() as a templated function. This way you are not forced to write both `DrawAShape-WhichIsARectangleOverAndOver()` and `DrawAShapeWhichIsACircleOverAndOver()`.

```
template<typename ShapeType>
void DrawAShapeOverAndOver(ShapeType* myShape)
{
  for(int i=0; i<10000; i++)
  {
    myShape->DrawOutline();
  }
}
```

```
Rectangle *myRectangle = new Rectangle;
DrawAShapeOverAndOver(myRectangle);
delete myRectangle;
```

Hey! Now you're getting somewhere! You can pass in any kind of `Shape` to `DrawAShapeOverAndOver()`, just like before, except this time there is no runtime checking of `myShape`'s type! Interestingly enough, `Rectangle` and `Circle` don't even have to be derived from `Shape`. They just have to be classes with a `DrawOutline()` function.

Making Life More Difficult

Let's go back to the original example, but this time let's make more use of the other features of subclassing. After all, derived classes and base classes with no private members, nontrivial constructors, or internal calls of virtual functions are a rather severe oversimplification of subclassing. Let's also supply an actual implementation of `DrawOutline()` and `DrawFill()`, albeit using a completely fictional `Graphics` object that will nevertheless allow me to illustrate how functions in derived classes may use functions in base classes. Okay, let's pull out the big guns:

```
class Shape
{
public:
  Shape(const Point &initialLocation,
    const std::string &initialOutlineColor,
    const std::string &initialFillColor) :
    location(initialLocation),
    outlineColor(initialOutlineColor),
    fillColor(initialFillColor)
```

```cpp
  {
  }

  virtual ~Shape()
  {
  }

  virtual void DrawOutline() const = 0;
  virtual void DrawFill() const = 0;

  void SetOutlineColor(const std::string &newOutlineColor)
  {
    outlineColor = newOutlineColor;
  }

  void SetFillColor(const std::string &newFillColor)
  {
    fillColor = newFillColor;
  }

  void SetLocation(const Point & newLocation)
  {
    location = newLocation;
  }

  const std::string &GetOutlineColor() const
  {
    return outlineColor;
  }

  const std::string &GetFillColor() const
  {
    return fillColor;
  }

  const Point &GetLocation() const
  {
    return location;
  }

  void DrawFilled() const
  {
    DrawOutline();
```

```
      DrawFill();
  }

private:
  std::string outlineColor;

  std::string fillColor;

  Point location;
};

class Rectangle : public Shape
{
public:
  Rectangle(const Point &initialLocation,
      const std::string &initialOutlineColor,
      const std::string &initialFillColor(),
      double initialHeight,
      double initialWidth) :
    Shape(initialLocation, initialOutlineColor,
          initialFillColor),
    height(initialHeight),
    width(initialWidth)
  {
  }

  virtual ~Rectangle()
  {
  }

  virtual void DrawOutline() const
  {
    Graphics::SetColor(GetOutlineColor());
    Graphics::GoToPoint(GetLocation());
    Graphics::DrawRectangleLines(height, width);
  }

  virtual void DrawFill() const
  {
    Graphics::SetColor(GetOutlineColor());
    Graphics::GoToPoint(GetLocation());
    Graphics::DrawRectangleFill(height, width);
  }
```

```cpp
    void SetHeight(double newHeight)
    {
      height = newHeight;
    }

    void SetWidth(double newWidth)
    {
      width = newWidth;
    }

    double GetHeight() const
    {
      return height;
    }

    double GetWidth() const
    {
      return width;
    }

private:
  double height;
  double width;
};

class Circle : public Shape
{
public:
  Circle(const Point &initialLocation,
     const std::string &initialOutlineColor,
     const std::string &initialFillColor,
     double initialRadius) :
     Shape(initialLocation, initialOutlineColor,
          initialFillColor),
     radius(initialRadius)
  {
  }

  virtual ~Circle()
  {
  }

  virtual void DrawOutline() const
```

```
  {
    Graphics::SetColor(GetOutlineColor());
    Graphics::GoToPoint(GetLocation());
    Graphics::DrawCircularLine(radius);
  }

  virtual void DrawFill() const
  {
    Graphics::SetColor(GetOutlineColor());
    Graphics::GoToPoint(GetLocation());
    Graphics::DrawCircularFill(radius);
  }

  void SetRadius(double newRadius)
  {
    radius = newRadius;
  }

  double GetRadius() const
  {
    return radius;
  }
private:
  double radius;
};
```

Whew! Let's see what's added there. First of all, `Shape` objects now have data members. All `Shape` objects have a location, and an `outlineColor` and a `fillColor`. In addition, `Rectangle` objects have a height and a width, and `Circle` objects have a radius. Each of these members has corresponding getter and setter functions. The most important new addition is the `DrawFilled()` method, which draws both the outline and the fill in one step by delegating these methods to the derived class.

You Can Rebuild It—You Have the Technology

Now that you have this all set up, let's rip it apart! Let's tear it down and rebuild it into a class structure that invites compile-time polymorphism.

First, let's remove the virtual keyword from the declarations of `DrawOutline()` and `DrawFill()`. As I touched on earlier, virtual functions add runtime overhead, which is precisely what you are trying to avoid. For that matter, let's go one step further and remove the declarations of those functions from the base class altogether, as they do no good anyway. Let's leave them in as comments, though, so it remains clear that they were omitted on purpose.

Now, what have you broken? Not much, actually. If you have a rectangle, you can get and set its height and width and colors and location, and you can draw it. Life is good. However, one thing that you have broken is the `DrawFilled()` function, which calls the now nonexistent base class functions `DrawOutline()` and `DrawFill()`. Base classes can only call functions of derived classes if those functions are declared as virtual in the base class—which is precisely what you do not want.

In order to fix the broken `DrawFilled()` function, you will use templates in a very strange and interesting way. Here's a bit of code to broadly illustrate the insanity that is to come: template <typename ShapeType>

```
class Shape
{

...
protected:
  Shape( ... )
  {
  }

};

class Rectangle : public Shape<Rectangle>
{

public:
  Rectangle( ... ) :
    Shape<Rectangle>( ... )
  {
  }
...


};
```

Whaaa? That's right: `Rectangle` no longer inherits from `Shape`; now it inherits from a special *kind* of `Shape`. `Rectangle` creates its own special `Shape` class,

Shape<Rectangle>, to inherit from. In fact, Rectangle is the only class that inherits from this specially crafted Shape<Rectangle>. To enforce this, you declare as protected the constructor of the templated Shape class so that an object of this type cannot be instanced directly. Instead, this special kind of Shape must be inherited from and instanced within the public constructor of the derived class.

Yes, it's legal. Yes, it's strange. Yes, it's necessary. It's called the "Curiously Recurring Template Pattern" (or "Idiom," depending on who you ask). But why? What could this strange code possibly gain for you??

What you gain is the template parameter. The base class Shape now knows that it really is the Shape part of a Rectangle because you have told it so through the template parameter and because you have taken a solemn oath that the only class that ever inherits Shape<Rectangle> is Rectangle. If Shape<ShapeType> ever wonders what subclass it's a part of, it can just check its ShapeType template parameter.

What this knowledge gains you, in turn, is the ability to downcast. *Downcasting* is taking an object of a base class and casting it as an object of a derived class. It's what dynamic_cast does for virtual classes, and it's what virtual function calls do. It's also what I tried to do way back near the beginning of this article, when I tried to use static_cast to convince the compiler that myShape was a rectangle. Now that the functions aren't virtual anymore, however, this will work much better (in other words, it'll work). Let's use it to rewrite DrawFilled().

```
template <typename ShapeType>
class Shape
{
  void DrawFilled()
  {
    static_cast<const ShapeType *>(this)->DrawOutline();
    static_cast<const ShapeType *>(this)->DrawFill();
  }
};
```

Take a moment to cogitate on this code. It's possibly the most crucial part of this entire article. When DrawFilled() is called on a Rectangle, even though it is a method defined in Shape and thus called with a this pointer of type Shape, it knows that it can safely treat itself as a Rectangle. This lets Shape static_cast itself down to a Rectangle and from there call DrawOutline() on the resultant Rectangle. Ditto with DrawFill().

Putting It All Together

So here it is:

```cpp
template<typename ShapeType>
class Shape
{
public:
  ~Shape()
  {
  }

/* Omitted from the base class and
   declared instead in subclasses */
/* void DrawOutline() const = 0; */
/* void DrawFill() const = 0; */

  void SetOutlineColor(const std::string &newOutlineColor)
  {
    outlineColor = newOutlineColor;
  }

  void SetFillColor(const std::string &newFillColor)
  {
    fillColor = newFillColor;
  }

  void SetLocation(const Point &newLocation)
  {
    location = newLocation;
  }

  const std::string &GetOutlineColor() const
  {
    return outlineColor;
  }

  const std::string &GetFillColor() const
  {
    return fillColor;
  }

  const Point &GetLocation() const
```

```
  {
    return location;
  }

  void DrawFilled() const
  {
    static_cast<const ShapeType *>(this)->DrawOutline();
    static_cast<const ShapeType *>(this)->DrawFill();
  }

protected:
  Shape(const Point &initialLocation,
    const std::string &initialOutlineColor,
    const std::string &initialFillColor) :
    location(initialLocation),
    outlineColor(initialOutlineColor),
    fillColor(initialFillColor)
  {
  }

private:
  std::string outlineColor;

  std::string fillColor;

  Point location;
};

class Rectangle : public Shape<Rectangle>
{
public:
  Rectangle(const Point &initialLocation,
        const std::string &initialOutlineColor,
        const std::string &initialFillColor,
        double initialHeight,
        double initialWidth) :
    Shape<Rectangle>(initialLocation, initialOutlineColor,
                     initialFillColor),
    height(initialHeight),
    width(initialWidth)
  {
  }
```

```cpp
  ~Rectangle()
  {
  }

  void DrawOutline() const
  {
    Graphics::SetColor(GetOutlineColor());
    Graphics::GoToPoint(GetLocation());
    Graphics::DrawRectangleLines(height, width);
  }

  void DrawFill() const
  {
    Graphics::SetColor(GetOutlineColor());
    Graphics::GoToPoint(GetLocation());
    Graphics::DrawRectangleFill(height, width);
  }

  void SetHeight(double newHeight)
  {
    height = newHeight;
  }

  void SetWidth(double newWidth)
  {
    width = newWidth;
  }

  double GetHeight() const
  {
    return height;
  }

  double GetWidth() const
  {
    return width;
  }
private:
  double height;
  double width;
};
```

```
class Circle : public Shape<Circle>
{
public:
  Circle(const Point &initialLocation,
      const std::string &initialOutlineColor,
      const std::string &initialFillColor,
      double initialRadius) :
    Shape<Circle>(initialLocation, initialOutlineColor,
                  initialFillColor),
    radius(initialRadius)
  {
  }

  ~Circle()
  {
  }

  void DrawOutline() const
  {
    Graphics::SetColor(GetOutlineColor());
    Graphics::GoToPoint(GetLocation());
    Graphics::DrawCircularLine(radius);
  }

  void DrawFill() const
  {
    Graphics::SetColor(GetOutlineColor());
    Graphics::GoToPoint(GetLocation());
    Graphics::DrawCircularFill(radius);
  }

  void SetRadius(double newRadius)
  {
    radius = newRadius;
  }

  double GetRadius() const
  {
    return radius;
  }
private:
  double radius;
};
```

This is just what you need! Base class functions can defer certain functionality to derived classes, and derived classes can decide which base class functions to override. If you had declared a non-virtual `DrawOutline()` function in `Shape` (rather than leaving it in only as a comment), it would be optional for `Circle` and `Rectangle` to override it. This approach allows programmers using a class to not concern themselves with whether a function is in the derived class or inherited from the base class. It's the functionality that you had in the last section, but without the added overhead of runtime polymorphism.

So, let's rewrite `DrawAShapeOverAndOver()`.

```
template<typename ShapeType>
void DrawAShapeOverAndOver(ShapeType* myShape)
{
  for(int i=0; i<10000; i++)
  {
    myShape->DrawOutline();
    // OR
    myShape->DrawFilled();
  }
}

Rectangle *rectangle = new Rectangle;
DrawAShapeOverAndOver(rectangle);
delete rectangle;
```

Notice that you can call member functions declared either in the derived class or the base class. Of course, if the templated function uses member functions defined in only a particular derived class (such as `GetRadius()`), the templated function will not compile if used with a class that does not have those member functions. For example, calling `GetRadius()` on a `Rectangle` will not compile.

Limitations

The biggest limitation of compile-time polymorphism is that it's compile-time. In other words, if you want to call a function on a `Rectangle`, you can't do it through a pointer to a `Shape`. In fact, there is no such thing as a pointer to a `Shape`, since there is no `Shape` class without a `template` argument. This is less of a limitation than you might think. Take another look at the rewritten `DrawAShapeOverAndOver()`:

```
template<typename ShapeType>
void DrawAShapeOverAndOver(ShapeType* myShape)
```

```
{
  for(int i=0; i<10000; i++)
  {
    myShape->DrawOutline();
  }
}
```

Essentially, wherever you once had functions that took in base class pointers, you now have templated functions that take in derived class pointers (or derived classes). The responsibility for calling the correct member function is delegated to the outer templated function, not to the object.

Templates have drawbacks. Although the best way to get a feel for these drawbacks is to experience them yourself, it's also a good idea for a programmer to have an idea of what to expect. First and foremost is that most compilers require templates to be declared inline. This means that all your templated functions will have to go in the header, which can make your code less tidy. (If you're using the Comeau compiler, this doesn't apply to you. Congratulations.)

Secondly, templates can lead to code bloat, since different versions of the functions must be compiled for each data type they are used with. How *much* code bloat is very specific to the project (switching all of my content-loading functions to use this model increased my stripped executable size by about 50k). As always, the best source of wisdom is your own tests.

Summary

Using templates for compile-time polymorphism can increase performance when they are used to avoid needless virtual function binding. With careful design, templates can be used to give non-virtual classes all the capabilities that virtual classes have, except for runtime binding. Although such compile-time polymorphism is not appropriate for every situation, a careful decision by the programmer as to where virtual functions are actually needed can dramatically improve code performance, without incurring a loss of flexibility or readability.

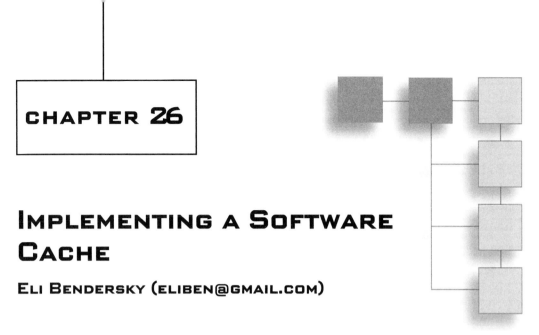

CHAPTER 26

IMPLEMENTING A SOFTWARE CACHE

ELI BENDERSKY (ELIBEN@GMAIL.COM)

In this article, I'll implement a complete caching class that can be readily applied to any problem, and you'll see a concrete example of using the cache to speed up calculations.

Software vs. Hardware Cache

If you read something on your computer, you are most likely already using a cache. Your computer caches what you see on the screen and thus is able to work faster. This cache is a hardware cache, deep in the hierarchy of computer architecture/hardware/software. It is completely *transparent* to us, the simple PC users.

It was noticed a long time ago that while CPU (central processing unit) speeds accelerate quickly, the speed of computer memory (DRAM, or dynamic random access memory) and the bus to the memory (front side bus in a PC, or FSB) can't keep up. Each access to the memory is expensive, and the CPU spends many cycles just waiting for the data to arrive. Thus caches were invented. A *hardware cache* is a small and extremely fast memory that is usually located on the same chip with the CPU. Its access time is almost as fast as the CPU itself, and there is no external bus to wait for. When the CPU accesses some memory location, it stores it in the cache, and future accesses are done much more quickly. Caches usually guess that if the CPU reads some memory location, there's a good chance that it'll read the next one as well; so they store a whole chunk of memory, which often results in a very high cache *hit rate* (the percentage of memory accesses that find what they want in the cache).

In reality, things are much more complicated. Caches pre-fetch data from the memory with methods based on the principles of time and space locality. These days, there are at least two (sometimes three) levels of cache in a computer. Complex algorithms are involved in cleaning up the cache and keeping it coherent (in sync) with the main memory, especially when multiple CPUs/cores are working together. This is a fascinating topic, and if you're interested, there's a lot of free and well-written information floating on the web—just run a web search.

But this is all hardware cache. In this article, I want to discuss software caches. A *software cache* is a programming technique used to speed up repetitive calculations. The implementation level may be different, but the principles are the same. All you really want is to remember computations you already did and not repeat them unnecessarily.

Basic Requirements and Definitions

A cache has to store results of computations—that is, for inputs, it stores outputs. Therefore, a cache is somewhat similar to a dictionary data structure—it stores key/value pairs—given a key, we want to quickly find the value. A hardware cache, for example, stores the contents of memory locations. Therefore, its key is a memory address, and its value is the address's contents.

How fast should a cache be? The obvious answer—as fast as possible—is not accurate. It depends on the keys you use. A solution that works fastest in the most general case is not always the solution that works fastest for some specific cases. I'll get back to this a bit later.

To Infinity and Beyond?

There is an important complication with caches that still needs to be considered, however. Caches, like all data structures (and physical structures), have some finite size. Can you store all the calculations you'll ever need in a cache? Can you store the contents of all memory locations in a hardware cache?

The answer to both questions is, of course, no. Hardware caches, for example, are far smaller than the main memory (caches are made of fast hardware, which makes them very expensive). Since the amount of memory is finite, you can't let software caches grow forever. Therefore, the cache must have a limited size. The exact limit depends heavily on the application, the data, and the amount of available memory, so it's best to let the user of the cache decide how large he wants it to be.

Cache Removal

So now you know the cache should be of limited size. This raises an important question: what to do when the cache is full? You can just stop and not add new keys, but this is obviously a bad solution. The alternative is to make free space for new keys by removing old ones, or *cache removal.*

There are many algorithms and methods of cache removal, some of which depend on the data. Here are some of the more popular approaches:

- **Random:** Using this approach, when the cache is full and you want to add a new key to it, you just throw out some old key at random.

- **LRU:** LRU stands for "least recently used." Using this approach, you throw out the key that is the oldest—that is, it was accessed least recently.

- **MRU:** MRU is "most recently used." You throw out the newest key, or the one accessed most recently.

All three have their merits and may be useful for certain types of data. In this cache implementation, I will use LRU because I believe it fits the more common applications of a cache and has a certain logical sense. After all, if there is some key that has been accessed more recently than another, it makes sense that the more recent key takes part in the current computations and the older key is the one that should be thrown away.

Requirements Revisited

Let's define the operations that the cache needs to perform:

- **Creation and initialization**: I'd like to specify the cache size upon its creation—that is the maximum number of keys it stores.

- **Lookup**: I'd like to ask the cache for a key and get the value, or an indication that this key doesn't exist in the cache.

- **Insertion**: I'd like to add keys to the cache. If the key already exists in the cache, its value will be updated with the latest value. If there's no such key in the cache, it will be added to the cache. If the cache is full, the LRU key will be removed to make space for the new key.

Design

You certainly need a data structure that lets you look up values for keys efficiently. This will be the core cache table. You can use the C++ standard map container for this purpose—it provides logarithmic lookup and insertion (O(log N) where N is the cache size).

But how do you implement LRU removal? You can keep some count of "recent access time stamp" for each key, but how do you know which to throw away? Going over the whole cache to find the LRU key is a O(N) operation—too slow.

You solve this using a very common programming trick—sacrifice space for time. Such problems are usually solved by using another data structure that provides the special requirement quickly and is kept fully coherent with the main data structure. What you need here, for example, is a *priority queue*—keys sorted in a linear structure with the most recent key in some known location, like the front of the queue, which lets you remove it quickly.

This leaves the question of how to implement the queue. You could go for a simple array, but that won't do. (Can you figure out why?) The problem is that when there's a lookup on some cache key, it immediately becomes the most recently used key and should be marked as such, for example, by being moved to the back of the queue. This operation is called *splicing*—take an item from the middle of a container and put it at the end. Splicing in arrays is expensive (O(N)), which is unacceptable.

Fortunately, there is a solution: a linked list. In a linked list, insertion and removal at both ends is O(1), and so is splicing, given that you already have a pointer/handle to the key you want to splice. But that can be arranged by holding such a pointer in the main cache data structure.

So, I'll go for two data structures: a map for the table and a list (another container in the C++ standard library) for the recent usage queue. For each key, the table will hold the value and a pointer to the key in the queue, which makes it trivial to mark it as recent on lookups.

So, enough babbling, let's get to the code.

Implementation

The source code package provided on this book's companion web site (www.courseptr.com/downloads) contains a file named cache.h—this is the implementation of the cache (it is wholly in an .h file because it's templated):

```
template <typename key_type, typename value_type>
class cache
```

This cache can work for any key type and value type given to it at creation as template arguments. Here is a portion of the cache class that lists its data members:

```
typedef typename list<key_type>::iterator list_iter;
struct cached_value
{
  cached_value(value_type value_, list_iter cache_i_) :
    value(value_), cache_i(cache_i_)
  {
  }
  value_type value;
  list_iter cache_i;
};
typedef typename map<key_type, cached_value<::iterator table_iter;
/// Maximal cache size.
///
unsigned maxsize;
/// Orders keys by time of last access. MRU (most recently used)
/// in the front, and LRU (least recently used) in the back.
///
/// Note: the elements in lru_list and table are always
/// the same.
///
list<key_type> lru_list;
/// Table storing cache elements for quick access.
///
map<key_type, cached_value> table;
```

maxsize is the maximal size given to the cache at creation. table is the main cache table—for each key, it holds a value and a pointer to the queue. lru_list is the queue—a list sorted by recent use (with the most recently used key in the front).

Note that the class also defines a cache_statistics subtype. This is to collect statistics of cache usage. The implementation of statistics is simple enough that I won't mention it here. It can be very useful, however, when you plan to use the cache for your needs and want to analyze its performance.

Lookup of keys in the cache is done as follows:

```
value_type* find(const key_type& key)
{
  table_iter ti = table.find(key);
  IF_DEBUG(stats.finds++);
  if (ti == table.end())
    return 0;
  IF_DEBUG(stats.finds_hit++);
  list_iter li = ti->second.cache_i;
  lru_list.splice(lru_list.begin(), lru_list, li);
  return &(ti->second.value);
}
```

The key is looked up in the table, which has efficient lookups. If the key wasn't found, you simply return 0. If the key was found, you have to splice the accessed key out of its place in the queue and place it in the front (since now this key is the most recently used). Then, you return the value of the key.

Insertion is just a little more complex:

```
void insert(const key_type& key, const value_type& value)
{
  value_type* valptr = find(key);
  if (valptr)
  {
    *valptr = value;
  }
  else
  {
    lru_list.push_front(key);
    cached_value cv(value, lru_list.begin());
    table.insert(make_pair(key, cv));
    if (lru_list.size() > maxsize)
    {
```

```
        key_type lru_key = lru_list.back();
        table.erase(lru_key);
        lru_list.pop_back();
        IF_DEBUG(stats.removed++);
    }
  }
}
```

First you look for the key in the table. Note that the local cache function find() is used here, because if you do find the element, you want it marked as MRU.

If the key was found, you just update its value and return. More interesting is what happens when the key is not found—here the insertion takes place. After adding the key to the cache, you check to see if the cache size is exceeded. If it is, you throw out the key that's in the back of lru_list, which is, if you recall, the LRU key—just what you need!

Using the Cache

Using this cache is very simple. Here's a small demonstration:

```
cache cc(4);
cc.insert("pi", 3.14);
cc.insert("e", 2.71);
cc.insert("gold", 1.61);
cc.insert("sq2", 1.41);
cc.debug_dump();
cc.insert("zero", 0);
cc.debug_dump();
double* e_value = cc.find("e");
cc.insert("one", 1);
cc.debug_dump();
cc.statistics();
for (int i = 0; i < 30; ++i)
  double* one_value = cc.find("one");
cc.statistics();
```

Run this (don't forget to #include cache.h and run in debug mode so that statistics will be collected and printed). Try to predict what the state of the cache is during the execution.

In the first dump, you see the items you inserted, in MRU order. In the second dump, you don't see "pi". That's because it's LRU and was removed when "zero" was added. In the second dump you don't see "gold". Why not "e", which was inserted before "gold"? Because "e" was accessed by find and thus was marked MRU.

Efficiency Revisited

The way the cache is currently implemented, it does all operations in O(log N), with N being the cache size. LRU removal/splicing is very efficient (O(1)). What takes the most time is the map lookups. Can't you make those more efficient?

As a matter of fact, you can—well, in most cases. By using a hash table instead of map (which uses trees and, hence, is logarithmic), you can make all cache operations O(1). There's only one catch though—this can be done only if you have good hashing functions for your keys. But since most of the keys would be either numbers or strings, and good hashing functions for those exist, it's not a real problem.

Interestingly, the C++ standard library has an extension container named hash_map, which is a hash table. Since it's not standard yet (it's only an extension), its implementations differ and aren't very stable. Bruce Eckel, in his book *Thinking in C++* (Prentice Hall, 2nd edition, 2000), creates a benchmark that gives him 4x speedup with hash_map against map.

Maybe his implementation of hash_map is better, but I didn't get such results with my tests (on Microsoft Visual C++ .NET's implementation of STL). I got only a minimal (about 20%) speedup for integer keys (Eckel's benchmark, in my opinion, is very dubious—the data he uses isn't too good for reliable benchmarking). When I tried strings as keys, hash_map was in fact twice as slow as map.

Hence, I stuck with map, but I'm confident that given a good implementation of a hash map and a good hashing function for the keys, the cache can be made more efficient. The fact that the cache size is limited and known beforehand only helps to create a very speedy hash table. This is left as an exercise for the astute reader.

INDEX